Getting Started with SAS/CALC™ Spreadsheet Applications

Version 6
First Edition

SAS Institute Inc.
SAS Campus Drive
Cary, NC 27513

The correct bibliographic citation for this manual is as follows: SAS Institute Inc., *Getting Started with SAS/CALC" Spreadsheet Applications, Version 6, First Edition*, Cary, NC: SAS Institute Inc., 1991. 224 pp.

Getting Started with SAS/CALC" Spreadsheet Applications, Version 6, First Edition

Copyright © 1991 by SAS Institute Inc., Cary, NC, USA.

ISBN 1-55544-455-5

Restricted Rights Legend. Use, duplication, or disclosure by the U.S. Government is subject to restrictions as set forth in subparagraph (c)(1)(ii) of the Rights in Technical Data and Computer Software clause at DFARS 252.227-7013.

SAS Institute Inc., SAS Campus Drive, Cary, North Carolina 27513.

All rights reserved. Printed in the United States of America. No part of this publication may be reproduced, stored in a retrieval system, or transmitted, in any form or by any means, electronic, mechanical, photocopying, or otherwise, without the prior written permission of the publisher, SAS Institute Inc.

1st printing, November 1991
2nd printing, February 1995

Note that text corrections may have been made at each printing.

The SAS® System is an integrated system of software providing complete control over data access, management, analysis, and presentation. Base SAS software is the foundation of the SAS System. Products within the SAS System include SAS/ACCESS® SAS/AF® SAS/ASSIST® SAS/CALC® SAS/CONNECT® SAS/CPE® SAS/DMI® SAS/EIS® SAS/ENGLISH® SAS/ETS® SAS/FSP® SAS/GRAPH® SAS/IMAGE® SAS/IML® SAS/IMS-DL/I® SAS/INSIGHT® SAS/LAB® SAS/NVISION® SAS/OR® SAS/PH-Clinical® SAS/QC® SAS/REPLAY-CICS® SAS/SESSION® SAS/SHARE® SAS/STAT® SAS/TOOLKIT® SAS/TRADER® SAS/TUTOR® SAS/DB2™ SAS/GEO™ SAS/GIS™ SAS/PH-Kinetics™ SAS/SHARE*NET™ SAS/SPECTRAVIEW™ and SAS/SQL-DS™ software. Other SAS Institute products are SYSTEM 2000® Data Management Software, with basic SYSTEM 2000, CREATE™ Multi-User™ QueX™ Screen Writer™ and CICS interface software; InfoTap™ software; NeoVisuals® software; JMP® JMP IN® JMP Serve® and JMP *Design*® software; SAS/RTERM® software; and the SAS/C® Compiler and the SAS/CX® Compiler; VisualSpace™ software; and Emulus® software. MultiVendor Architecture™ and MVA™ are trademarks of SAS Institute Inc. SAS Institute also offers SAS Consulting® SAS Video Productions® Ambassador Select® and On-Site Ambassador™ services. A*uthorline*® Books by Users™ The Encore Series™ *Observations*® *SAS Communications*® *SAS Training*® *SAS Views*® the SASware Ballot® and *JMPer Cable*® are published by SAS Institute Inc. The SAS Video Productions logo and the Books by Users SAS Institute's Author Service logo are registered service marks and the Helplus logo and The Encore Series logo are trademarks of SAS Institute Inc. All trademarks above are registered trademarks or trademarks of SAS Institute Inc. in the USA and other countries. ® indicates USA registration.

The Institute is a private company devoted to the support and further development of its software and related services.

Other brand and product names are registered trademarks or trademarks of their respective companies.

Doc P19, 110691

Contents

Reference Aids   v

Credits   xiii

Using This Book   xv

Part 1 - Introduction   1

Chapter 1 - Introducing SAS/CALC Software   3

Introducing SAS/CALC Software   3

What the Tutorials Cover   12

Part 2 - The Tutorial Chapters   17

Chapter 2 - Creating Your First Spreadsheet   19

Creating Your First Spreadsheet   19

Chapter 3 - Modifying Your Spreadsheet   55

Modifying Your Spreadsheet   55

Chapter 4 - Producing Spreadsheet Reports and Generating Graphics   75

Producing Spreadsheet Reports   75

Generating Graphics   95

Chapter 5 - Creating a Three-Dimensional Spreadsheet   105

Creating a Three-Dimensional Spreadsheet   105

Chapter 6 - Linking Spreadsheets   131

Linking Spreadsheets   131

Chapter 7 - Using Programs with SAS/CALC Software   157

Using Programs with SAS/CALC Software   157

Part 3 - Appendices   189

Appendix 1 - Accessing and Using the Online Help Facility and COPY Command   191

Accessing the Online Help Facility   191

Using the COPY Command   197

Appendix 2 - Troubleshooting Information 203

Common User Errors 203

Common Programming Errors 205

Appendix 3 - Video References 207

Glossary 209

Index 217

Reference Aids

Displays

1.1 The Spreadsheet Window   4
1.2 A Default Spreadsheet   5
1.3 A Spreadsheet with Entered Values   6
1.4 Edit Pull-down Menu   7
1.5 Change Dialog Box   8
1.6 Selecting Keys   10
1.7 Keys Window   10
1.8 The FORWARD Command   11
1.9 File Pull-down Menu   12
1.10 The EASTERN Spreadsheet   13
1.11 Enhanced EASTERN Spreadsheet   13
1.12 Default Pie Chart   14
1.13 The COMPANY Spreadsheet   15
2.1 The EASTERN Spreadsheet   19
2.2 Selecting Globals   21
2.3 Selecting Desktop   21
2.4 Selecting Spreadsheet...   22
2.5 Default Spreadsheet... Dialog Box   22
2.6 Typing SASUSER in the Spreadsheet... Dialog Box   23
2.7 Typing CALC in the Spreadsheet... Dialog Box   24
2.8 DIRECTORY Window   25
2.9 The PROC CALC Step   26
2.10 Submitting the PROC CALC Step   26
2.11 DIRECTORY Window   27
2.12 Selecting New...   28
2.13 Default New... Dialog Box   28
2.14 New... Dialog Box with EASTERN   29
2.15 Default Additional Options Dialog Box   30
2.16 Modified Additional Options Dialog Box   31
2.17 The EASTERN Spreadsheet with Default Row and Column Names   32
2.18 New Column and Row Names   33

2.19	Selecting Delete	34
2.20	Delete Dialog Box	35
2.21	Delete Rows Dialog Box	36
2.22	Result of Deleting Rows and Columns	37
2.23	The EASTERN Spreadsheet with Cell Values	38
2.24	Selecting Enter Formula	39
2.25	Default Formula Entry Area	40
2.26	Formula Entry Area for EXPENSES.QTR1	41
2.27	Formula for EXPENSES.QTR1	42
2.28	Result of the Formula	43
2.29	Ending Formula Entry	44
2.30	Marking the Source Cell	45
2.31	EXPENSES.QTR1 as the Source Cell	46
2.32	The Target Cells	47
2.33	Copying the Formula	48
2.34	Results of Copying	48
2.35	The Saved Spreadsheet	49
2.36	Closing a Spreadsheet	50
2.37	DIRECTORY Window with EASTERN.CALC Entry	51
2.38	Ending the SAS/CALC Software Session	51
2.39	The PROGRAM EDITOR Window	52
2.40	Ending the SAS System Session	52
3.1	Enhanced EASTERN Spreadsheet	55
3.2	Opening the EASTERN Spreadsheet	56
3.3	The EASTERN Spreadsheet	57
3.4	Selecting Insert...	58
3.5	Inserting a Row	59
3.6	The NET Row	60
3.7	Inserting Columns	60
3.8	The ACTUAL and VARIANCE Columns	61
3.9	The Marked Column Names	62
3.10	Changing Column Widths	63
3.11	New Column Widths	64
3.12	New Value for SALARY.ACTUAL	65
3.13	New Value for SALARY.VARIANCE	66
3.14	Computed Values for ACTUAL and VARIANCE	68

Reference Aids **vii**

3.15 New Value for NET.QTR1   68

3.16 The EASTERN Spreadsheet with Computed Values   69

3.17 Assigning Cell Formats   70

3.18 Formatted Values   71

3.19 The Help Window   72

4.1 Default Pie Chart   77

4.2 Default Bar Chart   78

4.3 File Pull-Down Menu   80

4.4 Selecting Send Default Report   81

4.5 Selecting Free   82

4.6 New... Dialog Box with ENHANCED   84

4.7 ENHANCED.REPORT Dialog Box   85

4.8 Default Page Format Dialog Box   86

4.9 Modified Page Format Dialog Box   87

4.10 TRANS.REPORT Dialog Box   88

4.11 Free Style Specification Window   89

4.12 Specifying Rows, Columns, and Pages   90

4.13 Sending an Alternate Report   91

4.14 Entry Definition Dialog Box   92

4.15 Three New Report Entries   94

4.16 Selecting Pie Chart...   96

4.17 Default Pie Chart   96

4.18 Selecting Other Attributes...   97

4.19 Default Additional Pie Attributes Dialog Box   98

4.20 Selecting Percentage   99

4.21 Selecting BENEFITS to Explode   100

4.22 Enhanced Pie Chart   101

4.23 Label Attributes Dialog Box   101

4.24 Enhanced Pie Chart with Title   102

4.25 Default Bar Chart   103

5.1 The EASTERN Spreadsheet   107

5.2 Changing Perspective   108

5.3 Viewing Pages and Columns   109

5.4 Results of Copying PAGE1   110

5.5 The Renamed Pages   111

5.6 Go to... Dialog Box   112

5.7 Clearing Marked Areas   113
5.8 Clearing Data Only   114
5.9 SERVICE Page with Cleared Cell Values   114
5.10 Recomputed Values   115
5.11 Selecting Autocalc Off   116
5.12 RECALC Displayed in Window   117
5.13 Entered Values   118
5.14 Selecting Recalc All   119
5.15 The SERVICE Page   120
5.16 Inserting a Summary Page   121
5.17 PAGE3   122
5.18 Computing Total Salaries   123
5.19 Result of the Formula   124
5.20 PAGE3 with Computed Values   125
5.21 Formatted Values   126
5.22 Renamed Page   127
5.23 The SALES Page   128
6.1 Enhanced COMPANY Spreadsheet   132
6.2 Selecting Copy an Entry   133
6.3 Copy An Entry... Dialog Box   134
6.4 Libnames Window   134
6.5 SASHELP Directory Window   135
6.6 Selecting SASHELP CALC CATALOG   135
6.7 Selecting WESTERN CALC from the Catalog Directory Window   136
6.8 Assign New Names Dialog Box   137
6.9 DIRECTORY Window with WESTERN Entry   138
6.10 The WESTERN Spreadsheet   139
6.11 New Column Width   140
6.12 Selecting Set Link...   142
6.13 Define a New Link Dialog Box with ELINK   143
6.14 Selecting EASTERN from the Catalog Directory Window   144
6.15 Define a New Link Dialog Box   145
6.16 ELINK Has Been Assigned   145
6.17 Formula for SALARY.QTR1   147
6.18 Result of the Formula   148
6.19 The COMPANY Spreadsheet with Computed Values   149

6.20	Enhanced COMPANY Spreadsheet	150
6.21	Selecting Drilldown	151
6.22	Drilldown Window	152
6.23	Selecting ELINK	153
6.24	Selecting Deactivate	153
6.25	Selecting Open	154
6.26	The COMPANY Spreadsheet without EASTERN Cell Values	154
7.1	Selecting the Spreadsheets	158
7.2	Assign New Names Dialog Box	159
7.3	DIRECTORY Window	159
7.4	SALES Page of EASTERN2	160
7.5	SERVICE Page of EASTERN2	161
7.6	SUMMARY Page of EASTERN2	162
7.7	Default New... Dialog Box	163
7.8	New... Dialog Box with REGION	164
7.9	PGM Window	165
7.10	Assignment Statements for the REGION.PGM Entry	166
7.11	EASTERN2 without Computed Cell Values	168
7.12	Selecting Run	169
7.13	Default Run Dialog Box	170
7.14	Specifying REGION in the Run Dialog Box	170
7.15	SALES Page of EASTERN2 with Computed Cell Values	171
7.16	SERVICE Page with Computed Cell Values	172
7.17	SUMMARY Page with Computed Cell Values	173
7.18	DIRECTORY Window with REGION.PGM Entry	174
7.19	SALES Page of WESTERN2	175
7.20	Specifying REGION in the Run Dialog Box	176
7.21	SALES Page of WESTERN2 with Computed Cell Values	177
7.22	COMPANY2 with No Cell Values	178
7.23	Naming the SUMMARY PGM Entry	179
7.24	Assignment Statement for PAGE1 of COMPANY2	180
7.25	COMPANY2 without Computed Cell Values	181
7.26	Running the SUMMARY.PGM Entry	182
7.27	COMPANY2 with Computed Cell Values	183
7.28	DIRECTORY Window with SUMMARY.PGM Entry	184
A1.1	Selecting Help and CALC Index	191

x   *Reference Aids*

A1.2	CALC: Index Window 192
A1.3	SAS/CALC Software Introduction 192
A1.4	PROC CALC Syntax 193
A1.5	CATALOG Option Information 193
A1.6	Windows Information 194
A1.7	First Display of Available SAS/CALC Software Commands 195
A1.8	Second Display of Available SAS/CALC Software Commands 195
A1.9	COPY Command Help 196
A1.10	Selecting Global Options 197
A1.11	Selecting Action Bar Off 198
A1.12	A Command Line 198
A1.13	Copying a Formula with the COPY Command 199
A1.14	Result of the COPY Command 200
A1.15	Copying a Formula with the COPY Command 201
A1.16	Result of the COPY Command 202

Figures

1.1	Three-Dimensional EASTERN Spreadsheet 6
1.2	Three-Dimensional EASTERN Spreadsheet 15
4.1	Steps for Generating a Printed Report 79
5.1	Three-Dimensional EASTERN Spreadsheet 106
6.1	Purpose of the Expression 148
7.1	Purpose of Assignment Statements in REGION.PGM 167
7.2	Purpose of Assignment Statement in SUMMARY.PGM 181
7.3	Formulas versus Programs 185

Output

4.1	Default Spreadsheet Report 75
4.2	Enhanced Spreadsheet Report 76
4.3	Transposed Spreadsheet Report 76
4.4	Page 1 of a Multipage Spreadsheet Report 77
4.5	Default Spreadsheet Report 83
4.6	Enhanced Spreadsheet Report 93
4.7	Transposed Spreadsheet Report 93
4.8	Page 1 of a Multipage Spreadsheet Report 94

Tables

A2.1   Common User Problems   203

A2.2   Common User Errors   203

A2.3   Error Messages   206

A3.1   Video References   207

Credits

Documentation

This book was formatted using SAS/PUBLISH software, currently in development at SAS Institute Inc., and output on a PostScript printer.

Composition	Eloise M. Currie, Blanche W. Phillips, Carol M. Thompson
Graphic Design	Creative Services Department
Proofreading	Kandy B. Newton, Cathy L. Brinsfield
Technical Review	Rhonda D. Ayscue, David J. Biesack, Cathy L. Brinsfield, Jim Goodling, Velerie M. Howell, Susan C. Johnson, Carl L. LaChapelle, Elly Sato, Larry Stewart, Cindy Swamp, Walter F. Teague, Carol M. Thompson, Linda L. Wharton
Writing and Editing	Cathy L. Brinsfield, Velerie M. Howell, N. Elizabeth Malcom, Larry Stewart, Walter F. Teague, Curt Yeo

Software

Release 6.07 of SAS/CALC software was developed by the Display Products Division. Product development includes design, programming, debugging, support, and documentation.

Interface	Patti M. Brideson, Douglas E. Jackson, K. Deva Kumar, Carl L. LaChapelle
Graphics	Jim Adams, Glen R. Walker
Drilldown	Jim Adams, Douglas E. Jackson
SAS/CALC Language	David J. Biesack, Gary W. Black, Yao Chen, Sue H. Her, Douglas E. Jackson, Al Kulik
PMENU action bars and menus	Patti M. Brideson, Douglas E. Jackson, Pamela A. Katchuk, Elly Sato
HELP System	Elly Sato, Kyoko U. Tidball
Sample Library	Velerie M. Howell
Reports	Patti M. Brideson
CPORT, CIMPORT and V5TOV6	LanChien Hsueh
Testing	Rhonda D. Ayscue, Teresa Dickerson, Jim Goodling, Susan C. Johnson, Larnell Lennon, Linda L. Wharton

Support Groups

Technical Support	David A. Driggs
Quality Assurance Testing	Richard A. Ragland, Elizabeth L. Hill, Todd M. Dalness, Patricia L. Berryman, Daniel P. O'Connor, Marilyn Adams

Using This Book

Purpose

Getting Started with SAS/CALC Spreadsheet Applications, Version 6, First Edition provides step-by-step instructions for using SAS/CALC software. This book provides a series of tutorial chapters that teach you how to use many features of SAS/CALC software. However, it does not attempt to cover all the components of the software.

You should read the remainder of "Using This Book" as it contains important information that will assist you as you use this book. This information describes the intended audience, the audience's prerequisite knowledge, and the book's organization and conventions. This book can also be used in conjunction with the SAS/CALC video tutorial titled "Getting Started with SAS/CALC Spreadsheet Applications."

Audience

Getting Started with SAS/CALC Spreadsheet Applications is intended for novice users of both spreadsheets and the SAS System. However, experienced spreadsheet or SAS System users will also benefit from this book. Users familiar with the FSCALC procedure in Version 5 SAS/FSP software will find this primer useful for learning the CALC procedure in Release 6.07 SAS/CALC software.

Specifically, this book is intended for users with

- little or no spreadsheet experience
- no SAS/CALC software experience
- little or no programming experience
- some SAS System experience.

Prerequisites

To use SAS/CALC software you need to know how to invoke the SAS System at your site. Your SAS Software Consultant can provide instructions on invoking the SAS System.

The following SAS software must be licensed and installed on the system you are using:

- base SAS software, Release 6.07
- SAS/CALC software, Release 6.07.

Additionally, you need a terminal that supports interactive displays.

How to Use This Book

The section provides an overview of the organization and content of this book.

Organization

This book is divided into three parts.

Part 1: Introduction

Part 1 contains one chapter that introduces you to SAS/CALC software.

Chapter 1, "Introducing SAS/CALC Software"
describes the SAS/CALC software environment for creating and managing your spreadsheets.

Part 2: The Tutorial Chapters

Part 2 contains six chapters that teach you the fundamental concepts of SAS/CALC software as well as advanced features for using it.

Chapter 2, "Creating Your First Spreadsheet"
teaches you how to invoke SAS/CALC software, name a spreadsheet, change row and column names, delete rows and columns, enter cell values, define formulas for computing cell values, copy formulas, save a spreadsheet, close a spreadsheet, and end the SAS/CALC session.

Chapter 3, "Modifying Your Spreadsheet"
teaches you how to open an existing spreadsheet, add rows and columns, change column widths, define and copy formulas, and change cell formats.

Chapter 4, "Producing Spreadsheet Reports and Generating Graphics"
teaches you how to print default and enhanced spreadsheet reports as well as how to generate pie charts and bar charts based on their spreadsheet data.

Chapter 5, "Creating a Three-Dimensional Spreadsheet"
teaches you the concept of a three-dimensional (3D) spreadsheet. This chapter explains how to copy and insert pages to create a 3D spreadsheet, clear cell values but retain formulas, and summarize values across pages in a spreadsheet.

Chapter 6, "Linking Spreadsheets"
teaches you the concept of linking spreadsheets. This chapter explains how to define links for creating new spreadsheets, summarize cell values across multiple spreadsheets, and use the drilldown facility to verify links and deactivate spreadsheets.

Chapter 7, "Using Programs with SAS/CALC Software"
teaches you how to use SAS/CALC programs to compute cell values. This chapter also compares programs and formulas.

Part 3: Appendices

Part 3 contains three appendices that provide additional information for using SAS/CALC software.

Appendix 1: "Accessing and Using the Online Help Facility and Copy Command"
: introduces the online help facility for SAS/CALC software, shows you how to use the help facility, and provides examples of using SAS/CALC software commands.

Appendix 2: "Troubleshooting Information"
: discusses common user errors and programming errors in SAS/CALC software applications.

Appendix 3: "Video References"
: provides information for referencing the SAS/CALC video tutorial "Getting Started with SAS/CALC Spreadsheet Applications."

What You Should Read

You should read this book from beginning to end in order. Each tutorial chapter builds on a spreadsheet created or modified in a previous chapter.

Reference Aids

Getting Started with SAS/CALC Spreadsheet Applications includes two additional sections to help you locate the information you need. The following sections at the back of this book provide information about special SAS/CALC software topics:

Index
: provides a cross-reference of the pages where specific topics, procedures, statements, commands, or options are discussed.

Glossary
: provides definitions of SAS/CALC terms used in the book.

The graphic on the inside front cover provides an overview of the action bar and pull-down menu selections available in SAS/CALC software.

Conventions

This section explains the various conventions this book uses, including typographical and syntax conventions.

Typographical Conventions

You will see several type styles used in this book. The following list explains the meaning of each style:

roman
: is the standard type style used for most text in this book.

UPPERCASE ROMAN	is used for SAS statements, commands, variable names, and other SAS language elements when they appear in the text.
italic	defines new terms or concepts. Italic is also used for book titles when they are referenced in text.
`monospace`	is used to shown examples of SAS programming code. In most cases, this book uses lowercase type for SAS code, with the exception of some title characters. You can enter your own SAS code in lowercase, uppercase, or a mixture of the two. However, titles, footnotes, and character variable values must be entered exactly as you want them to appear. Monospace is also used for field values when they appear in text. These can be values that you type into the fields, or values that you select by positioning the cursor and pressing ENTER, or pointing and clicking with a mouse, or by typing a value.

Syntax Conventions

Type styles have special meanings when used in the presentation of SAS/CALC procedure syntax and commands in this book. The following list explains the style conventions for the syntax sections:

UPPERCASE BOLD	identifies SAS keywords, such as the names of statements and procedures.
UPPERCASE ROMAN	identifies command names, arguments, and literal values that must be spelled exactly as shown (although they do not necessarily have to be entered in uppercase).
italic	identifies arguments or values that you supply. Italic is also used for generic terms that represent classes of arguments.

Additional Documentation

SAS Institute provides many publications about SAS System products. For a complete list of available publications, refer to the current issue of the SAS Institute *Publications Catalog*. The catalog is published twice yearly. You can obtain a free copy of the catalog by writing to the following address or calling the following telephone number:

SAS Institute Inc.
Book Sales Department
SAS Campus Drive
Cary, NC 27513
919-677-8000

- *SAS/CALC Software: Usage and Reference, Version 6, First Edition* (order #A56035) provides both usage and reference information about the CALC procedure, windows, and commands provided in Release 6.07 of SAS/CALC software.

- *SAS Language and Procedures: Introduction, Version 6, First Edition* (order #A56074) gets you started if you are unfamiliar with the SAS System or any other programming language.

- *SAS Language: Reference, Version 6, First Edition* (order #A56076) provides detailed reference information on base SAS software, the SAS programming language, and the types of applications the SAS System can perform.

- The SAS companion or other SAS documentation for your operating system provides information about the operating system specific features of the SAS System under your operating system.

Part 1
Introduction

Chapter 1   Introducing SAS/CALC ™ Software

Chapter 1 Introducing SAS/CALC™ Software

Introducing SAS/CALC Software 3
Fundamental Concepts of a SAS/CALC Software Spreadsheet 3
The PMENU Facility 7
Action Bar and Pull-down Menu Selections 9
Using Function Keys 9

What the Tutorials Cover 12

Introducing SAS/CALC Software

SAS/CALC software provides an interactive windowing environment that enables you to create electronic spreadsheets.

Electronic spreadsheets are computer versions of the familiar accountant's pad. Although spreadsheets are typically used for financial applications and other applications that use numbers, you can put any information that you can represent as a table of rows and columns into a spreadsheet. You use SAS/CALC software to enter data into a spreadsheet, define formulas to compute values, generate reports and graphics, consolidate information from several spreadsheets into a single spreadsheet, perform drilldowns, create SAS data sets, and fetch data from SAS data sets.

Fundamental Concepts of a SAS/CALC Software Spreadsheet

When you use SAS/CALC software to create spreadsheets, you work within a spreadsheet window, as shown in Display 1.1.

Display 1.1
The Spreadsheet Window

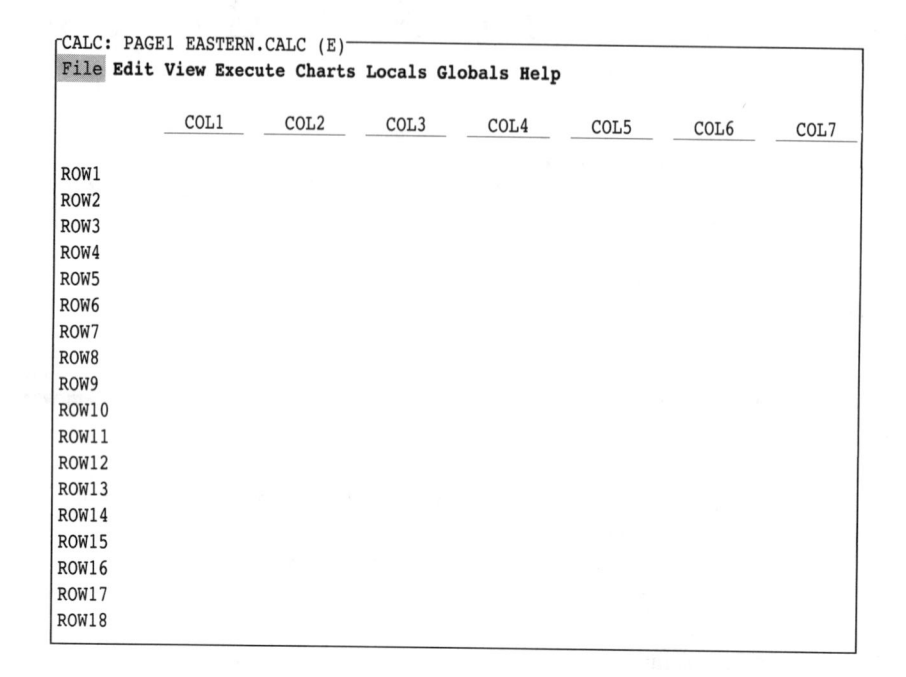

```
┌CALC: PAGE1 EASTERN.CALC (E)─────────────────────────────────┐
│ File Edit View Execute Charts Locals Globals Help           │
│                                                             │
│          COL1    COL2    COL3    COL4    COL5    COL6    COL7│
│  ROW1                                                        │
│  ROW2                                                        │
│  ROW3                                                        │
│  ROW4                                                        │
│  ROW5                                                        │
│  ROW6                                                        │
│  ROW7                                                        │
│  ROW8                                                        │
│  ROW9                                                        │
│  ROW10                                                       │
│  ROW11                                                       │
│  ROW12                                                       │
│  ROW13                                                       │
│  ROW14                                                       │
│  ROW15                                                       │
│  ROW16                                                       │
│  ROW17                                                       │
│  ROW18                                                       │
└─────────────────────────────────────────────────────────────┘
```

Notice the upper-left corner of the window contains the procedure's name, CALC, and the name of the spreadsheet, EASTERN.CALC.

Also, notice that the spreadsheet window contains an action bar. This action bar enables you to perform specific tasks in the spreadsheet window. The selections in this action bar will be discussed in more detail later in this chapter.

You actually build a spreadsheet in the text area of the spreadsheet window.

Spreadsheets created with SAS/CALC software consist of rows and columns, which are assigned default names. All rows have the root name ROW and are sequentially numbered. Similarly, all columns have the root name COL and are sequentially numbered. A default SAS/CALC software spreadsheet is shown in Display 1.2.

The intersection of each row and column in the spreadsheet is called a *cell*. Each cell is identified by its row and column coordinates. For example, the cell at the intersection of ROW1 and COL1 is called cell ROW1.COL1.

Display 1.2
A Default Spreadsheet

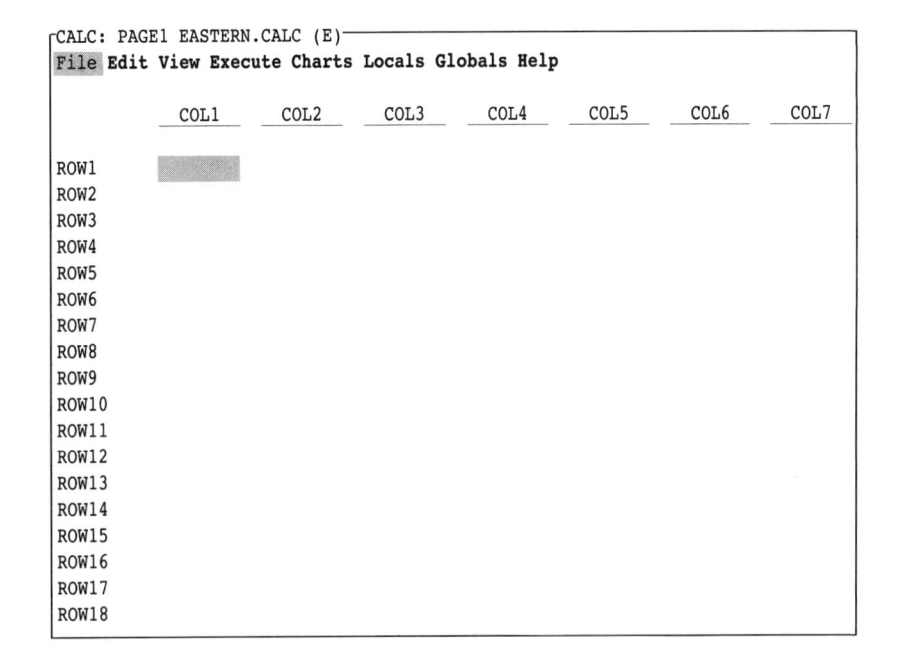

```
┌CALC: PAGE1 EASTERN.CALC (E)──────────────────────────────────┐
│ File Edit View Execute Charts Locals Globals Help            │
│                                                              │
│             COL1     COL2     COL3     COL4     COL5     COL6     COL7 │
│    ROW1   ▓▓▓▓▓                                              │
│    ROW2                                                      │
│    ROW3                                                      │
│    ROW4                                                      │
│    ROW5                                                      │
│    ROW6                                                      │
│    ROW7                                                      │
│    ROW8                                                      │
│    ROW9                                                      │
│    ROW10                                                     │
│    ROW11                                                     │
│    ROW12                                                     │
│    ROW13                                                     │
│    ROW14                                                     │
│    ROW15                                                     │
│    ROW16                                                     │
│    ROW17                                                     │
│    ROW18                                                     │
└──────────────────────────────────────────────────────────────┘
```

You can assign values to cells by manually entering the values, calculating values with formulas or SAS/CALC programs, or retrieving values from a SAS data set or another spreadsheet. Display 1.3 shows a spreadsheet with modified row and column names and entered values.

Display 1.3
A Spreadsheet with Entered Values

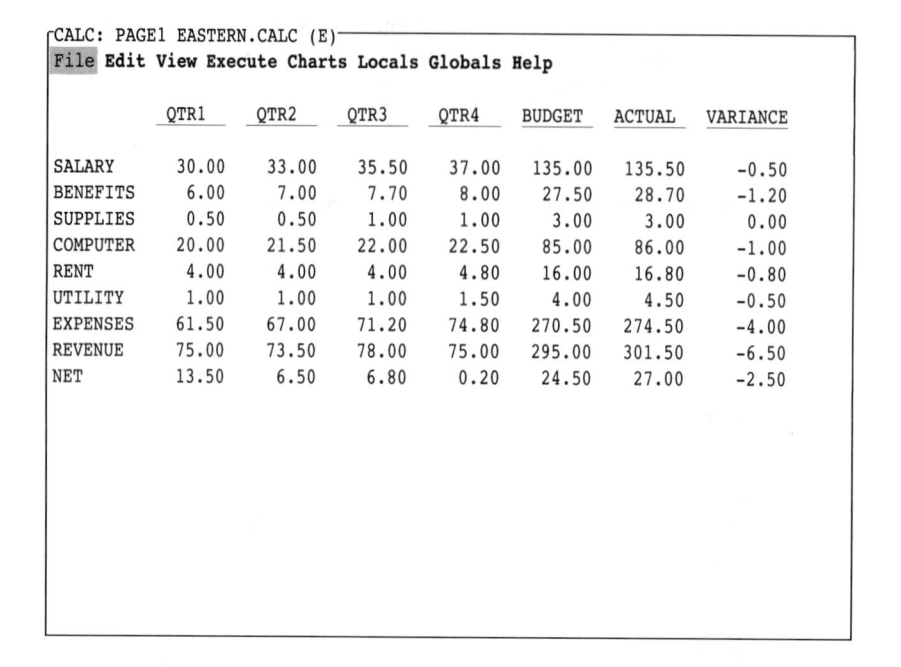

```
┌CALC: PAGE1 EASTERN.CALC (E)─────────────────────────────────────┐
│ File Edit View Execute Charts Locals Globals Help               │
│                                                                 │
│              QTR1    QTR2    QTR3    QTR4   BUDGET  ACTUAL  VARIANCE │
│                                                                 │
│    SALARY    30.00   33.00   35.50   37.00  135.00  135.50  -0.50   │
│    BENEFITS   6.00    7.00    7.70    8.00   27.50   28.70  -1.20   │
│    SUPPLIES   0.50    0.50    1.00    1.00    3.00    3.00   0.00   │
│    COMPUTER  20.00   21.50   22.00   22.50   85.00   86.00  -1.00   │
│    RENT       4.00    4.00    4.00    4.80   16.00   16.80  -0.80   │
│    UTILITY    1.00    1.00    1.00    1.50    4.00    4.50  -0.50   │
│    EXPENSES  61.50   67.00   71.20   74.80  270.50  274.50  -4.00   │
│    REVENUE   75.00   73.50   78.00   75.00  295.00  301.50  -6.50   │
│    NET       13.50    6.50    6.80    0.20   24.50   27.00  -2.50   │
│                                                                 │
└─────────────────────────────────────────────────────────────────┘
```

The spreadsheet shown in Display 1.3 has two dimensions, rows and columns. The two dimensions represent the intersection of a row and a column. As Figure 1.1 illustrates, you can create three-dimensional spreadsheets with SAS/CALC software. The third dimension represents pages of the spreadsheet. Together, the three dimensions represent the intersection of a row, a column, and a page.

Figure 1.1   *Three-Dimensional EASTERN Spreadsheet*

```
CALC: SUMMARY EASTERN.CALC──────────────────────────────────────────┐
            QTR1     QTR2    QTR3    QTR4   BUDGET  ACTUAL  VARIANCE │
                                                                     │
  SALARY    62.00   67.00   69.50   71.50  265.00  270.00   -5.00    │
  BE  CALC: SERVICE EASTERN.CALC──────────────────────────────────────┐
  SU │         QTR1    QTR2    QTR3    QTR4   BUDGET  ACTUAL  VARIANCE │
  CO │                                                                 │
  RE │ SALARY   32.00   34.00   34.00   34.50  130.00  134.50  -04.50  │
  UT │ BE  CALC: SALES EASTERN.CALC────────────────────────────────────┐
  EX │ SU │         QTR1    QTR2    QTR3    QTR4   BUDGET  ACTUAL  VARIANCE │
  RE │ CO │                                                                 │
  NE │ RE │ SALARY    30.00   33.00   35.50   37.00  135.00  135.50  -0.50  │
     │ UT │ BENEFITS   6.00    7.00    7.70    8.00   27.50   28.70  -1.20  │
     │ EX │ SUPPLIES   0.50    0.50    1.00    1.00    3.00    3.00   0.00  │
     │ RE │ COMPUTER  20.00   21.50   22.00   22.50   85.00   86.00  -1.00  │
     │ NE │ RENT       4.00    4.00    4.00    4.80   16.00   16.80  -0.80  │
     └────│ UTILITY    1.00    1.00    1.00    1.50    4.00    4.50  -0.50  │
          │ EXPENSES  61.50   67.00   71.20   74.80  270.50  274.50  -4.00  │
          │ REVENUE   75.00   73.50   78.00   75.00  295.00  301.50  -6.50  │
          │ NET       13.50    6.50    6.80    0.20   24.50   27.00  -2.50  │
          └─────────────────────────────────────────────────────────────────┘
```

You manipulate your spreadsheet and its values by issuing commands in the spreadsheet window. These commands are issued in any of three ways: you can use an action bar and pull-down menus, function keys, or type commands on a command line. This book uses pull-down menus and function keys to issue commands and perform specific tasks.

The PMENU Facility

Pull-down menus are activated from the action bar at the top of the SAS/CALC software windows. Each pull-down menu contains items that you select to perform specific tasks.

Note: Some commands, such as END, can be issued with function keys. Performing an action using function keys often requires fewer keystrokes than performing an action using pull-down menus or commands.

To select an item from an action bar or pull-down menu, use one of the following methods:

- press the TAB or BACKTAB key to move the cursor to the item and press ENTER

- use the arrow keys to position the cursor on the item and press ENTER

- use a mouse to point and click on the item.

If you select an item such as Edit from the action bar, a pull-down menu is automatically displayed for that item, as shown in the Display 1.4.

Display 1.4
Edit Pull-down Menu

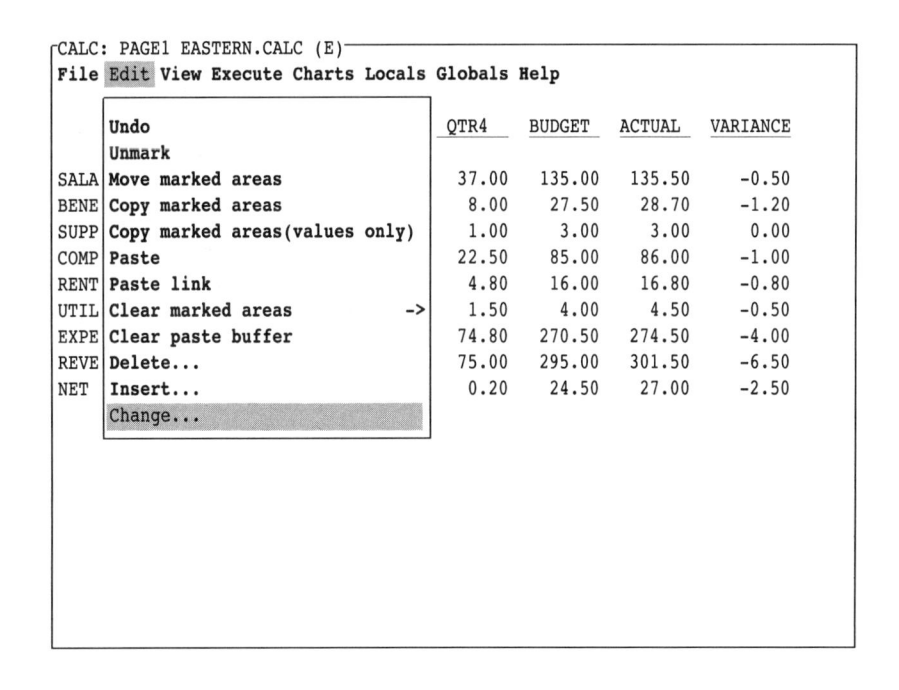

```
┌CALC: PAGE1 EASTERN.CALC (E)─────────────────────────────────────────┐
│File Edit View Execute Charts Locals Globals Help                    │
│    ┌─────────────────────────────────┐                              │
│    │Undo                             │   QTR4   BUDGET  ACTUAL  VARIANCE
│    │Unmark                           │                              │
│SALA│Move marked areas                │  37.00   135.00  135.50   -0.50
│BENE│Copy marked areas                │   8.00    27.50   28.70   -1.20
│SUPP│Copy marked areas(values only)   │   1.00     3.00    3.00    0.00
│COMP│Paste                            │  22.50    85.00   86.00   -1.00
│RENT│Paste link                       │   4.80    16.00   16.80   -0.80
│UTIL│Clear marked areas           ->  │   1.50     4.00    4.50   -0.50
│EXPE│Clear paste buffer               │  74.80   270.50  274.50   -4.00
│REVE│Delete...                        │  75.00   295.00  301.50   -6.50
│NET │Insert...                        │   0.20    24.50   27.00   -2.50
│    │Change...                        │                              │
│    └─────────────────────────────────┘                              │
│                                                                     │
│                                                                     │
│                                                                     │
│                                                                     │
└─────────────────────────────────────────────────────────────────────┘
```

8 *Introducing SAS/CALC Software* □ *Chapter 1*

To perform an action, you select an item such as Change... from the Edit pull-down menu.

Pull-down menu tasks that have ellipses following the item name, such as Change..., automatically open other windows, called dialog boxes, such as the Change dialog box shown in Display 1.5.

Display 1.5
Change Dialog Box

```
┌CALC: PAGE1 EASTERN.CALC (E)─────────────────────────────────┐
│File Edit View Execute Charts Locals Globals Help            │
│ ┌CALC: Change──────────────────────────────────────────────┐│
│ │                                                          ││
│ │    Target: [                                           ] ││
│ │SA                                                        ││
│ │BE  □ Cell type   □ Data type      □ Justification        ││
│ │SU    o Data        o Numeric        o Left               ││
│ │CO    o Label       o Character      o Right              ││
│ │RE    o Title                        o Center             ││
│ │UT    o Subtitle                     o None               ││
│ │EX                                                        ││
│ │RE  Options:                                              ││
│ │NE   □ Round   □ Caps    □ Hide    □ Protect  □ Consolidate││
│ │      o On      o On      o On      o On       o On       ││
│ │      o Off     o Off     o Off     o Off      o Off      ││
│ │                                                          ││
│ │    Others:                                               ││
│ │     □ Color:     [        ]   □ Format:  [            ]  ││
│ │     □ Attribute: [        ]   □ Informat:[            ]  ││
│ │     □ Width:     [  ]         □ Space:   [    ]          ││
│ │                                                          ││
│ │        [ OK ]        [ Cancel ]        [ Help ]          ││
│ └──────────────────────────────────────────────────────────┘│
└─────────────────────────────────────────────────────────────┘
```

These *dialog boxes* provide additional selections or request more information. When you are finished making your selections or supplying more information, the dialog box automatically disappears and the action is performed.

Note: If you need to exit any pull-down menu without making a selection, use the arrow keys or a mouse to position the cursor anywhere outside the pull-down menu, and press ENTER. Make sure the cursor is not positioned on another item on the action bar or on an item on the display or that item will be selected when you press ENTER. If you need to exit a dialog box, select the **Cancel** button.

A brief discussion of the types of tasks that you can perform in each pull-down menu item is presented in the following section. Individual selections within each menu are explained as they are needed throughout the following chapters.

Action Bar and Pull-down Menu Selections

File	enables you to open other spreadsheets, print spreadsheets, and close and save spreadsheets.
Edit	enables you to delete or insert rows or columns, change the widths and formats of columns, and copy marked areas.
View	enables you to view the spreadsheet from different perspectives, scroll to a specific row or column within a spreadsheet, and control the size and position of the spreadsheet window on your display.
Execute	enables you to run programs to perform computations in the spreadsheet, define formulas to perform calculations, and control execution of the programs and formulas.
Charts	enables you to produce plots and charts graphically representing the spreadsheet data.
Locals	enables you to perform tasks that are designed for SAS/CALC software, such as define ranges for use in formulas and programs, link to other spreadsheets, and perform drilldowns.
Globals	enables you to perform tasks that are global to the SAS System, such as move to the LOG, OUTPUT, and PROGRAM EDITOR windows, and turn pull-down menus on and off.
Help	enables you to access online help, such as help for the entire SAS System, help for SAS/CALC software, and current function key definitions.

Using Function Keys

An alternative to selecting items from an action bar is to perform an action directly using a function key. *Function keys* are keyboard keys that can be assigned commands to perform specific tasks. Using the SAS/CALC function keys can help you perform some tasks faster than using the action bar and pull-down menus.

10 *Introducing SAS/CALC Software* □ *Chapter 1*

To see how each function key is defined for SAS/CALC software:

1. Select **Help** from the action bar in the spreadsheet window.
2. Select **Keys** from the Help pull-down menu as shown in Display 1.6.

Display 1.6
Selecting Keys

```
┌CALC: PAGE1 EASTERN.CALC (E)─────────────────────────────────────┐
│File Edit View Execute Charts Locals Globals Help                │
│                                                                 │
│            QTR1    QTR2    QTR3    QTR4  ┌Extended help┐ L  VARIANCE
│                                          │Keys         │
│  SALARY   30.00   33.00   35.50   37.00  │SAS System   │ 50   -0.50
│  BENEFITS  6.00    7.00    7.70    8.00  │CALC Index   │ 70   -1.20
│  SUPPLIES  0.50    0.50    1.00    1.00  └─────────────┘ 00    0.00
│  COMPUTER 20.00   21.50   22.00   22.50   85.00   86.00  -1.00
│  RENT      4.00    4.00    4.00    4.80   16.00   16.80  -0.80
│  UTILITY   1.00    1.00    1.00    1.50    4.00    4.50  -0.50
│  EXPENSES 61.50   67.00   71.20   74.80  270.50  274.50  -4.00
│  REVENUE  75.00   73.50   78.00   75.00  295.00  301.50  -6.50
│  NET      13.50    6.50    6.80    0.20   24.50   27.00  -2.50
│                                                                 │
│                                                                 │
└─────────────────────────────────────────────────────────────────┘
```

Selecting **Keys** displays the Keys window shown in Display 1.7.

Display 1.7
Keys Window

```
┌CALC: SALES EASTERN.CALC (E)──────────┐┌KEYS <CALC>─────────────────┐
│File Edit View Execute Charts Locals Glo││File Edit View Globals Help│
│                                        ││                            │
│            QTR1    QTR2    QTR3    QT ││ Key       Definition       │
│                                        ││                            │
│  SALARY   30.00   33.00   35.50     3 ││ F0        compile          │
│  BENEFITS  6.00    7.00    7.70       ││ F1        copy             │
│  SUPPLIES  0.50    0.50    1.00       ││ F2        unmark           │
│  COMPUTER 20.00   21.50   22.00     2 ││ F3        formula          │
│  RENT      4.00    4.00    4.00       ││ F4        paste            │
│  UTILITY   1.00    1.00    1.00       ││ F5        change           │
│  EXPENSES 61.50   67.00   71.20     7 ││ F6        forward cell     │
│  REVENUE  75.00   73.50   78.00     7 ││ F7        down cell        │
│  NET      13.50    6.50    6.80       ││ F8        pmenu            │
│                                        ││ F9        command          │
│                                        ││ SHF F0    keys             │
│                                        ││ SHF F1    undo             │
│                                        ││ SHF F2    help             │
│                                        ││ SHF F3    zoom             │
│                                        ││ SHF F4    end              │
│                                        ││ SHF F5    mark block       │
│                                        ││ SHF F6    insert           │
│                                        ││ SHF F7    msg              │
└────────────────────────────────────────┘└────────────────────────────┘
```

Note: Because function key definitions are system-dependent, your function keys may be defined differently from those shown in this primer.

The frequently issued commands in SAS/CALC software that are assigned to function keys, include

END	saves and closes a window or display. If you do not have a mouse, using the END key can be faster than selecting END from the File pull-down menu.
MARK BLOCK	marks a cell or range of cells for copying and moving.
BACKWARD	scrolls a display backward.
FORWARD	scrolls a display forward.
RIGHT	scrolls a display to the right.
LEFT	scrolls a display to the left.

To scroll forward to see additional function key definitions:

1. Select **Globals** from the action bar and **Command** from the Globals pull-down menu.

2. Select **Command...** from the Command pull-down menu to display the Command... dialog box.

3. Type FORWARD on the command line, as shown in Display 1.8, and select **OK**. You can type FORWARD in uppercase or lowercase.

Display 1.8
The FORWARD Command

```
┌CALC: PAGE1 EASTERN.CALC (E)──────────┬KEYS <CALC>─────────────────────┐
│File Edit View Execute Charts Locals Glo│File Edit View Globals Help     │
│                                        │                                 │
│          QTR1    QTR2    QTR3    QT│Key      Defin│SAS/ASSIST           │
│                                        │              │SAS/EIS              │
│ SALARY   30.00   33.00   35.50    3│F0       compi│Program Editor       │
│ BENEFITS  6.00    7.00    7.70     │F1       copy │Log                  │
│ SUPPLIES  0.50    0.50    1.00     │F2       unmar│Output               │
│ COMPUTER 20.00   21.50   22.00    2│F3       formu│Output Manager       │
│ RENT      4.00    4.00    4.00     │F4       paste│Graph Manager        │
│ UTILITY   1.00    1.00    1.00     │F5       chang│Access               │
│ EXPENSES 61.50   67.00   71.20    7│F6       forwa│Invoke application ->│
│ REVENUE  75.00   73.50   78.00    7│F7       down │Data management    ->│
│ NET      13.50    6.50    6.80     │F8       pmenu│Desktop            ->│
│                                        │F9       comma│Comma┌──────────────┐
├Command...─────────────────────────────┤                                 │
│                                        │                                 │
│  Command ===> FORWARD                  │                                 │
│                                        │                                 │
│                  ┌────┐        ┌──────┐│                                 │
│                  │ OK │        │Cancel││                                 │
│                  └────┘        └──────┘│                                 │
│                                   ┌────┴──┐                             │
│                                   │SHF F7 │ msg                         │
└────────────────────────────────────┴───────┴─────────────────────────────┘
```

You may want to make a note of the FORWARD, RIGHT, and LEFT function keys for future reference.

4. To exit the KEYS window using the action bar, select **File** from the action bar and **End** from the File pull-down menu as shown in Display 1.9. Selecting End closes the keys window.

Display 1.9
File Pull-down Menu

```
┌CALC: PAGE1 EASTERN.CALC (E)─────────┬─KEYS <CALC>──────────────┐
│File Edit View Execute Charts Locals Glo│File Edit View Globals Help│
│                                     │                          │
│           QTR1    QTR2    QTR3    QT│Open...      inition     │
│                                     │Save                      │
│SALARY    30.00   33.00   35.50    3│Save as...   mand        │
│BENEFITS   6.00    7.00    7.70     │Cancel       s           │
│SUPPLIES   0.50    0.50    1.00     │End          o           │
│COMPUTER  20.00   21.50   22.00    2│             p           │
│RENT       4.00    4.00    4.00     │SHF F3    zoom           │
│UTILITY    1.00    1.00    1.00     │SHF F4    end            │
│EXPENSES  61.50   67.00   71.20    7│SHF F5    mark block     │
│REVENUE   75.00   73.50   78.00    7│SHF F6    insert         │
│NET       13.50    6.50    6.80     │SHF F7    msg            │
│                                     │SHF F8    backward       │
│                                     │SHF F9    forward        │
│                                     │CTL F0    swap           │
│                                     │CTL F1    left           │
│                                     │CTL F2    right          │
│                                     │CTL F3    home           │
│                                     │CTL F4                   │
│                                     │CTL F5                   │
│                                     │CTL F6                   │
└─────────────────────────────────────┴──────────────────────────┘
```

Note: To exit the KEYS window using a function key, press the function key assigned to the END command.

This concludes your introduction to SAS/CALC software. The remainder of this chapter introduces you to the tutorial chapters within this book. The tutorial chapters provide you with step-by-step instructions for learning and using SAS/CALC software.

What the Tutorials Cover

In the following chapters you learn how to access SAS/CALC software to create multiple spreadsheets, reports, and graphics. This section provides an overview of what each chapter covers and introduces some terminology related to spreadsheets.

The spreadsheets in the chapters represent financial data for a fictitious company. The company currently has two regional offices (East and West) with two divisions (Sales and Service) in each office.

The first tutorial chapter (Chapter 2, "Creating Your First Spreadsheet) teaches you how to invoke SAS/CALC software and build a simple two-dimensional spreadsheet, named EASTERN, that shows revenue and expenses for the Sales Division in the East regional office. The spreadsheet is shown in Display 1.10. The row and column names have been changed from the defaults, and the cells in the row named **EXPENSES** use formulas to compute total expenses.

Display 1.10
The EASTERN Spreadsheet

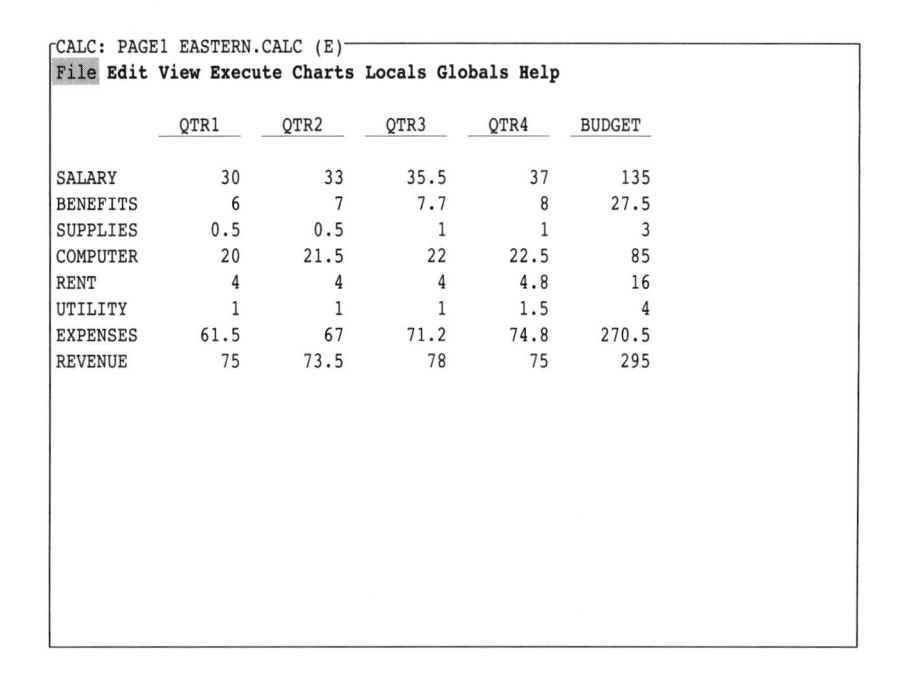

```
┌CALC: PAGE1 EASTERN.CALC (E)─────────────────────────────┐
│ File Edit View Execute Charts Locals Globals Help       │
│                                                         │
│               QTR1     QTR2     QTR3     QTR4    BUDGET │
│                                                         │
│  SALARY         30       33     35.5       37       135 │
│  BENEFITS        6        7      7.7        8      27.5 │
│  SUPPLIES      0.5      0.5        1        1         3 │
│  COMPUTER       20     21.5       22     22.5        85 │
│  RENT            4        4        4      4.8        16 │
│  UTILITY         1        1        1      1.5         4 │
│  EXPENSES     61.5       67     71.2     74.8     270.5 │
│  REVENUE        75     73.5       78       75       295 │
│                                                         │
└─────────────────────────────────────────────────────────┘
```

In the second tutorial chapter (Chapter 3, "Modifying Your Spreadsheet), you enhance the EASTERN spreadsheet by inserting a row and two columns as shown in Display 1.11. The row named **NET** represents net income, the column named **ACTUAL** represents the total year-to-date actual expenses, and the column named **VARIANCE** shows the difference between the **BUDGET** and **ACTUAL** columns. Additionally, the column widths have been decreased from the defaults so the new columns are visible on the display without scrolling, and formats have been added to improve the appearance and readability of the spreadsheet.

Display 1.11
Enhanced EASTERN Spreadsheet

```
┌CALC: PAGE1 EASTERN.CALC (E)─────────────────────────────────────┐
│ File Edit View Execute Charts Locals Globals Help               │
│                                                                 │
│           QTR1    QTR2    QTR3    QTR4   BUDGET  ACTUAL VARIANCE│
│                                                                 │
│  SALARY   30.00   33.00   35.50   37.00  135.00  135.50   -0.50 │
│  BENEFITS  6.00    7.00    7.70    8.00   27.50   28.70   -1.20 │
│  SUPPLIES  0.50    0.50    1.00    1.00    3.00    3.00    0.00 │
│  COMPUTER 20.00   21.50   22.00   22.50   85.00   86.00   -1.00 │
│  RENT      4.00    4.00    4.00    4.80   16.00   16.80   -0.80 │
│  UTILITY   1.00    1.00    1.00    1.50    4.00    4.50   -0.50 │
│  EXPENSES 61.50   67.00   71.20   74.80  270.50  274.50   -4.00 │
│  REVENUE  75.00   73.50   78.00   75.00  295.00  301.50   -6.50 │
│  NET      13.50    6.50    6.80    0.20   24.50   27.00   -2.50 │
│                                                                 │
└─────────────────────────────────────────────────────────────────┘
```

14 *What the Tutorials Cover* □ *Chapter 1*

The third tutorial chapter (Chapter 4, "Producing Spreadsheet Reports and Generating Graphics") teaches you how to produce reports and generate graphics from a spreadsheet. The following display shows a simple pie chart based on the budget data in the EASTERN spreadsheet.

Display 1.12
Default Pie Chart

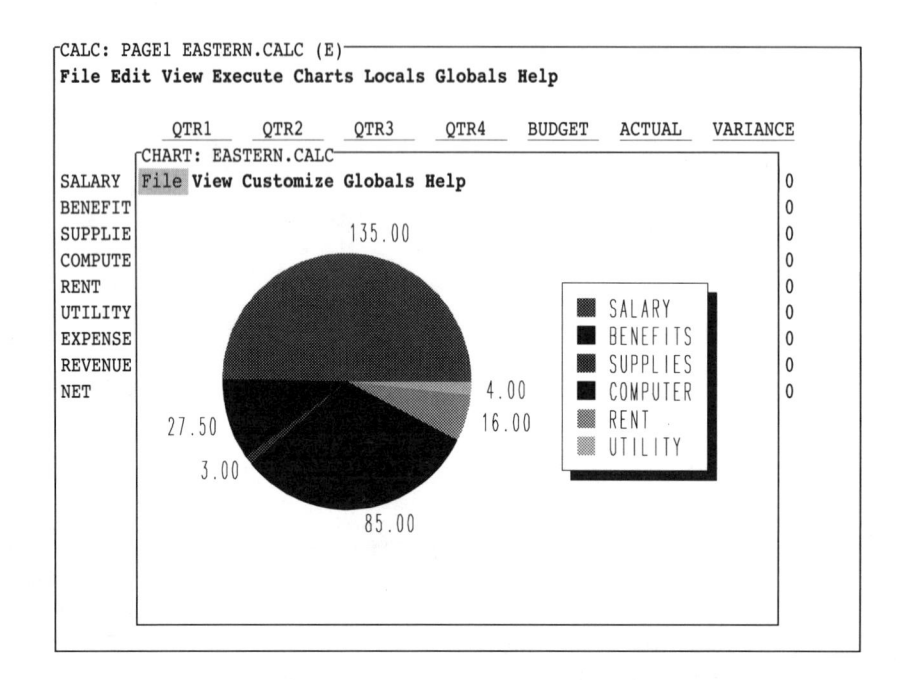

```
┌CALC: PAGE1 EASTERN.CALC (E)─────────────────────────────────┐
│File Edit View Execute Charts Locals Globals Help            │
│                                                             │
│         QTR1    QTR2    QTR3    QTR4   BUDGET  ACTUAL  VARIANCE│
│      ┌CHART: EASTERN.CALC─────────────────────────┐         │
│SALARY│File View Customize Globals Help            │       0 │
│BENEFIT│                                           │       0 │
│SUPPLIE│              135.00                       │       0 │
│COMPUTE│                                           │       0 │
│RENT  │                                            │       0 │
│UTILITY│                                           │       0 │
│EXPENSE│                      ┌──────────────┐     │       0 │
│REVENUE│                      │ ■ SALARY     │     │       0 │
│NET   │                 4.00  │ ■ BENEFITS   │     │       0 │
│      │        27.50   16.00  │ ■ SUPPLIES   │     │         │
│      │         3.00          │ ■ COMPUTER   │     │         │
│      │                       │ ■ RENT       │     │         │
│      │          85.00        │ ■ UTILITY    │     │         │
│      │                       └──────────────┘     │         │
│      └────────────────────────────────────────────┘         │
└─────────────────────────────────────────────────────────────┘
```

In the fourth tutorial chapter (Chapter 5, "Creating a Three-Dimensional Spreadsheet"), the EASTERN spreadsheet is expanded to three dimensions by adding a page for the Service Division. Additionally, a summary page is added to show totals from both divisions in the eastern region. Figure 1.2 illustrates the three-dimensional EASTERN spreadsheet.

Figure 1.2 *Three-Dimensional EASTERN Spreadsheet*

```
┌CALC: SUMMARY EASTERN.CALC─────────────────────────────────────────┐
│          QTR1     QTR2     QTR3     QTR4    BUDGET   ACTUAL  VARIANCE
│
│SALARY   62.00    67.00    69.50    71.50   265.00   270.00   -5.00
│BE ┌CALC: SERVICE EASTERN.CALC──────────────────────────────────────┐
│SU │          QTR1     QTR2     QTR3     QTR4    BUDGET   ACTUAL  VARIANCE
│CO │
│RE │SALARY   32.00    34.00    34.00    34.50   130.00   134.50  -04.50
│UT │BE ┌CALC: SALES EASTERN.CALC──────────────────────────────────────┐
│EX │SU │          QTR1     QTR2     QTR3     QTR4    BUDGET   ACTUAL  VARIANCE
│RE │CO │
│NE │RE │SALARY   30.00    33.00    35.50    37.00   135.00   135.50   -0.50
│   │UT │BENEFITS  6.00     7.00     7.70     8.00    27.50    28.70   -1.20
│   │EX │SUPPLIES  0.50     0.50     1.00     1.00     3.00     3.00    0.00
│   │RE │COMPUTER 20.00    21.50    22.00    22.50    85.00    86.00   -1.00
│   │NE │RENT      4.00     4.00     4.00     4.80    16.00    16.80   -0.80
│   └───│UTILITY   1.00     1.00     1.00     1.50     4.00     4.50   -0.50
│       │EXPENSES 61.50    67.00    71.20    74.80   270.50   274.50   -4.00
│       │REVENUE  75.00    73.50    78.00    75.00   295.00   301.50   -6.50
│       │NET      13.50     6.50     6.80     0.20    24.50    27.00   -2.50
│       └──────────────────────────────────────────────────────────────┘
```

The fifth tutorial chapter (Chapter 6, "Linking Spreadsheets") introduces some advanced features of SAS/CALC software. First, a new three-dimensional spreadsheet, named WESTERN, is introduced. It contains information for the West regional office. Next, a COMPANY spreadsheet, shown in the Display 1.13, is created by linking to the summary pages of the EASTERN and WESTERN spreadsheets to obtain totals across both regions.

Display 1.13
The COMPANY Spreadsheet

```
┌CALC: PAGE1 COMPANY.CALC (E)──────────────────────────────────────┐
│ File Edit View Execute Charts Locals Globals Help
│
│            QTR1     QTR2     QTR3     QTR4    BUDGET   ACTUAL  VARIANCE
│
│  SALARY   128.00   133.50   137.00   139.00   535.00   537.50   -2.50
│  BENEFITS  26.40    27.40    28.80    30.20   113.00   112.80    0.20
│  SUPPLIES   6.50     7.50     8.40     9.20    29.00    31.60   -2.60
│  COMPUTER  85.00    86.80    88.20    88.70   356.00   348.70    7.30
│  RENT      19.00    19.00    19.00    22.60    82.80    79.60    3.20
│  EXPENSES   6.00     6.50     6.50     8.00    30.00    27.00    3.00
│  REVENUE  270.90   280.70   287.90   297.70  1145.80  1137.20    8.60
│  NET      298.00   308.70   305.00   308.00  1250.00  1219.70   30.30
│
└──────────────────────────────────────────────────────────────────┘
```

Finally, the sixth tutorial chapter (Chapter 7, "Using Programs with SAS/CALC Software") teaches you how to write and execute programs using SAS/CALC software. You create three spreadsheets, EASTERN2, WESTERN2, and COMPANY2, using SAS/CALC language statements.

Part 2
The Tutorial Chapters

Chapter 2	**Creating Your First Spreadsheet**
Chapter 3	**Modifying Your Spreadsheet**
Chapter 4	**Producing Spreadsheet Reports and Generating Graphics**
Chapter 5	**Creating a Three-Dimensional Spreadsheet**
Chapter 6	**Linking Spreadsheets**
Chapter 7	**Using Programs with SAS/CALC™ Software**

Chapter 2 Creating Your First Spreadsheet

Creating Your First Spreadsheet 19
    Lesson 2.1: Invoking SAS/CALC Software 20
    Lesson 2.2: Creating a New Spreadsheet 27
    Lesson 2.3: Defining Initial Parameters 30
    Lesson 2.4: Changing the Default Row and Column Names 32
    Lesson 2.5: Deleting Rows and Columns 34
    Lesson 2.6: Entering the Cell Values 38
    Lesson 2.7: Defining Formulas 39
    Lesson 2.8: Copying Formulas 44
    Lesson 2.9: Saving a Spreadsheet 49
    Lesson 2.10: Closing a Spreadsheet 50
    Lesson 2.11: Ending the SAS/CALC Software Session 51
    Lesson 2.12: Ending the SAS System Session 52
Chapter Summary 53

Creating Your First Spreadsheet

In this chapter you learn how to create a simple spreadsheet using SAS/CALC software.
    Specifically, you learn how to create a spreadsheet, define initial parameters such as the number of rows and columns in the spreadsheet, define row and column names, delete rows and columns, enter values into cells, and define formulas to compute cell values.

    In this tutorial, you create the spreadsheet shown in Display 2.1. This spreadsheet contains financial data showing the amounts budgeted for and actually spent on expense items within the Sales Division for the eastern region of a corporation.

Display 2.1
The EASTERN Spreadsheet

```
┌CALC: PAGE1 EASTERN.CALC (E)─────────────────────────────┐
│ File Edit View Execute Charts Locals Globals Help       │
│                                                         │
│              QTR1      QTR2      QTR3     QTR4   BUDGET │
│                                                         │
│   SALARY       30        33      35.5       37      135 │
│   BENEFITS      6         7       7.7        8     27.5 │
│   SUPPLIES    0.5       0.5         1        1        3 │
│   COMPUTER     20      21.5        22     22.5       85 │
│   RENT          4         4         4      4.8       16 │
│   UTILITY       1         1         1      1.5        4 │
│   EXPENSES   61.5        67      71.2     74.8    270.5 │
│   REVENUE      75      73.5        78       75      295 │
│                                                         │
│                                                         │
│                                                         │
│                                                         │
│                                                         │
│                                                         │
└─────────────────────────────────────────────────────────┘
```

The spreadsheet contains the following columns:

QTR1-QTR4   are the actual expenditures for the quarters of the year for each item.

BUDGET   is the amount of money budgeted for the year for each item.

The spreadsheet contains the following rows:

SALARY   contains salary values.

BENEFITS   contains costs for employee benefits.

SUPPLIES   contains costs for supplies.

COMPUTER   contains costs for computer equipment.

RENT   contains rental costs.

UTILITY   contains costs for utilities.

EXPENSES   contains total costs for each quarter and the total budget.

REVENUE   contains revenue amounts for each quarter and the projected yearly revenue for the division.

Note: The cell values represent thousands of dollars.

Lesson 2.1: Invoking SAS/CALC Software

This tutorial uses pull-down menus to execute many commands. If your display has a command line instead of an action bar, type PMENU on the command line and press ENTER to activate the pull-down menus.

Creating Your First Spreadsheet □ *Creating Your First Spreadsheet* **21**

To invoke SAS/CALC software and create a new spreadsheet:

1. Select **Globals** from the action bar at the top of the PROGRAM EDITOR window as shown in Display 2.2.

Display 2.2
Selecting Globals

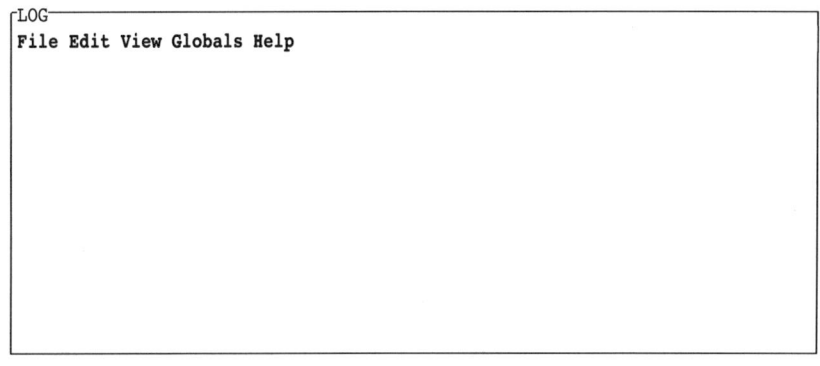

```
┌LOG─────────────────────────────────────────────────┐
│File Edit View Globals Help                         │
│                                                    │
│                                                    │
│                                                    │
│                                                    │
│                                                    │
│                                                    │
└────────────────────────────────────────────────────┘
┌PROGRAM EDITOR──────────────────────────────────────┐
│File Edit View Locals Globals Help                  │
│                                                    │
│00001                                               │
│00002                                               │
│00003                                               │
│00004                                               │
│00005                                               │
│00006                                               │
└────────────────────────────────────────────────────┘
```

2. Select **Desktop** from the Globals pull-down menu as shown in Display 2.3.

Display 2.3
Selecting Desktop

```
┌LOG─────────────────────────────────────────────────┐
│File Edit View Globals Help                         │
│                                                    │
│                                                    │
│                                            ┌──────────────────────┐
│                                            │SAS/ASSIST            │
│                                            │SAS/EIS               │
│                                            │Program Editor        │
│                                            │Log                   │
┌PROGRAM EDITOR──────────────────────────────│Output                │
│File Edit View Locals                       │Output Manager        │
│                                            │Graph Manager         │
│00001                                       │Access                │
│00002                                       │Invoke application  ->│
│00003                                       │Data management    ->│
│00004                                       │Desktop             ->│
│00005                                       │Command             ->│
│00006                                       │Global options      ->│
                                             └──────────────────────┘
```

22 *Creating Your First Spreadsheet* □ *Chapter 2*

3. Select **Spreadsheet...** from the Desktop pull-down menu as shown in Display 2.4.

Display 2.4
Selecting Spreadsheet...

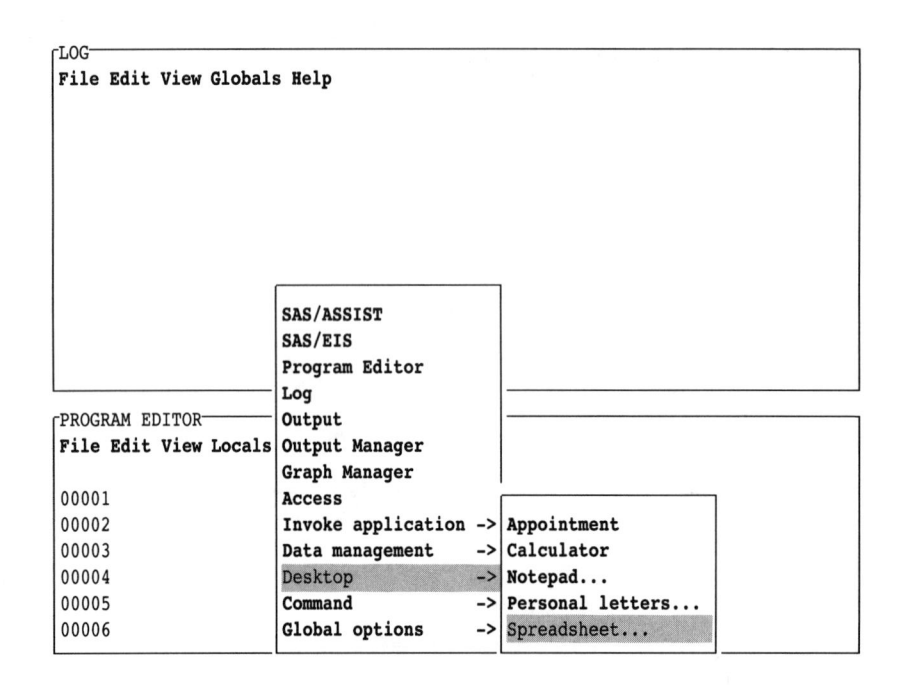

```
┌LOG─────────────────────────────────────────────────────────┐
│File Edit View Globals Help                                 │
│                                                            │
│                                                            │
│                                                            │
│                          ┌─────────────────┐               │
│                          │ SAS/ASSIST      │               │
│                          │ SAS/EIS         │               │
│                          │ Program Editor  │               │
│                          │ Log             │               │
│ ┌PROGRAM EDITOR──────────│ Output          │───────────────│
│ │File Edit View Locals   │ Output Manager  │               │
│ │                        │ Graph Manager   │               │
│ │00001                   │ Access          │               │
│ │00002                   │ Invoke application ->│ Appointment    │
│ │00003                   │ Data management    ->│ Calculator     │
│ │00004                   │ Desktop            ->│ Notepad...     │
│ │00005                   │ Command            ->│ Personal letters...│
│ │00006                   │ Global options     ->│ Spreadsheet... │
```

Selecting **Spreadsheet...** opens the Spreadsheet... dialog box, shown in Display 2.5, enabling you to name the catalog where you want to store your spreadsheets.

Display 2.5
Default Spreadsheet... Dialog Box

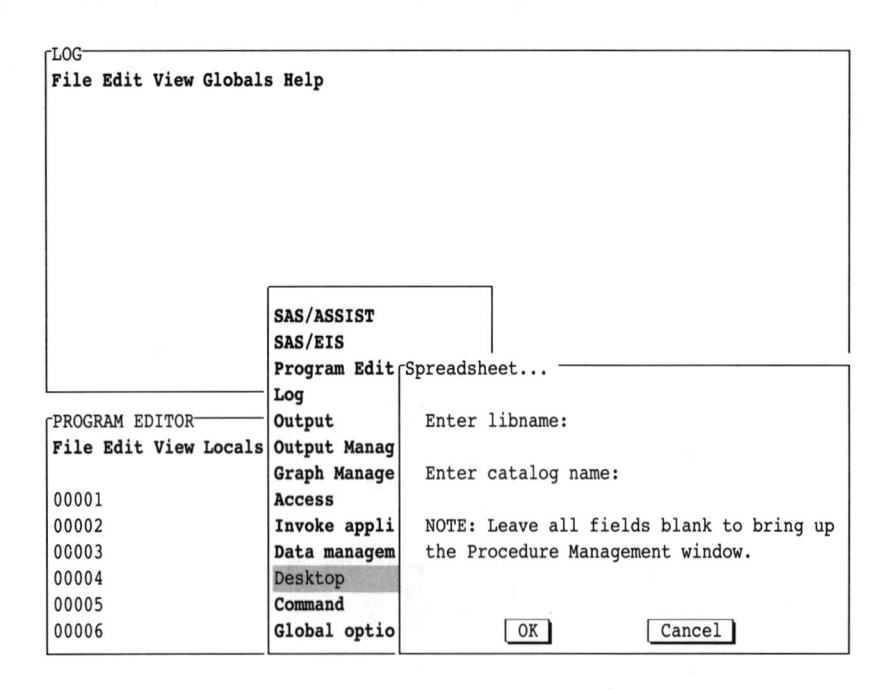

```
┌LOG─────────────────────────────────────────────────────────┐
│File Edit View Globals Help                                 │
│                                                            │
│                                                            │
│                          SAS/ASSIST                        │
│                          SAS/EIS                           │
│                          Program Edit┌Spreadsheet...──────┐│
│                          Log         │                    ││
│ ┌PROGRAM EDITOR──────────Output      │ Enter libname:     ││
│ │File Edit View Locals   Output Manag│                    ││
│ │                        Graph Manage│ Enter catalog name:││
│ │00001                   Access      │                    ││
│ │00002                   Invoke appli│ NOTE: Leave all fields blank to bring up│
│ │00003                   Data managem│ the Procedure Management window.│
│ │00004                   Desktop     │                    ││
│ │00005                   Command     │                    ││
│ │00006                   Global optio│  [ OK ]   [ Cancel ]││
```

4. Type SASUSER next to **Enter libname** as shown in Display 2.6. You can type SASUSER in uppercase or lowercase.

    The libname SASUSER indicates the SASUSER library as the location for storing your new spreadsheet. You do not need to create the SASUSER library. It is automatically created for you when you invoke the SAS System for the first time.

Display 2.6
Typing SASUSER in the Spreadsheet... Dialog Box

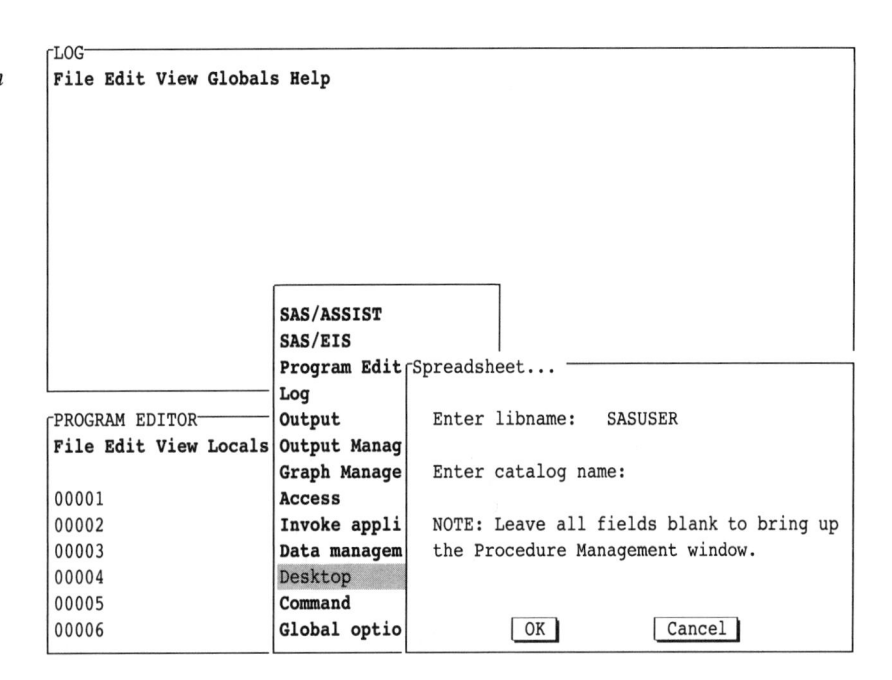

```
┌LOG─────────────────────────────────────────────────────────────────────┐
│File Edit View Globals Help                                             │
│                                                                        │
│                                                                        │
│                                                    │
│                          ┌─────────────────┐                          │
│                          │SAS/ASSIST       │                          │
│                          │SAS/EIS          │                          │
│                          │Program Edit┌Spreadsheet...──────────────┐  │
│                          │Log         │                             │  │
│┌PROGRAM EDITOR──────────┐│Output      │ Enter libname:   SASUSER   │  │
││File Edit View Locals   ││Output Manag│                             │  │
││                        ││Graph Manage│ Enter catalog name:         │  │
││00001                   ││Access      │                             │  │
││00002                   ││Invoke appli│ NOTE: Leave all fields blank to bring up │
││00003                   ││Data managem│ the Procedure Management window.         │
││00004                   ││Desktop     │                             │  │
││00005                   ││Command     │                             │  │
││00006                   ││Global optio│    [ OK ]        [ Cancel ] │  │
│                          └────────────┴─────────────────────────────┘  │
└────────────────────────────────────────────────────────────────────────┘
```

24 *Creating Your First Spreadsheet □ Chapter 2*

5. Type CALC next to **Enter catalog name** as shown in Display 2.7. You can type CALC in uppercase or lowercase.

   The catalog CALC identifies the catalog in the SASUSER library where the spreadsheet will be stored. If the CALC catalog does not already exist, SAS/CALC software creates the catalog.

Display 2.7
Typing CALC in the Spreadsheet... Dialog Box

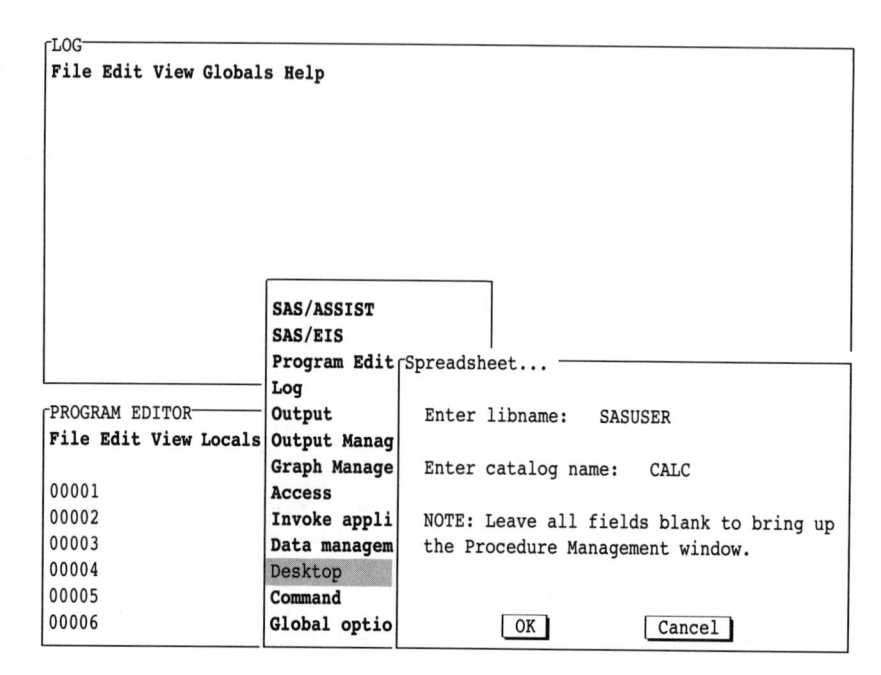

```
┌LOG─────────────────────────────────────────────────────────────┐
│File Edit View Globals Help                                      │
│                                                                 │
│                                                                 │
│                                                                 │
│                                                                 │
│                                                                 │
│                          ┌──────────────┐                       │
│                          │SAS/ASSIST    │                       │
│                          │SAS/EIS       │                       │
│                          │Program Edit ┌─Spreadsheet...─────────┐
│                          │Log          │                        │
│  ┌PROGRAM EDITOR─────────┤Output       │ Enter libname:  SASUSER│
│  │File Edit View Locals  │Output Manag │                        │
│  │                       │Graph Manage │ Enter catalog name: CALC│
│  │00001                  │Access       │                        │
│  │00002                  │Invoke appli │ NOTE: Leave all fields blank to bring up
│  │00003                  │Data managem │ the Procedure Management window.
│  │00004                  │Desktop      │                        │
│  │00005                  │Command      │                        │
│  │00006                  │Global optio │  [  OK  ]    [ Cancel ]│
│                          └──────────────┴────────────────────────┘
```

Note: Consult *SAS/CALC Software: Usage and Reference, Version 6, First Edition* for more information regarding the Procedure Management window.

6. Select **OK** in the Spreadsheet... dialog box to display the DIRECTORY window shown in Display 2.8.

Display 2.8
DIRECTORY Window

```
┌CALC: DIRECTORY SASUSER.CALC (E)──────────────────────────────┐
│ File Edit View Locals Globals Help                           │
│                                                              │
│    Name    Type    Description                     Updated   │
│                                                              │
│                                                              │
│                                                              │
│                                                              │
│                                                              │
│                                                              │
│                                                              │
│                                                              │
│                                                              │
│                                                              │
│                                                              │
│                                                              │
└──────────────────────────────────────────────────────────────┘
```

An alternative to using the pull-down menus to invoke SAS/CALC software is to submit a CALC procedure step.

To invoke SAS/CALC software with a PROC CALC step:

1. Type the PROC CALC step, as shown in Display 2.9, in the PROGRAM EDITOR window.

    The CATALOG= option in the PROC CALC statement identifies the catalog, CALC, in the SASUSER library where the spreadsheet will be stored.

26 *Creating Your First Spreadsheet* □ *Chapter 2*

Display 2.9
The PROC CALC Step

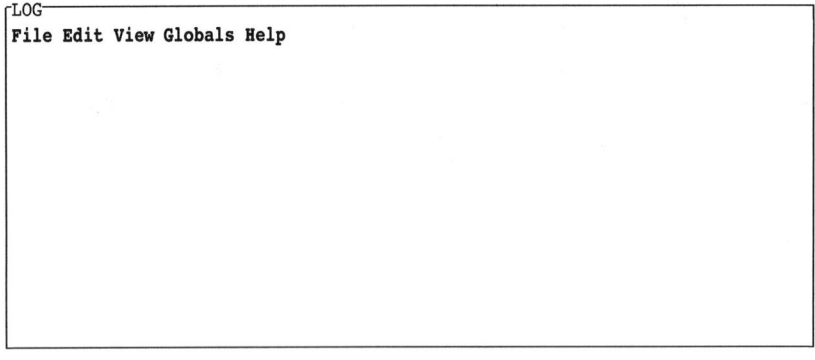

```
LOG
File Edit View Globals Help




```

```
PROGRAM EDITOR
File Edit View Locals Globals Help

00001 proc calc catalog=sasuser.calc;
00002 run;
00003
00004
00005
00006
```

2. Select **Locals** from the action bar and **Submit** from the Locals pull-down menu, as shown in Display 2.10.

Display 2.10
Submitting the PROC CALC Step

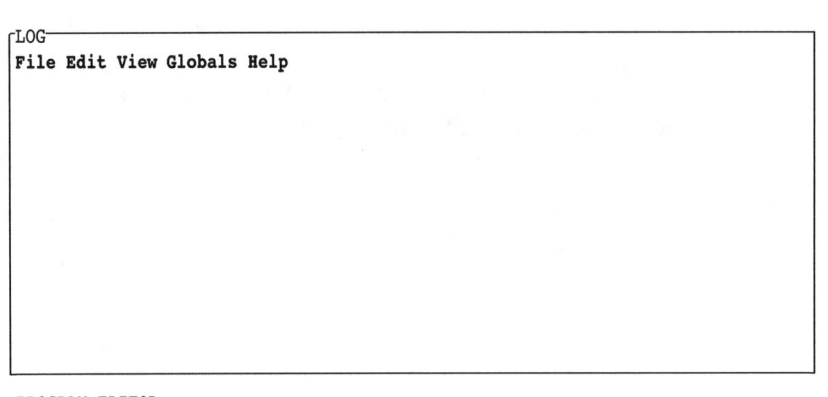

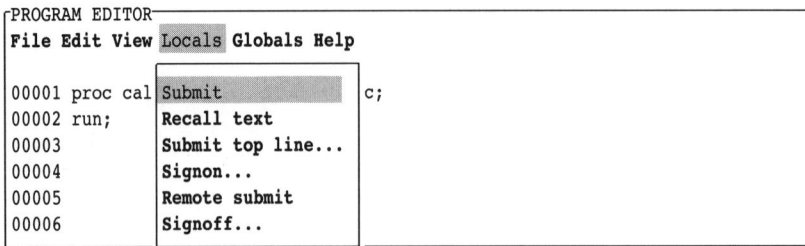

```
LOG
File Edit View Globals Help




```

```
PROGRAM EDITOR
File Edit View Locals Globals Help

00001 proc cal  Submit          c;
00002 run;      Recall text
00003           Submit top line...
00004           Signon...
00005           Remote submit
00006           Signoff...
```

Selecting **Submit** passes the PROC CALC step to the SAS System for processing and displays the DIRECTORY window shown in Display 2.11.

Display 2.11
DIRECTORY Window

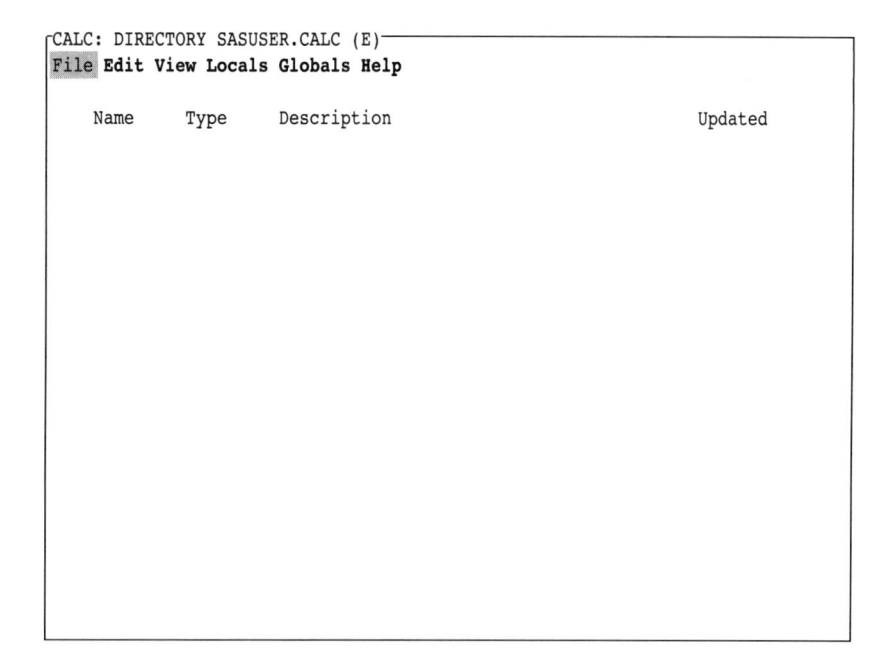

```
┌CALC: DIRECTORY SASUSER.CALC (E)──────────────────────────────┐
│ File Edit View Locals Globals Help                           │
│                                                              │
│    Name    Type    Description              Updated          │
│                                                              │
│                                                              │
│                                                              │
│                                                              │
│                                                              │
│                                                              │
│                                                              │
│                                                              │
│                                                              │
│                                                              │
│                                                              │
│                                                              │
└──────────────────────────────────────────────────────────────┘
```

The DIRECTORY window enables you to create new spreadsheets and modify existing spreadsheets.

Lesson 2.2: Creating a New Spreadsheet

To create a new spreadsheet:

1. Select **File** from the action bar at the top of the DIRECTORY window and **New...** from the File pull-down menu, as shown in Display 2.12.

28 *Creating Your First Spreadsheet* □ *Chapter 2*

Display 2.12
Selecting New...

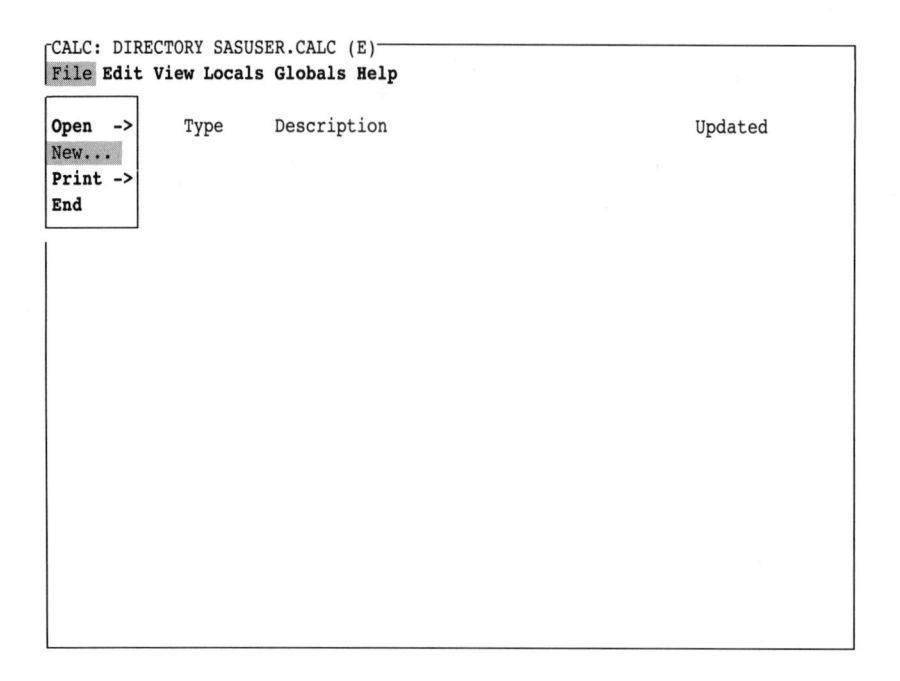

```
┌CALC: DIRECTORY SASUSER.CALC (E)─────────────────────────────┐
│ File Edit View Locals Globals Help                          │
│                                                             │
│ ┌──────────┐                                                │
│ │ Open  -> │  Type    Description              Updated      │
│ │ New...   │                                                │
│ │ Print -> │                                                │
│ │ End      │                                                │
│ └──────────┘                                                │
│                                                             │
│                                                             │
│                                                             │
│                                                             │
│                                                             │
│                                                             │
└─────────────────────────────────────────────────────────────┘
```

After selecting **New...**, the New... dialog box, shown in Display 2.13, appears enabling you to name and define your spreadsheet.

Display 2.13
Default New...
Dialog Box

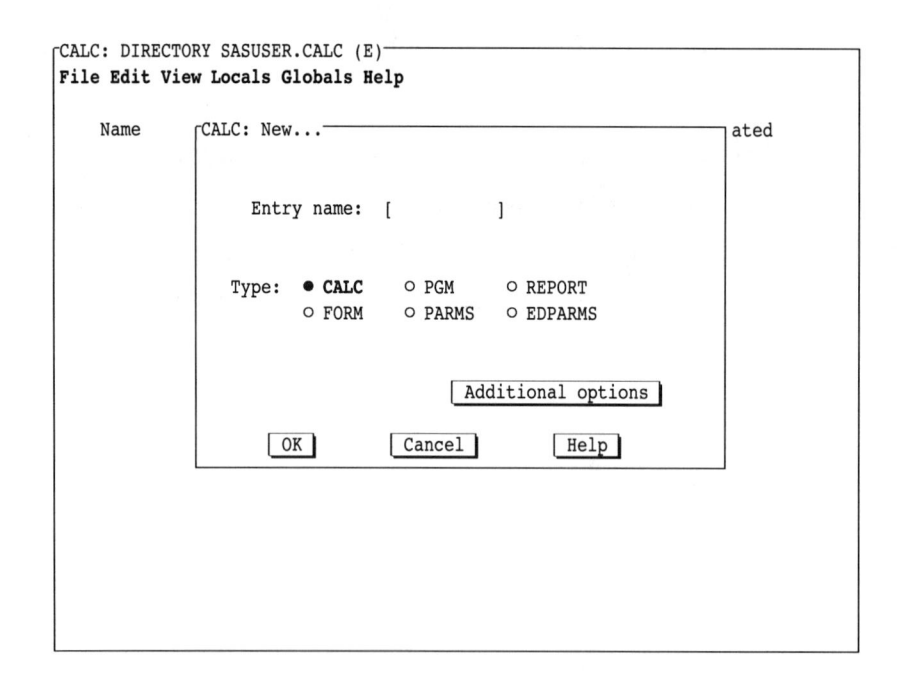

```
┌CALC: DIRECTORY SASUSER.CALC (E)─────────────────────────────┐
│ File Edit View Locals Globals Help                          │
│                                                             │
│   Name   ┌CALC: New...──────────────────────────┐  ated     │
│          │                                      │           │
│          │     Entry name: [          ]         │           │
│          │                                      │           │
│          │     Type:  ● CALC   ○ PGM    ○ REPORT│           │
│          │            ○ FORM   ○ PARMS  ○ EDPARMS│          │
│          │                                      │           │
│          │                      ┌─────────────────┐│         │
│          │                      │Additional options││        │
│          │     ┌──┐   ┌──────┐   └─────────────────┘│        │
│          │     │OK│   │Cancel│        │Help │      │         │
│          │     └──┘   └──────┘        └─────┘      │         │
│          └──────────────────────────────────────────┘         │
│                                                             │
└─────────────────────────────────────────────────────────────┘
```

2. Name your spreadsheet by typing the spreadsheet name, EASTERN, in the **Entry name** field, as shown in Display 2.14, and pressing ENTER. You can type EASTERN in uppercase or lowercase. When you press ENTER, the spreadsheet name is automatically translated to uppercase and the **Additional options** button becomes active.

Display 2.14
New... Dialog Box with EASTERN

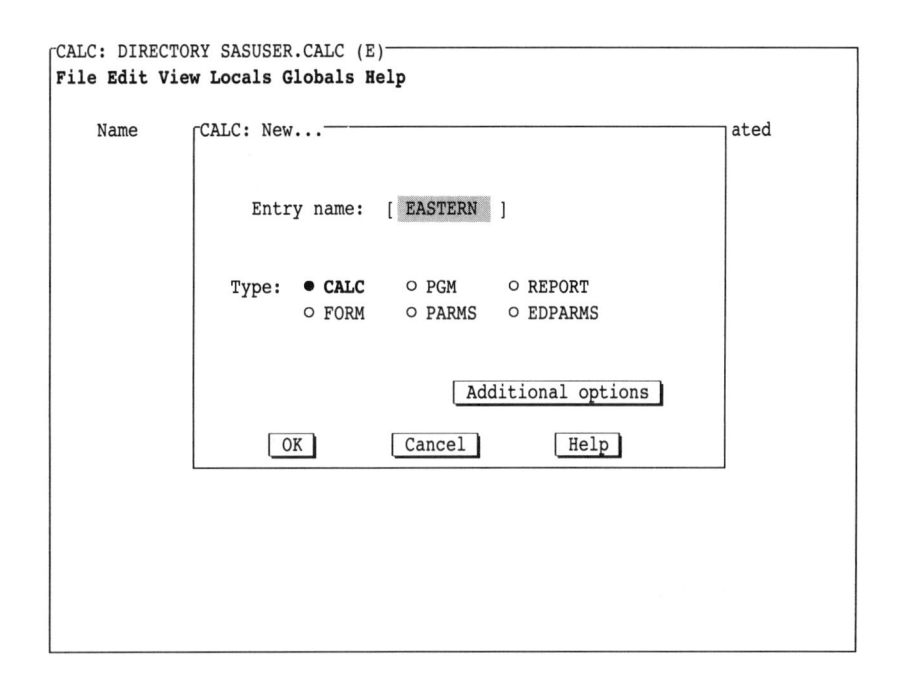

```
┌CALC: DIRECTORY SASUSER.CALC (E)─────────────────────────┐
│File Edit View Locals Globals Help                       │
│                                                         │
│    Name    ┌CALC: New...──────────────────────┐ated     │
│            │                                  │         │
│            │    Entry name:  [ EASTERN ]      │         │
│            │                                  │         │
│            │    Type:  ● CALC   ○ PGM   ○ REPORT │      │
│            │           ○ FORM   ○ PARMS ○ EDPARMS│      │
│            │                                  │         │
│            │                  [Additional options]    │
│            │   [OK]   [Cancel]     [Help]     │         │
│            └──────────────────────────────────┘         │
│                                                         │
└─────────────────────────────────────────────────────────┘
```

3. Because **Type** defaults to **CALC**, which is the appropriate type for a spreadsheet, you do not need to select a type.

4. Select **Additional options** to define initial parameters for your spreadsheet.

   Note: Defining initial parameters for a new spreadsheet is optional.
   Selecting **Additional options** displays the Additional Options dialog box shown in Display 2.15. This box enables you to define the initial number of rows and columns, maximum rows and columns, password protection, and column widths for your spreadsheet.

Display 2.15
Default Additional Options Dialog Box

```
┌CALC: DIRECTORY SASUSER.CALC (E)─────────────────────────┐
│File Edit View Locals Globals Help                       │
│┌CALC: Additional Options──────────────────────────────┐ │
││                                                      │ │
││       Spreadsheet specification for: EASTERN         │ │
││                                                      │ │
││              Initial number of rows: [ 20    ]       │ │
││           Initial number of columns: [ 20    ]       │ │
││             Initial number of pages: [ 1     ]       │ │
││                                                      │ │
││              Maximum number of rows: [ 25    ]       │ │
││           Maximum number of columns: [ 25    ]       │ │
││                                                      │ │
││     Column width: [ 8   ]         Column space: [ 2 ]│ │
││        Password: [         ]                         │ │
││                                                      │ │
││                                       │Fetch a data set││
││     │OK│           │Cancel│             │Help│       │ │
│└──────────────────────────────────────────────────────┘ │
└─────────────────────────────────────────────────────────┘
```

By default, all spreadsheets have 20 rows and 20 columns for a total of 400 cells. If you need more or fewer cells, you can change these default values. Because the EASTERN spreadsheet does not need 400 cells, you can reduce the initial number of rows and columns by typing new values in the initial rows and initial columns fields.

Lesson 2.3: Defining Initial Parameters

1. Move the cursor to **Initial number of rows** and change the value from 20 to 15 as shown in Display 2.16.

2. Move the cursor to **Initial number of columns** and change the value from 20 to 8 as shown in Display 2.16.

Display 2.16
Modified Additional Options Dialog Box

```
┌CALC: DIRECTORY SASUSER.CALC (E)──────────────────────────────┐
│File Edit View Locals Globals Help                            │
│                                                              │
│┌CALC: Additional Options─────────────────────────────────────┐
││                                                             │
││              Spreadsheet specification for: EASTERN         │
││                                                             │
││                    Initial number of rows: [ 15    ]        │
││                 Initial number of columns: [ 8     ]        │
││                   Initial number of pages: [ 1     ]        │
││                                                             │
││                    Maximum number of rows: [ 25    ]        │
││                 Maximum number of columns: [ 25    ]        │
││                                                             │
││      Column width: [ 8   ]          Column space: [ 2 ]     │
││         Password: [          ]                              │
││                                                             │
││                                           [Fetch a data set]│
││   [ OK ]            [Cancel]              [Help]            │
│└─────────────────────────────────────────────────────────────┘
│                                                              │
└──────────────────────────────────────────────────────────────┘
```

3. After defining the initial number of rows and columns, select **OK** to return to the New... dialog box.

4. Select **OK** in the New... dialog box to open the EASTERN spreadsheet shown in Display 2.17.

   Note: The number of columns and rows that appear on the display depends on your hardware.

   Note: Consult *SAS/CALC Software: Usage and Reference* for more information regarding the Additional Options dialog box.

Display 2.17
The EASTERN Spreadsheet with Default Row and Column Names

```
┌CALC: PAGE1 EASTERN.CALC (E)─────────────────────────────────────┐
│ File Edit View Execute Charts Locals Globals Help               │
│                                                                 │
│           COL1    COL2    COL3    COL4    COL5    COL6    COL7  │
│  ROW1                                                           │
│  ROW2                                                           │
│  ROW3                                                           │
│  ROW4                                                           │
│  ROW5                                                           │
│  ROW6                                                           │
│  ROW7                                                           │
│  ROW8                                                           │
│  ROW9                                                           │
│  ROW10                                                          │
│  ROW11                                                          │
│  ROW12                                                          │
│  ROW13                                                          │
│  ROW14                                                          │
│  ROW15                                                          │
│                                                                 │
└─────────────────────────────────────────────────────────────────┘
```

You are now ready to define the rows and columns for the EASTERN spreadsheet.

Lesson 2.4: Changing the Default Row and Column Names

Column and row names

- contain 1 to 8 characters
- begin with a letter A-Z or an underscore
- continue with any combination of letters, numbers, or underscores.

Change the column names COL1 through COL5 to QTR1, QTR2, QTR3, QTR4, and BUDGET, respectively. You can type the names in uppercase or lowercase.

To define the column names:

1. Move the cursor to each column heading.

2. Type the new name over the existing name. Be sure to delete the default column name completely.

3. Press ENTER.

   Note: The column names are centered and translated to uppercase.

Change the row names `ROW1` through `ROW8` to `SALARY`, `BENEFITS`, `SUPPLIES`, `COMPUTER`, `RENT`, `UTILITY`, `EXPENSES`, and `REVENUE`, respectively. You can type the names in uppercase or lowercase.

To define the row names:

1. Move the cursor to each row name.

2. Type the new name over the existing name. Be sure to delete the default row name completely.

3. Press ENTER.

   Note: The row names are translated to uppercase.
   The new column and row names appear in Display 2.18.

Display 2.18
New Column and Row Names

```
┌CALC: PAGE1 EASTERN.CALC (E)─────────────────────────────────────┐
│ File Edit View Execute Charts Locals Globals Help               │
│                                                                 │
│              QTR1      QTR2      QTR3      QTR4    BUDGET    COL6    COL7 │
│                                                                 │
│  SALARY                                                         │
│  BENEFITS                                                       │
│  SUPPLIES                                                       │
│  COMPUTER                                                       │
│  RENT                                                           │
│  UTILITY                                                        │
│  EXPENSES                                                       │
│  REVENUE                                                        │
│  ROW9                                                           │
│  ROW10                                                          │
│  ROW11                                                          │
│  ROW12                                                          │
│  ROW13                                                          │
│  ROW14                                                          │
│  ROW15                                                          │
│                                                                 │
│                                                                 │
└─────────────────────────────────────────────────────────────────┘
```

As you can see, the EASTERN spreadsheet contains more rows and columns than are actually needed.

34 *Creating Your First Spreadsheet* □ *Chapter 2*

Lesson 2.5: Deleting Rows and Columns

To delete rows from the spreadsheet:

1. Select **Edit** from the action bar and **Delete...** from the Edit pull-down menu as shown in Display 2.19.

Display 2.19
Selecting Delete

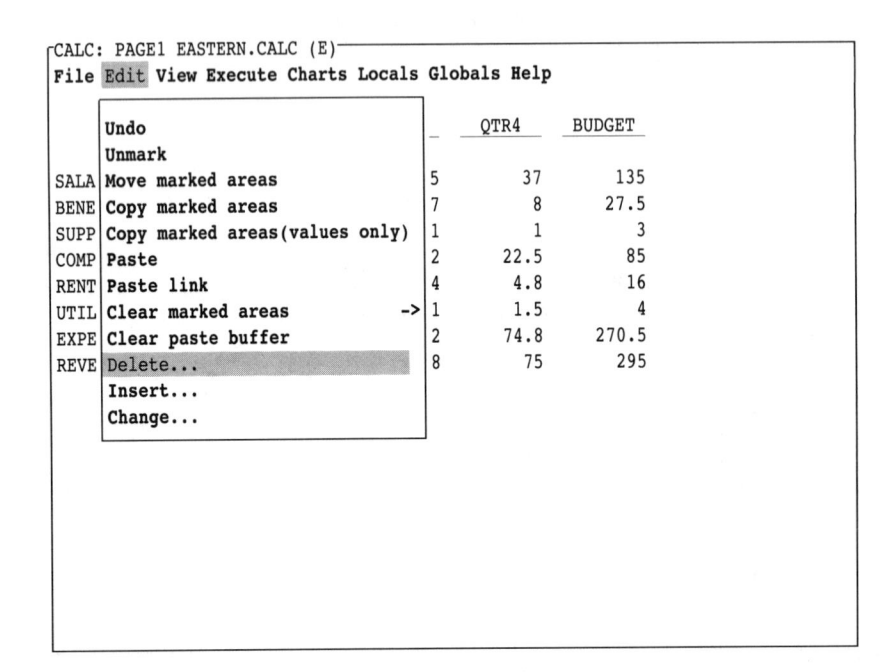

```
┌CALC: PAGE1 EASTERN.CALC (E)─────────────────────────────────┐
│File Edit View Execute Charts Locals Globals Help            │
│     ┌──────────────────────────────────┐                    │
│     │Undo                              │    QTR4    BUDGET  │
│     │Unmark                            │                    │
│SALA │Move marked areas                 │ 5    37      135   │
│BENE │Copy marked areas                 │ 7     8     27.5   │
│SUPP │Copy marked areas(values only)    │ 1     1        3   │
│COMP │Paste                             │ 2   22.5      85   │
│RENT │Paste link                        │ 4    4.8      16   │
│UTIL │Clear marked areas            ->  │ 1    1.5       4   │
│EXPE │Clear paste buffer                │ 2   74.8    270.5  │
│REVE │Delete...                         │ 8    75      295   │
│     │Insert...                         │                    │
│     │Change...                         │                    │
│     └──────────────────────────────────┘                    │
│                                                             │
└─────────────────────────────────────────────────────────────┘
```

2. Select **Rows...** from the Delete dialog box, as shown in Display 2.20, to open the Delete rows dialog box.

Display 2.20
Delete Dialog Box

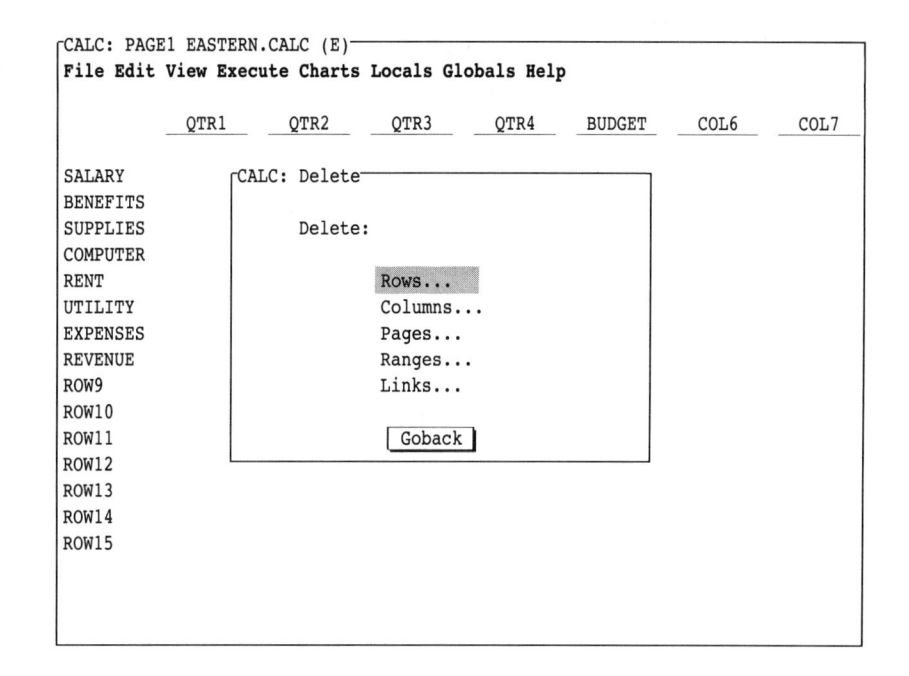

```
┌CALC: PAGE1 EASTERN.CALC (E)─────────────────────────────────────┐
│File Edit View Execute Charts Locals Globals Help                │
│                                                                  │
│             QTR1     QTR2      QTR3     QTR4    BUDGET   COL6   COL7
│                                                                  │
│  SALARY    ┌CALC: Delete─────────────────────┐                  │
│  BENEFITS  │                                 │                  │
│  SUPPLIES  │      Delete:                    │                  │
│  COMPUTER  │                                 │                  │
│  RENT      │           Rows...               │                  │
│  UTILITY   │           Columns...            │                  │
│  EXPENSES  │           Pages...              │                  │
│  REVENUE   │           Ranges...             │                  │
│  ROW9      │           Links...              │                  │
│  ROW10     │                                 │                  │
│  ROW11     │          ┌ Goback ┐             │                  │
│  ROW12     │          └────────┘             │                  │
│  ROW13     └─────────────────────────────────┘                  │
│  ROW14                                                          │
│  ROW15                                                          │
│                                                                  │
└──────────────────────────────────────────────────────────────────┘
```

36 *Creating Your First Spreadsheet □ Chapter 2*

3. Select the first row name you want to delete, **ROW9**, by moving the cursor to **ROW9** and pressing ENTER or, if you are using a mouse, by pointing and clicking on the row name.

   An asterisk is displayed, as shown in Display 2.21, indicating the column will be deleted. The cursor automatically moves to the next row name, **ROW10**.

4. Continue selecting each individual row to delete as shown in Display 2.21.

   Note: SAS/CALC software automatically scrolls the list of row names if you select the last item in the list.

   Note: If you select a row by mistake, reselect the row name to remove the asterisk.

Display 2.21
Delete Rows Dialog Box

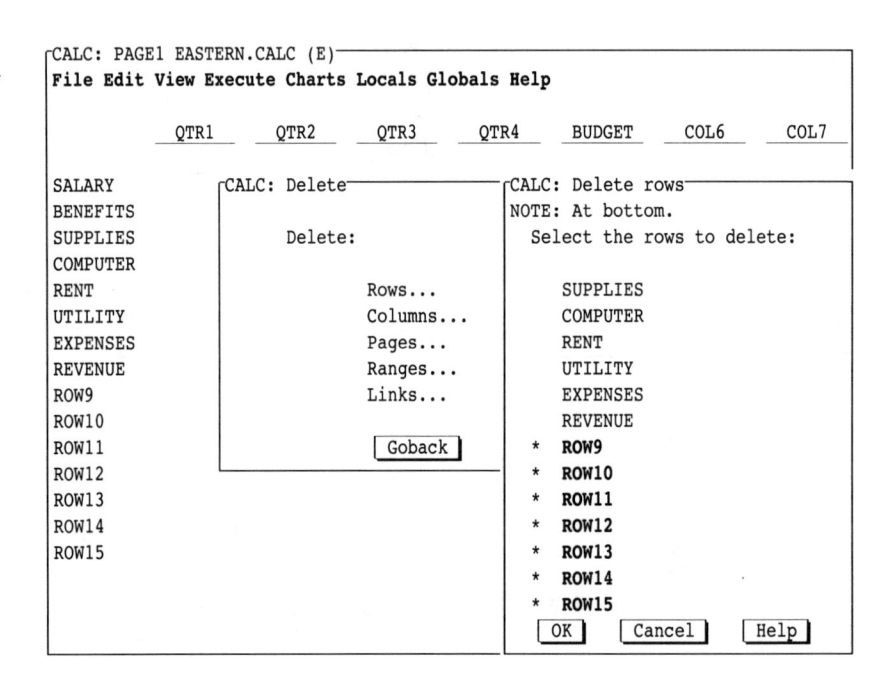

```
┌CALC: PAGE1 EASTERN.CALC (E)─────────────────────────────────────────┐
│File Edit View Execute Charts Locals Globals Help                    │
│                                                                      │
│              QTR1      QTR2     QTR3     QTR4    BUDGET   COL6   COL7│
│                                                                      │
│   SALARY       ┌CALC: Delete──────┐  ┌CALC: Delete rows─────────┐    │
│   BENEFITS     │                  │  │NOTE: At bottom.          │    │
│   SUPPLIES     │   Delete:        │  │   Select the rows to delete:│ │
│   COMPUTER     │                  │  │                          │    │
│   RENT         │        Rows...   │  │     SUPPLIES             │    │
│   UTILITY      │        Columns...│  │     COMPUTER             │    │
│   EXPENSES     │        Pages...  │  │     RENT                 │    │
│   REVENUE      │        Ranges... │  │     UTILITY              │    │
│   ROW9         │        Links...  │  │     EXPENSES             │    │
│   ROW10        │                  │  │     REVENUE              │    │
│   ROW11        │      [ Goback ]  │  │  *  ROW9                 │    │
│   ROW12        │                  │  │  *  ROW10                │    │
│   ROW13        └──────────────────┘  │  *  ROW11                │    │
│   ROW14                              │  *  ROW12                │    │
│   ROW15                              │  *  ROW13                │    │
│                                      │  *  ROW14                │    │
│                                      │  *  ROW15                │    │
│                                      │  [ OK ] [ Cancel ] [ Help ]│  │
│                                      └──────────────────────────┘    │
└──────────────────────────────────────────────────────────────────────┘
```

5. Once you have selected all of the desired rows, select **OK** to delete the rows and redisplay the EASTERN spreadsheet.

To delete columns from the spreadsheet:

1. Select **Edit** from the action bar and **Delete...** from the Edit pull-down menu.

2. Select **Columns...** from the Delete dialog box to open the Delete columns dialog box.

3. Select the first column name you want to delete, **COL6**, by moving the cursor to the column name and pressing ENTER or by pointing and clicking with a mouse.

4. Continue selecting **COL7** and **COL8**.

    Note: SAS/CALC software automatically scrolls the list of column names if you select the last item in the list.

    Note: If you select a column by mistake, reselect the column to remove the asterisk.

5. Once you have selected all of the desired columns, select **OK** to delete the columns and redisplay the EASTERN spreadsheet shown in Display 2.22.

Display 2.22
Result of Deleting Rows and Columns

```
┌CALC: PAGE1 EASTERN.CALC (E)──────────────────────────────────┐
│ File Edit View Execute Charts Locals Globals Help            │
│                                                              │
│              QTR1      QTR2      QTR3      QTR4     BUDGET   │
│   SALARY                                                     │
│   BENEFITS                                                   │
│   SUPPLIES                                                   │
│   COMPUTER                                                   │
│   RENT                                                       │
│   UTLITY                                                     │
│   EXPENSES                                                   │
│   REVENUE                                                    │
│                                                              │
│                                                              │
│                                                              │
│                                                              │
│                                                              │
└──────────────────────────────────────────────────────────────┘
```

Now that you have deleted the excess columns and rows from the spreadsheet, you are ready to enter data values into the cells.

Lesson 2.6: Entering the Cell Values

To enter the cell values:

1. Move the cursor to the first cell, SALARY.QTR1, and type 30.

2. Move the cursor to the appropriate cells and continue entering the values shown in Display 2.23.

Display 2.23
The EASTERN Spreadsheet with Cell Values

```
┌CALC: PAGE1 EASTERN.CALC (E)─────────────────────────────
File Edit View Execute Charts Locals Globals Help

              QTR1      QTR2      QTR3      QTR4     BUDGET

SALARY         30        33       35.5       37       135
BENEFITS        6         7        7.7        8        27.5
SUPPLIES      0.5       0.5        1          1         3
COMPUTER       20       21.5      22         22.5      85
RENT            4         4        4          4.8      16
UTILITY         1         1        1          1.5       4
EXPENSES
REVENUE        75       73.5      78         75       295
```

3. Once you have entered all the values, press ENTER. By default, numeric values are right justified.

After you have entered values into the spreadsheet, you write a formula to compute the values for the EXPENSES row by summing the expense values within each column in the spreadsheet.

Lesson 2.7: Defining Formulas

A *formula* is an expression that performs a calculation on cell values in the spreadsheet. The syntax of a formula is

```
=expression
```

The expression can include constant values, cell names, arithmetic operators, logical operators, and functions. In this spreadsheet, you need to compute the value for each cell in the EXPENSES row.

To define a formula to compute the total expenses in the first quarter (cell EXPENSES.QTR1):

1. Select **Execute** from the action bar and **Enter formula** from the Execute pull-down menu as shown in Display 2.24.

Display 2.24
Selecting Enter Formula

```
┌CALC: PAGE1 EASTERN.CALC (E)─────────────────────────────────┐
│ File Edit View Execute Charts Locals Globals Help           │
│                                                             │
│                  QT┌Enter formula    ┐R3     QTR4    BUDGET │
│                    │End formula entry│                      │
│          SALARY    │Run...           │35.5     37      135  │
│          BENEFITS  │Recalc           │ 7.7      8     27.5  │
│          SUPPLIES  │Recalc all       │  1       1        3  │
│          COMPUTER  │Compile...       │ 22     22.5      85  │
│          RENT      │Runopts...       │  4      4.8      16  │
│          UTILITY   │Clear pgm        │  1      1.5       4  │
│          EXPENSES  │Autocalc      -> │                      │
│          REVENUE   └─────────────────┘ 78      75      295  │
│                                                             │
│                                                             │
│                                                             │
│                                                             │
│                                                             │
└─────────────────────────────────────────────────────────────┘
```

40 *Creating Your First Spreadsheet* □ *Chapter 2*

After selecting **Enter formula**, the formula entry area appears below the action bar as shown in Display 2.25. Initially, the value for the cell in the first row and first column in the spreadsheet is displayed in the formula entry area. Notice the cell SALARY.QTR1 is highlighted and the cell name, SALARY.QTR1.PAGE1, appears to the left of the formula entry area. This indicates that the cell value, **30**, currently displayed in the formula entry area applies to that cell.

Display 2.25
Default Formula Entry Area

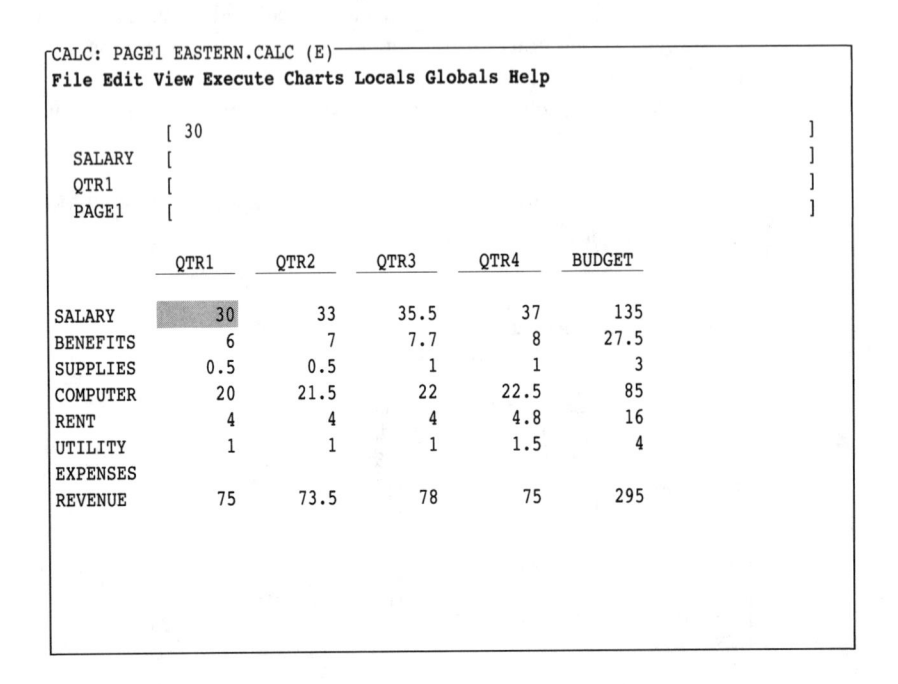

```
┌CALC: PAGE1 EASTERN.CALC (E)─────────────────────────────────────────┐
│File Edit View Execute Charts Locals Globals Help                    │
│                                                                     │
│              [ 30                                                 ] │
│     SALARY   [                                                    ] │
│     QTR1     [                                                    ] │
│     PAGE1    [                                                    ] │
│                                                                     │
│                  QTR1     QTR2     QTR3     QTR4    BUDGET          │
│                                                                     │
│     SALARY        30       33      35.5      37      135            │
│     BENEFITS       6        7       7.7       8      27.5           │
│     SUPPLIES      0.5      0.5       1        1        3            │
│     COMPUTER      20      21.5      22      22.5      85            │
│     RENT           4        4        4       4.8      16            │
│     UTILITY        1        1        1       1.5       4            │
│     EXPENSES                                                        │
│     REVENUE       75      73.5      78       75      295            │
│                                                                     │
│                                                                     │
│                                                                     │
└─────────────────────────────────────────────────────────────────────┘
```

Before you define a formula, you must place the cursor on the cell where the formula applies.

2. Select the EXPENSES.QTR1 cell by using the cursor keys to move the cursor to the cell and pressing ENTER or by pointing and clicking with a mouse.

▶ *Caution* .... *Using the TAB Key*
Do not use the TAB key to move the cursor to the EXPENSES.QTR1 cell. The TAB key moves the cursor to the action bar. ▲

After selecting the EXPENSES.QTR1 cell, the cell is highlighted, as shown in Display 2.26, indicating that the formula you enter applies to that cell.

Display 2.26
Formula Entry Area for EXPENSES.QTR1

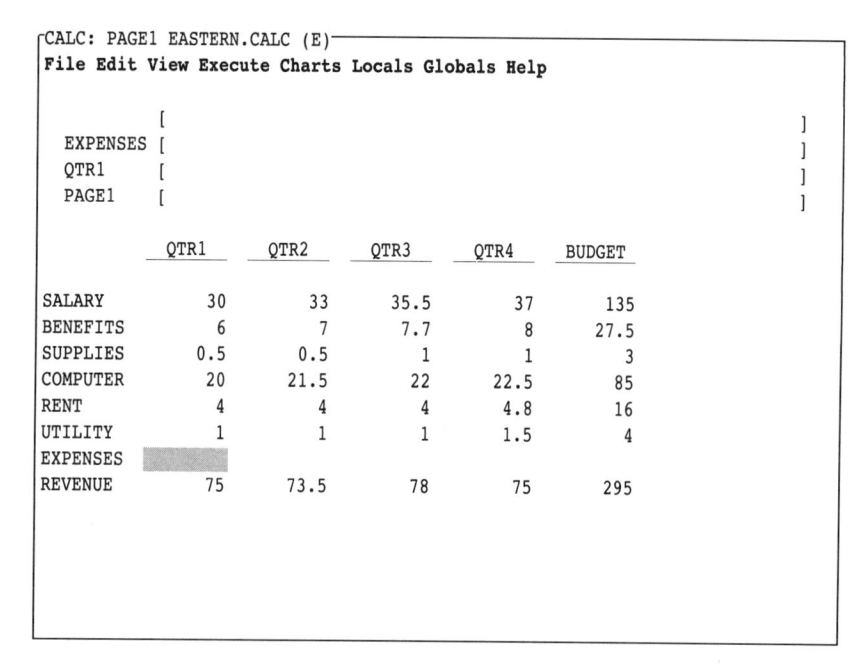

```
┌CALC: PAGE1 EASTERN.CALC (E)─────────────────────────────────┐
│File Edit View Execute Charts Locals Globals Help            │
│                                                             │
│              [                                            ] │
│    EXPENSES  [                                            ] │
│    QTR1      [                                            ] │
│    PAGE1     [                                            ] │
│                                                             │
│              QTR1      QTR2      QTR3      QTR4     BUDGET  │
│                                                             │
│   SALARY      30        33       35.5       37       135    │
│   BENEFITS     6         7        7.7        8       27.5   │
│   SUPPLIES    0.5       0.5        1         1         3    │
│   COMPUTER    20       21.5       22       22.5       85    │
│   RENT         4         4         4        4.8       16    │
│   UTILITY      1         1         1        1.5        4    │
│   EXPENSES  ▓▓▓▓▓                                           │
│   REVENUE     75       73.5       78        75       295    │
│                                                             │
│                                                             │
└─────────────────────────────────────────────────────────────┘
```

3. Move the cursor to the formula entry area at the top of the display under the action bar and type the formula shown in Display 2.27.

   Note: Because this formula is too long to type on one line in the formula entry area, type as much of the formula as possible on the first line, move the cursor to the next line, and complete the formula.

▶ *Caution* . . . . **Pressing ENTER in the Formula Entry Area**
Pressing ENTER while the formula entry area is open automatically executes the formula. If you press ENTER before you have finished typing the formula, you are executing an incomplete formula. ▲

Display 2.27
Formula for EXPENSES.QTR1

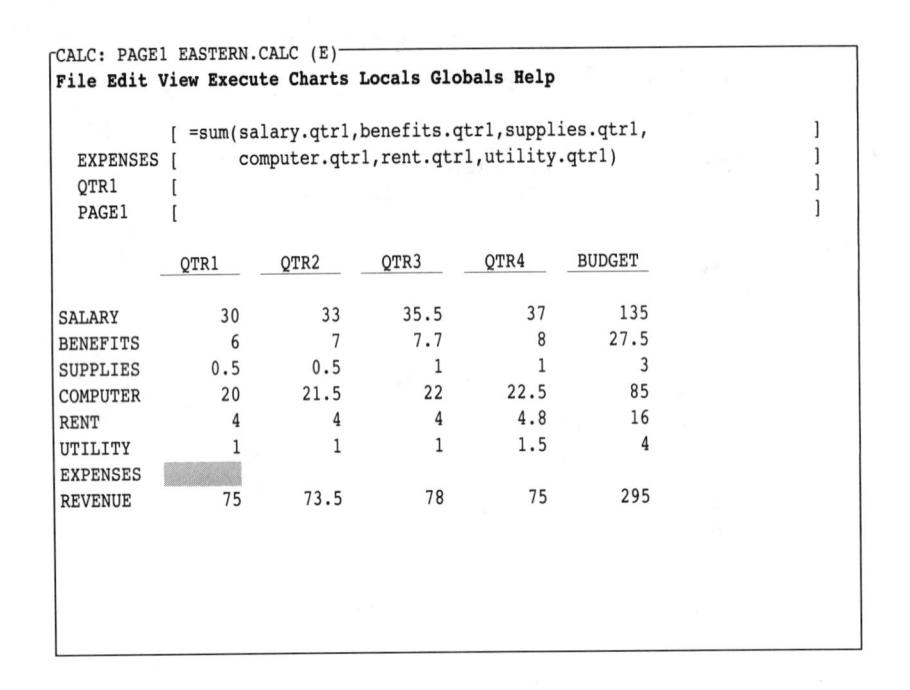

```
┌CALC: PAGE1 EASTERN.CALC (E)─────────────────────────────────┐
│ File Edit View Execute Charts Locals Globals Help           │
│                                                             │
│              [ =sum(salary.qtr1,benefits.qtr1,supplies.qtr1,]
│   EXPENSES   [    computer.qtr1,rent.qtr1,utility.qtr1)     ]
│   QTR1       [                                              ]
│   PAGE1      [                                              ]
│
│              QTR1      QTR2      QTR3     QTR4    BUDGET
│
│   SALARY      30        33       35.5      37      135
│   BENEFITS     6         7        7.7       8       27.5
│   SUPPLIES    0.5       0.5       1         1        3
│   COMPUTER   20        21.5      22        22.5     85
│   RENT        4         4         4         4.8     16
│   UTILITY     1         1         1         1.5      4
│   EXPENSES  ▓▓▓▓▓
│   REVENUE   75        73.5       78        75      295
│
└─────────────────────────────────────────────────────────────┘
```

Formulas begin with an equal sign (=) followed by an expression. In this example, the expression consists of the SUM function to add the values of the six expense items in the QTR1 column. Note that the names of the cells being processed by the SUM function are separated by commas. These cells are the arguments for the SUM function. You can type the formula in uppercase or lowercase. If you enter the formula in lowercase, pressing ENTER translates the formula to uppercase.

Note: In Chapter 3, "Modifying Your Spreadsheet," you learn how to abbreviate lists of cells in formulas, making formula entry easier and less error prone. Consult *SAS/CALC Software: Usage and Reference* for more information about formulas.

4. Press ENTER. Pressing ENTER enables SAS/CALC software to check the syntax of the formula, including proper placement of the equal sign and parentheses, and correct spelling of the row and column names. Once SAS/CALC software verifies the syntax, the formula executes and values are displayed in the EXPENSES.QTR1 cell, as shown in Display 2.28. Notice the formula is automatically translated to uppercase.

Display 2.28
Result of the Formula

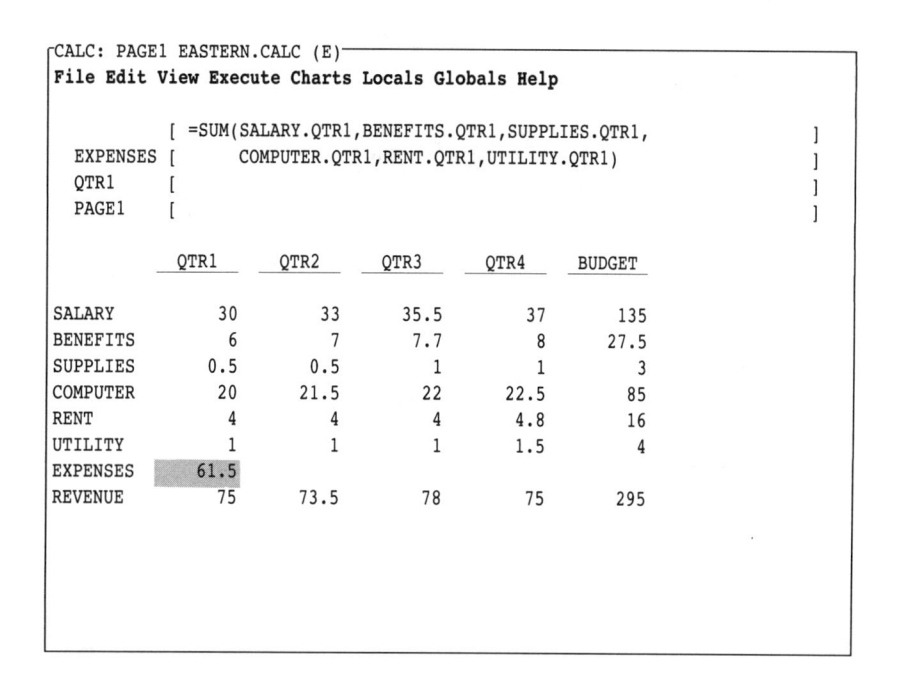

```
┌CALC: PAGE1 EASTERN.CALC (E)─────────────────────────────────┐
│File Edit View Execute Charts Locals Globals Help            │
│                                                             │
│           [ =SUM(SALARY.QTR1,BENEFITS.QTR1,SUPPLIES.QTR1,  ]│
│  EXPENSES [       COMPUTER.QTR1,RENT.QTR1,UTILITY.QTR1)    ]│
│  QTR1     [                                                ]│
│  PAGE1    [                                                ]│
│                                                             │
│                QTR1      QTR2     QTR3     QTR4    BUDGET   │
│                                                             │
│   SALARY        30        33      35.5      37      135     │
│   BENEFITS       6         7       7.7       8       27.5   │
│   SUPPLIES      0.5       0.5       1        1        3     │
│   COMPUTER      20       21.5      22      22.5      85     │
│   RENT           4         4        4       4.8      16     │
│   UTILITY        1         1        1       1.5       4     │
│   EXPENSES    │61.5│                                        │
│   REVENUE       75       73.5      78       75      295     │
│                                                             │
│                                                             │
└─────────────────────────────────────────────────────────────┘
```

▶ *Caution* .... ***Errors During Formula Entry***
   If you obtain errors during formula entry, select **Locals** from the action bar and **Message window** from the Locals pull-down menu. Select **Go to message window** to open the Message window. Read the error messages and correct the formula. For additional information, consult Appendix 2, ''Troubleshooting Information,'' in this book. ▲

5. Select **Execute** from the action bar and **End formula entry** from the Execute pull-down menu, as shown in Display 2.29, to close the formula entry area.

▶ *Caution* .... ***Closing the Formula Entry Area***
   Do not select **File** from the action bar and **End** from the File pull-down menu to close the formula entry area. Selecting **File** and **End** closes the spreadsheet. ▲

Display 2.29
Ending Formula Entry

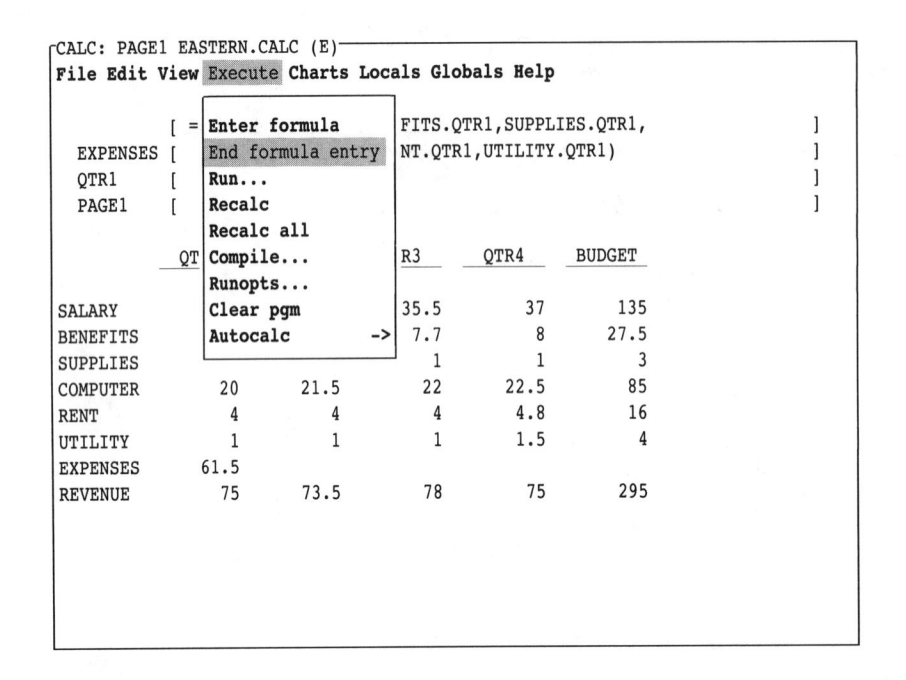

```
┌CALC: PAGE1 EASTERN.CALC (E)─────────────────────────────────┐
│File Edit View Execute Charts Locals Globals Help            │
│                                                             │
│            [ =│Enter formula   │FITS.QTR1,SUPPLIES.QTR1,   ]│
│  EXPENSES  [  │End formula entry│NT.QTR1,UTILITY.QTR1)     ]│
│  QTR1      [  │Run...          │                           ]│
│  PAGE1     [  │Recalc          │                           ]│
│               │Recalc all      │                            │
│           QT  │Compile...      │R3      QTR4     BUDGET     │
│               │Runopts...      │                            │
│  SALARY       │Clear pgm       │35.5    37       135        │
│  BENEFITS     │Autocalc    -> │ 7.7     8       27.5       │
│  SUPPLIES     └────────────────┘ 1       1        3        │
│  COMPUTER       20      21.5     22     22.5      85       │
│  RENT            4       4        4      4.8      16       │
│  UTILITY         1       1        1      1.5       4       │
│  EXPENSES       61.5                                        │
│  REVENUE        75      73.5     78     75       295        │
│                                                             │
└─────────────────────────────────────────────────────────────┘
```

By default, cells that contain formulas are automatically protected. This protection prevents accidental or unauthorized changes that can destroy your formulas. For example, if the EXPENSES.QTR1 cell is not protected and you accidentally type a value in that cell, you automatically overwrite the formula with the new value.

Note: Consult *SAS/CALC Software: Usage and Reference* for information about disabling the automatic protection.

Now, you need to define formulas for the remaining cells in the EXPENSES row. You can define the formulas by manually highlighting each cell and typing the appropriate formula, or you can copy the formula in the EXPENSES.QTR1 cell to the other cells.

Lesson 2.8: Copying Formulas

When you copy a cell that contains a formula, the formula is copied to the target cell or cells and automatically adjusted to use the appropriate data. When using pull-down menus to copy a cell, you issue MARK BLOCK commands to mark the source and target cells and then issue a COPY command to copy the source cell to the target cell.

Note: You must use a function key to issue the MARK BLOCK command when you are using pull-down menus. To view or change your current function key definitions, select **Help** from the action bar and **Keys** from the Help pull-down menu.

To copy the cell EXPENSES.QTR1 (including the formula):

1. Move the cursor to the EXPENSES.QTR1 cell, using the cursor keys or pointing and clicking with a mouse, and press the function key assigned to the MARK BLOCK command.

▶ *Caution* .... *Using the TAB Key*
Do not use the TAB key to move to the EXPENSES.QTR1 cell. You cannot tab to the EXPENSES.QTR1 cell because it contains a formula and is protected by default. ▲

As shown in Display 2.30, the EXPENSES.QTR1 cell is highlighted, the cursor remains on the cell, and the word Mark appears at the bottom of the window indicating you have issued the MARK BLOCK command.

Display 2.30
Marking the Source Cell

```
┌CALC: PAGE1 EASTERN.CALC (E)─────────────────────────────────┐
│File Edit View Execute Charts Locals Globals Help            │
│                                                             │
│              QTR1      QTR2      QTR3      QTR4    BUDGET   │
│                                                             │
│SALARY         30        33       35.5       37      135     │
│BENEFITS        6         7        7.7        8       27.5   │
│SUPPLIES       0.5       0.5        1         1        3     │
│COMPUTER       20        21.5      22        22.5     85     │
│RENT            4         4         4         4.8     16     │
│UTILITY         1         1         1         1.5      4     │
│EXPENSES      61.5                                           │
│REVENUE        75        73.5      78        75      295     │
│                                                             │
│                                                             │
│                                                             │
│                                                     Mark    │
└─────────────────────────────────────────────────────────────┘
```

46 *Creating Your First Spreadsheet* □ *Chapter 2*

2. Because you are copying only the EXPENSES.QTR1 cell, press the MARK BLOCK function key again to end the MARK command.

   Notice the word Mark no longer appears at the bottom of the display, as shown in Display 2.31, indicating the MARK BLOCK command is finished. The EXPENSES.QTR1 cell remains highlighted indicating it is the source cell and ready to be copied.

Display 2.31
EXPENSES.QTR1 as the Source Cell

```
┌CALC: PAGE1 EASTERN.CALC (E)─────────────────────────────────┐
│File Edit View Execute Charts Locals Globals Help            │
│                                                             │
│                QTR1     QTR2     QTR3     QTR4    BUDGET    │
│                                                             │
│   SALARY        30       33      35.5      37      135      │
│   BENEFITS       6        7       7.7       8      27.5     │
│   SUPPLIES     0.5      0.5        1        1        3      │
│   COMPUTER      20      21.5      22      22.5      85      │
│   RENT           4        4        4       4.8      16      │
│   UTILITY        1        1        1       1.5       4      │
│   EXPENSES    61.5                                          │
│   REVENUE       75      73.5      78       75      295      │
│                                                             │
│                                                             │
│                                                             │
│                                                             │
│                                                             │
│                                                             │
└─────────────────────────────────────────────────────────────┘
```

▶ *Caution* . . . . *Incorrectly Marking Cells*

If you incorrectly mark a cell or a range of cells, select **Edit** from the action bar and **Unmark** from the Edit pull-down menu to remove all current marks. Then, remark the cell or cells. ▲

3. You are now ready to identify the target cells. Move the cursor to the EXPENSES.QTR2 cell and press the MARK BLOCK function key.

    The cell is highlighted indicating that it is selected. Because you want to copy the formula to a range of cells, move the cursor to the EXPENSES.BUDGET cell and press the MARK BLOCK function key. All the cells in the **EXPENSES** row from the **QTR2** column to the **BUDGET** column are highlighted, as shown in Display 2.32, indicating they are all target cells.

Display 2.32
The Target Cells

```
┌CALC: PAGE1 EASTERN.CALC (E)─────────────────────────────────┐
│File Edit View Execute Charts Locals Globals Help            │
│                                                             │
│              QTR1      QTR2      QTR3      QTR4     BUDGET  │
│                                                             │
│   SALARY      30        33       35.5       37       135    │
│   BENEFITS     6         7        7.7        8       27.5   │
│   SUPPLIES   0.5       0.5         1         1         3    │
│   COMPUTER    20       21.5       22       22.5       85    │
│   RENT         4         4         4        4.8       16    │
│   UTILITY      1         1         1        1.5        4    │
│   EXPENSES   61.5     ▓▓▓▓▓    ▓▓▓▓▓    ▓▓▓▓▓     ▓▓▓▓▓    │
│   REVENUE     75       73.5       78        75       295    │
│                                                             │
│                                                             │
│                                                             │
│                                                             │
│                                                             │
└─────────────────────────────────────────────────────────────┘
```

4. Select **Edit** from the action bar and **Copy marked areas** from the Edit pull-down menu, as shown in Display 2.33, to copy the formula to the target cells.

▶ *Caution* .... *Copy marked areas (values only)*
Notice there is another selection in the Edit pull-down menu, **Copy marked areas(values only)**. This selection copies only the cell value or values in the source range, not the formula. ▲

48 *Creating Your First Spreadsheet □ Chapter 2*

Display 2.33
Copying the Formula

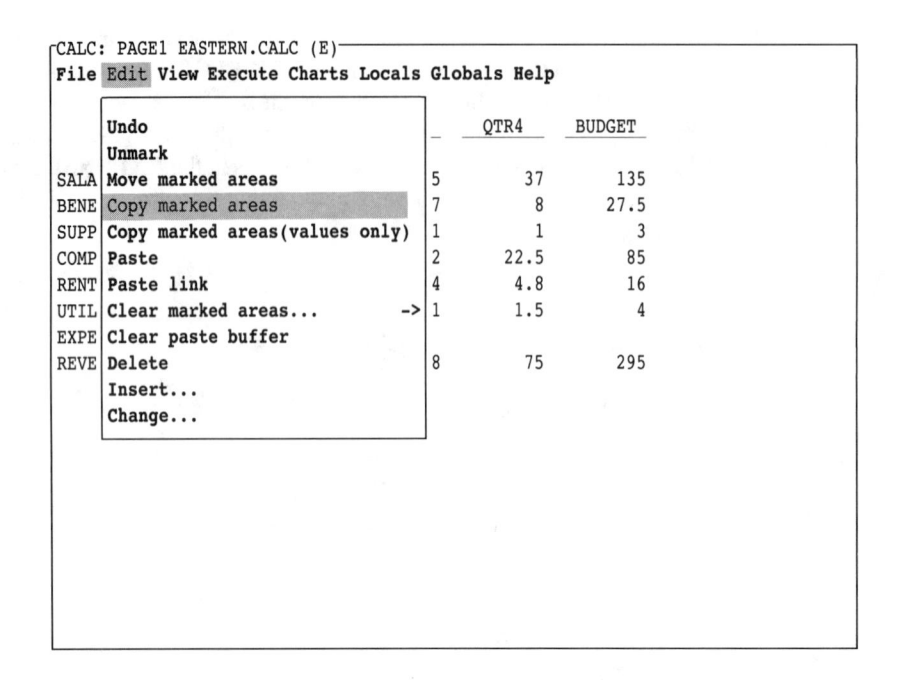

```
┌CALC: PAGE1 EASTERN.CALC (E)─────────────────────────────┐
│ File Edit View Execute Charts Locals Globals Help       │
│     ┌─────────────────────────────────┐                 │
│     │ Undo                            │    QTR4  BUDGET │
│     │ Unmark                          │                 │
│ SALA│ Move marked areas               │ 5    37    135  │
│ BENE│ Copy marked areas               │ 7     8   27.5  │
│ SUPP│ Copy marked areas(values only)  │ 1     1      3  │
│ COMP│ Paste                           │ 2  22.5     85  │
│ RENT│ Paste link                      │ 4   4.8     16  │
│ UTIL│ Clear marked areas...       -> │ 1   1.5      4  │
│ EXPE│ Clear paste buffer              │                 │
│ REVE│ Delete                          │ 8    75    295  │
│     │ Insert...                       │                 │
│     │ Change...                       │                 │
│     └─────────────────────────────────┘                 │
│                                                         │
└─────────────────────────────────────────────────────────┘
```

Notice that you now have values displayed in all the cells in the **EXPENSES** row, as shown in Display 2.34.

Display 2.34
Results of Copying

```
┌CALC: PAGE1 EASTERN.CALC (E)─────────────────────────────┐
│ File Edit View Execute Charts Locals Globals Help       │
│                                                         │
│              QTR1    QTR2    QTR3    QTR4   BUDGET      │
│                                                         │
│  SALARY       30      33    35.5      37     135        │
│  BENEFITS      6       7     7.7       8    27.5        │
│  SUPPLIES    0.5     0.5       1       1       3        │
│  COMPUTER     20    21.5      22    22.5      85        │
│  RENT          4       4       4     4.8      16        │
│  UTILITY       1       1       1     1.5       4        │
│  EXPENSES   61.5      67    71.2    74.8   270.5        │
│  REVENUE      75    73.5      78      75     295        │
│                                                         │
└─────────────────────────────────────────────────────────┘
```

To verify that the formula is copied correctly:

1. Select **Execute** from the action bar and **Enter formula** from the Execute pull-down menu.

2. Select the EXPENSES.QTR4 cell to highlight the cell and display the cell formula in the formula entry area. Use the cursor keys or a mouse to move the cursor to the EXPENSES.QTR4 cell.
   Note that the formula is automatically adjusted to use the data in the QTR4 column. Check the formulas in the remaining target cells if you desire.

3. Select **Execute** from the action bar and **End formula entry** to close the formula entry area.

Once you finish working on a spreadsheet, you need to save the spreadsheet.

Lesson 2.9: Saving a Spreadsheet

To save a spreadsheet:

1. Select **File** from the action bar.

2. Select **Save** from the File pull-down menu as shown in Display 2.35. A note appears indicating that the spreadsheet has been saved.

Display 2.35
The Saved Spreadsheet

```
┌CALC: PAGE1 EASTERN.CALC (E)─────────────────────────────────────┐
│ File Edit View Execute Charts Locals Globals Help               │
│ NOTE: Member EASTERN.CALC has been saved.                       │
│              QTR1      QTR2      QTR3      QTR4      BUDGET    │
│                                                                 │
│ SALARY        30        33       35.5       37        135       │
│ BENEFITS       6         7        7.7        8        27.5      │
│ SUPPLIES      0.5       0.5        1         1          3       │
│ COMPUTER      20       21.5       22       22.5       85        │
│ RENT           4         4         4        4.8       16        │
│ UTILITY        1         1         1        1.5        4        │
│ EXPENSES     61.5       67       71.2      74.8      270.5      │
│ REVENUE       75       73.5       78        75        295       │
│                                                                 │
│                                                                 │
│                                                                 │
│                                                                 │
│                                                                 │
└─────────────────────────────────────────────────────────────────┘
```

You have completed the first tutorial chapter. If you want to continue with Chapter 3, turn to Chapter 3 now. If you are finished working on the tutorial, follow the steps below to close your spreadsheet, end the SAS/CALC software session, and end the SAS System session.

Lesson 2.10: Closing a Spreadsheet

To close a spreadsheet:

1. Select **File** from the action bar.

2. Select **End** from the File pull-down menu as shown in Display 2.36.

Display 2.36
Closing a Spreadsheet

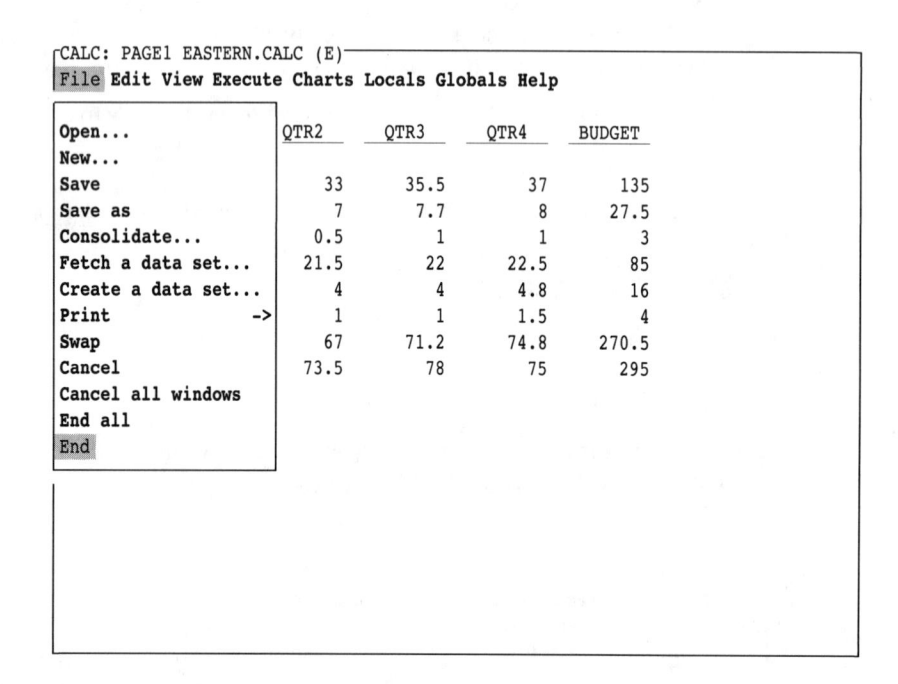

```
┌CALC: PAGE1 EASTERN.CALC (E)─────────────────────────────────────┐
│ File  Edit View Execute Charts Locals Globals Help              │
│ ┌────────────────────┐                                          │
│ │Open...             │ QTR2      QTR3      QTR4     BUDGET      │
│ │New...              │                                          │
│ │Save                │   33      35.5        37       135       │
│ │Save as             │    7       7.7         8      27.5       │
│ │Consolidate...      │  0.5         1         1         3       │
│ │Fetch a data set... │ 21.5        22      22.5        85       │
│ │Create a data set...│    4         4       4.8        16       │
│ │Print            -> │    1         1       1.5         4       │
│ │Swap                │   67      71.2      74.8     270.5       │
│ │Cancel              │ 73.5        78        75       295       │
│ │Cancel all windows  │                                          │
│ │End all             │                                          │
│ │ End                │                                          │
│ └────────────────────┘                                          │
│                                                                 │
│                                                                 │
│                                                                 │
└─────────────────────────────────────────────────────────────────┘
```

3. Selecting **End** automatically saves your spreadsheet, closes the spreadsheet, and redisplays the DIRECTORY window shown in Display 2.37. Notice the EASTERN.CALC entry.

Display 2.37
DIRECTORY Window with EASTERN.CALC Entry

```
┌CALC: DIRECTORY SASUSER.CALC (E)─────────────────────────────┐
│File Edit View Locals Globals Help                           │
│NOTE: Member EASTERN.CALC has not been modified since last save.│
│    Name      Type     Description                  Updated  │
│                                                             │
│ _  EASTERN   CALC     EASTERN.CALC                 08/21/91 │
│                                                             │
│                                                             │
│                                                             │
│                                                             │
│                                                             │
│                                                             │
│                                                             │
│                                                             │
│                                                             │
│                                                             │
│                                                             │
└─────────────────────────────────────────────────────────────┘
```

Lesson 2.11: Ending the SAS/CALC Software Session

To end the SAS/CALC software session:

1. Select **File** from the action bar in the DIRECTORY window.

2. Select **End** from the File pull-down menu as shown in Display 2.38.

Display 2.38
Ending the SAS/CALC Software Session

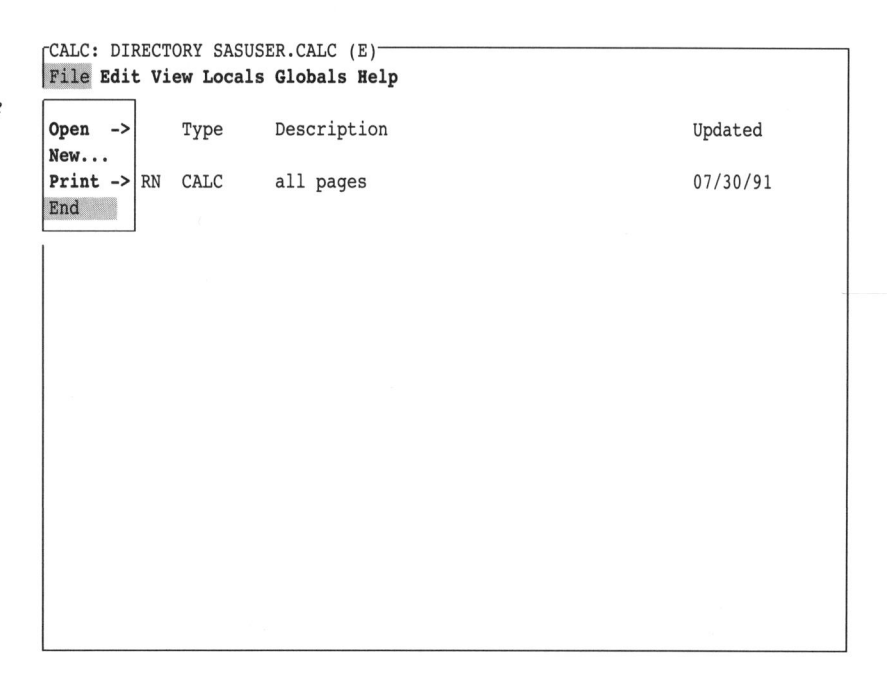

```
┌CALC: DIRECTORY SASUSER.CALC (E)─────────────────────────────┐
│File Edit View Locals Globals Help                           │
│┌──────────┐                                                 │
││Open   -> │  Type    Description                  Updated   │
││New...    │                                                 │
││Print  -> │RN CALC   all pages                    07/30/91  │
││End       │                                                 │
│└──────────┘                                                 │
│                                                             │
│                                                             │
│                                                             │
│                                                             │
│                                                             │
│                                                             │
│                                                             │
│                                                             │
└─────────────────────────────────────────────────────────────┘
```

Selecting **End** displays the PROGRAM EDITOR window as shown in Display 2.39.

Display 2.39
The PROGRAM EDITOR Window

```
┌LOG─────────────────────────────────────────────┐
│File Edit View Globals Help                     │
│                                                │
│12   proc calc c=sasuser.calc;run;              │
│                                                │
│NOTE: The PROCEDURE CALC used 4.00 seconds.     │
│NOTE: The PROCEDURE CALC used 2.68 seconds cpu time. │
│                                                │
│                                                │
│                                                │
└────────────────────────────────────────────────┘

┌PROGRAM EDITOR──────────────────────────────────┐
│File Edit View Locals Globals Help              │
│                                                │
│00001                                           │
│00002                                           │
│00003                                           │
│00004                                           │
│00005                                           │
│00006                                           │
└────────────────────────────────────────────────┘
```

Lesson 2.12: Ending the SAS System Session

To end the SAS session:

1. Select **File** from the action bar in the PROGRAM EDITOR window.

2. Select **Exit...** from the File pull-down menu.

Display 2.40
Ending the SAS System Session

```
┌LOG─────────────────────────────────────────────┐
│File Edit View Globals Help                     │
│                                                │
│1                                               │
│2                                               │
│3                                               │
│4                                               │
│5        proc calc c=sasuser.calc;run;          │
│                                                │
│NOTE: The PROCEDURE CALC used 7.00 seconds.     │
│NOTE: The PROCEDURE CALC used 3.43 seconds cpu time. │
│                                                │
└────────────────────────────────────────────────┘

┌PROGRAM EDITOR──────────────────────────────────┐
│File Edit View Locals Globals Help              │
│     ┌Exit...─────────────────────────────┐     │
│Open  ->                                        │
│Save      Are you sure you really want to terminate the │
│Save as ->  SAS session?                        │
│Print ->                                        │
│Exit...                                         │
│           [ OK ]      [ Cancel ]               │
│     └────────────────────────────────────┘     │
└────────────────────────────────────────────────┘
```

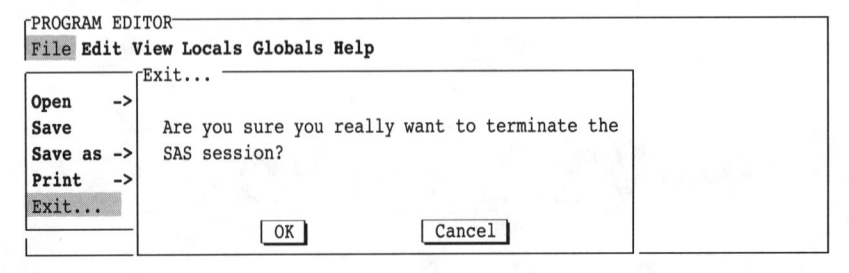

Selecting **Exit...** opens the Exit... dialog box shown in Display 2.40.

3. Select **OK** to end the SAS session and return to your operating system.

Chapter Summary

This chapter introduces the basic concepts of using SAS/CALC software and creating and saving SAS/CALC software spreadsheets.

To begin the chapter, you learn two methods for invoking SAS/CALC software: using action bar and pull-down menu selections or using a PROC CALC step.

You also learn that spreadsheets are stored as entries in catalogs in SAS data libraries.

From within SAS/CALC software, you learn how to create a spreadsheet named EASTERN, which contains quarterly data for the eastern region of a company. While creating EASTERN, you learn how to name a spreadsheet, define initial parameters such as the number of rows and columns, how to rename and delete rows and columns, enter cell values, and define a formula to compute automatically the total quarterly expenses for the eastern region. You also learn how to mark a source and target range for copying your formulas from one cell to another.

At the end of the chapter, you learn how to save the EASTERN spreadsheet, end the SAS/CALC session, and end the SAS System session.

After completing this chapter, you are ready to learn additional features of SAS/CALC software, including inserting rows and columns, defining multiple formulas, and enhancing the general appearance of the EASTERN spreadsheet.

Chapter 3 Modifying Your Spreadsheet

Modifying Your Spreadsheet 55
    Lesson 3.1: Invoking SAS/CALC Software 56
    Lesson 3.2: Opening an Existing Spreadsheet 56
    Lesson 3.3: Inserting New Rows and Columns 57
    Lesson 3.3: Inserting a Row 58
    Lesson 3.4: Inserting a Column 60
    Lesson 3.5: Changing Column Widths 61
    Lesson 3.6: Defining Formulas 64
    Lesson 3.7: Copying Formulas 67
    Lesson 3.8: Assigning Cell Formats 70
    Lesson 3.9: Verifying Cell Attributes 72
Chapter Summary 73

Modifying Your Spreadsheet

In the first tutorial chapter you learned how to create a spreadsheet, enter values into the cells, use formulas to compute cell values, copy formulas, and save your spreadsheet.

In this chapter, you create the spreadsheet shown in Display 3.1 by enhancing the EASTERN spreadsheet from Chapter 2, "Creating Your First Spreadsheet." Specifically, you learn how to insert rows and columns into the spreadsheet, alter column widths, and use ranges to perform actions on a group of cells.

Display 3.1
Enhanced EASTERN Spreadsheet

```
┌CALC: PAGE1 EASTERN.CALC (E)─────────────────────────────────────┐
│ File Edit View Execute Charts Locals Globals Help               │
│                                                                 │
│             QTR1     QTR2     QTR3     QTR4   BUDGET   ACTUAL   VARIANCE │
│                                                                 │
│   SALARY    30.00    33.00    35.50    37.00   135.00   135.50    -0.50 │
│   BENEFITS   6.00     7.00     7.70     8.00    27.50    28.70    -1.20 │
│   SUPPLIES   0.50     0.50     1.00     1.00     3.00     3.00     0.00 │
│   COMPUTER  20.00    21.50    22.00    22.50    85.00    86.00    -1.00 │
│   RENT       4.00     4.00     4.00     4.80    16.00    16.80    -0.80 │
│   UTILITY    1.00     1.00     1.00     1.50     4.00     4.50    -0.50 │
│   EXPENSES  61.50    67.00    71.20    74.80   270.50   274.50    -4.00 │
│   REVENUE   75.00    73.50    78.00    75.00   295.00   301.50    -6.50 │
│   NET       13.50     6.50     6.80     0.20    24.50    27.00    -2.50 │
│                                                                 │
│                                                                 │
└─────────────────────────────────────────────────────────────────┘
```

If you ended the SAS/CALC software session after Chapter 2, begin this chapter with Lesson 3.1. If you did not close your spreadsheet and end the SAS/CALC software session after Chapter 2, read Lesson 3.2 and begin this chapter with Lesson 3.3, "Inserting New Rows and Columns."

Lesson 3.1: Invoking SAS/CALC Software

To invoke SAS/CALC software:

1. Select **Globals** from the action bar at the top of the PROGRAM EDITOR window and **Desktop** from the Globals pull-down menu.

2. Select **Spreadsheet...** from the Desktop pull-down menu to open the Spreadsheet... dialog box.

3. Type SASUSER next to **Enter libname** and CALC next to **Enter catalog name**.

4. Select **OK** in the DIRECTORY dialog box to display the DIRECTORY window shown in Display 3.2.

Lesson 3.2: Opening an Existing Spreadsheet

To open an existing spreadsheet:

1. Type the letter O in the selection field beside **EASTERN**, as shown in Display 3.2.

Display 3.2
Opening the EASTERN Spreadsheet

```
┌CALC: DIRECTORY SASUSER.CALC (E)─────────────────────────────┐
│File Edit View Locals Globals Help                           │
│                                                             │
│    Name     Type     Description              Updated       │
│                                                             │
│ [O] EASTERN  CALC     EASTERN.CALC             06/11/91     │
│                                                             │
│                                                             │
│                                                             │
│                                                             │
│                                                             │
│                                                             │
│                                                             │
│                                                             │
│                                                             │
└─────────────────────────────────────────────────────────────┘
```

2. Press ENTER to display the spreadsheet shown in Display 3.3.

Display 3.3
The EASTERN Spreadsheet

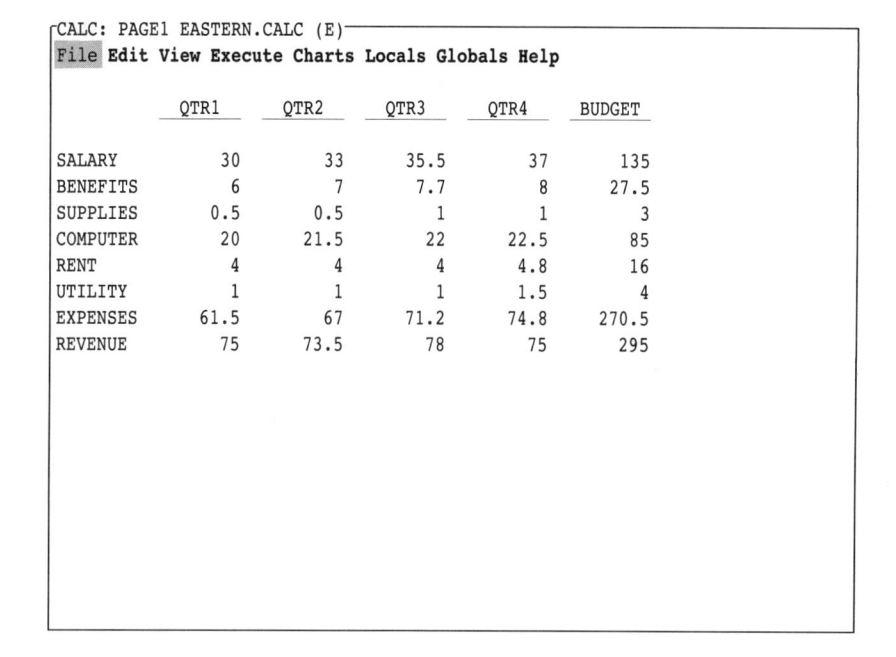

```
┌CALC: PAGE1 EASTERN.CALC (E)─────────────────────────────────┐
│ File Edit View Execute Charts Locals Globals Help           │
│                                                             │
│                QTR1      QTR2      QTR3      QTR4    BUDGET │
│                                                             │
│    SALARY        30        33      35.5        37       135 │
│    BENEFITS       6         7       7.7         8      27.5 │
│    SUPPLIES     0.5       0.5         1         1         3 │
│    COMPUTER      20      21.5        22      22.5        85 │
│    RENT           4         4         4       4.8        16 │
│    UTILITY        1         1         1       1.5         4 │
│    EXPENSES    61.5        67      71.2      74.8     270.5 │
│    REVENUE       75      73.5        78        75       295 │
│                                                             │
│                                                             │
│                                                             │
│                                                             │
│                                                             │
│                                                             │
└─────────────────────────────────────────────────────────────┘
```

Lesson 3.3: Inserting New Rows and Columns

In this section, you insert one new row, NET, and two new columns, ACTUAL and VARIANCE. The row NET represents the difference between the rows named REVENUE and EXPENSES. The column ACTUAL represents actual year-to-date expenses and revenues, and the column VARIANCE represents the difference between the columns, ACTUAL and BUDGET.

Lesson 3.3: Inserting a Row

To insert the new row named NET:

1. Select **Edit** from the action bar and **Insert...** from the Edit pull-down menu as shown in Display 3.4.

Display 3.4
Selecting Insert...

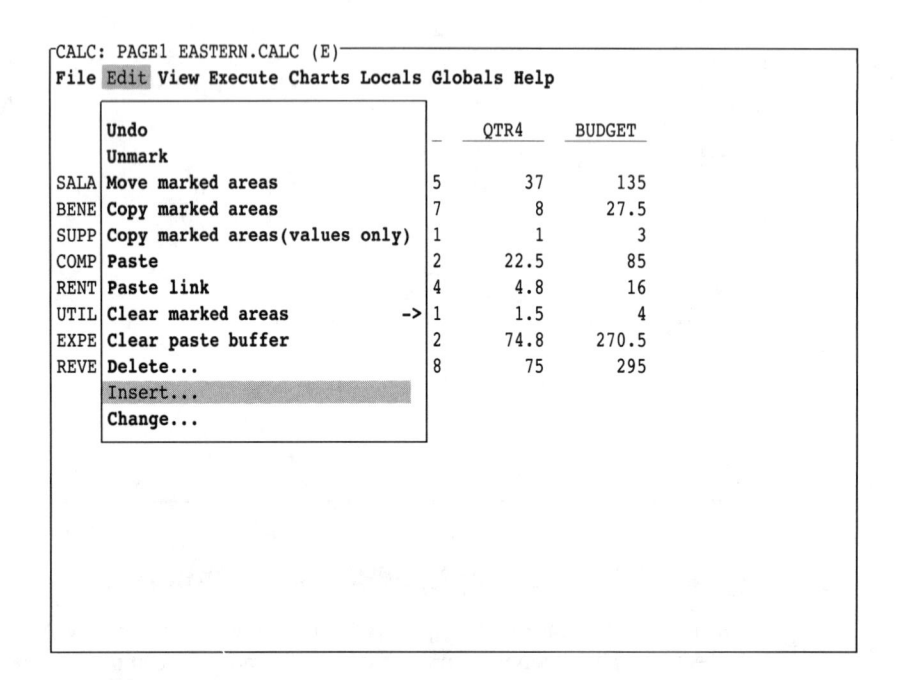

```
┌CALC: PAGE1 EASTERN.CALC (E)─────────────────────────────────────┐
│ File Edit View Execute Charts Locals Globals Help               │
│      ┌─────────────────────────────────────┐                    │
│      │ Undo                                │    QTR4    BUDGET  │
│      │ Unmark                              │                    │
│ SALA │ Move marked areas                   │ 5    37      135   │
│ BENE │ Copy marked areas                   │ 7     8       27.5 │
│ SUPP │ Copy marked areas(values only)      │ 1     1        3   │
│ COMP │ Paste                               │ 2    22.5     85   │
│ RENT │ Paste link                          │ 4     4.8     16   │
│ UTIL │ Clear marked areas               -> │ 1     1.5      4   │
│ EXPE │ Clear paste buffer                  │ 2    74.8    270.5 │
│ REVE │ Delete...                           │ 8    75      295   │
│      │ Insert...                           │                    │
│      │ Change...                           │                    │
│      └─────────────────────────────────────┘                    │
│                                                                 │
└─────────────────────────────────────────────────────────────────┘
```

These selections display the Insert... dialog box shown in Display 3.5. You use this dialog box to supply information about the type of insertion you want to perform.

Display 3.5
Inserting a Row

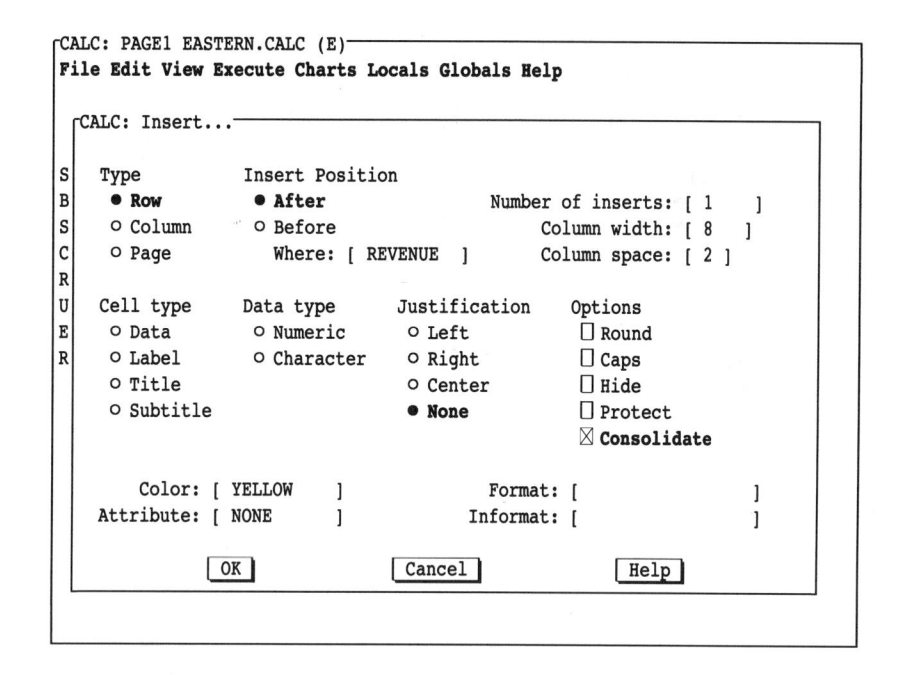

```
┌CALC: PAGE1 EASTERN.CALC (E)─────────────────────────────────┐
│ File Edit View Execute Charts Locals Globals Help           │
│                                                             │
│   ┌CALC: Insert...──────────────────────────────────────┐   │
│ S │                                                     │   │
│ B │  Type            Insert Position                    │   │
│ S │  ● Row           ● After         Number of inserts: [ 1    ]│
│ C │  ○ Column        ○ Before        Column width:      [ 8    ]│
│ R │  ○ Page          Where: [ REVENUE ]  Column space:  [ 2    ]│
│ U │                                                     │   │
│ E │  Cell type       Data type       Justification   Options│
│ R │  ○ Data          ○ Numeric       ○ Left          ☐ Round│
│   │  ○ Label         ○ Character     ○ Right         ☐ Caps │
│   │  ○ Title                         ○ Center        ☐ Hide │
│   │  ○ Subtitle                      ● None          ☐ Protect│
│   │                                                  ☒ Consolidate│
│   │                                                     │   │
│   │        Color: [ YELLOW    ]      Format:  [              ]│
│   │    Attribute: [ NONE      ]      Informat:[              ]│
│   │                                                     │   │
│   │          [ OK ]        [ Cancel ]        [ Help ]   │   │
│   └─────────────────────────────────────────────────────┘   │
│                                                             │
└─────────────────────────────────────────────────────────────┘
```

2. Select **Row** in the **Type** field of the Insert... dialog box.

3. Specify that the desired location of the NET row is after the REVENUE row by accepting the default **After** in the **Insert Position** field.

4. Specify the number of rows you want to insert. In this case, the default value of **1** in the **Number of inserts** field is correct, indicating that you want to insert one row after REVENUE.

5. Type REVENUE in the brackets following the **Where** field. You can type REVENUE in uppercase or lowercase.

   As you can see, there are numerous other fields in the dialog box that you can use to supply additional information about the inserted row. In this example, you can accept the defaults. Consult *SAS/CALC Software: Usage and Reference. Version 6, First Edition* for more information about the Insert... dialog box.

6. After supplying the appropriate information, select **OK** to close the Insert... dialog box and redisplay the EASTERN spreadsheet with the new row, ROW16. The original spreadsheet had 15 rows. SAS/CALC software automatically increments inserted rows by one.

7. Change the row name to **NET**, as shown in Display 3.6, by typing over the default name. Remember to delete the default row name completely.

60 *Modifying Your Spreadsheet □ Chapter 3*

Display 3.6
The NET Row

```
┌CALC: PAGE1 EASTERN.CALC (E)─────────────────────────────┐
│File Edit View Execute Charts Locals Globals Help        │
│                                                          │
│              QTR1      QTR2      QTR3      QTR4    BUDGET│
│                                                          │
│   SALARY      30        33      35.5        37       135 │
│   BENEFITS     6         7       7.7         8      27.5 │
│   SUPPLIES   0.5       0.5         1         1         3 │
│   COMPUTER    20      21.5        22      22.5        85 │
│   RENT         4         4         4       4.8        16 │
│   UTILITY      1         1         1       1.5         4 │
│   EXPENSES  61.5        67      71.2      74.8     270.5 │
│   REVENUE     75      73.5        78        75       295 │
│   NET                                                    │
│                                                          │
│                                                          │
│                                                          │
│                                                          │
└──────────────────────────────────────────────────────────┘
```

Lesson 3.4: Inserting a Column

To insert the new columns, follow the same procedure you used to insert the rows:

1. Select **Edit** from the action bar and **Insert...** from the Edit pull-down menu to display the Insert... dialog box.

2. Select **Column** for the **Type** field as shown in Display 3.7.

Display 3.7
Inserting Columns

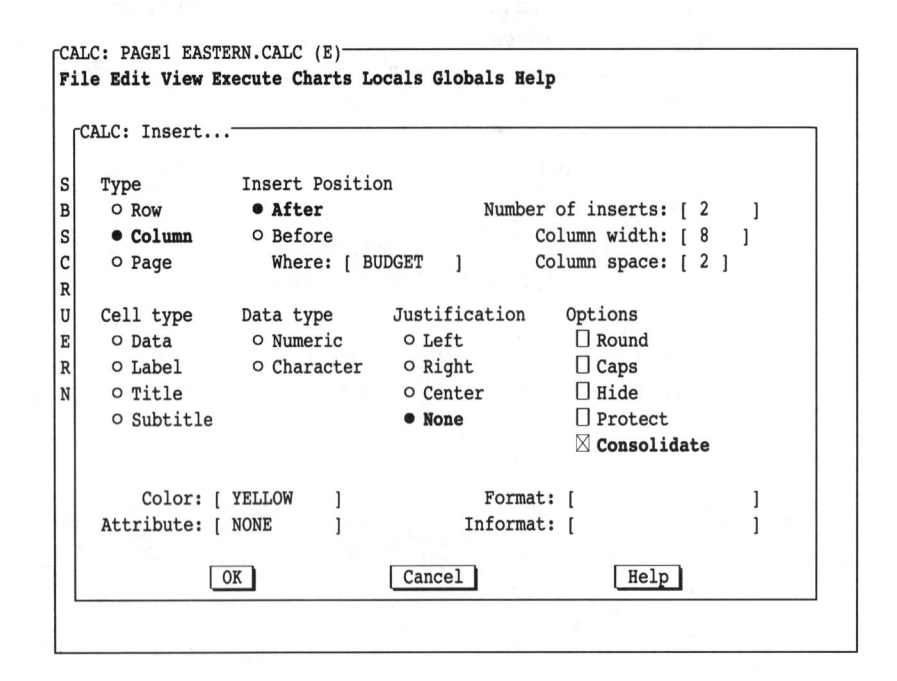

```
┌CALC: PAGE1 EASTERN.CALC (E)─────────────────────────────┐
│File Edit View Execute Charts Locals Globals Help        │
│  ┌CALC: Insert...─────────────────────────────────────┐ │
│S │                                                    │ │
│  │  Type         Insert Position                      │ │
│B │   ○ Row        ● After          Number of inserts: [ 2   ] │
│S │   ● Column     ○ Before         Column width:  [ 8   ]    │
│C │   ○ Page        Where: [ BUDGET    ]  Column space: [ 2 ] │
│R │                                                    │ │
│U │  Cell type    Data type     Justification   Options│ │
│E │   ○ Data       ○ Numeric      ○ Left        □ Round│ │
│R │   ○ Label      ○ Character    ○ Right       □ Caps │ │
│N │   ○ Title                     ○ Center      □ Hide │ │
│  │   ○ Subtitle                  ● None        □ Protect│ │
│  │                                             ⊠ Consolidate│ │
│  │                                                    │ │
│  │       Color: [ YELLOW   ]        Format: [          ] │ │
│  │   Attribute: [ NONE     ]       Informat: [          ] │ │
│  │           [ OK ]      [ Cancel ]         [ Help ]  │ │
│  └────────────────────────────────────────────────────┘ │
└──────────────────────────────────────────────────────────┘
```

3. Accept the default **After** in the **Insert Position** field.

4. Type 2 for the **Number of inserts** field indicating that you want to insert two columns after BUDGET.

5. Type BUDGET for the **Where** field. You can type BUDGET in uppercase or lowercase.

6. Select **OK** to close the Insert... dialog box and redisplay the EASTERN spreadsheet with the new columns, COL9 and COL10.

▶ *Caution* .... *Size of Display*
If your display is not wide enough to display all the columns, you can scroll to the right to see the new columns by pressing the function key assigned to the RIGHT command. ▲

7. Change the first new column name to ACTUAL and the second new column name to VARIANCE, as shown in Display 3.8, by typing over the default names.

Display 3.8
The ACTUAL and VARIANCE Columns

```
┌CALC: PAGE1 EASTERN.CALC (E)─────────────────────────────────┐
│ File Edit View Execute Charts Locals Globals Help           │
│                                                              │
│              QTR1    QTR2    QTR3    QTR4   BUDGET  ACTUAL  VARIANCE
│                                                              │
│ SALARY        30      33     35.5     37     135            │
│ BENEFITS       6       7      7.7      8     27.5           │
│ SUPPLIES     0.5     0.5       1       1       3            │
│ COMPUTER      20    21.5      22     22.5     85            │
│ RENT           4       4       4      4.8     16            │
│ UTILITY        1       1       1      1.5      4            │
│ EXPENSES    61.5      67     71.2    74.8   270.5           │
│ REVENUE       75    73.5      78      75     295            │
│ NET                                                          │
│                                                              │
└──────────────────────────────────────────────────────────────┘
```

If you scrolled to the right to see the new columns, press the function key assigned to the LEFT command to scroll back to the left.

Lesson 3.5: Changing Column Widths

To make the spreadsheet easier to read, you can reduce the column widths so that all the columns are visible on your display without having to scroll right and left.

To change the column widths, you make selections from the action bar and pull-down menus. To make these selections easier, you use the MARK BLOCK function key to mark the range of cells in the spreadsheet you want affected by the change.

62 *Modifying Your Spreadsheet* □ *Chapter 3*

To mark the cells you want to change:

1. Move the cursor to the column name **QTR1** and press the MARK BLOCK function key.

2. Move the cursor to the column name **ACTUAL** and press the MARK BLOCK function key.

▶ *Caution* .... *Incorrectly Marking Cells*
If you incorrectly mark a cell or a range of cells, select **Edit** from the action bar and **Unmark** from the Edit pull-down menu to remove all current marks. Then, mark the cell or cells again. ▲

Notice that all cells are highlighted, as shown in Display 3.9, except those in the **VARIANCE** column. The column width assigned to your cells affects the size of your column name. VARIANCE has 8 letters, which corresponds to the default column width. If you change the column width to a value less then 8, the column name VARIANCE is truncated on the display. As a result, VARIANCE is omitted from the column width change.

Display 3.9
The Marked Column Names

```
┌CALC: PAGE1 EASTERN.CALC (E)─────────────────────────────
│File Edit View Execute Charts Locals Globals Help
│
│              QTR1    QTR2    QTR3    QTR4   BUDGET  ACTUAL  VARIANCE
│
│   SALARY      30      33     35.5     37     135
│   BENEFITS     6       7      7.7      8      27.5
│   SUPPLIES    0.5     0.5     1        1       3
│   COMPUTER    20     21.5    22       22.5    85
│   RENT         4       4      4        4.8    16
│   UTILITY      1       1      1        1.5     4
│   EXPENSES   61.5    67      71.2    74.8   270.5
│   REVENUE    75      73.5    78       75    295
│   NET
│
│
│
│
│
│
└─────────────────────────────────────────────────────────
```

3. Select **Edit** from the action bar and **Change...** from the Edit pull-down menu to open the Change dialog box, shown in Display 3.10, which enables you to change cell attributes such as widths and formats.

Display 3.10
Changing Column Widths

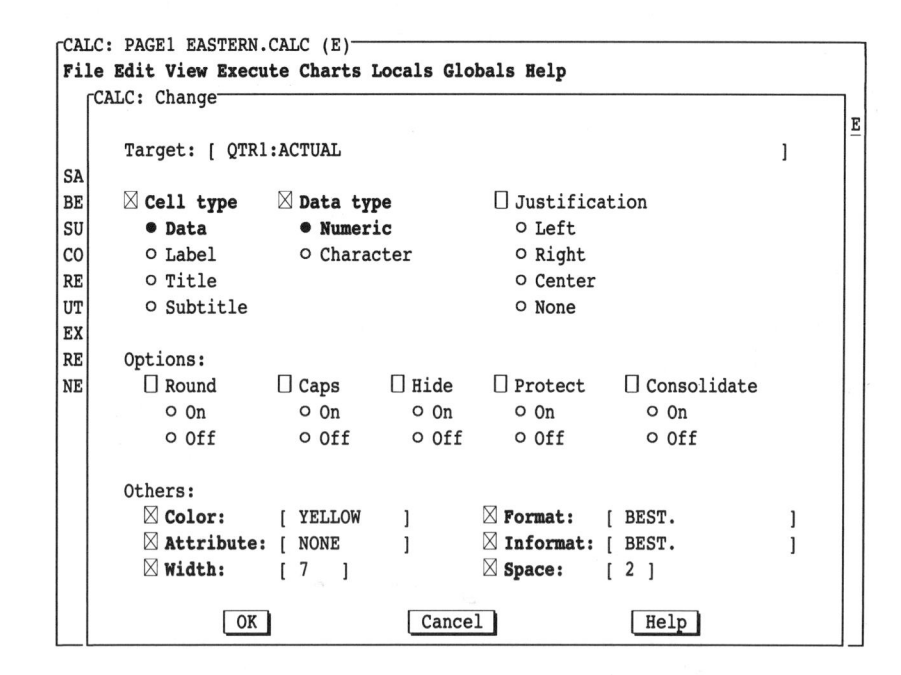

```
┌CALC: PAGE1 EASTERN.CALC (E)─────────────────────────────────────┐
│File Edit View Execute Charts Locals Globals Help                │
│ ┌CALC: Change──────────────────────────────────────────────┐   │E
│ │                                                          │   │─
│SA│  Target: [ QTR1:ACTUAL                              ]   │
│BE│                                                          │
│SU│  ⊠ Cell type      ⊠ Data type       ☐ Justification     │
│CO│    ● Data           ● Numeric         ○ Left             │
│RE│    ○ Label          ○ Character       ○ Right            │
│UT│    ○ Title                            ○ Center           │
│EX│    ○ Subtitle                         ○ None             │
│RE│                                                          │
│NE│  Options:                                                │
│  │    ☐ Round     ☐ Caps     ☐ Hide     ☐ Protect   ☐ Consolidate │
│  │      ○ On        ○ On       ○ On       ○ On        ○ On  │
│  │      ○ Off       ○ Off      ○ Off      ○ Off       ○ Off │
│  │                                                          │
│  │  Others:                                                 │
│  │    ⊠ Color:    [ YELLOW   ]    ⊠ Format:   [ BEST.    ] │
│  │    ⊠ Attribute:[ NONE     ]    ⊠ Informat: [ BEST.    ] │
│  │    ⊠ Width:    [ 7        ]    ⊠ Space:    [ 2        ] │
│  │                                                          │
│  │       [  OK  ]         [ Cancel ]          [ Help ]      │
│  └──────────────────────────────────────────────────────────┘
└─────────────────────────────────────────────────────────────────┘
```

Notice the **Target** field contains the column names **QTR1:ACTUAL**. This range name corresponds to the columns that you marked with the MARK BLOCK commands. Marking columns and cells before entering the Change dialog box saves typing.

Also, notice those attributes that can be changed within the dialog box are highlighted and have a mark in the selection field beside the attribute. Those selection fields with marks are active, while those selection fields without marks are inactive. Note the mark beside the **Width** field indicating the **Width** field is active.

4. Move the cursor to the **Width** field and type 7 over the current default width (8).

5. Select **OK** to close the Change dialog box and redisplay the EASTERN spreadsheet.

When the Change dialog box closes, a message is displayed indicating that six columns have been changed. All columns are now visible on the display as shown in Display 3.11.

Display 3.11
New Column Widths

```
┌CALC: PAGE1 EASTERN.CALC (E)─────────────────────────────────┐
│ File Edit View Execute Charts Locals Globals Help           │
│ NOTE: 6 column(s) have been changed.                        │
│             QTR1    QTR2    QTR3    QTR4   BUDGET  ACTUAL  VARIANCE │
│                                                             │
│ SALARY        30      33    35.5     37     135             │
│ BENEFITS       6       7     7.7      8    27.5             │
│ SUPPLIES     0.5     0.5       1      1       3             │
│ COMPUTER      20    21.5      22   22.5      85             │
│ RENT           4       4       4    4.8      16             │
│ UTILITY        1       1       1    1.5       4             │
│ EXPENSES    61.5      67    71.2   74.8   270.5             │
│ REVENUE       75    73.5      78     75     295             │
│ NET                                                         │
│                                                             │
│                                                             │
│                                                             │
│                                                             │
│                                                             │
└─────────────────────────────────────────────────────────────┘
```

Lesson 3.6: Defining Formulas

Now that you have added the appropriate row and columns to the spreadsheet, you can define formulas to compute the values for the cells in the new row and columns. To define formulas, as you saw in Chapter 2, you open the formula entry area, select the cell for which the formula applies, type your formula in the formula entry area, and press ENTER to display the computed value.

Formulas for the ACTUAL and VARIANCE columns are defined first, and then a formula for the NET row is defined.

In the first chapter, you learned how to define a formula in a cell and then copy that single cell containing the formula to other cells within the spreadsheet. In this chapter, you define formulas for the first cell in the ACTUAL and VARIANCE columns and then copy those two cells to the remaining cells in those columns.

Note: The programming capabilities of SAS/CALC software provide an alternative method of computing cell values. Once you understand how to use formulas for computing cell values, consult Chapter 7, "Using Programs with SAS/CALC Software," for information on computing cell values with programs.

To compute the values for the **ACTUAL** column:

1. Select **Execute** from the action bar and **Enter formula** from the Execute pull-down menu to display the formula entry area.

2. Select the SALARY.ACTUAL cell by using the cursor keys to move the cursor to the cell and pressing ENTER or by pointing and clicking with a mouse.

▶ *Caution* . . . . *Using the TAB Key*
Do not use the TAB key to move the cursor to the SALARY.ACTUAL cell. The TAB key moves the cursor to the action bar. ▲

As you saw in Chapter 2, you can sum the values of cells by listing each of the cells in the SUM function. You can avoid having to list all the cells you want to process by using a range of cells. When you changed the widths of columns earlier in this chapter, you saw that the Target field automatically contained the cell range QTR1:ACTUAL because you marked that range of column names prior to opening the Change dialog box. You can write your own cell ranges for use in formulas. You specify a range of cells by placing a colon (:) between the names of the first and last cell you want to process.

For the SALARY.ACTUAL cell, you want to sum the values of the cells SALARY.QTR1, SALARY.QTR2, SALARY.QTR3, and SALARY.QTR4. You can define a range of cells in the SUM function to sum the values of all four cells.

3. Move the cursor to the formula entry area and type the following formula as shown in Display 3.12.

    ```
    =sum(salary.qtr1:salary.qtr4)
    ```

4. Press ENTER to execute the formula.

    Pressing ENTER displays the resulting value in the SALARY.ACTUAL cell, as shown in Display 3.12.

Display 3.12
New Value for SALARY.ACTUAL

```
┌CALC: PAGE1 EASTERN.CALC (E)─────────────────────────────────────┐
│File Edit View Execute Charts Locals Globals Help                │
│                                                                 │
│              [ =SUM(SALARY.QTR1:SALARY.QTR4)                 ]  │
│     SALARY   [                                               ]  │
│     ACTUAL   [                                               ]  │
│     PAGE1    [                                               ]  │
│                                                                 │
│              QTR1    QTR2    QTR3    QTR4   BUDGET  ACTUAL  VARIANCE │
│                                                                 │
│   SALARY      30      33     35.5     37     135    135.5      │
│   BENEFITS     6       7      7.7      8     27.5              │
│   SUPPLIES   0.5     0.5       1       1       3               │
│   COMPUTER    20    21.5      22    22.5      85               │
│   RENT         4       4       4     4.8      16               │
│   UTILITY      1       1       1     1.5       4               │
│   EXPENSES  61.5      67    71.2    74.8   270.5               │
│   REVENUE     75    73.5      78      75     295               │
│   NET                                                          │
│                                                                 │
└─────────────────────────────────────────────────────────────────┘
```

Now, you are ready to enter the formulas for the cells in the VARIANCE column. For the SALARY.VARIANCE cell, you want to compute the difference between the values in the SALARY.BUDGET and SALARY.ACTUAL cells.

To compute the values for the **VARIANCE** column:

1. With the formula entry area visible on your display, select the SALARY.VARIANCE cell.

2. Move the cursor to the formula entry area and type the following formula, as shown in Display 3.13.

    ```
    =salary.budget-salary.actual
    ```

3. Press ENTER to execute the formula.
    Pressing ENTER displays the resulting value in the VARIANCE.SALARY cell, as shown in Display 3.13.

Display 3.13
New Value for SALARY.VARIANCE

```
┌CALC: PAGE1 EASTERN.CALC (E)─────────────────────────────────────────┐
│File Edit View Execute Charts Locals Globals Help                    │
│                                                                     │
│             [ =SALARY.BUDGET-SALARY.ACTUAL                        ] │
│   SALARY    [                                                     ] │
│   VARIANCE  [                                                     ] │
│   PAGE1     [                                                     ] │
│                                                                     │
│              QTR1    QTR2    QTR3    QTR4   BUDGET  ACTUAL  VARIANCE│
│                                                                     │
│   SALARY      30      33    35.5      37     135    135.5    -0.5  │
│   BENEFITS     6       7     7.7       8    27.5                   │
│   SUPPLIES   0.5     0.5       1       1       3                   │
│   COMPUTER    20    21.5      22    22.5      85                   │
│   RENT         4       4       4     4.8      16                   │
│   UTILITY      1       1       1     1.5       4                   │
│   EXPENSES  61.5      67    71.2    74.8   270.5                   │
│   REVENUE     75    73.5      78      75     295                   │
│   NET                                                               │
│                                                                     │
└─────────────────────────────────────────────────────────────────────┘
```

4. Select **Execute** from the action bar and **End formula entry** from the Execute pull-down menu to close the formula entry area.

Note: Although you do not need to close the formula entry area to perform tasks, such as copying, the display appears less cluttered.

The same computations you defined for the SALARY.ACTUAL and SALARY.VARIANCE cells must be defined for the remaining cells within those columns. As you saw in Chapter 2, you can copy the formulas you defined for the SALARY.ACTUAL and SALARY.VARIANCE cells to those remaining cells.

Lesson 3.7: Copying Formulas

To copy the SALARY.ACTUAL and SALARY.VARIANCE cells:

1. Mark the SALARY.ACTUAL cell by placing the cursor on that cell and pressing the MARK BLOCK function key. You are now ready to mark the target cells.

▶ *Caution* . . . . *Using the TAB Key*
Do not use the TAB key to move the cursor to the SALARY.ACTUAL cell. You cannot TAB to the SALARY.ACTUAL cell because it contains a formula and is protected by default. ▲

   Because you also want to copy the SALARY.VARIANCE cell, you must also mark that cell by placing the cursor on the cell and pressing the MARK BLOCK function key. Both cells are highlighted indicating they are the source range of cells you want to copy.

▶ *Caution* . . . . *Incorrectly Marking Cells*
If you incorrectly mark a cell or a range of cells, select **Edit** from the action bar and **Unmark** from the Edit pull-down menu to remove all current marks. Then, remark the correct cell or cells. ▲

2. Place the cursor on the BENEFITS.ACTUAL cell and press the MARK BLOCK function key.
   You have highlighted the first target cell. The BENEFITS.ACTUAL cell is the cell in the upper-left corner of a range of cells you want to mark.

3. Place the cursor on the REVENUE.VARIANCE cell and press the MARK BLOCK function key.
   The REVENUE.VARIANCE cell is the cell in the lower-right corner of the range of cells you want to mark. All cells within the target range are highlighted.

4. Select **Edit** from the action bar and **Copy marked areas** from the Edit pull-down menu to copy the formula from the source range to each target cell in the **ACTUAL** and **VARIANCE** columns.
   The highlight is removed, and the computed values are displayed, as shown in Display 3.14.

68 *Modifying Your Spreadsheet* □ *Chapter 3*

Display 3.14
Computed Values for ACTUAL and VARIANCE

```
┌CALC: PAGE1 EASTERN.CALC (E)─────────────────────────────────────────┐
│ File Edit View Execute Charts Locals Globals Help                   │
│                                                                     │
│                QTR1    QTR2    QTR3    QTR4   BUDGET  ACTUAL VARIANCE│
│                                                                     │
│   SALARY        30      33    35.5      37     135    135.5    -0.5 │
│   BENEFITS       6       7     7.7       8    27.5     28.7    -1.2 │
│   SUPPLIES     0.5     0.5       1       1       3        3       0 │
│   COMPUTER      20    21.5      22    22.5      85       86      -1 │
│   RENT           4       4       4     4.8      16     16.8    -0.8 │
│   UTILITY        1       1       1     1.5       4      4.5    -0.5 │
│   EXPENSES    61.5      67    71.2    74.8   270.5    274.5      -4 │
│   REVENUE       75    73.5      78      75     295    301.5    -6.5 │
│   NET                                                               │
│                                                                     │
│                                                                     │
│                                                                     │
│                                                                     │
└─────────────────────────────────────────────────────────────────────┘
```

Now, you are ready to enter the formulas for the cells in the NET row. For the NET.QTR1 cell, you want to compute the difference between the values in the REVENUE.QTR1 and EXPENSES.QTR1 cells.

To compute the values for the NET row, enter the following formula. After the formula is executed, the resulting value is displayed in the NET.QTR1 cell as shown in Display 3.15.

```
=revenue.qtr1-expenses.qtr1
```

Display 3.15
New Value for NET.QTR1

```
┌CALC: PAGE1 EASTERN.CALC (E)─────────────────────────────────────────┐
│ File Edit View Execute Charts Locals Globals Help                   │
│                                                                     │
│             [ =REVENUE.QTR1-EXPENSES.QTR1                         ] │
│   NET       [                                                     ] │
│   QTR1      [                                                     ] │
│   PAGE1     [                                                     ] │
│                                                                     │
│                QTR1    QTR2    QTR3    QTR4   BUDGET  ACTUAL VARIANCE│
│                                                                     │
│   SALARY        30      33    35.5      37     135    135.5    -0.5 │
│   BENEFITS       6       7     7.7       8    27.5     28.7    -1.2 │
│   SUPPLIES     0.5     0.5       1       1       3        3       0 │
│   COMPUTER      20    21.5      22    22.5      85       86      -1 │
│   RENT           4       4       4     4.8      16     16.8    -0.8 │
│   UTILITY        1       1       1     1.5       4      4.5    -0.5 │
│   EXPENSES    61.5      67    71.2    74.8   270.5    274.5      -4 │
│   REVENUE       75    73.5      78      75     295    301.5    -6.5 │
│   NET         13.5                                                  │
│                                                                     │
└─────────────────────────────────────────────────────────────────────┘
```

After the formula is executed, the resulting value is displayed in the NET.QTR1 cell as shown in Display 3.15.

Because the same computation you defined for the NET.QTR1 cell must be defined for the remaining cells within the row, copy the formula to those remaining cells.

1. Move the cursor to the NET.QTR1 cell and press the MARK BLOCK function key two times. Once to begin the MARK BLOCK command and once to end the MARK BLOCK command.

2. Move the cursor to the NET.QTR2 cell and press the MARK BLOCK function key.

3. Move the cursor to the NET.VARIANCE cell and press the MARK BLOCK function key.

4. Select **Edit** from the action bar and **Copy marked areas** from the Edit pull-down menu.

When you have finished defining and copying all the formulas, your spreadsheet appears, as shown in Display 3.16,

Display 3.16
The EASTERN Spreadsheet with Computed Values

```
┌CALC: PAGE1 EASTERN.CALC (E)─────────────────────────────────────┐
│File Edit View Execute Charts Locals Globals Help                │
│                                                                 │
│             QTR1     QTR2     QTR3     QTR4   BUDGET   ACTUAL   VARIANCE
│                                                                 │
│  SALARY       30       33     35.5       37      135    135.5     -0.5
│  BENEFITS      6        7      7.7        8     27.5     28.7     -1.2
│  SUPPLIES    0.5      0.5        1        1        3        3        0
│  COMPUTER     20     21.5       22     22.5       85       86       -1
│  RENT          4        4        4      4.8       16     16.8     -0.8
│  UTILITY       1        1        1      1.5        4      4.5     -0.5
│  EXPENSES   61.5       67     71.2     74.8    270.5    274.5       -4
│  REVENUE      75     73.5       78       75      295    301.5     -6.5
│  NET        13.5      6.5      6.8      0.2     24.5       27     -2.5
│                                                                 │
│                                                                 │
│                                                                 │
│                                                                 │
└─────────────────────────────────────────────────────────────────┘
```

Looking at the spreadsheet, you will notice that some cell values are displayed with one decimal place while others are displayed with no decimal places. By default, the cell values are displayed with a BEST. format indicating that SAS/CALC software selects the best form for displaying the values. To improve the look of your spreadsheet by displaying all cell values in the same form, you can replace the BEST. format with one that you select.

70 *Modifying Your Spreadsheet* □ *Chapter 3*

Lesson 3.8: Assigning Cell Formats

Follow the steps below to assign a format to each cell that displays the cell values with two decimal places.

1. Move the cursor to the SALARY.QTR1 cell and press the MARK BLOCK function key.

2. Move the cursor to the NET.VARIANCE cell and press the MARK BLOCK function key.
   All cells are highlighted indicating that you want to change all cells.

3. Select **Edit** from the action bar and **Change...** from the Edit pull-down menu to open the Change dialog box shown in Display 3.17.

Display 3.17
Assigning Cell Formats

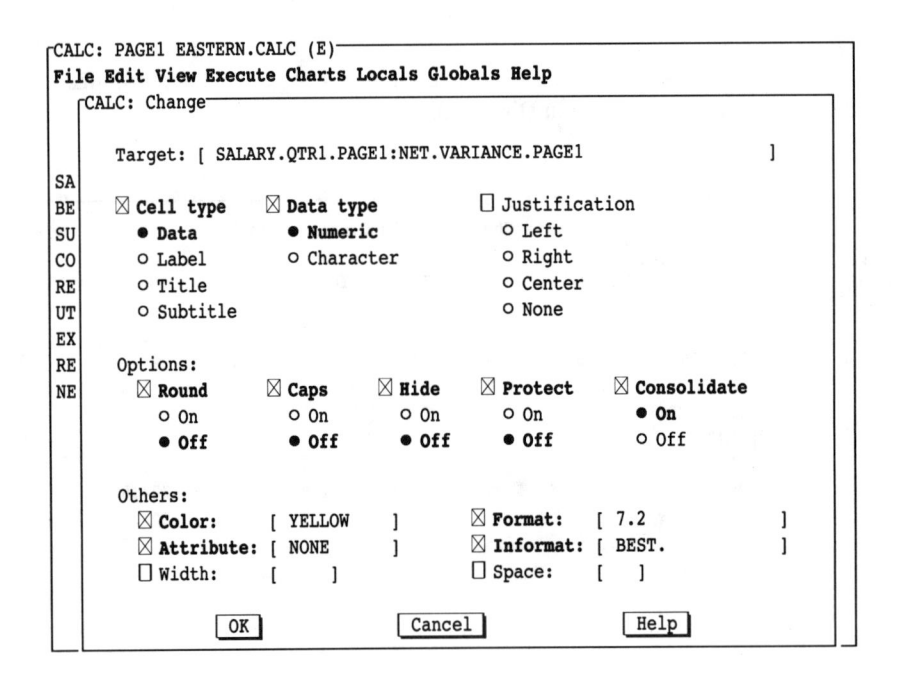

```
┌CALC: PAGE1 EASTERN.CALC (E)─────────────────────────────────┐
│File Edit View Execute Charts Locals Globals Help            │
│ ┌CALC: Change──────────────────────────────────────────────┐│
│ │                                                          ││
│ │   Target: [ SALARY.QTR1.PAGE1:NET.VARIANCE.PAGE1       ] ││
│SA│                                                          ││
│BE│   ⊠ Cell type    ⊠ Data type       □ Justification       ││
│SU│     ● Data         ● Numeric         ○ Left              ││
│CO│     ○ Label        ○ Character       ○ Right             ││
│RE│     ○ Title                          ○ Center            ││
│UT│     ○ Subtitle                       ○ None              ││
│EX│                                                          ││
│RE│   Options:                                               ││
│NE│    ⊠ Round    ⊠ Caps    ⊠ Hide    ⊠ Protect  ⊠ Consolidate││
│  │    ○ On       ○ On      ○ On       ○ On       ● On       ││
│  │    ● Off      ● Off     ● Off      ● Off      ○ Off      ││
│  │                                                          ││
│  │   Others:                                                ││
│  │    ⊠ Color:    [ YELLOW  ]    ⊠ Format:  [ 7.2     ]     ││
│  │    ⊠ Attribute:[ NONE    ]    ⊠ Informat:[ BEST.   ]     ││
│  │    □ Width:    [         ]    □ Space:   [       ]       ││
│  │         [ OK ]         [ Cancel ]          [ Help ]      ││
│ └──────────────────────────────────────────────────────────┘│
└─────────────────────────────────────────────────────────────┘
```

Notice the **Target** field contains the cell range **SALARY.QTR1.PAGE1:NET.VARIANCE.PAGE1** . This range name corresponds to the cells that you marked with the MARK BLOCK commands.

4. Move the cursor to the **Format** field and type 7.2 over the current format, **BEST.** Delete the default format name BEST. completely; a format of 7.2T. is invalid.
   Make sure there is a mark in the selection field for **Format**. The 7.2 format indicates that you want the cell values to be displayed in a maximum width of seven spaces including two digits to the right of the decimal point.

5. Select **OK** to display the spreadsheet shown in Display 3.18. A message is displayed indicating that 63 cells have been changed.

Display 3.18
Formatted Values

```
┌CALC: PAGE1 EASTERN.CALC (E)─────────────────────────────────┐
│ File Edit View Execute Charts Locals Globals Help           │
│ NOTE: 63 cell(s) have been changed.                         │
│          QTR1    QTR2    QTR3    QTR4   BUDGET  ACTUAL  VARIANCE│
│                                                             │
│ SALARY   30.00   33.00   35.50   37.00  135.00  135.50  -0.50│
│ BENEFITS  6.00    7.00    7.70    8.00   27.50   28.70  -1.20│
│ SUPPLIES  0.50    0.50    1.00    1.00    3.00    3.00   0.00│
│ COMPUTER 20.00   21.50   22.00   22.50   85.00   86.00  -1.00│
│ RENT      4.00    4.00    4.00    4.80   16.00   16.80  -0.80│
│ UTILITY   1.00    1.00    1.00    1.50    4.00    4.50  -0.50│
│ EXPENSES 61.50   67.00   71.20   74.80  270.50  274.50  -4.00│
│ REVENUE  75.00   73.50   78.00   75.00  295.00  301.50  -6.50│
│ NET      13.50    6.50    6.80    0.20   24.50   27.00  -2.50│
│                                                             │
│                                                             │
│                                                             │
└─────────────────────────────────────────────────────────────┘
```

You can use the HELP command to verify the cell formats and to obtain specific cell attribute information.

Note: You must use a function key to issue the HELP command when you are using pull-down menus. To view or change your current function key definitions, select **Help** from the action bar and **Keys** from the Help pull-down menu.

Lesson 3.9: Verifying Cell Attributes

To verify cell attributes:

1. Move the cursor to the NET.ACTUAL cell.

2. Press the function key assigned to the HELP command to display the Help window shown in Display 3.19.

Display 3.19
The Help Window

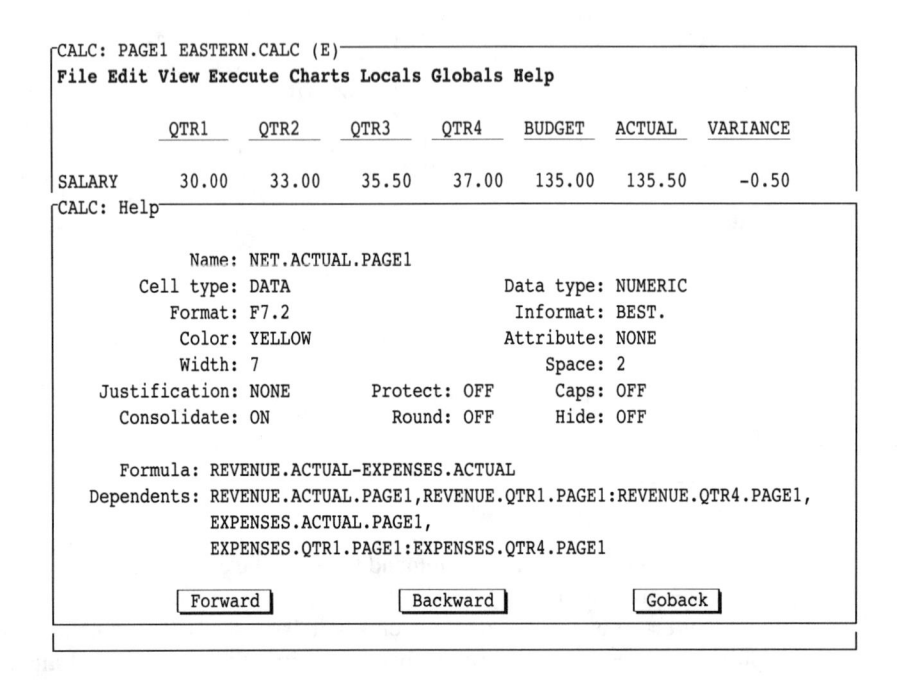

```
┌CALC: PAGE1 EASTERN.CALC (E)─────────────────────────────────────────┐
│File Edit View Execute Charts Locals Globals Help                    │
│                                                                     │
│              QTR1     QTR2     QTR3     QTR4    BUDGET  ACTUAL  VARIANCE │
│                                                                     │
│SALARY       30.00    33.00    35.50    37.00    135.00  135.50   -0.50  │
│┌CALC: Help─────────────────────────────────────────────────────────┐│
││                                                                   ││
││            Name: NET.ACTUAL.PAGE1                                 ││
││       Cell type: DATA                  Data type: NUMERIC         ││
││          Format: F7.2                   Informat: BEST.           ││
││           Color: YELLOW                Attribute: NONE            ││
││           Width: 7                         Space: 2               ││
││   Justification: NONE        Protect: OFF   Caps: OFF             ││
││     Consolidate: ON            Round: OFF   Hide: OFF             ││
││                                                                   ││
││         Formula: REVENUE.ACTUAL-EXPENSES.ACTUAL                   ││
││      Dependents: REVENUE.ACTUAL.PAGE1,REVENUE.QTR1.PAGE1:REVENUE.QTR4.PAGE1,││
││                  EXPENSES.ACTUAL.PAGE1,                           ││
││                  EXPENSES.QTR1.PAGE1:EXPENSES.QTR4.PAGE1          ││
││                                                                   ││
││         │ Forward │          │ Backward │         │ Goback │      ││
│└───────────────────────────────────────────────────────────────────┘│
└─────────────────────────────────────────────────────────────────────┘
```

Notice the cell name, **NET.ACTUAL.PAGE1**, in the **Name** field. Also, notice the format, **7.2**, and the cell width, **7**. The **Formula** field displays the formula that calculates the value for the NET.ACTUAL cell.

3. When you are finished viewing the Help window, select **Goback** to close the Help window and redisplay the EASTERN spreadsheet.

Note: Consult *SAS/CALC Software: Usage and Reference* for more information regarding the Help window.

You have now completed the second tutorial chapter. You can end your SAS/CALC software session, or you can continue with Chapter 4, ''Producing Spreadsheet Reports and Generating Graphics.''

If you want to end your spreadsheet and end the SAS/CALC software session, refer to Lessons 2.11 and 2.12 in Chapter 2 for assistance.

Chapter Summary

This chapter introduces many features of SAS/CALC software that enable you to modify and enhance your spreadsheets.

First, you learn how to open an existing spreadsheet. After opening the spreadsheet, you learn how to insert an additional row and two additional columns, and how to define formulas to compute the cell values for the new row and columns. You also learn how to change column widths, and specify a format to display cell values with two decimal places.

After completing this chapter, you have an enhanced EASTERN spreadsheet that you can use to produce spreadsheet reports and generate graphics.

Chapter 4 Producing Spreadsheet Reports and Generating Graphics

Producing Spreadsheet Reports 75
    Lesson 4.1: Sending a Default Report 80
    Lesson 4.2: Freeing the Print File 82
    Lesson 4.3: Creating an Enhanced REPORT Entry 84
    Lesson 4.4: Transposing Rows and Columns for a Report 87
    Lesson 4.5: Creating a Multipage REPORT Entry 89
    Lesson 4.6: Sending the Enhanced, Transposed, and Multipage Reports 91
    Lesson 4.7: Freeing the Print Files 93
Generating Graphics 95
    Lesson 4.8: Creating a Pie Chart 95
    Lesson 4.9: Enhancing a Pie Chart 97
    Lesson 4.10: Creating a Bar Chart 102
Chapter Summary 104

Producing Spreadsheet Reports

Once a spreadsheet is created, you can use the report generating capabilities of SAS/CALC software to print hardcopy of all or selected parts of your spreadsheet. In the first part of this chapter, you generate the reports shown in Output 4.1, Output 4.2, Output 4.3, and Output 4.4.

Output 4.1 is a default report that displays the entire EASTERN spreadsheet using default printing features.

Output 4.1
Default Spreadsheet Report

```
                                      Monday, October 7, 1991  12:42:58  PAGE 1
                                 EASTERN.CALC
                QTR1      QTR2      QTR3      QTR4    BUDGET    ACTUAL  VARIANCE
              -------   -------   -------   -------  -------   -------  --------
     SALARY     30.00     33.00     35.50     37.00   135.00    135.50     -0.50
   BENEFITS      6.00      7.00      7.70      8.00    27.50     28.70     -1.20
   SUPPLIES      0.50      0.50      1.00      1.00     3.00      3.00      0.00
   COMPUTER     20.00     21.50     22.00     22.50    85.00     86.00     -1.00
       RENT      4.00      4.00      4.00      4.80    16.00     16.80     -0.80
    UTILITY      1.00      1.00      1.00      1.50     4.00      4.50     -0.50
   EXPENSES     61.50     67.00     71.20     74.80   270.50    274.50     -4.00
    REVENUE     75.00     73.50     78.00     75.00   295.00    301.50     -6.50
        NET     13.50      6.50      6.80      0.20    24.50     27.00     -2.50
```

Output 4.2 is an enhanced report that uses options to print a report title, and suppress such items as the time, date, and page numbers.

Output 4.2
Enhanced Spreadsheet Report

```
                    Eastern Division Financial Report
             QTR1     QTR2     QTR3     QTR4    BUDGET   ACTUAL  VARIANCE
             -------  -------  -------  -------  -------  -------  --------
   SALARY    30.00    33.00    35.50    37.00   135.00   135.50    -0.50
   BENEFITS   6.00     7.00     7.70     8.00    27.50    28.70    -1.20
   SUPPLIES   0.50     0.50     1.00     1.00     3.00     3.00     0.00
   COMPUTER  20.00    21.50    22.00    22.50    85.00    86.00    -1.00
   RENT       4.00     4.00     4.00     4.80    16.00    16.80    -0.80
   UTILITY    1.00     1.00     1.00     1.50     4.00     4.50    -0.50
   EXPENSES  61.50    67.00    71.20    74.80   270.50   274.50    -4.00
   REVENUE   75.00    73.50    78.00    75.00   295.00   301.50    -6.50
   NET       13.50     6.50     6.80     0.20    24.50    27.00    -2.50
```

Output 4.3 is a report of the EASTERN spreadsheet with the spreadsheet rows and columns transposed.

Output 4.3 *Transposed Spreadsheet Report*

```
                         Transposed Rows and Columns
           SALARY  BENEFITS  SUPPLIES  COMPUTER   RENT   UTILITY  EXPENSES  REVENUE    NET
           ------  --------  --------  --------  ------  -------  --------  -------  ------
  QTR1      30.00     6.00      0.50    20.00     4.00    1.00     61.50    75.00   13.50
  QTR2      33.00     7.00      0.50    21.50     4.00    1.00     67.00    73.50    6.50
  QTR3      35.50     7.70      1.00    22.00     4.00    1.00     71.20    78.00    6.80
  QTR4      37.00     8.00      1.00    22.50     4.80    1.50     74.80    75.00    0.20
  BUDGET   135.00    27.50      3.00    85.00    16.00    4.00    270.50   295.00   24.50
  ACTUAL   135.50    28.70      3.00    86.00    16.80    4.50    274.50   301.50   27.00
  VARIANCE  -0.50    -1.20      0.00    -1.00    -0.80   -0.50     -4.00    -6.50   -2.50
```

Output 4.4 is the first page of a multipage report that displays the data for each quarter on a separate page.

Output 4.4
Page 1 of a Multipage Spreadsheet Report

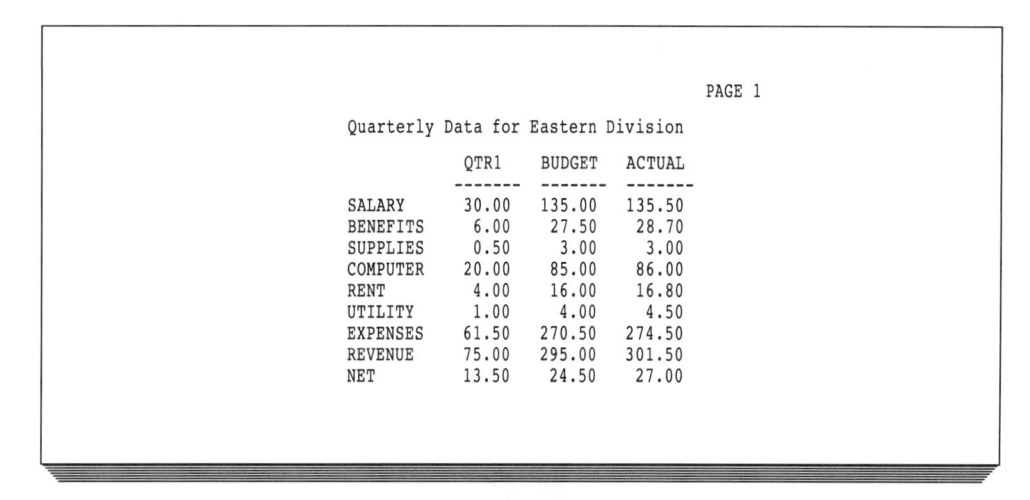

```
                                              PAGE 1
           Quarterly Data for Eastern Division
                     QTR1    BUDGET    ACTUAL
                    -------  -------   -------
          SALARY     30.00   135.00    135.50
          BENEFITS    6.00    27.50     28.70
          SUPPLIES    0.50     3.00      3.00
          COMPUTER   20.00    85.00     86.00
          RENT        4.00    16.00     16.80
          UTILITY     1.00     4.00      4.50
          EXPENSES   61.50   270.50    274.50
          REVENUE    75.00   295.00    301.50
          NET        13.50    24.50     27.00
```

You can also generate graphic reports such as pie charts, bar charts, and plots from the data in your spreadsheet.

In the second part of this chapter, you learn to generate the pie chart shown in Display 4.1 and the bar chart shown in Display 4.2.

The pie chart in Display 4.1 shows the percentage of money budgeted for each expenditure item.

Display 4.1
Default Pie Chart

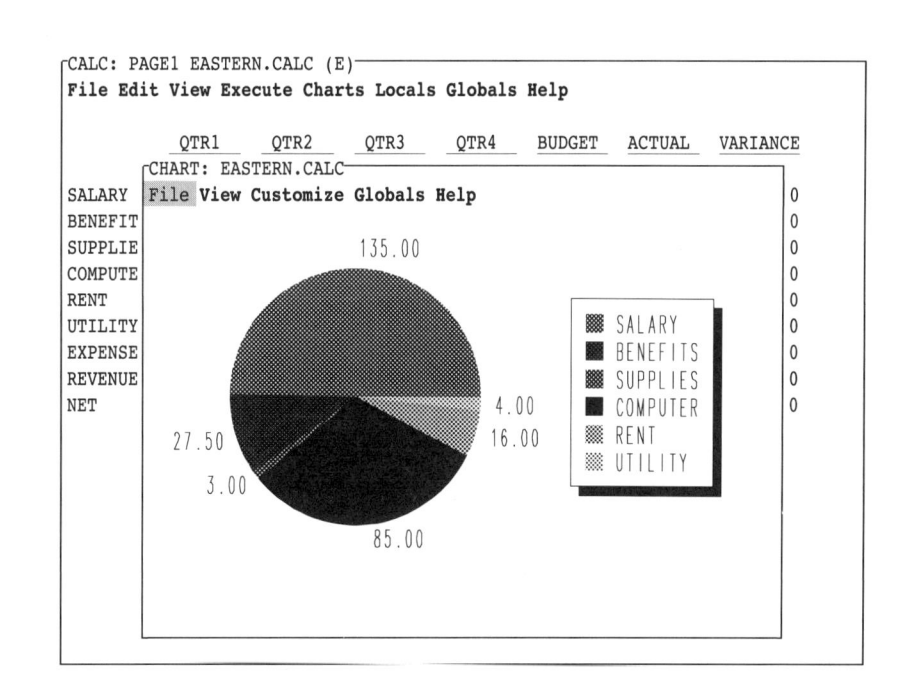

```
┌CALC: PAGE1 EASTERN.CALC (E)─────────────────────────────┐
│File Edit View Execute Charts Locals Globals Help        │
│                                                         │
│          QTR1    QTR2    QTR3    QTR4   BUDGET  ACTUAL  VARIANCE
│   ┌CHART: EASTERN.CALC────────────────────────────────┐ │
│ SALARY │File View Customize Globals Help             │ 0
│ BENEFIT│                                             │ 0
│ SUPPLIE│              135.00                         │ 0
│ COMPUTE│                                             │ 0
│ RENT   │                                             │ 0
│ UTILITY│                        ┌──────────────┐     │ 0
│ EXPENSE│                        │ ▓ SALARY     │     │ 0
│ REVENUE│                        │ ■ BENEFITS   │     │ 0
│ NET    │                        │ ▓ SUPPLIES   │     │ 0
│        │                  4.00  │ ■ COMPUTER   │     │
│        │        27.50    16.00  │ ▓ RENT       │     │
│        │         3.00           │ ▓ UTILITY    │     │
│        │                        └──────────────┘     │
│        │            85.00                            │
│        └─────────────────────────────────────────────┘ │
└─────────────────────────────────────────────────────────┘
```

78 *Producing Spreadsheet Reports* □ *Chapter 4*

The bar chart in Display 4.2 compares budgeted amounts to actual amounts for each expenditure item.

Display 4.2
Default Bar Chart

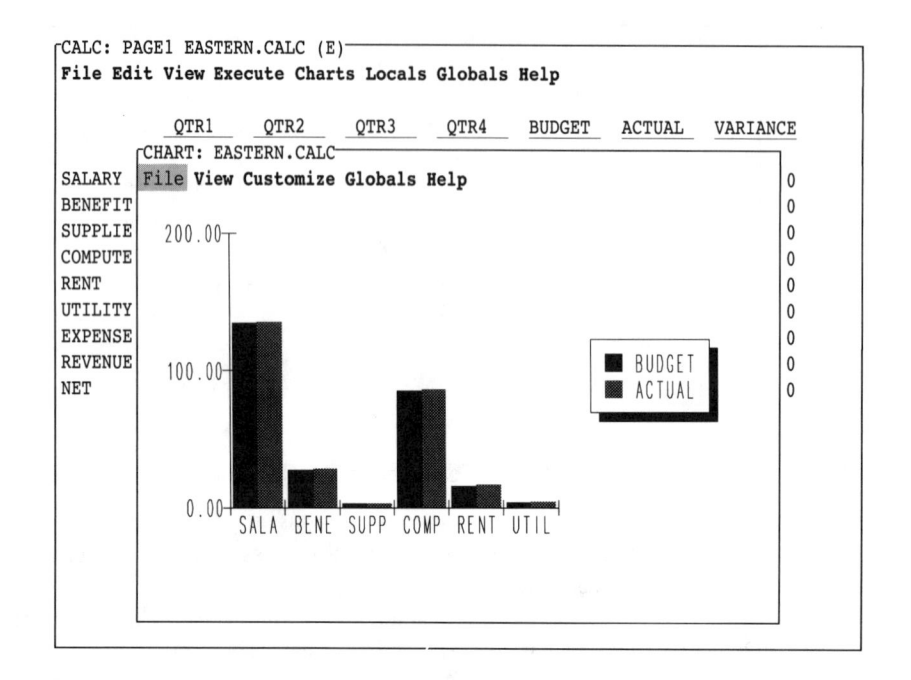

```
┌CALC: PAGE1 EASTERN.CALC (E)─────────────────────────────────┐
│File Edit View Execute Charts Locals Globals Help            │
│                                                             │
│         QTR1     QTR2     QTR3     QTR4    BUDGET  ACTUAL  VARIANCE
│ ┌CHART: EASTERN.CALC─────────────────────────────────┐      │
│ SALARY │File View Customize Globals Help             │   0  │
│ BENEFIT│                                             │   0  │
│ SUPPLIE│  200.00┬                                    │   0  │
│ COMPUTE│        │                                    │   0  │
│ RENT   │        │                                    │   0  │
│ UTILITY│        │                                    │   0  │
│ EXPENSE│        │      ■ ■                           │   0  │
│ REVENUE│  100.00┤      █ █        ┌──────────┐       │   0  │
│ NET    │        │      █ █        │ ■ BUDGET │       │   0  │
│        │        │      █ █  ■ ■   │ ■ ACTUAL │       │      │
│        │        │      █ █  █ █   └──────────┘       │      │
│        │    0.00┴──────█─█──█─█──────────────        │      │
│        │           SALA BENE SUPP COMP RENT UTIL     │      │
│        └─────────────────────────────────────────────┘      │
└─────────────────────────────────────────────────────────────┘
```

▶ *Caution* . . . . *Sending Reports to a Printer*
Before generating the reports in this chapter, contact the SAS Software Consultant at your site for informaton about printing at your site. ▲

The steps needed to generate a printed report from your spreadsheet are listed in Figure 4.1. These steps are explained briefly in the following figure and in more detail on the pages that follow.

Figure 4.1 *Steps for Generating a Printed Report*

Step	Purpose
1. Create a FORM entry (optional)	— defines the printer destination — controls the number of lines and characters per page — controls margin sizes
— A FORM entry must be associated with all reports that you generate. — A FORM entry can be used for any spreadsheet report you create during the current SAS session and across SAS sessions. — A default FORM entry named CALC.FORM is stored in the catalog SASHELP.CALC, which is provided with SAS/CALC software. This is the form that you use during this tutorial. Because the form automatically sends the reports to your default printer, contact your SAS Software Consultant for more information about your default printer.	
2. Create a REPORT entry (optional)	— controls how the report is formatted — defines titles and footnotes — controls the printing of page numbers and the date and time a report is generated — specifies which rows, columns, and pages appear on the report — specifies which rows and columns appear on each page of a multipage report
— Each REPORT entry you create identifies a specific report format. — You can create multiple REPORT entries that generate different reports from the same spreadsheet. — You can use a simple REPORT entry with any number of spreadsheets. — A default REPORT entry named DEFAULT.REPORT is stored in the catalog SASHELP.CALC, which is provided with SAS/CALC software. This REPORT entry uses the form CALC.FORM by default.	
3. Send the report	— reads the spreadsheet data — formats the report according to the REPORT entry — writes the report to a print file
4. After the report is written, you free the print file to the printer to get your hardcopy.	

80 *Producing Spreadsheet Reports □ Chapter 4*

In this chapter, you first use the default FORM and REPORT entries provided with the software. Then, you create three REPORT entries and store them in the same catalog that contains the EASTERN spreadsheet.

To generate the report shown in Output 4.1, you send a default report for the EASTERN spreadsheet to your printer.

If you ended the CALC session after Chapter 3, "Modifying Your Spreadsheet," refer to Lessons 2.1 and 2.2 in Chapter 2, "Creating Your First Spreadsheet," for information on invoking the CALC procedure and opening an existing spreadsheet. If you did not close your spreadsheet after Chapter 3, continue with this chapter.

Lesson 4.1: Sending a Default Report

To send a default report to the print file:

1. Open the EASTERN spreadsheet.

2. Select **File** from the action bar and **Print** from the File pull-down menu as shown in Display 4.3.

Display 4.3
File Pull-Down Menu

```
┌CALC: PAGE1 EASTERN.CALC (E)─────────────────────────────────────────┐
│ File Edit View Execute Charts Locals Globals Help                    │
│ ┌───────────────────┐                                                │
│ │Open...            │  R2     QTR3    QTR4    BUDGET   ACTUAL  VARIANCE│
│ │New...             │                                                │
│ │Save               │ 3.00   35.50   37.00   135.00   135.50   -0.50 │
│ │Save as            │ 7.00    7.70    8.00    27.50    28.70   -1.20 │
│ │Consolidate...     │ 0.50    1.00    1.00     3.00     3.00    0.00 │
│ │Fetch a data set...│ 1.50   22.00   22.50    85.00    86.00   -1.00 │
│ │Create a data set..│ 4.00    4.00    4.80    16.00    16.80   -0.80 │
│ │Print           -> │ 1.00    1.00    1.50     4.00     4.50   -0.50 │
│ │Swap               │ 7.00   71.20   74.80   270.50   274.50   -4.00 │
│ │Cancel             │ 3.50   78.00   75.00   295.00   301.50   -6.50 │
│ │Cancel all windows │ 6.50    6.80    0.20    24.50    27.00   -2.50 │
│ │End all            │                                                │
│ │End                │                                                │
│ └───────────────────┘                                                │
│                                                                      │
│                                                                      │
│                                                                      │
└──────────────────────────────────────────────────────────────────────┘
```

3. Select **Send default report** from the Print pull-down menu as shown in Display 4.4.

Display 4.4
Selecting Send Default Report

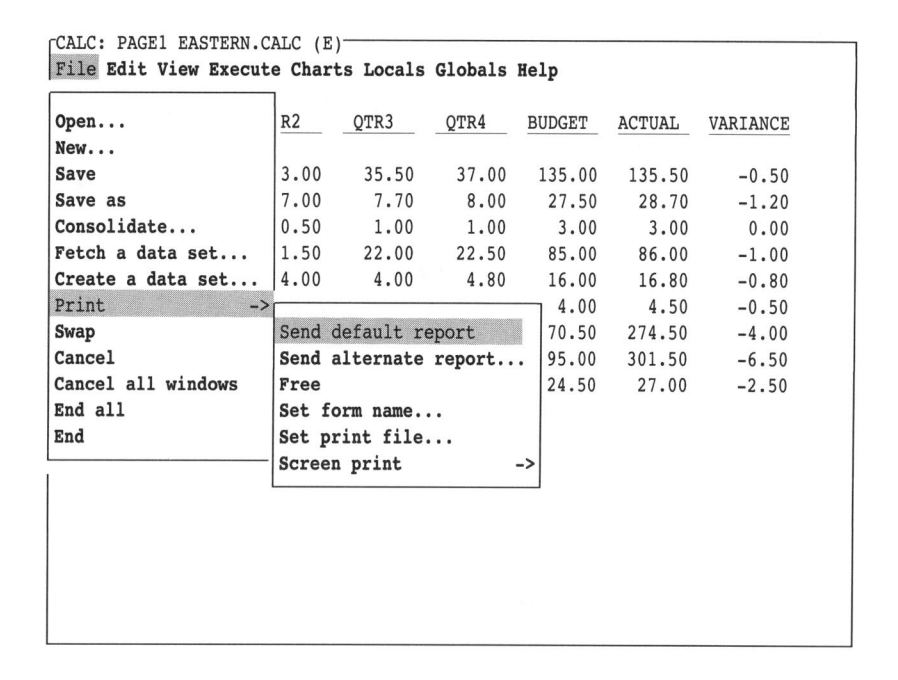

```
┌CALC: PAGE1 EASTERN.CALC (E)─────────────────────────────────────┐
│ File Edit View Execute Charts Locals Globals Help              │
│ ┌─────────────────┐                                            │
│ │Open...          │ R2      QTR3    QTR4    BUDGET  ACTUAL  VARIANCE
│ │New...           │                                            │
│ │Save             │ 3.00    35.50   37.00   135.00  135.50  -0.50
│ │Save as          │ 7.00    7.70    8.00    27.50   28.70   -1.20
│ │Consolidate...   │ 0.50    1.00    1.00    3.00    3.00    0.00
│ │Fetch a data set.│ 1.50    22.00   22.50   85.00   86.00   -1.00
│ │Create a data set│ 4.00    4.00    4.80    16.00   16.80   -0.80
│ │Print         -> │                         4.00    4.50    -0.50
│ │Swap             │┌─────────────────────┐  70.50   274.50  -4.00
│ │Cancel           ││Send default report  │  95.00   301.50  -6.50
│ │Cancel all window││Send alternate report│  24.50   27.00   -2.50
│ │End all          ││Free                 │
│ │End              ││Set form name...     │
│ └─────────────────┘│Set print file...    │
│                    │Screen print      -> │
│                    └─────────────────────┘
└─────────────────────────────────────────────────────────────────┘
```

A note is displayed verifying that the report was sent to the print file. A print file is an external file containing carriage-control (printer-control) information. To produce hardcopy of the report, you must free the report to the printer.

82 *Producing Spreadsheet Reports* □ *Chapter 4*

Lesson 4.2: Freeing the Print File

To free the print file:

1. Select **File** from the action bar and **Print** from the File pull-down menu.

2. Select **Free** from the Print pull-down menu as shown in Display 4.5. After you select **Free**, the report is sent to the printer.

Display 4.5
Selecting Free

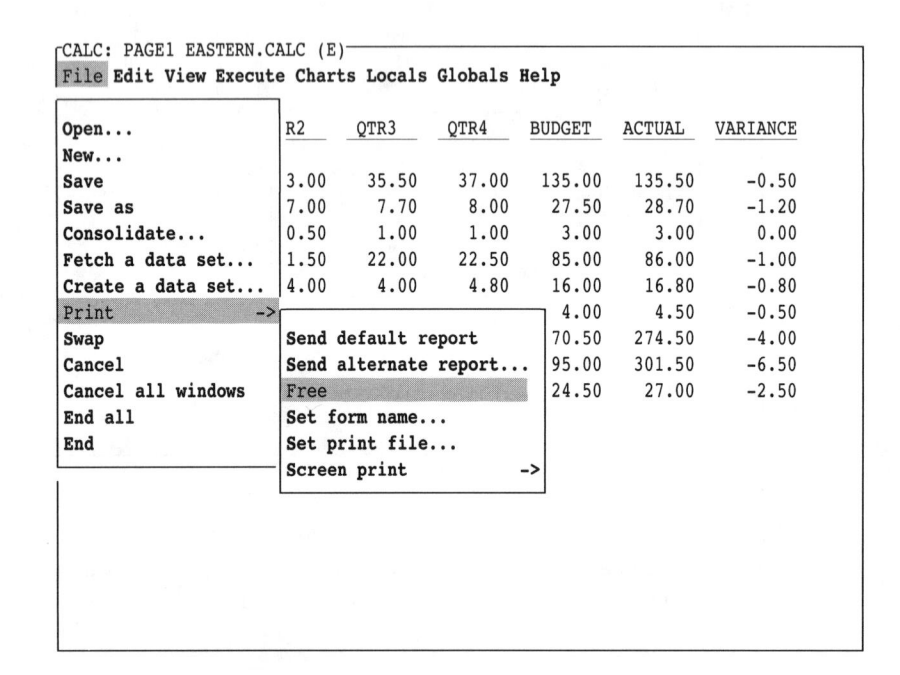

```
┌CALC: PAGE1 EASTERN.CALC (E)─────────────────────────────────────────────┐
│ File Edit View Execute Charts Locals Globals Help                        │
│ ┌─────────────────────┐                                                  │
│ │ Open...             │   R2      QTR3     QTR4    BUDGET   ACTUAL   VARIANCE │
│ │ New...              │                                                  │
│ │ Save                │  3.00    35.50    37.00   135.00   135.50    -0.50 │
│ │ Save as             │  7.00     7.70     8.00    27.50    28.70    -1.20 │
│ │ Consolidate...      │  0.50     1.00     1.00     3.00     3.00     0.00 │
│ │ Fetch a data set... │  1.50    22.00    22.50    85.00    86.00    -1.00 │
│ │ Create a data set...│  4.00     4.00     4.80    16.00    16.80    -0.80 │
│ │ Print           ->  │─┐                          4.00     4.50    -0.50 │
│ │ Swap                │ │ Send default report     70.50   274.50    -4.00 │
│ │ Cancel              │ │ Send alternate report...│95.00   301.50    -6.50 │
│ │ Cancel all windows  │ │ Free                    │24.50    27.00    -2.50 │
│ │ End all             │ │ Set form name...        │                       │
│ │ End                 │ │ Set print file...       │                       │
│ └─────────────────────┘ │ Screen print        ->  │                       │
│                         └─────────────────────────┘                       │
│                                                                           │
└───────────────────────────────────────────────────────────────────────────┘
```

The resulting report is shown in Output 4.5.

Output 4.5
Default Spreadsheet Report

```
                                      Monday, October 7, 1991  12:42:58  PAGE 1
                                   EASTERN.CALC
                QTR1     QTR2     QTR3     QTR4    BUDGET    ACTUAL   VARIANCE
                -------  -------  -------  -------  -------  -------  --------
      SALARY    30.00    33.00    35.50    37.00   135.00   135.50    -0.50
      BENEFITS   6.00     7.00     7.70     8.00    27.50    28.70    -1.20
      SUPPLIES   0.50     0.50     1.00     1.00     3.00     3.00     0.00
      COMPUTER  20.00    21.50    22.00    22.50    85.00    86.00    -1.00
      RENT       4.00     4.00     4.00     4.80    16.00    16.80    -0.80
      UTILITY    1.00     1.00     1.00     1.50     4.00     4.50    -0.50
      EXPENSES  61.50    67.00    71.20    74.80   270.50   274.50    -4.00
      REVENUE   75.00    73.50    78.00    75.00   295.00   301.50    -6.50
      NET       13.50     6.50     6.80     0.20    24.50    27.00    -2.50
```

Notice the report contains the following default features:

- the date
- the time
- the page number
- the global title, which is the spreadsheet name
- the information centered on the page.

Note: If you do not use the default form provided with the software, you must create your own form. Consult ''FORM'' in Chapter 17, ''SAS Display Manager Windows,'' in *SAS Language: Reference, Version 6, First Edition* for information on creating a form.

Remember that the REPORT entry controls how your report is formatted. Next, you create a REPORT entry named ENHANCED that alters some of the default formatting features.

Specifically, the ENHANCED entry:

- suppresses the time, date, and page number
- suppresses the global title
- prints a report title.

84 *Producing Spreadsheet Reports* □ *Chapter 4*

Lesson 4.3: Creating an Enhanced REPORT Entry

To create a REPORT entry:

1. Select **File** from the action bar and **New...** from the File pull-down menu to display the New... dialog box.

2. Type the name of the report, ENHANCED, in the **Entry name** field.

3. Select **REPORT** in the **Type** field, as shown in Display 4.6.

Display 4.6
New... Dialog Box with ENHANCED

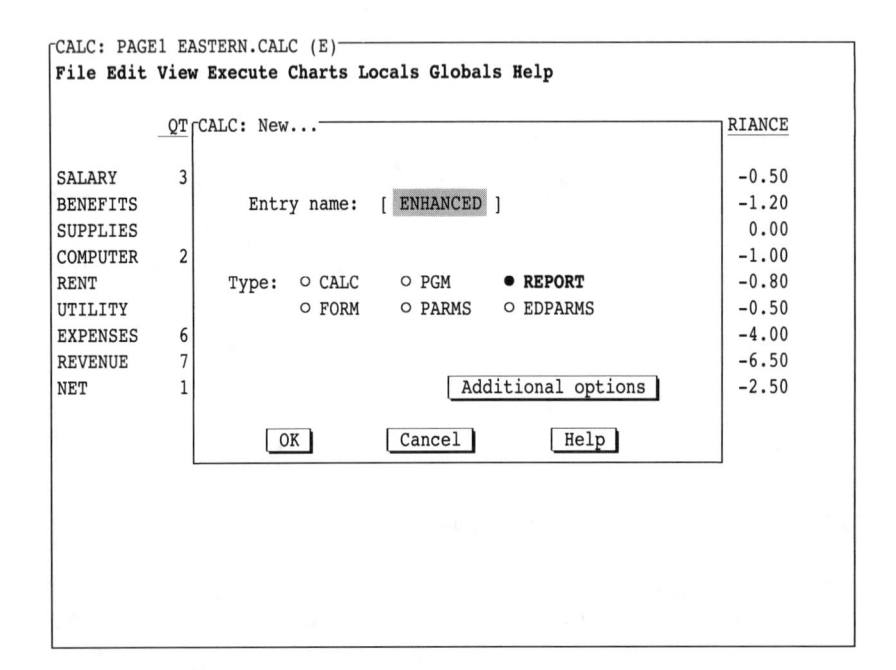

```
┌CALC: PAGE1 EASTERN.CALC (E)─────────────────────────────────────┐
│File Edit View Execute Charts Locals Globals Help                │
│                                                                 │
│            QT ┌CALC: New...──────────────────────────┐   RIANCE │
│               │                                      │          │
│  SALARY    3  │                                      │   -0.50  │
│  BENEFITS     │    Entry name:  [ ENHANCED ]         │   -1.20  │
│  SUPPLIES     │                                      │    0.00  │
│  COMPUTER  2  │                                      │   -1.00  │
│  RENT         │    Type:  ○ CALC    ○ PGM   ● REPORT │   -0.80  │
│  UTILITY      │           ○ FORM    ○ PARMS ○ EDPARMS│   -0.50  │
│  EXPENSES  6  │                                      │   -4.00  │
│  REVENUE   7  │                                      │   -6.50  │
│  NET       1  │              ┌──────────────────┐    │   -2.50  │
│               │              │Additional options│    │          │
│               │              └──────────────────┘    │          │
│               │   ┌────┐   ┌──────┐     ┌────┐       │          │
│               │   │ OK │   │Cancel│     │Help│       │          │
│               │   └────┘   └──────┘     └────┘       │          │
│               └──────────────────────────────────────┘          │
│                                                                 │
└─────────────────────────────────────────────────────────────────┘
```

4. Select **OK** to display the ENHANCED.REPORT dialog box shown in Display 4.7. You use this dialog box to specify which FORM entry to use and how to format the report.

The following note is displayed, **The current setting for CHECK is ON**. CHECK is a SAS/CALC software command that compares information you enter when creating a REPORT entry, such as row and column names, against a spreadsheet.

When creating a REPORT entry from within a spreadsheet, such as EASTERN, CHECK is set to ON because EASTERN is open and available for comparison. When creating a REPORT entry from within the DIRECTORY window, CHECK is set to OFF because no spreadsheet is open for comparison.

Display 4.7
ENHANCED.REPORT Dialog Box

```
┌CALC: PAGE1 EASTERN.CALC (E)─────────────────────────────────────────┐
│File Edit View Execute Charts Locals Globals Help                    │
│                                                                     │
│          QTR1     QTR2     QTR3     QTR4    BUDGET   ACTUAL  VARIANCE│
│                                                                     │
│ SALARY  ┌CALC: ENHANCED.REPORT (E)──────────────────────────────┐   │
│ BENEFITS│File Locals Globals Help                                │   │
│ SUPPLIES│Note: The current setting for CHECK is ON.              │   │
│ COMPUTER│   Report description: [ Enhanced Report              ] │   │
│ RENT    │                                                        │   │
│ UTILITY │         Report title: [ Eastern Division Financial Report ] │
│ EXPENSES│                       [                              ] │   │
│ REVENUE │                                                        │   │
│ NET     │                 Form: [ CALC    ]                      │   │
│         │                                                        │   │
│         │        Report columns:   ○ Rows   ● Columns   ○ Pages  │   │
│         │           Report rows:   ● Rows   ○ Columns   ○ Pages  │   │
│         │                                                        │   │
│         │         Report format:  ● Row/column/page specification... │
│         │                         ○ Free style specification...  │   │
│         │                                                        │   │
│         │             [ Page format ]  [ Additional information ]│   │
│         │                                                        │   │
│         └────────────────────────────────────────────────────────┘   │
└─────────────────────────────────────────────────────────────────────┘
```

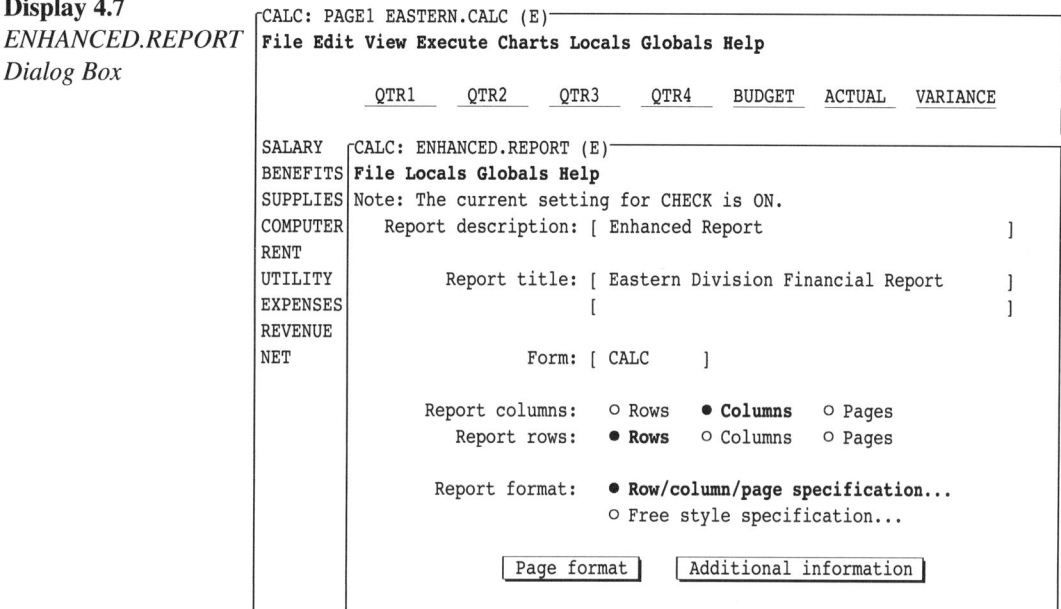

5. Move the cursor to the **Report description** field and type the text, `Enhanced Report`, for your report description, which appears in the DIRECTORY window beside the REPORT entry.

6. Move the cursor to the **Report title** field and type the text, `Eastern Division Financial Report`, for your report title.
   This field defines the text for the report title, but it does not cause the text to print in the report. You must indicate that you want to print the text by controlling the page format.

7. Accept the default form, **CALC**, in the **Form** field.

8. Select the **Page format** button to display the Page Format dialog box shown in Display 4.8.

86 *Producing Spreadsheet Reports* □ *Chapter 4*

Display 4.8
Default Page Format Dialog Box

```
┌CALC: PAGE1 EASTERN.CALC (E)──────────────────────────────┐
│File Edit View Execute Charts Locals Globals Help         │
│                                                          │
│         QTR1    QTR2    QTR3    QTR4   BUDGET  ACTUAL  VARIANCE │
│                                                          │
│SALARY  ┌CALC: ENHANCED.REPORT (E)─────────────────────┐  │
│BENEFITS│File Locals Globals Help                      │  │
│SUPPLIES│┌CALC: Page Format──────────────────────────┐ │ ]│
│COMPUTER││                                           │ │  │
│RENT    ││   Select:                                 │ │  │
│UTILITY ││     ☐ Convert all alphabetic text to uppercase. │ ]│
│EXPENSES││     ☐ Ignore user pagination.             │ │ ]│
│REVENUE ││     ☒ Center text on page.                │ │  │
│NET     ││     ☒ Print global title.                 │ │  │
│        ││     ☐ Print report title.                 │ │  │
│        ││     ☒ Print report column headings.       │ │  │
│        ││     ☒ Print report row headings.          │ │  │
│        ││     ☐ Left-justify page information.      │ │  │
│        ││     ☒ Print page number.                  │ │  │
│        ││     ☒ Print date.    Date format: [ WEEKDATE29. ] │ │  │
│        ││     ☒ Print time.    Time format: [ TIME8.    ]   │ │  │
│        ││                                           │ │  │
│        ││       [ OK ]      [ Cancel ]     [ Help ] │ │  │
│        │└───────────────────────────────────────────┘ │  │
└────────┴──────────────────────────────────────────────┴──┘
```

This dialog box enables you to control many formatting features. The features with a mark beside them are selected by default. You select or deselect these features by selecting the box or text. If a mark is present, it is removed; and if a mark is absent, it is entered.

9. Select **Print global title** to suppress the global title (spreadsheet name). Notice that the mark beside the item is removed.

10. Request the report title you want to print by selecting **Print report title**. Notice that a mark is entered beside the item. This selection causes the text you enter in the **Report title** field in the ENHANCED.REPORT dialog box to print.

11. Select **Print page number** to suppress the page number.

12. Select **Print date** to suppress the date.

13. Select **Print time** to suppress the time. The final Page Format dialog box is shown in Display 4.9.

Display 4.9
Modified Page Format Dialog Box

```
┌CALC: PAGE1 EASTERN.CALC (E)─────────────────────────────────────
│File Edit View Execute Charts Locals Globals Help
│
│           QTR1      QTR2      QTR3      QTR4    BUDGET   ACTUAL   VARIANCE
│
│SALARY  ┌CALC: ENHANCED.REPORT (E)──────────────────────────────
│BENEFITS│File Locals Globals Help
│SUPPLIES│┌CALC: Page Format─────────────────────────────────────
│COMPUTER││                                                              ]
│RENT    ││   Select:
│UTILITY ││     ☐ Convert all alphabetic text to uppercase.             ]
│EXPENSES││     ☐ Ignore user pagination.                               ]
│REVENUE ││     ☒ Center text on page.
│NET     ││     ☐ Print global title.
│        ││     ☒ Print report title.
│        ││     ☒ Print report column headings.
│        ││     ☒ Print report row headings.
│        ││     ☐ Left-justify page information.
│        ││     ☐ Print page number.
│        ││     ☐ Print date.    Date format: [ WEEKDATE29. ]
│        ││     ☐ Print time.    Time format: [ TIME8.      ]
│        ││
│        ││       [ OK ]          [ Cancel ]         [ Help ]
```

14. Select **OK** to redisplay the ENHANCED.REPORT dialog box.

15. Select **File** from the action bar and **End** from the File pull-down menu to close the ENHANCED.REPORT dialog box and redisplay the EASTERN spreadsheet. A note is displayed indicating the ENHANCED.REPORT entry has been saved.

At this point, you can send a report using the new ENHANCED entry to the print file. However, in this chapter you create two more REPORT entries, TRANS and MULTI, and then you send all three reports to the print file.

In addition to the features you used in the ENHANCED entry, there are features that enable you to transpose rows and columns for a report, create multipage reports, and specify which rows and columns appear on a report and the location of rows and columns in the report.

Lesson 4.4: Transposing Rows and Columns for a Report

Sometimes you may want to generate a report based on your spreadsheet but transpose the rows and columns. In other words, you want the rows in your spreadsheet to be the columns in your report and the columns in your spreadsheet to be the rows in your report. Transposing the rows and columns provides a different view of your data.

The TRANS entry you create in this lesson generates a report that transposes the rows and columns.

To transpose the rows and columns in a report:

1. Select **File** from the action bar and **New...** from the File pull-down menu to create a new REPORT entry.

2. Type **TRANS** in the **Entry name** field.

3. Select **REPORT** in the **Type** field.

4. Select **OK** to display the TRANS.REPORT dialog box as shown in Display 4.10.

88 *Producing Spreadsheet Reports* □ *Chapter 4*

5. In the TRANS.REPORT dialog box type the text, `Transposed Report`, in the **Report description** field.

6. Type the text, `Transposed Rows and Columns`, in the **Report title** field.

7. Accept the default form, **CALC**, in the **Form** field.

8. Select **Rows** in the **Report columns** field.
   By default, the selection is **Columns** indicating that the columns in the report correspond to the columns in the spreadsheet. By selecting **Rows**, you are redefining the columns in the report to correspond to the rows in the spreadsheet.

Display 4.10
TRANS.REPORT Dialog Box

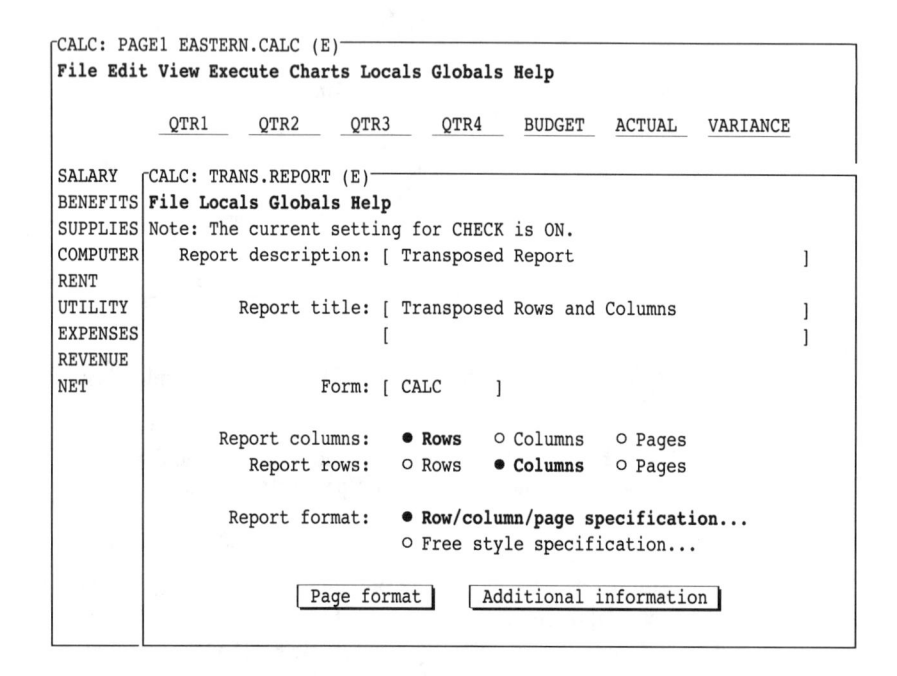

```
┌CALC: PAGE1 EASTERN.CALC (E)─────────────────────────────────────────┐
│File Edit View Execute Charts Locals Globals Help                    │
│                                                                     │
│           QTR1     QTR2     QTR3     QTR4    BUDGET   ACTUAL  VARIANCE│
│SALARY  ┌CALC: TRANS.REPORT (E)──────────────────────────────────┐   │
│BENEFITS│File Locals Globals Help                                │   │
│SUPPLIES│Note: The current setting for CHECK is ON.              │   │
│COMPUTER│    Report description: [ Transposed Report          ]  │   │
│RENT    │                                                        │   │
│UTILITY │        Report title: [ Transposed Rows and Columns  ]  │   │
│EXPENSES│                      [                               ] │   │
│REVENUE │                                                        │   │
│NET     │                 Form: [ CALC     ]                     │   │
│        │                                                        │   │
│        │       Report columns:  ● Rows    ○ Columns   ○ Pages   │   │
│        │          Report rows:  ○ Rows    ● Columns   ○ Pages   │   │
│        │                                                        │   │
│        │        Report format:  ● Row/column/page specification...│  │
│        │                        ○ Free style specification...   │   │
│        │                                                        │   │
│        │           [ Page format ]   [ Additional information ] │   │
│        │                                                        │   │
│        └────────────────────────────────────────────────────────┘   │
└─────────────────────────────────────────────────────────────────────┘
```

9. Select **Columns** in the **Report rows** field.
   By default, the selection is **Rows** indicating that the rows in the report correspond to the rows in the spreadsheet. By selecting **Columns**, you are redefining the rows in the report to correspond to the columns in the spreadsheet.

10. Select the **Page format** button to display the Page Format dialog box.

11. Suppress the global title, date, time, and page number options.

12. Select the **Print report title** option.

13. Select **OK** to redisplay the TRANS.REPORT dialog box.

14. Select **File** from the action bar and **End** from the File pull-down menu to redisplay the EASTERN spreadsheet.
    A note is displayed indicating the TRANS.REPORT entry has been saved.

At this time, you can send a report using the new TRANS entry, however, for this example, you need to define one more REPORT entry, MULTI, and then send all three reports together.

Lesson 4.5: Creating a Multipage REPORT Entry

MULTI, the last REPORT entry that you create

- produces a separate page in the report for each quarter
- includes the yearly budget (BUDGET column) on each page
- includes the total expenditures (ACTUAL column) on each page.

To create the MULTI.REPORT entry:

1. Select **File** from the action bar and **New...** from the File pull-down menu to create a new REPORT entry.

2. Type `MULTI` in the **Entry name** field.

3. Select **REPORT** in the **Type** field.

4. Select **OK**.

5. In the MULTI.REPORT dialog box type the text, `Multipage Report`, in the **Report description** field.

6. Type the text, `Quarterly Data for Eastern Division`, in the **Report title** field.

7. Accept the default form, **CALC**, in the **Form** field.

8. Select the **Free style specification** button to display the Free Style Specification window shown in Display 4.11. This window provides a text editor that you use to specify exactly which rows and columns you want printed on the report and where you want them printed. By default, line numbers are not displayed in the window. You can display them with the NUMBERS or NUMS command.

Display 4.11
Free Style Specification Window

```
┌CALC: PAGE3 EASTERN.CALC (E)─────────────────────────────────────
 File Edit View Execute Charts Locals Globals Help

            QTR1      QTR2      QTR3      QTR4    BUDGET   ACTUAL    VARIANCE

 SALARY  ┌CALC: MULTI.REPORT (E)──────────────────────────────────
 BENEFITS│File Locals Globals Help
 SUPPLIES│
 COMPUTER│    Report description: [ Multipage Report                      ]
 RENT    │
 UTILITY │         Report title: [ Quarterly Data for Eastern Division   ]
 EXPENSES│                       [                                        ]
         ┌CALC: Free Style Specification──────────────────────────
         Command ===>




```

9. Type NUMS on the command line and press ENTER.

    You can issue line commands for deleting, copying, and moving lines by typing the commands on the line numbers in the display and pressing ENTER.

    Note: Consult *SAS Language: Reference*, Chapter 19, ''SAS Text Editor Commands,'' for information regarding these line commands.

10. Type the following text on the first four lines as shown in Display 4.12.

    ```
    qtr1 budget actual /
    qtr2 budget actual /
    qtr3 budget actual /
    qtr4 budget actual
    ```

Display 4.12
Specifying Rows, Columns, and Pages

```
┌CALC: PAGE1 EASTERN.CALC (E)─────────────────────────────────────┐
│File Edit View Execute Charts Locals Globals Help                │
│                                                                 │
│           QTR1    QTR2    QTR3    QTR4    BUDGET  ACTUAL  VARIANCE │
│                                                                 │
│SALARY  ┌CALC: MULTI.REPORT (E)──────────────────────────────┐  │
│BENEFITS│File Locals Globals Help                            │  │
│SUPPLIES│                                                    │  │
│COMPUTER│   Report description: [ Multipage Report        ]  │  │
│RENT    │                                                    │  │
│UTILITY │        Report title: [ Quarterly Data for Eastern Division ] │
│EXPENSES│                      [                          ]  │  │
┌CALC: Free Style Specification──────────────────────────────────┐
│Command ===> end                                                │
│                                                                │
│00001 qtr1 budget actual /                                      │
│00002 qtr2 budget actual /                                      │
│00003 qtr3 budget actual /                                      │
│00004 qtr4 budget actual                                        │
│00005                                                           │
│00006                                                           │
│00007                                                           │
│00008                                                           │
└────────────────────────────────────────────────────────────────┘
```

The slashes are page breaks, which enable you to specify the number of pages you want in your report and which rows and columns you want on each page. The specification above prints columns QTR1, BUDGET, and ACTUAL on the first page; QTR2, BUDGET, and ACTUAL on the second page; QTR3, BUDGET, and ACTUAL on the third page; and QTR4, BUDGET, and ACTUAL on the fourth page. Notice that you can print any column as many times as you want. Additionally, you can list row names in the above specification to control which rows are printed on each page. In this example, no row names are listed, which causes all rows to print on each page of the report.

11. Issue the END command to close the Free Style Specification window, save the report specification, and redisplay the MULTI.REPORT dialog box.

    Note: Consult *SAS/CALC Software: Usage and Reference, Version 6, First Edition* for more information on using the Free Style Specification window.

12. Select the **Page Format** button to display the Page Format dialog box.

13. Suppress the global title, date, and time options.

14. Enable the **Print report title** option.

15. Select **OK** to redisplay the TRANS.REPORT dialog box.

16. Select **File** from the action bar and **End** from the File pull-down menu to redisplay the EASTERN spreadsheet.
    A note is displayed indicating the MULTI.REPORT entry has been saved.

Now that you have generated the three report entries, you are ready to send them to the printer.

Lesson 4.6: Sending the Enhanced, Transposed, and Multipage Reports

To send the reports:

1. Select **File** from the action bar and **Print** from the File pull-down menu.

2. Select **Send alternate report...** from the Print pull-down menu as shown in Display 4.13.

Display 4.13
Sending an Alternate Report

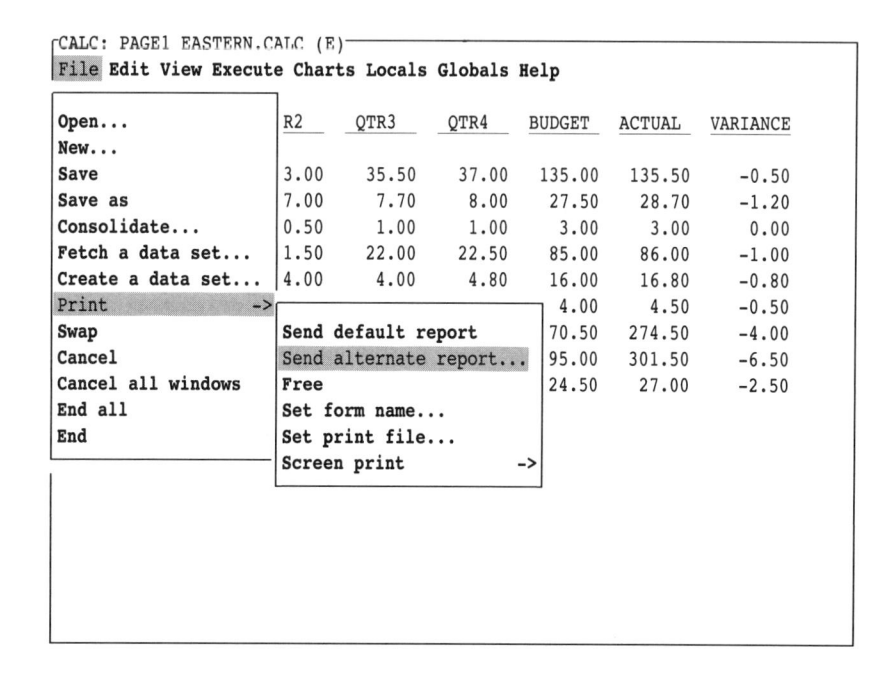

```
┌CALC: PAGE1 EASTERN.CALC (E)─────────────────────────────────────────────┐
│ File  Edit View Execute Charts Locals Globals Help                      │
│                                                                          │
│ Open...              R2       QTR3     QTR4    BUDGET   ACTUAL  VARIANCE │
│ New...                                                                   │
│ Save                 3.00     35.50    37.00   135.00   135.50    -0.50  │
│ Save as              7.00      7.70     8.00    27.50    28.70    -1.20  │
│ Consolidate...       0.50      1.00     1.00     3.00     3.00     0.00  │
│ Fetch a data set...  1.50     22.00    22.50    85.00    86.00    -1.00  │
│ Create a data set... 4.00      4.00     4.80    16.00    16.80    -0.80  │
│ Print             ->                             4.00     4.50    -0.50  │
│ Swap                 ┌Send default report─┐     70.50   274.50    -4.00  │
│ Cancel               │Send alternate report...│ 95.00   301.50    -6.50  │
│ Cancel all windows   │Free                    │ 24.50    27.00    -2.50  │
│ End all              │Set form name...        │                          │
│ End                  │Set print file...       │                          │
│                      │Screen print         -> │                          │
│                      └────────────────────────┘                          │
│                                                                          │
│                                                                          │
│                                                                          │
└──────────────────────────────────────────────────────────────────────────┘
```

92 *Producing Spreadsheet Reports* □ *Chapter 4*

> Selecting **Send alternate report...** displays the Entry Definition dialog box.

3. Type ENHANCED in the **Entry** field as shown in Display 4.14. The ENHANCED entry contains the report specifications for the enhanced report.

Display 4.14
Entry Definition Dialog Box

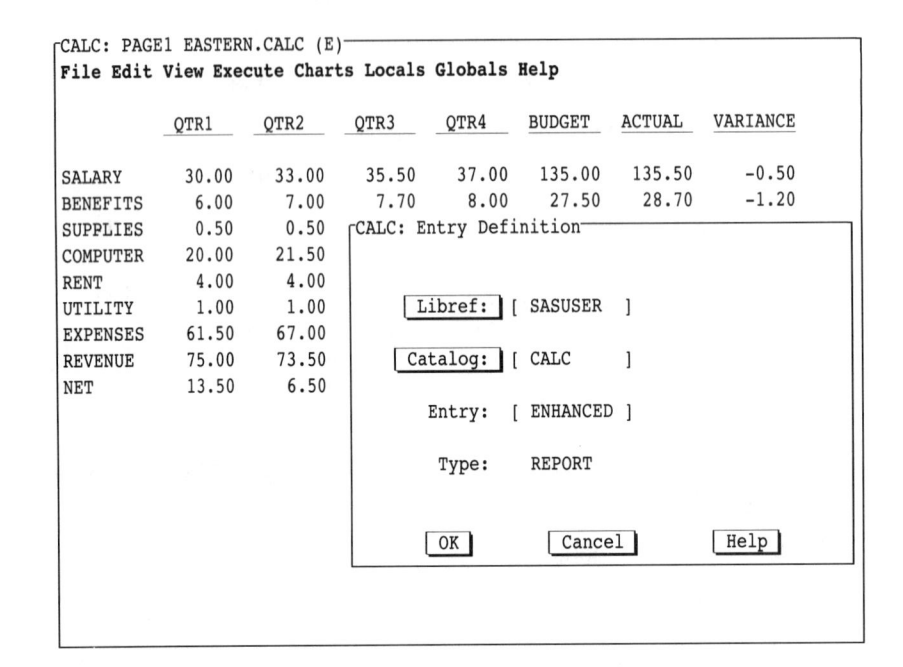

```
┌CALC: PAGE1 EASTERN.CALC (E)─────────────────────────────────┐
│File Edit View Execute Charts Locals Globals Help            │
│                                                             │
│              QTR1    QTR2    QTR3    QTR4   BUDGET  ACTUAL  VARIANCE │
│                                                             │
│  SALARY     30.00   33.00   35.50   37.00   135.00  135.50   -0.50  │
│  BENEFITS    6.00    7.00    7.70    8.00    27.50   28.70   -1.20  │
│  SUPPLIES    0.50    0.50  ┌CALC: Entry Definition──────────────┐   │
│  COMPUTER   20.00   21.50  │                                    │   │
│  RENT        4.00    4.00  │                                    │   │
│  UTILITY     1.00    1.00  │      │Libref:│ [ SASUSER ]         │   │
│  EXPENSES   61.50   67.00  │                                    │   │
│  REVENUE    75.00   73.50  │      │Catalog:│ [ CALC    ]        │   │
│  NET        13.50    6.50  │                                    │   │
│                            │        Entry: [ ENHANCED ]         │   │
│                            │                                    │   │
│                            │         Type:   REPORT             │   │
│                            │                                    │   │
│                            │      │OK│      │Cancel│    │Help│  │   │
│                            └────────────────────────────────────┘   │
│                                                             │
└─────────────────────────────────────────────────────────────┘
```

4. Select **OK**. A note is displayed verifying that the report was sent.

5. Select **File** from the action bar and **Print** from the File pull-down menu.

6. Select **Send alternate report...** from the Print pull-down menu.

7. Type TRANS in the **Entry** field of the Entry Definition dialog box. The TRANS entry contains the report specifications for the transposed rows and columns.

8. Select **OK**. A note is displayed verifying that the report was sent.

9. Select **File** from the action bar and **Print** from the File pull-down menu.

10. Select **Send alternate report...** from the Print pull-down menu.

11. Type MULTI in the **Entry** field of the Entry Definition dialog box. The MULTI entry contains the report specifications for the multipage report.

12. Select **OK**. A note is displayed verifying that the report was sent.

You have now sent three reports to the print file. Remember, once the reports are sent, you must release them to the printer.

Lesson 4.7: Freeing the Print Files

To free the print file:

1. Select **File** from the action bar and **Print** from the File pull-down menu.

2. Select **Free** from the Print pull-down menu.
   Selecting **Free** releases all three reports to the printer. The resulting reports are shown in Output 4.6, Output 4.7, and Output 4.8.

Output 4.6
Enhanced Spreadsheet Report

```
                    Eastern Division Financial Report
              QTR1     QTR2     QTR3     QTR4    BUDGET   ACTUAL   VARIANCE
              -------  -------  -------  -------  -------  -------  --------
     SALARY   30.00    33.00    35.50    37.00   135.00   135.50    -0.50
     BENEFITS  6.00     7.00     7.70     8.00    27.50    28.70    -1.20
     SUPPLIES  0.50     0.50     1.00     1.00     3.00     3.00     0.00
     COMPUTER 20.00    21.50    22.00    22.50    85.00    86.00    -1.00
     RENT      4.00     4.00     4.00     4.80    16.00    16.80    -0.80
     UTILITY   1.00     1.00     1.00     1.50     4.00     4.50    -0.50
     EXPENSES 61.50    67.00    71.20    74.80   270.50   274.50    -4.00
     REVENUE  75.00    73.50    78.00    75.00   295.00   301.50    -6.50
     NET      13.50     6.50     6.80     0.20    24.50    27.00    -2.50
```

Output 4.7 *Transposed Spreadsheet Report*

```
                         Transposed Rows and Columns
           SALARY  BENEFITS  SUPPLIES  COMPUTER   RENT   UTILITY  EXPENSES  REVENUE    NET
           ------  --------  --------  --------  ------  -------  --------  -------  ------
  QTR1      30.00     6.00      0.50     20.00    4.00     1.00     61.50    75.00   13.50
  QTR2      33.00     7.00      0.50     21.50    4.00     1.00     67.00    73.50    6.50
  QTR3      35.50     7.70      1.00     22.00    4.00     1.00     71.20    78.00    6.80
  QTR4      37.00     8.00      1.00     22.50    4.80     1.50     74.80    75.00    0.20
  BUDGET   135.00    27.50      3.00     85.00   16.00     4.00    270.50   295.00   24.50
  ACTUAL   135.50    28.70      3.00     86.00   16.80     4.50    274.50   301.50   27.00
  VARIANCE  -0.50    -1.20      0.00     -1.00   -0.80    -0.50     -4.00    -6.50   -2.50
```

Output 4.8
Page 1 of a Multipage Spreadsheet Report

```
                                              PAGE 1
              Quarterly Data for Eastern Division
                         QTR1    BUDGET   ACTUAL
                        ------   ------   ------
              SALARY     30.00   135.00   135.50
              BENEFITS    6.00    27.50    28.70
              SUPPLIES    0.50     3.00     3.00
              COMPUTER   20.00    85.00    86.00
              RENT        4.00    16.00    16.80
              UTILITY     1.00     4.00     4.50
              EXPENSES   61.50   270.50   274.50
              REVENUE    75.00   295.00   301.50
              NET        13.50    24.50    27.00
```

3. Select **File** from the action bar and **End** from the File pull-down menu to close the EASTERN spreadsheet and display the DIRECTORY window.

   Notice the three REPORT entries are displayed in the DIRECTORY window as shown in Display 4.15.

Display 4.15
Three New Report Entries

```
 CALC: DIRECTORY SASUSER.CALC (E)
 File Edit View Locals Globals Help

    Name      Type     Description                    Updated

  _ EASTERN   CALC     EASTERN.CALC                   08/01/91
  _ ENHANCED  REPORT   Enhanced Report                08/01/91
  _ MULTI     REPORT   Multipage Report               08/01/91
  _ TRANS     REPORT   Transposed Report              08/01/91
```

Reports showing various columns, rows, and formats are powerful means of presenting your data. The use of graphs is another way of presenting your data. In some situations, graphs can provide more insight into the meaning of your data than a simple spreadsheet or report. Graphs can highlight differences and relationships between data; they can make trends more obvious and show subtle influences that you can miss looking at a spreadsheet.

Generating Graphics

In the second half of this chapter, you learn how to produce pie and bar charts based on all or part of your data.

The CALC procedure enables you to create three basic types of graphic reports: pie charts, bar charts, and plots. In this chapter, you use the EASTERN spreadsheet to create default and enhanced pie charts and bar charts.

▶ *Caution* .... *Graphics Device*
The charts generated in this chapter require a graphics device. Before generating the charts in this chapter, contact the SAS Software Consultant at your site to verify that you have a graphics device. ▲

Before you begin creating graphs with SAS/CALC software, you must first decide what data you want to chart. For your first pie chart, you want to compare the BUDGET allowed for each expense item in the EASTERN spreadsheet.

In Chapter 3 you learned how to mark a range of cells when you wanted to change the cell widths or formats. You also mark a range of cells when you are defining the data that you want to chart.

Lesson 4.8: Creating a Pie Chart

To create a pie chart:

1. In the DIRECTORY window, type the letter O beside **EASTERN** and press ENTER to open the spreadsheet.

2. Move the cursor to the SALARY.BUDGET cell and press the MARK BLOCK function key.

3. Move the cursor to the UTILITY.BUDGET cell and press the MARK BLOCK function key.
   The EXPENSES, REVENUE, and NET rows have been omitted because they do not contribute to the budget data. By marking cells SALARY.BUDGET through UTILITY.BUDGET, you are excluding the other rows from processing.

96 *Generating Graphics □ Chapter 4*

    4. Select **Charts** from the action bar and **Pie chart...** from the Charts pull-down menu, as shown in Display 4.16, to display the CHART window and your pie chart for BUDGET, as shown in Display 4.17.

Display 4.16
Selecting Pie Chart...

```
┌CALC: PAGE1 EASTERN.CALC (E)─────────────────────────────────────┐
│File Edit View Execute Charts Locals Globals Help                │
│                                                                  │
│              QTR1     QT Pie chart...  QTR4   BUDGET  ACTUAL  VARIANCE
│                          X-Y plot
│   SALARY    30.00    3  Sequence plot  37.00  135.00  135.50   -0.50
│   BENEFITS   6.00       Bar chart...    8.00   27.50   28.70   -1.20
│   SUPPLIES   0.50       Default chart   1.00    3.00    3.00    0.00
│   COMPUTER  20.00    2                 22.50   85.00   86.00   -1.00
│   RENT       4.00    4.00    4.00       4.80   16.00   16.80   -0.80
│   UTILITY    1.00    1.00    1.00       1.50    4.00    4.50   -0.50
│   EXPENSES  61.50   67.00   71.20      74.80  270.50  274.50   -4.00
│   REVENUE   75.00   73.50   78.00      75.00  295.00  301.50   -6.50
│   NET       13.50    6.50    6.80       0.20   24.50   27.00   -2.50
│                                                                  │
└──────────────────────────────────────────────────────────────────┘
```

Display 4.17
Default Pie Chart

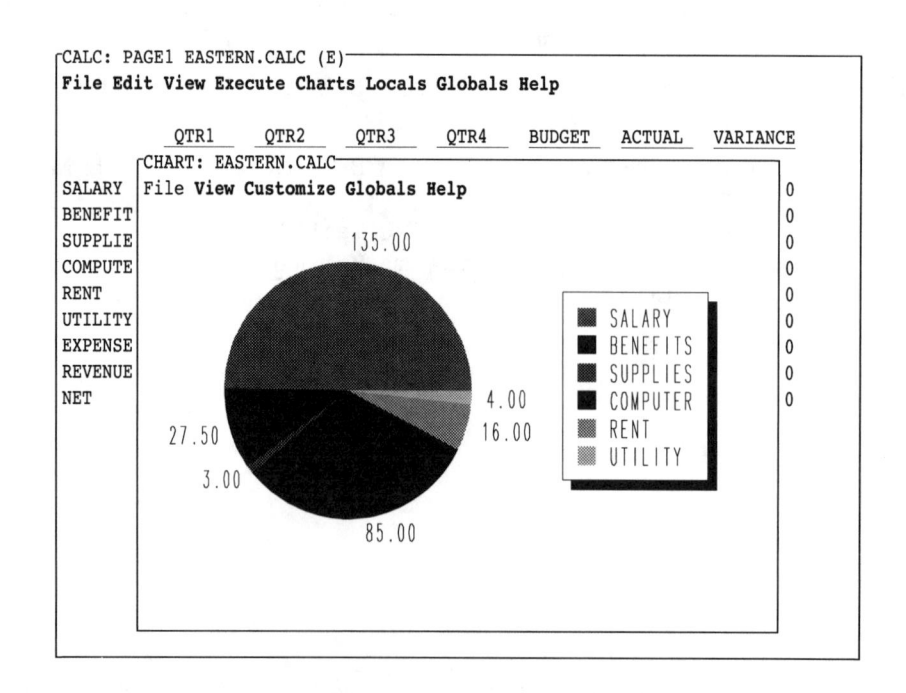

```
┌CALC: PAGE1 EASTERN.CALC (E)─────────────────────────────────────┐
│File Edit View Execute Charts Locals Globals Help                │
│                                                                  │
│              QTR1    QTR2    QTR3    QTR4   BUDGET  ACTUAL  VARIANCE
│         ┌CHART: EASTERN.CALC────────────────────────────────┐   0
│ SALARY  │File View Customize Globals Help                   │   0
│ BENEFIT │                                                   │   0
│ SUPPLIE │              135.00                               │   0
│ COMPUTE │                                                   │   0
│ RENT    │                                                   │   0
│ UTILITY │              (pie chart)         ■ SALARY         │   0
│ EXPENSE │                                  ■ BENEFITS       │   0
│ REVENUE │                                  ■ SUPPLIES       │   0
│ NET     │                           4.00   ■ COMPUTER       │   0
│         │   27.50             16.00        ■ RENT           │
│         │      3.00                        ■ UTILITY        │
│         │              85.00                                │
│         └───────────────────────────────────────────────────┘
└──────────────────────────────────────────────────────────────────┘
```

    By default, you get one pie slice for each row within the target range. The size of the pie slice reflects the percentage each row value contributes to the overall budget. The legend to the right of the chart shows the colors and the row names that correspond to each pie slice. The colors selected are defined by your graphics device driver.

The numbers outside the pie slices indicate the actual cell values for the rows within the target range. Because the slices in the pie chart represent a percentage of the whole, you may prefer displaying the actual percentage amounts outside the slices rather than the cell values.

Lesson 4.9: Enhancing a Pie Chart

By setting special attributes for your pie chart, you can specify percentage values, explode pie slices, and add titles to your final chart.

To enhance your pie chart:

1. In the CHART window, select **Customize** from the action bar and **Set specific attributes** from the Customize pull-down menu.

2. Select **Other attributes...** from the Set specific attributes pull-down menu, as shown in Display 4.18.

Display 4.18
Selecting Other Attributes...

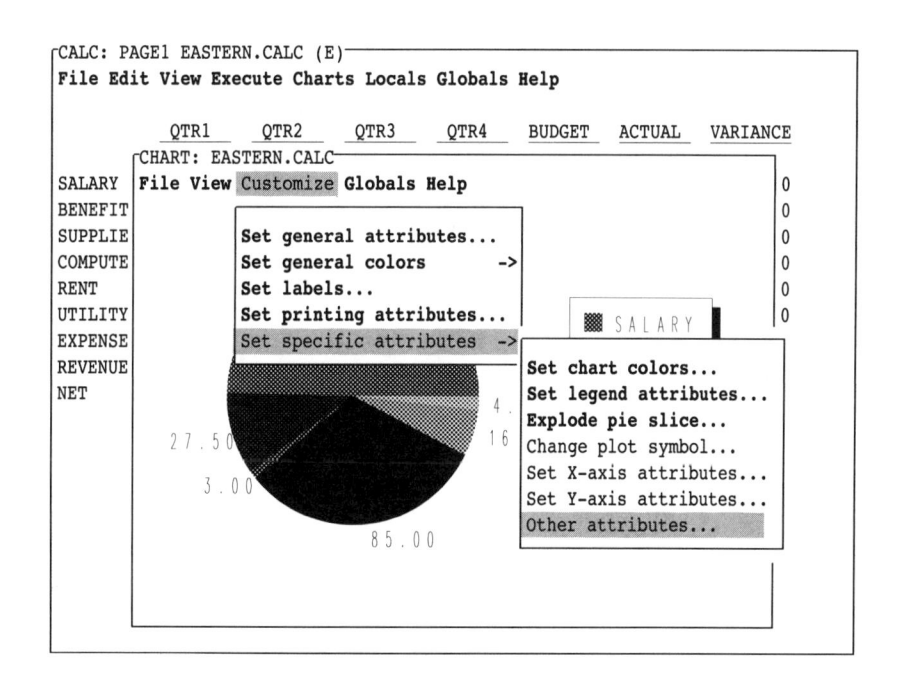

```
┌CALC: PAGE1 EASTERN.CALC (E)─────────────────────────────────────┐
│File Edit View Execute Charts Locals Globals Help                │
│                                                                 │
│           QTR1    QTR2    QTR3    QTR4   BUDGET  ACTUAL  VARIANCE│
│         ┌CHART: EASTERN.CALC─────────────────────────────────┐  │
│  SALARY │File View Customize Globals Help                   │0 │
│ BENEFIT │                                                   │0 │
│ SUPPLIE │    ┌─────────────────────────────┐                │0 │
│ COMPUTE │    │ Set general attributes...   │                │0 │
│    RENT │    │ Set general colors      -> │                 │0 │
│ UTILITY │    │ Set labels...               │                │0 │
│ EXPENSE │    │ Set printing attributes...  │   ▓ S A L A R Y│  │
│ REVENUE │    │ Set specific attributes -> │┌─────────────────┐│
│     NET │    └─────────────────────────────┘│ Set chart colors...│
│         │                              4.  │ Set legend attributes...│
│         │        27.50           16  │ Explode pie slice...│
│         │                                   │ Change plot symbol...│
│         │           3.00                    │ Set X-axis attributes...│
│         │                                   │ Set Y-axis attributes...│
│         │                  85.00            │ Other attributes...│
│         │                                   └─────────────────┘│
│         └──────────────────────────────────────────────────┘    │
└─────────────────────────────────────────────────────────────────┘
```

Selecting **Other attributes...** displays the Additional Pie Attributes dialog box shown in Display 4.19.

Display 4.19
Default Additional Pie Attributes Dialog Box

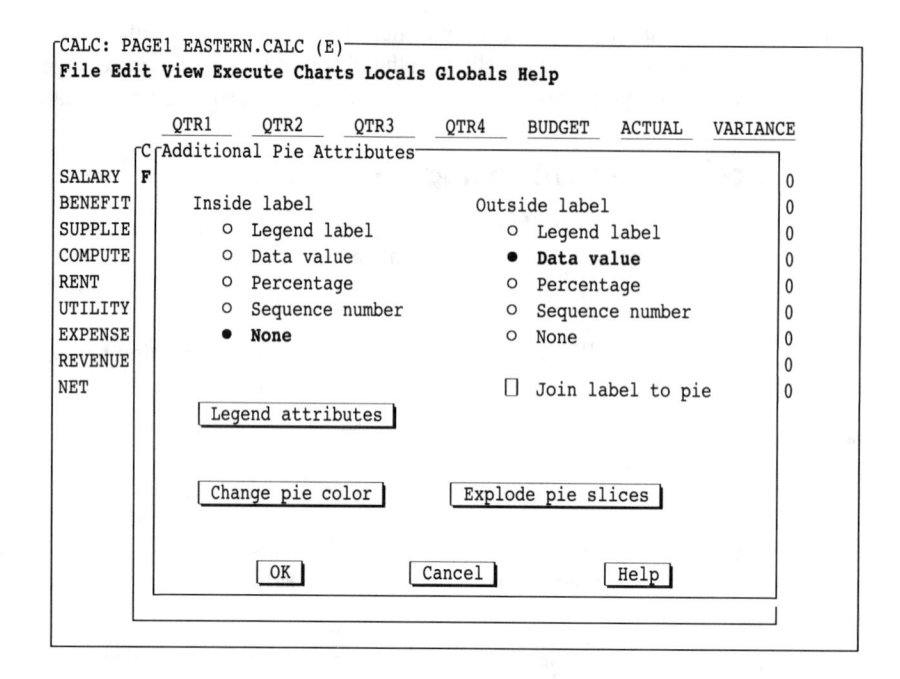

```
┌CALC: PAGE1 EASTERN.CALC (E)─────────────────────────────────
│File Edit View Execute Charts Locals Globals Help
│
│           QTR1      QTR2      QTR3      QTR4     BUDGET    ACTUAL    VARIANCE
│       ┌─C┌Additional Pie Attributes──────────────────────────────┐
│SALARY │ F│                                                        │  0
│BENEFIT│  │  Inside label               Outside label              │  0
│SUPPLIE│  │    ○ Legend label             ○ Legend label           │  0
│COMPUTE│  │    ○ Data value               ● Data value             │  0
│RENT   │  │    ○ Percentage               ○ Percentage             │  0
│UTILITY│  │    ○ Sequence number          ○ Sequence number        │  0
│EXPENSE│  │    ● None                     ○ None                   │  0
│REVENUE│  │                                                        │  0
│NET    │  │                               □ Join label to pie      │  0
│       │  │  ┌─────────────────┐                                   │
│       │  │  │ Legend attributes│                                   │
│       │  │  └─────────────────┘                                   │
│       │  │                                                        │
│       │  │  ┌─────────────────┐     ┌──────────────────┐          │
│       │  │  │ Change pie color│     │ Explode pie slices│         │
│       │  │  └─────────────────┘     └──────────────────┘          │
│       │  │                                                        │
│       │  │     ┌────┐        ┌────────┐          ┌──────┐         │
│       │  │     │ OK │        │ Cancel │          │ Help │         │
│       │  │     └────┘        └────────┘          └──────┘         │
│       │  └────────────────────────────────────────────────────────┘
└──────────────────────────────────────────────────────────────────────
```

Notice the **Outside label** selection group. By default, **Data value** is selected indicating that the actual cell data value is displayed outside each pie slice.

3. In the **Outside label** column, select **Percentage** as shown in Display 4.20.

    Selecting **Percentage** indicates that the slices of the pie represent percentages and the percent values are displayed on the outside of the pie slices.

Display 4.20
Selecting Percentage

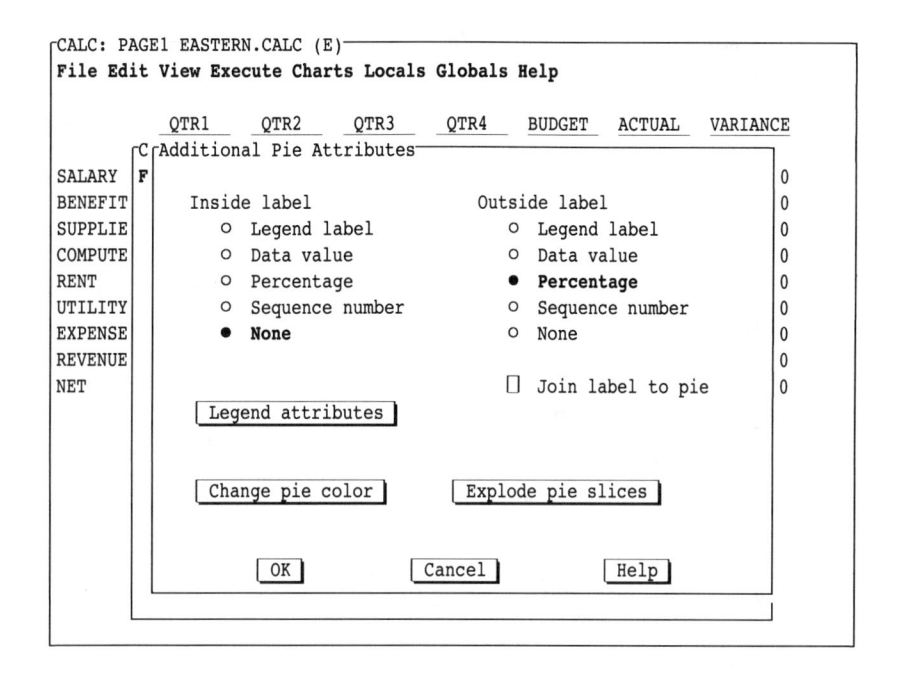

```
┌CALC: PAGE1 EASTERN.CALC (E)─────────────────────────────────────┐
│File Edit View Execute Charts Locals Globals Help                │
│                                                                 │
│          QTR1     QTR2     QTR3     QTR4    BUDGET  ACTUAL  VARIANCE│
│       ┌C┌Additional Pie Attributes───────────────────────────┐  │
│SALARY │F│                                                    │0 │
│BENEFIT│ │  Inside label              Outside label           │0 │
│SUPPLIE│ │    o  Legend label           o  Legend label       │0 │
│COMPUTE│ │    o  Data value             o  Data value         │0 │
│RENT   │ │    o  Percentage             ●  Percentage         │0 │
│UTILITY│ │    o  Sequence number        o  Sequence number    │0 │
│EXPENSE│ │    ●  None                   o  None               │0 │
│REVENUE│ │                                                    │0 │
│NET    │ │                              ☐  Join label to pie  │0 │
│       │ │   ┌─────────────────┐                              │  │
│       │ │   │ Legend attributes│                             │  │
│       │ │   └─────────────────┘                              │  │
│       │ │                                                    │  │
│       │ │  ┌──────────────────┐      ┌────────────────────┐  │  │
│       │ │  │ Change pie color │      │ Explode pie slices │  │  │
│       │ │  └──────────────────┘      └────────────────────┘  │  │
│       │ │                                                    │  │
│       │ │        ┌────┐       ┌────────┐      ┌──────┐       │  │
│       │ │        │ OK │       │ Cancel │      │ Help │       │  │
│       │ │        └────┘       └────────┘      └──────┘       │  │
│       │ └────────────────────────────────────────────────────┘  │
└─────────────────────────────────────────────────────────────────┘
```

At this point you may want to separate, or explode, one or more slices of the pie to emphasize the percentage of the budget that the slice requires.

For example, by exploding the BENEFITS slice, you create a clearer picture of how much of the budget BENEFITS requires.

100 *Generating Graphics* □ *Chapter 4*

4. Select **Explode pie slices**, as shown in Display 4.20.

    Selecting **Explode pie slices** displays the Select Data dialog box shown in Display 4.21.

Display 4.21
Selecting BENEFITS to Explode

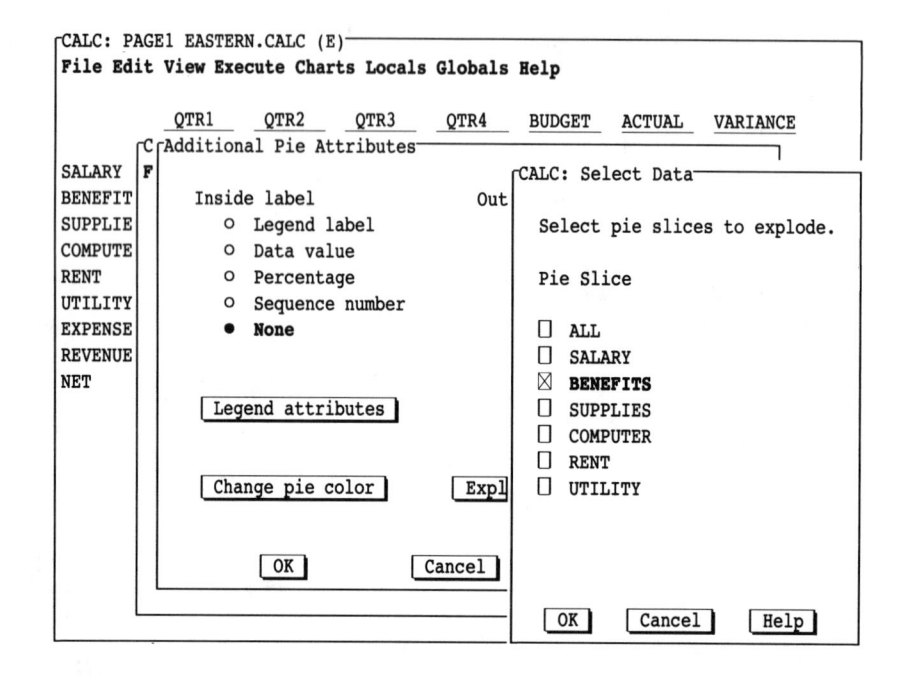

```
┌CALC: PAGE1 EASTERN.CALC (E)─────────────────────────────────────
│ File Edit View Execute Charts Locals Globals Help
│
│          QTR1     QTR2     QTR3    QTR4    BUDGET   ACTUAL   VARIANCE
│       ┌─C┌Additional Pie Attributes─────────────────────────────────────┐
│ SALARY │F │                                                             │
│ BENEFIT│  │   Inside label              Out  ┌CALC: Select Data──────┐  │
│ SUPPLIE│  │     o  Legend label              │                       │  │
│ COMPUTE│  │     o  Data value                │ Select pie slices to explode. │
│ RENT   │  │     o  Percentage                │                       │  │
│ UTILITY│  │     o  Sequence number           │ Pie Slice             │  │
│ EXPENSE│  │     ●  None                      │                       │  │
│ REVENUE│  │                                  │  ☐  ALL               │  │
│ NET    │  │                                  │  ☐  SALARY            │  │
│        │  │                                  │  ☒  BENEFITS          │  │
│        │  │   ┌Legend attributes┐            │  ☐  SUPPLIES          │  │
│        │  │   └─────────────────┘            │  ☐  COMPUTER          │  │
│        │  │                                  │  ☐  RENT              │  │
│        │  │   ┌Change pie color┐   ┌Expl┐    │  ☐  UTILITY           │  │
│        │  │   └────────────────┘   └────┘    │                       │  │
│        │  │       ┌OK┐       ┌Cancel┐        │                       │  │
│        │  │       └──┘       └──────┘        │ ┌OK┐ ┌Cancel┐ ┌Help┐  │  │
│        │  │                                  │ └──┘ └──────┘ └────┘  │  │
│        │  └──────────────────────────────────┴───────────────────────┘  │
```

5. Select **BENEFITS**, as shown in Display 4.21, to explode the BENEFITS pie slice from the remaining pie.

6. Select **OK** to redisplay the Additional Pie Attributes dialog box.

7. Select **OK** to display the enhanced pie chart shown in Display 4.22.

Display 4.22
Enhanced Pie Chart

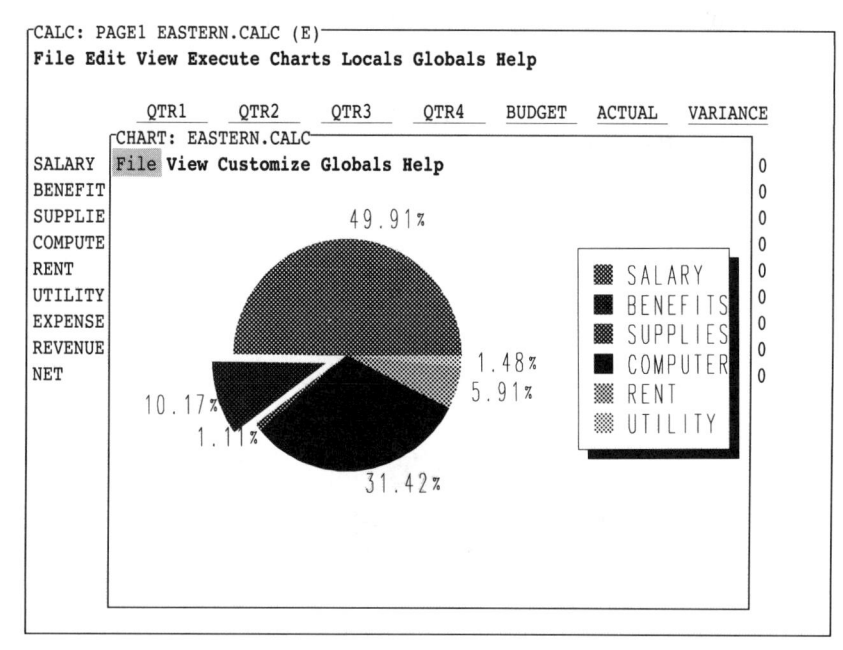

```
┌CALC: PAGE1 EASTERN.CALC (E)─────────────────────────────────┐
│ File Edit View Execute Charts Locals Globals Help           │
│                                                             │
│             QTR1    QTR2    QTR3    QTR4   BUDGET  ACTUAL   VARIANCE
│       ┌CHART: EASTERN.CALC────────────────────────────────┐ │
│ SALARY│ File View Customize Globals Help                  │0│
│ BENEFIT│                                                  │0│
│ SUPPLIE│                    49.91%                        │0│
│ COMPUTE│                                                  │0│
│ RENT  │                                     ┌──────────┐  │0│
│ UTILITY│                                    │▓ SALARY  │  │0│
│ EXPENSE│                                    │█ BENEFITS│  │0│
│ REVENUE│                              1.48% │▒ SUPPLIES│  │0│
│ NET   │              10.17%          5.91%  │█ COMPUTER│  │0│
│       │              1.11%                  │░ RENT    │  │
│       │                                     │░ UTILITY │  │
│       │                                     └──────────┘  │
│       │                    31.42%                         │
│       └───────────────────────────────────────────────────┘ │
└─────────────────────────────────────────────────────────────┘
```

To further enhance your chart you can add appropriate titles.

8. Select **Customize** from the action bar and **Set labels...** from the Customize pull-down menu to display the Label Attributes dialog box shown in Display 4.23.

Display 4.23
Label Attributes Dialog Box

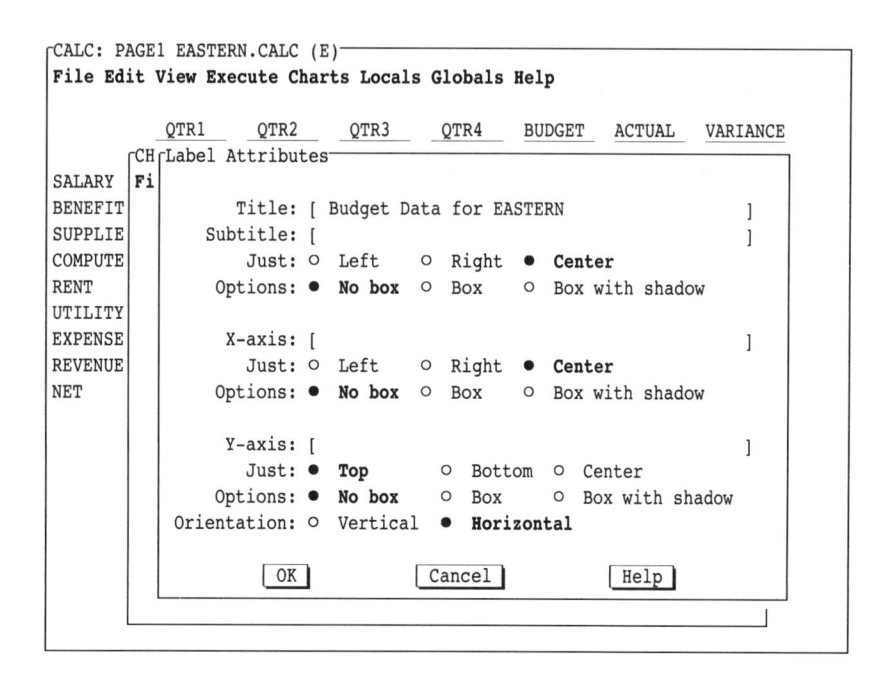

```
┌CALC: PAGE1 EASTERN.CALC (E)─────────────────────────────────┐
│ File Edit View Execute Charts Locals Globals Help           │
│                                                             │
│             QTR1    QTR2    QTR3    QTR4   BUDGET  ACTUAL   VARIANCE
│       ┌CH┌Label Attributes─────────────────────────────────┐│
│ SALARY│Fi│                                                 ││
│ BENEFIT│  │      Title: [ Budget Data for EASTERN        ] ││
│ SUPPLIE│  │   Subtitle: [                                ] ││
│ COMPUTE│  │       Just: ○ Left     ○ Right   ● Center      ││
│ RENT   │  │    Options: ● No box   ○ Box     ○ Box with shadow││
│ UTILITY│  │                                                 ││
│ EXPENSE│  │     X-axis: [                                ] ││
│ REVENUE│  │       Just: ○ Left     ○ Right   ● Center      ││
│ NET    │  │    Options: ● No box   ○ Box     ○ Box with shadow││
│        │  │                                                 ││
│        │  │     Y-axis: [                                ] ││
│        │  │       Just: ● Top      ○ Bottom  ○ Center      ││
│        │  │    Options: ● No box   ○ Box     ○ Box with shadow││
│        │  │Orientation: ○ Vertical ● Horizontal             ││
│        │  │         [ OK ]    [ Cancel ]    [ Help ]        ││
│        │  └─────────────────────────────────────────────────┘│
└─────────────────────────────────────────────────────────────┘
```

9. Type the text, `Budget Data for EASTERN`, in the **Title** field, as shown in Display 4.23.

102 *Generating Graphics* □ *Chapter 4*

10. Select **OK** to display your enhanced pie chart with the title, as shown in Display 4.24.

Display 4.24
Enhanced Pie Chart with Title

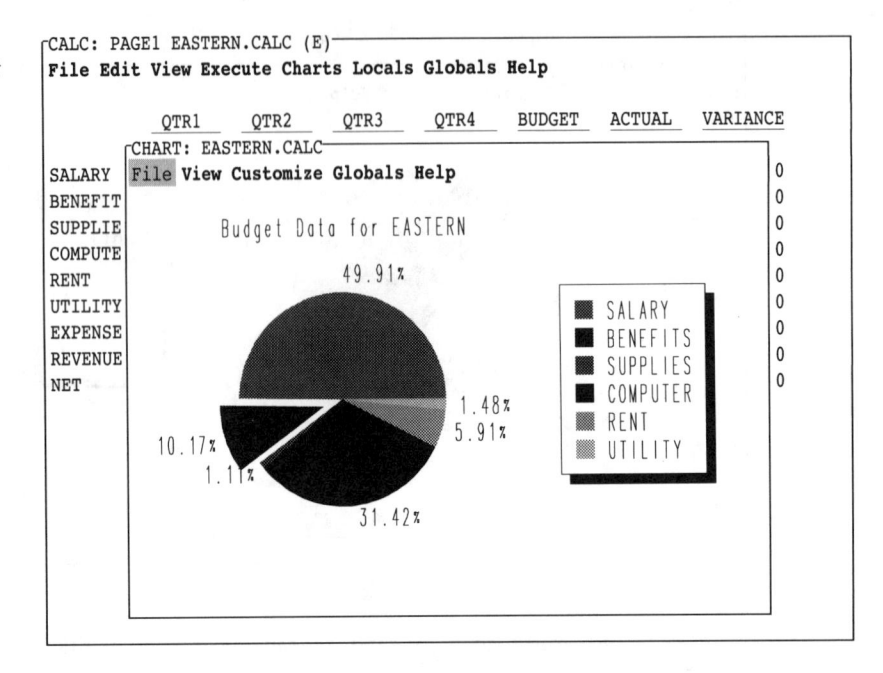

```
┌CALC: PAGE1 EASTERN.CALC (E)─────────────────────────────┐
│File Edit View Execute Charts Locals Globals Help        │
│                                                          │
│         QTR1    QTR2    QTR3    QTR4   BUDGET  ACTUAL  VARIANCE
│   ┌CHART: EASTERN.CALC───────────────────────────────┐  0
│SALARY │File View Customize Globals Help              │  0
│BENEFIT│                                              │  0
│SUPPLIE│         Budget Data for EASTERN              │  0
│COMPUTE│              49.91%                          │  0
│RENT   │                        ┌──────────┐          │  0
│UTILITY│                        │ ■ SALARY │          │  0
│EXPENSE│                        │ ■ BENEFITS│         │  0
│REVENUE│                        │ ■ SUPPLIES│         │  0
│NET    │                        │ ■ COMPUTER│         │
│       │            1.48%       │ ■ RENT   │          │
│       │    10.17%  5.91%       │ ■ UTILITY│          │
│       │        1.1%            └──────────┘          │
│       │         31.42%                               │
│       └──────────────────────────────────────────────┘
└──────────────────────────────────────────────────────────┘
```

11. When you are finished viewing your pie chart, select **File** from the action bar and **End** from the File pull-down menu to redisplay the EASTERN spreadsheet.

   Note: For more information on these and other options for enhancing your pie charts consult *SAS/CALC Software: Usage and Reference*.

Lesson 4.10: Creating a Bar Chart

While pie charts are an effective way of displaying percentages, bar charts are a great way of comparing two or more items. In this lesson, you create a bar chart that compares the BUDGET data to the ACTUAL data.

To create a bar chart:

1. Move the cursor to the SALARY.BUDGET cell and press the MARK BLOCK function key.

2. Move the cursor to the UTILITY.ACTUAL cell and press the MARK BLOCK function key.
      The EXPENSES, REVENUE, and NET rows have been omitted because they do not contribute to the budget data. By marking cells SALARY.BUDGET through UTILITY.ACTUAL, you are excluding the other rows from processing.

3. Select **Charts** from the action bar and **Bar chart...** from the Charts pull-down menu to display the CHART window and your bar chart comparing BUDGET and ACTUAL, as shown in Display 4.25.

Display 4.25
Default Bar Chart

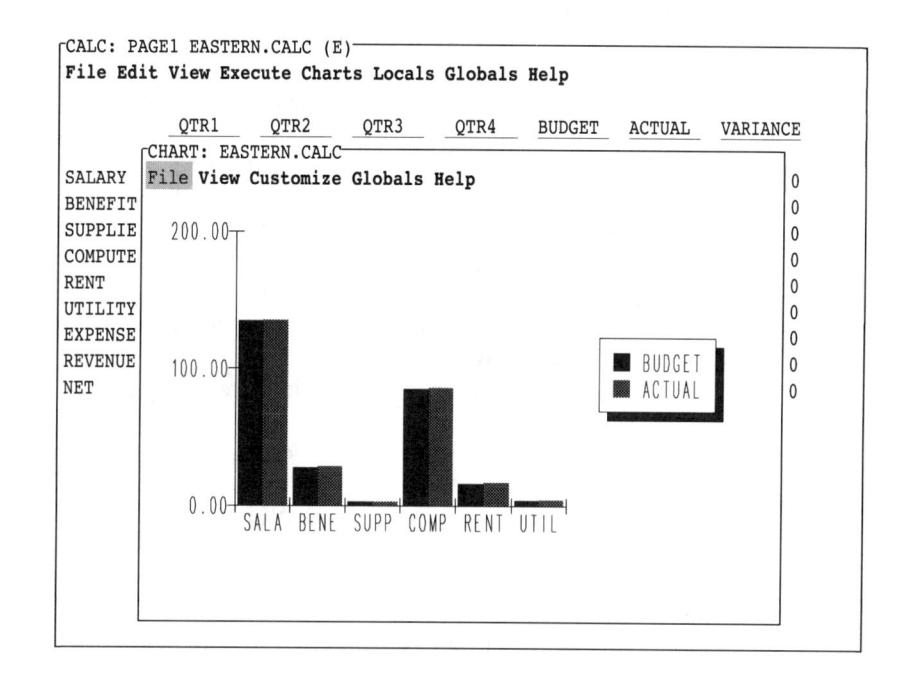

```
┌CALC: PAGE1 EASTERN.CALC (E)─────────────────────────────────────┐
│File Edit View Execute Charts Locals Globals Help                │
│                                                                 │
│            QTR1     QTR2     QTR3     QTR4   BUDGET  ACTUAL  VARIANCE │
│        ┌CHART: EASTERN.CALC─────────────────────────────┐       │
│ SALARY │File View Customize Globals Help                │    0  │
│ BENEFIT│                                                │    0  │
│ SUPPLIE│  200.00┐                                       │    0  │
│ COMPUTE│        │                                       │    0  │
│ RENT   │        │                                       │    0  │
│ UTILITY│        │                                       │    0  │
│ EXPENSE│        │    ██                                 │    0  │
│ REVENUE│        │    ██            ┌─────────┐          │    0  │
│ NET    │  100.00┤    ██            │ ■ BUDGET│          │    0  │
│        │        │    ██    ██      │ ■ ACTUAL│          │       │
│        │        │    ██▓▓  ▓▓      └─────────┘          │       │
│        │        │    ████  ██                           │       │
│        │    0.00┤    ████  ██  ▁▁  ████  ▁▁  ▁▁         │       │
│        │         SALA BENE SUPP COMP RENT UTIL          │       │
│        │                                                │       │
│        └────────────────────────────────────────────────┘       │
└─────────────────────────────────────────────────────────────────┘
```

Because you are charting two columns, BUDGET and ACTUAL, you get a vertical bar chart with the bars for each quarter grouped side by side on the chart. The height of the bars reflects the actual cell values within the spreadsheet. Notice the legend to the right of the chart shows the colors and column names that correspond to each bar.

4. When you are finished viewing your chart, select **File** from the action bar and **End** from the File pull-down menu to redisplay the EASTERN spreadsheet.

Note: For more information and for other options for enhancing your bar charts consult *SAS/CALC Software: Usage and Reference*.

You have finished the third tutorial chapter. You can end your spreadsheet and the SAS/CALC software session or continue with Chapter 5, "Creating a Three-Dimensional Spreadsheet."

If you want to end the SAS/CALC software session, refer to Lesson 2.11 and 2.12 in Chapter 2.

Chapter Summary

This chapter provides an excellent introduction to the various types of reports and graphics available in SAS/CALC software.

To begin the chapter, you learn how to generate and print a default report based on the EASTERN spreadsheet data.

From here, you learn how to generate an enhanced report by creating your own REPORT entry, named ENHANCED. This REPORT entry suppresses the time, date, and page numbers on your report, and specifies a report title.

The third report uses a REPORT entry named TRANS, which transposes the rows and columns of the EASTERN spreadsheet for your report. Transposing your rows and columns provides a different view of your spreadsheet data.

Finally, you create a third REPORT entry named MULTI, which produces a four-page report, displaying the actual and budgeted data for each quarter of the EASTERN spreadsheet on a separate page.

Once you understand the concept of creating spreadsheet reports, you create two types of graphics: pie charts and bar charts.

First, you generate a default pie chart, which shows the percentage of money budgeted for each expense item in the EASTERN spreadsheet. You enhance this pie chart by modifying the outside labels, exploding the BENEFITS pie slice for emphasis, and assigning an appropriate title.

Finally, you generate a bar chart, which compares the actual and budgeted data for the EASTERN spreadsheet.

After completing this chapter, you are ready to learn more advanced features of SAS/CALC software, including the concepts of three-dimensional spreadsheets, linking, drilldown, and SAS/CALC programs.

Chapter 5 Creating a Three-Dimensional Spreadsheet

Creating a Three-Dimensional Spreadsheet 105
 Lesson 5.1: Changing the Spreadsheet Perspective 108
 Lesson 5.2: Copying a Page 109
 Lesson 5.3: Renaming Pages 111
 Lesson 5.4: Going to a Page 112
 Lesson 5.5: Clearing Cell Values 113
 Lesson 5.6: Entering Cell Values and Reexecuting Formulas 115
 Lesson 5.7: Turning Off the AUTOCALC Option 116
 Lesson 5.8: Turning On the AUTOCALC Option 120
 Lesson 5.9: Inserting a Page 121
 Lesson 5.10: Summarizing Data 122
 Lesson 5.11: Renaming a Page 127
Chapter Summary 129

Creating a Three-Dimensional Spreadsheet

This chapter introduces the concept of a three-dimensional (3D) spreadsheet. The three dimensions of a spreadsheet are rows, columns, and pages. Currently, the EASTERN spreadsheet you built in the first two chapters contains rows and columns on one page. Because there is only one page, the spreadsheet is called a two-dimensional (2D) spreadsheet. The two dimensions are the rows and columns and the data represent financial information for the Sales Division in the eastern region of a corporation.

In this chapter, you convert the EASTERN spreadsheet to a 3D spreadsheet by adding two new pages. Specifically, you add a page that contains financial information for the Service Division in the eastern region of the corporation, and a summary page that contains totals from the two divisions.

Additionally, you learn how to copy pages, rename pages, change your view of the spreadsheet, and write formulas that access cell values on different pages.

The three-dimensional spreadsheet that you create in this chapter is shown in Figure 5.1. Each page in the spreadsheet contains the same rows and columns that are currently in the two-dimensional spreadsheet you completed in Chapter 3, ''Modifying Your Spreadsheet.''

Figure 5.1 *Three-Dimensional EASTERN Spreadsheet*

```
CALC: SUMMARY EASTERN.CALC─────────────────────────────────────────────┐
│          QTR1       QTR2       QTR3       QTR4      BUDGET     ACTUAL    VARIANCE │
│                                                                                    │
│SALARY    62.00      67.00      69.50      71.50     265.00     270.00     -5.00   │
│BE  CALC: SERVICE EASTERN.CALC─────────────────────────────────────────────┐
│SU │          QTR1       QTR2       QTR3       QTR4      BUDGET     ACTUAL    VARIANCE │
│CO │                                                                                    │
│RE │SALARY    32.00      34.00      34.00      34.50     130.00     134.50    -04.50  │
│UT │BE  CALC: SALES EASTERN.CALC─────────────────────────────────────────────┐
│EX │SU │          QTR1       QTR2       QTR3       QTR4      BUDGET     ACTUAL    VARIANCE │
│RE │CO │                                                                                    │
│NE │RE │SALARY    30.00      33.00      35.50      37.00     135.00     135.50     -0.50  │
│   │UT │BENEFITS   6.00       7.00       7.70       8.00      27.50      28.70     -1.20  │
│   │EX │SUPPLIES   0.50       0.50       1.00       1.00       3.00       3.00      0.00  │
│   │RE │COMPUTER  20.00      21.50      22.00      22.50      85.00      86.00     -1.00  │
│   │NE │RENT       4.00       4.00       4.00       4.80      16.00      16.80     -0.80  │
│       │UTILITY    1.00       1.00       1.00       1.50       4.00       4.50     -0.50  │
│       │EXPENSES  61.50      67.00      71.20      74.80     270.50     274.50     -4.00  │
│       │REVENUE   75.00      73.50      78.00      75.00     295.00     301.50     -6.50  │
│       │NET       13.50       6.50       6.80       0.20      24.50      27.00     -2.50  │
└───────┴───────────────────────────────────────────────────────────────────────────────┘
```

If you ended the SAS/CALC software session after Chapter 4, ''Producing Spreadsheet Reports and Generating Graphics,'' refer to Lessons 3.1 and 3.2 in Chapter 3 for information on invoking SAS/CALC software and opening an existing spreadsheet. If you did not close your spreadsheet and end the SAS/CALC software session after Chapter 4, continue with this chapter.

In Chapter 3 you learned how to insert rows and columns into your spreadsheet using the Insert... dialog box. In this chapter, you learn how to insert pages. You can insert the new pages by copying an existing page or by using the Insert... dialog box you used in Chapter 3 to insert rows and columns. Both techniques are presented here.

First, you copy the Sales Division page to create the Service Division page. Copying is used because the two pages have exactly the same row and column names and use the same formulas. By copying the first page, all cell values and formulas are automatically copied. After copying the page, you clear the cell values so you have a second page that contains formulas but no cell values. Although you have to re-enter some cell values to reflect the Service Division data, you do not have to re-enter the formulas.

You use the Insert... dialog box to insert the summary page. Although the summary page has the same rows and columns as the first two pages, the formulas are all different. Thus, there is no advantage to copying an existing page.

The easiest way to copy a page is to change your view (or perspective) of the spreadsheet before you identify the page you want to copy.

You are currently viewing the rows and columns of PAGE1 of your spreadsheet, as shown in Display 5.1.

Display 5.1
The EASTERN Spreadsheet

```
┌CALC: PAGE1 EASTERN.CALC (E)─────────────────────────────────┐
│ File Edit View Execute Charts Locals Globals Help           │
│                                                             │
│              QTR1    QTR2    QTR3    QTR4   BUDGET  ACTUAL  VARIANCE │
│                                                             │
│  SALARY     30.00   33.00   35.50   37.00   135.00  135.50   -0.50  │
│  BENEFITS    6.00    7.00    7.70    8.00    27.50   28.70   -1.20  │
│  SUPPLIES    0.50    0.50    1.00    1.00     3.00    3.00    0.00  │
│  COMPUTER   20.00   21.50   22.00   22.50    85.00   86.00   -1.00  │
│  RENT        4.00    4.00    4.00    4.80    16.00   16.80   -0.80  │
│  UTILITY     1.00    1.00    1.00    1.50     4.00    4.50   -0.50  │
│  EXPENSES   61.50   67.00   71.20   74.80   270.50  274.50   -4.00  │
│  REVENUE    75.00   73.50   78.00   75.00   295.00  301.50   -6.50  │
│  NET        13.50    6.50    6.80    0.20    24.50   27.00   -2.50  │
│                                                             │
│                                                             │
└─────────────────────────────────────────────────────────────┘
```

To view the names of all the pages, you can change the perspective by displaying the pages and columns instead of the rows and columns.

Lesson 5.1: Changing the Spreadsheet Perspective

To change the perspective:

1. Select **View** from the action bar.

2. Select **Change perspective** from the View pull-down menu.

3. Select **View pages and columns** from the Change perspective pull-down menu as shown in Display 5.2.

Display 5.2
Changing Perspective

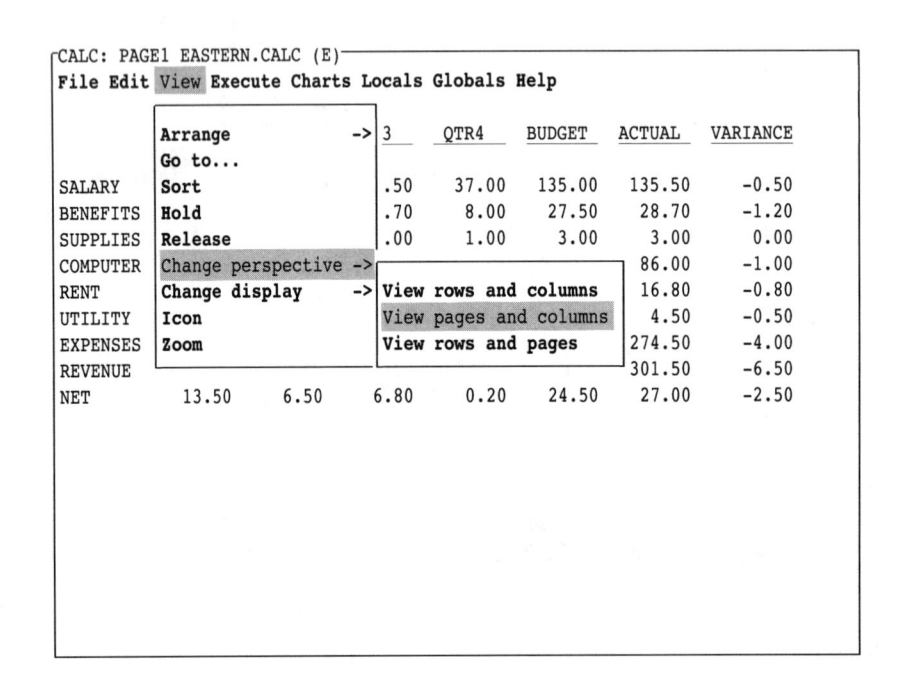

```
┌CALC: PAGE1 EASTERN.CALC (E)──────────────────────────────────────────┐
│File Edit View Execute Charts Locals Globals Help                     │
│        ┌─────────────────────────┐                                   │
│        │Arrange            -> │3     QTR4    BUDGET   ACTUAL  VARIANCE│
│        │Go to...              │                                       │
│ SALARY │Sort                  │.50   37.00   135.00   135.50   -0.50 │
│ BENEFITS│Hold                 │.70    8.00    27.50    28.70   -1.20 │
│ SUPPLIES│Release              │.00    1.00     3.00     3.00    0.00 │
│ COMPUTER│Change perspective ->│                         86.00   -1.00│
│ RENT   │Change display    -> │View rows and columns    16.80   -0.80 │
│ UTILITY│Icon                 │View pages and columns    4.50   -0.50 │
│ EXPENSES│Zoom                │View rows and pages     274.50   -4.00 │
│ REVENUE└─────────────────────┴─────────────────────────┘301.50   -6.50│
│ NET       13.50     6.50     6.80    0.20    24.50    27.00   -2.50  │
│                                                                      │
└──────────────────────────────────────────────────────────────────────┘
```

You are now viewing the pages and columns in the spreadsheet as shown in Display 5.3. Notice that there is only one page, **PAGE1**.

Display 5.3
Viewing Pages and Columns

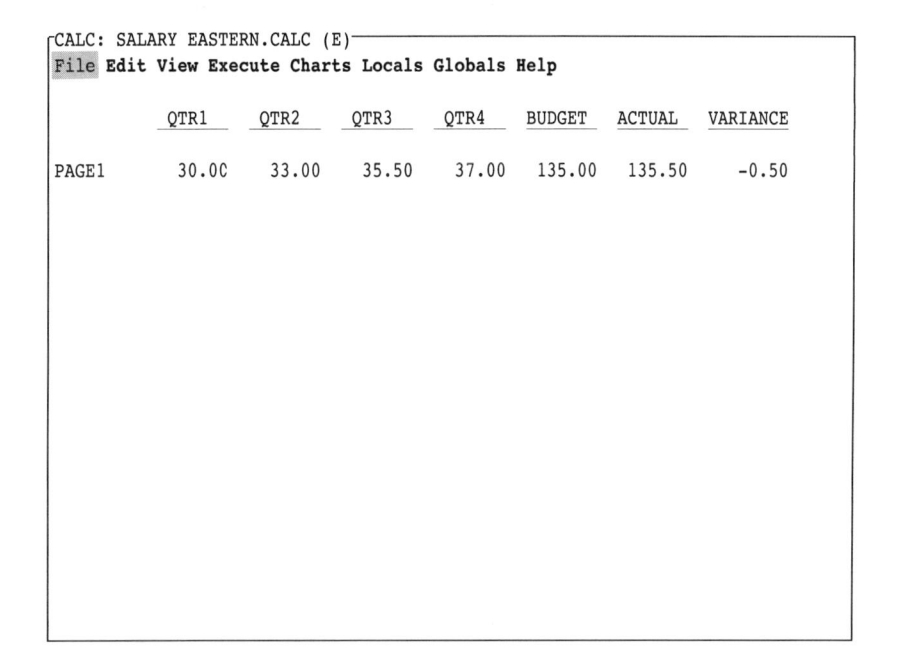

```
┌CALC: SALARY EASTERN.CALC (E)─────────────────────────────┐
│ File Edit View Execute Charts Locals Globals Help        │
│                                                          │
│              QTR1    QTR2    QTR3    QTR4   BUDGET  ACTUAL  VARIANCE │
│                                                          │
│     PAGE1   30.00   33.00   35.50   37.00   135.00  135.50   -0.50   │
│                                                          │
│                                                          │
│                                                          │
│                                                          │
│                                                          │
│                                                          │
│                                                          │
│                                                          │
└──────────────────────────────────────────────────────────┘
```

To create a second page you must copy PAGE1. Copying PAGE1 is different from other copies you performed in earlier chapters.

Lesson 5.2: Copying a Page

To copy PAGE1 (the SALES Division data) and create PAGE2 (the Service Division data):

1. Move the cursor to the name of the page you want to copy, **PAGE1**, and press the MARK BLOCK function key one time. The page name is highlighted indicating it is marked as the source range.
   Now, you must copy PAGE1 to a paste buffer because you cannot mark PAGE1 as both a source and a target range. A paste buffer is a temporary storage location that holds the contents of text stored with the Copy marked areas command. The contents of the paste buffer remain in effect for the duration of the current SAS session.

2. Select **Edit** from the action bar and **Copy marked areas** from the Edit pull-down menu. A note is displayed indicating that one page was copied to the paste buffer.

3. Move the cursor to the name of the page you want the copy to follow, **PAGE1**, and press the MARK BLOCK function key one time. The page name is highlighted indicating it is marked as the target range.

4. Select **Edit** from the action bar and **Paste** from the Edit pull-down menu to copy PAGE1 and display PAGE2.

The new page, PAGE2, appears in the spreadsheet, as shown in Display 5.4.

Display 5.4
Results of Copying PAGE1

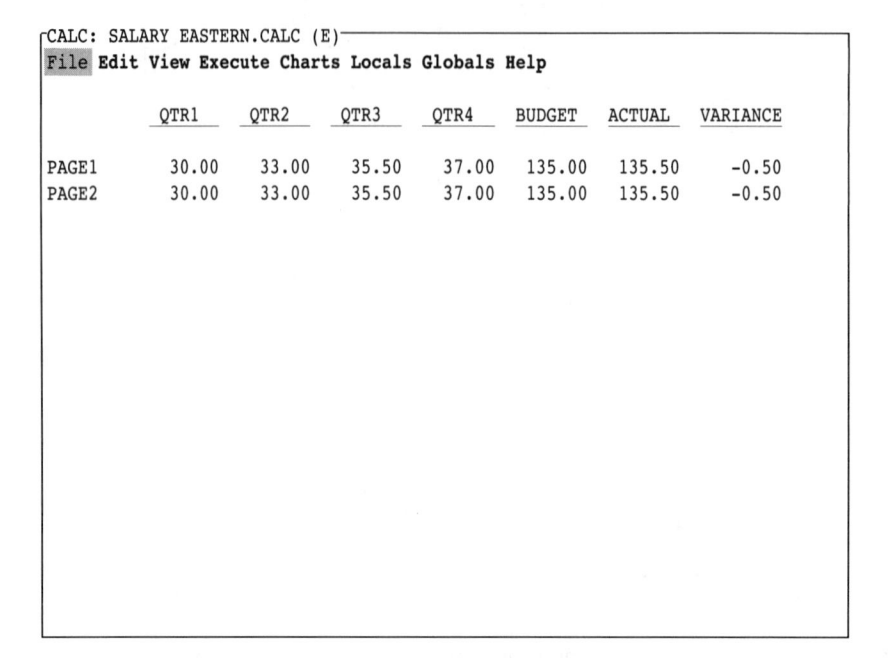

```
┌CALC: SALARY EASTERN.CALC (E)─────────────────────────────┐
│ File Edit View Execute Charts Locals Globals Help        │
│                                                          │
│               QTR1    QTR2    QTR3    QTR4   BUDGET  ACTUAL  VARIANCE │
│                                                          │
│       PAGE1  30.00   33.00   35.50   37.00   135.00  135.50   -0.50   │
│       PAGE2  30.00   33.00   35.50   37.00   135.00  135.50   -0.50   │
│                                                          │
│                                                          │
└──────────────────────────────────────────────────────────┘
```

The spreadsheet is easier to use if the names of the first two pages match the division names, Sales and Service. As with row and column names, you can type new page names over existing page names.

Lesson 5.3: Renaming Pages

To change the page names:

1. Type SALES over PAGE1.

2. Type SERVICE over PAGE2. You can type the names in uppercase or lowercase.

3. Press ENTER. When you press ENTER the names are translated to uppercase, as shown in Display 5.5.

Display 5.5
The Renamed Pages

```
┌CALC: SALARY EASTERN.CALC (E)─────────────────────────────────┐
│File Edit View Execute Charts Locals Globals Help             │
│                                                              │
│              QTR1    QTR2    QTR3    QTR4    BUDGET  ACTUAL  VARIANCE │
│                                                              │
│     SALES    30.00   33.00   35.50   37.00   135.00  135.50   -0.50 │
│     SERVICE  30.00   33.00   35.50   37.00   135.00  135.50   -0.50 │
│                                                              │
│                                                              │
└──────────────────────────────────────────────────────────────┘
```

You are currently viewing the pages and columns of the EASTERN spreadsheet. As a result, you cannot see all the cells for SERVICE. To view the entire page, you need to change the perspective back to rows and columns.

To change the perspective:

1. Select **View** from the action bar.

2. Select **Change perspective** from the View pull-down menu.

3. Select **View rows and columns** from the Change perspective pull-down menu.

After you change the perspective to rows and columns, the SALES page is displayed. Notice the page name in the upper-left corner of the window.

Lesson 5.4: Going to a Page

To go to the SERVICE page:

1. Select **View** from the action bar.

2. Select **Go to...** from the View pull-down menu to display the Go to... dialog box, shown in Display 5.6.

Display 5.6
Go to... Dialog Box

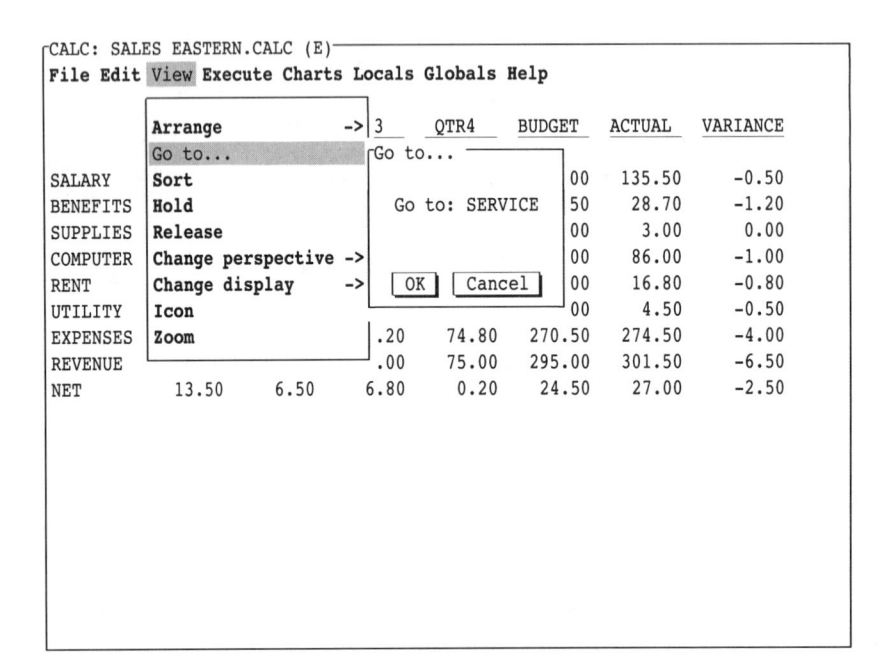

```
┌CALC: SALES EASTERN.CALC (E)─────────────────────────────────────────┐
│ File Edit View Execute Charts Locals Globals Help                    │
│                                                                       │
│          ┌Arrange            ->│ 3     QTR4    BUDGET   ACTUAL  VARIANCE
│          │Go to...             ┌Go to...────────────┐
│ SALARY   │Sort                 │                    │00    135.50   -0.50
│ BENEFITS │Hold                 │   Go to: SERVICE   │50     28.70   -1.20
│ SUPPLIES │Release              │                    │00      3.00    0.00
│ COMPUTER │Change perspective ->│                    │00     86.00   -1.00
│ RENT     │Change display     ->│   [ OK ]  [Cancel] │00     16.80   -0.80
│ UTILITY  │Icon                 └────────────────────┘00      4.50   -0.50
│ EXPENSES │Zoom              │.20    74.80   270.50   274.50   -4.00
│ REVENUE  └──────────────────┘.00    75.00   295.00   301.50   -6.50
│ NET          13.50    6.50    6.80    0.20    24.50    27.00   -2.50
│                                                                       │
└───────────────────────────────────────────────────────────────────────┘
```

3. Type `SERVICE` in the **Go to** field, as shown in Display 5.6. You can type `SERVICE` in uppercase or lowercase.

4. Select **OK** to display the SERVICE page of the EASTERN spreadsheet.

Notice the values in SERVICE are identical to the values in SALES. To change the values to reflect the Service Division's information, you can type over the current values with the correct data, or you can first clear the current data values and then enter the new data values for SERVICE. Remember that all values in the ACTUAL and CHANGE columns and the EXPENSES and NET rows are computed with formulas. Because the formulas were automatically copied from PAGE1 to PAGE2, you do not need to enter cell values or formulas for the cells in those rows and columns. SAS/CALC software has adjusted the formulas to use the values for the new page, SERVICE.

Lesson 5.5: Clearing Cell Values

To clear the cell values in SERVICE:

1. Move the cursor to the SALARY.QTR1 cell and press the MARK BLOCK function key.

2. Move the cursor to the NET.VARIANCE cell and press the MARK BLOCK function key.

3. Select **Edit** from the action bar and **Clear marked areas...** from the Edit pull-down menu, as shown in Display 5.7.

Display 5.7
Clearing Marked Areas

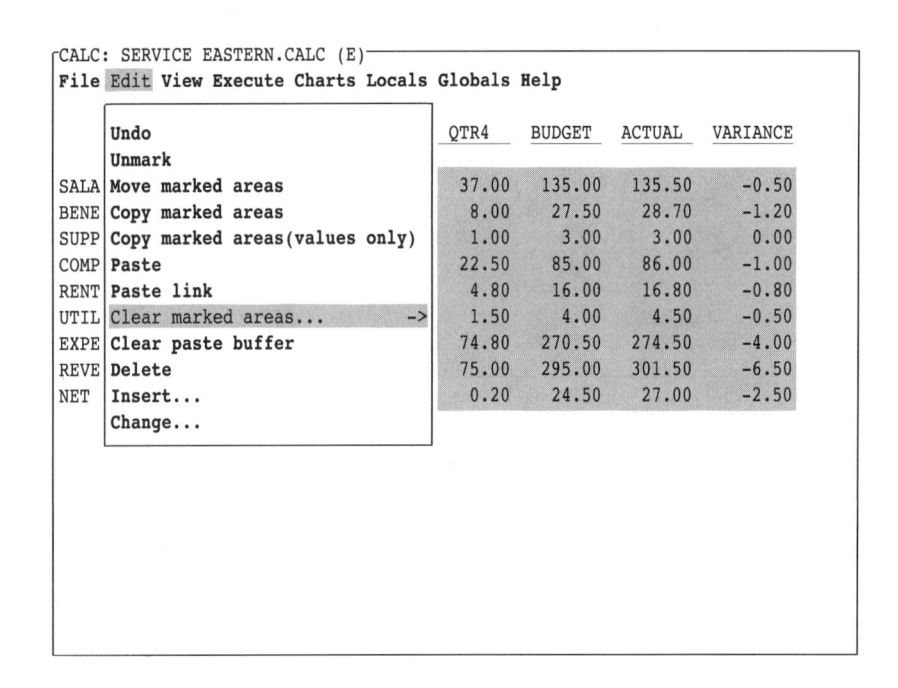

```
┌CALC: SERVICE EASTERN.CALC (E)─────────────────────────────────────┐
│ File Edit View Execute Charts Locals Globals Help                 │
│     ┌──────────────────────────────────┐                          │
│     │ Undo                             │  QTR4   BUDGET  ACTUAL  VARIANCE
│     │ Unmark                           │                          │
│ SALA│ Move marked areas                │ 37.00   135.00  135.50   -0.50
│ BENE│ Copy marked areas                │  8.00    27.50   28.70   -1.20
│ SUPP│ Copy marked areas(values only)   │  1.00     3.00    3.00    0.00
│ COMP│ Paste                            │ 22.50    85.00   86.00   -1.00
│ RENT│ Paste link                       │  4.80    16.00   16.80   -0.80
│ UTIL│ Clear marked areas...         -> │  1.50     4.00    4.50   -0.50
│ EXPE│ Clear paste buffer               │ 74.80   270.50  274.50   -4.00
│ REVE│ Delete                           │ 75.00   295.00  301.50   -6.50
│ NET │ Insert...                        │  0.20    24.50   27.00   -2.50
│     │ Change...                        │
│     └──────────────────────────────────┘
│                                                                   │
└───────────────────────────────────────────────────────────────────┘
```

114 *Creating a Three-Dimensional Spreadsheet* □ *Chapter 5*

4. Select **Clear data only** from the Clear marked areas… pull-down menu, as shown in Display 5.8.

Display 5.8
Clearing Data Only

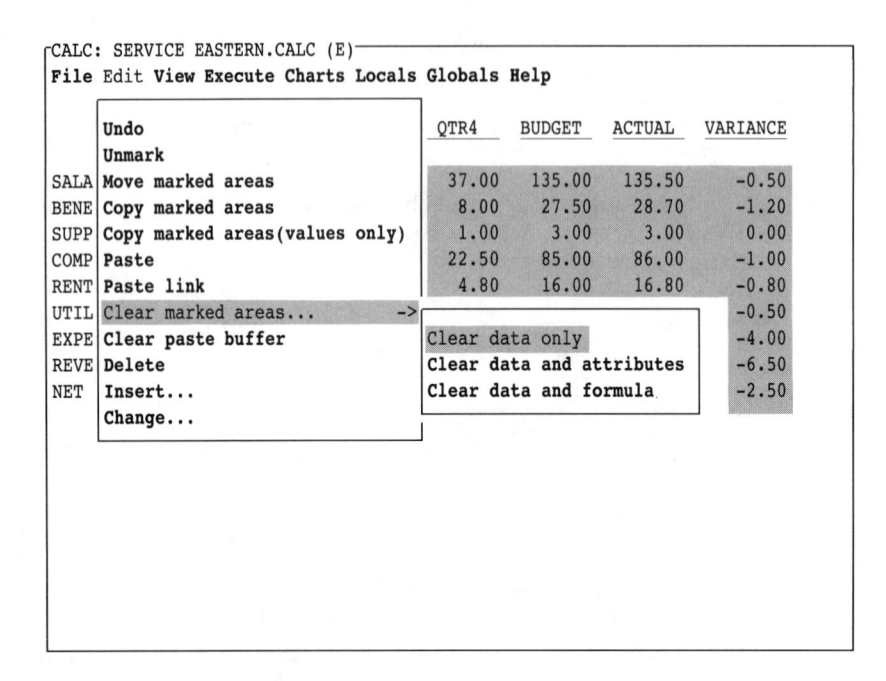

```
┌CALC: SERVICE EASTERN.CALC (E)─────────────────────────────────┐
│ File Edit View Execute Charts Locals Globals Help             │
│     ┌─────────────────────────────┐                           │
│     │ Undo                        │  QTR4   BUDGET  ACTUAL  VARIANCE │
│     │ Unmark                      │                           │
│ SALA│ Move marked areas           │  37.00  135.00  135.50  -0.50   │
│ BENE│ Copy marked areas           │   8.00   27.50   28.70  -1.20   │
│ SUPP│ Copy marked areas(values only)│ 1.00    3.00    3.00   0.00   │
│ COMP│ Paste                       │  22.50   85.00   86.00  -1.00   │
│ RENT│ Paste link                  │   4.80   16.00   16.80  -0.80   │
│ UTIL│ Clear marked areas...    ─> │                         -0.50   │
│ EXPE│ Clear paste buffer          │ ┌─────────────────────┐ -4.00   │
│ REVE│ Delete                      │ │ Clear data only     │ -6.50   │
│ NET │ Insert...                   │ │ Clear data and attributes │ -2.50 │
│     │ Change...                   │ │ Clear data and formula │       │
│     └─────────────────────────────┘ └─────────────────────┘       │
│                                                               │
└───────────────────────────────────────────────────────────────┘
```

Selecting **Clear data only** clears the data values in the marked range, as shown in Display 5.9. A note is displayed indicating the cells have been cleared. Those cells containing formulas have a value of zero. The formulas in those cells remain present and active.

Display 5.9
SERVICE Page with Cleared Cell Values

```
┌CALC: SERVICE EASTERN.CALC (E)─────────────────────────────────┐
│ File Edit View Execute Charts Locals Globals Help             │
│ NOTE: The cells have been cleared.                            │
│         QTR1    QTR2    QTR3    QTR4   BUDGET  ACTUAL  VARIANCE │
│                                                               │
│ SALARY                                          0.00    0.00  │
│ BENEFITS                                        0.00    0.00  │
│ SUPPLIES                                        0.00    0.00  │
│ COMPUTER                                        0.00    0.00  │
│ RENT                                            0.00    0.00  │
│ UTILITY                                         0.00    0.00  │
│ EXPENSES 0.00    0.00    0.00    0.00    0.00   0.00    0.00  │
│ REVENUE                                         0.00    0.00  │
│ NET      0.00    0.00    0.00    0.00    0.00   0.00    0.00  │
│                                                               │
└───────────────────────────────────────────────────────────────┘
```

Lesson 5.6: Entering Cell Values and Reexecuting Formulas

Type the new value, 32, for the cell SALARY.QTR1 in SERVICE and press ENTER. Notice that the values of the cells in the QTR1 column and the SALARY row that contain formulas are automatically recomputed, as shown in Display 5.10.

Display 5.10
Recomputed Values

```
┌CALC: SERVICE EASTERN.CALC (E)─────────────────────────────────┐
│File Edit View Execute Charts Locals Globals Help              │
│                                                                │
│             QTR1    QTR2    QTR3    QTR4   BUDGET  ACTUAL  VARIANCE│
│                                                                │
│  SALARY    32.00                                    32.00   -32.00│
│  BENEFITS                                            0.00     0.00│
│  SUPPLIES                                            0.00     0.00│
│  COMPUTER                                            0.00     0.00│
│  RENT                                                0.00     0.00│
│  UTILITY                                             0.00     0.00│
│  EXPENSES  32.00    0.00    0.00    0.00    0.00    32.00   -32.00│
│  REVENUE                                             0.00     0.00│
│  NET      -32.00    0.00    0.00    0.00    0.00   -32.00    32.00│
│                                                                │
│                                                                │
│                                                                │
│                                                                │
└────────────────────────────────────────────────────────────────┘
```

In fact, each time you alter a value in the spreadsheet and press ENTER or a function key, the formulas execute. This automatic execution of formulas is controlled by the AUTOCALC option. By default, the AUTOCALC option is turned on. You can conserve resources by controlling when the formulas execute.

In this application, you do not need to execute the formulas until you have entered all the data for the Service Division. One way to prevent the automatic execution of the formulas is to enter all cell values before you press ENTER or a function key. Another way is to turn the AUTOCALC option off, which prevents formulas from executing even when ENTER or a function key is pressed. You can then turn the option back on to resume automatic execution of formulas, or you can request execution of formulas without turning on automatic execution.

Lesson 5.7: Turning Off the AUTOCALC Option

To turn off the AUTOCALC option:

1. Select **Execute** from the action bar.

2. Select **Autocalc** from the Execute pull-down menu.

3. Select **Autocalc off** from the Autocalc pull-down menu, as shown in Display 5.11.

Display 5.11
Selecting Autocalc Off

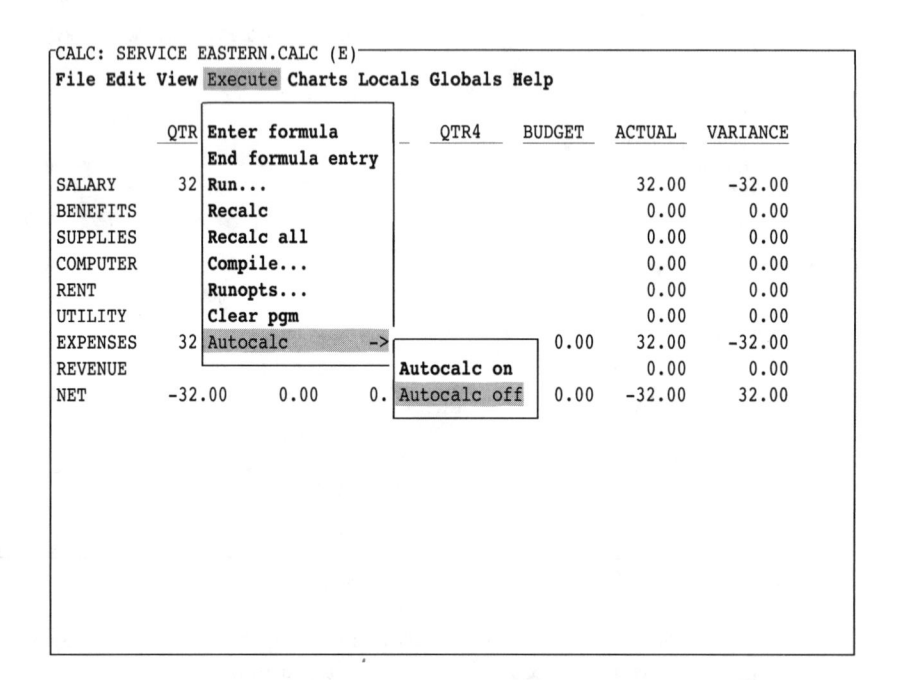

```
┌CALC: SERVICE EASTERN.CALC (E)─────────────────────────────────────────┐
│File Edit View Execute Charts Locals Globals Help                      │
│                                                                        │
│              QTR Enter formula        QTR4    BUDGET   ACTUAL  VARIANCE│
│                  End formula entry                                     │
│    SALARY     32 Run...                                  32.00   -32.00│
│    BENEFITS      Recalc                                   0.00     0.00│
│    SUPPLIES      Recalc all                               0.00     0.00│
│    COMPUTER      Compile...                               0.00     0.00│
│    RENT          Runopts...                               0.00     0.00│
│    UTILITY       Clear pgm                                0.00     0.00│
│    EXPENSES   32 Autocalc         ->            0.00     32.00   -32.00│
│    REVENUE                           ┌Autocalc on         0.00     0.00│
│    NET       -32.00    0.00     0.  │Autocalc off│ 0.00  -32.00    32.00│
│                                      └────────────┘                    │
│                                                                        │
│                                                                        │
│                                                                        │
│                                                                        │
└────────────────────────────────────────────────────────────────────────┘
```

A note is displayed indicating that the AUTOCALC option has been turned off.

Now, type the value 34 into the cell SALARY.QTR2 and press ENTER. Notice that the values of the cells that are computed with formulas in the SALARY row and the QTR2 column do not change. Instead, the word **RECALC** is displayed in the upper-right corner of the window, as shown in Display 5.12, indicating that at least one value has been typed into a cell since the last execution of the formulas. Once RECALC is displayed, it remains displayed until the formulas execute.

Display 5.12
RECALC Displayed in Window

```
┌CALC: SERVICE EASTERN.CALC (E)──────────────────────────────RECALC┐
│File Edit View Execute Charts Locals Globals Help                  │
│                                                                   │
│              QTR1    QTR2    QTR3    QTR4   BUDGET  ACTUAL VARIANCE│
│                                                                   │
│     SALARY   32.00   34.00                          32.00  -32.00 │
│     BENEFITS                                         0.00    0.00 │
│     SUPPLIES                                         0.00    0.00 │
│     COMPUTER                                         0.00    0.00 │
│     RENT                                             0.00    0.00 │
│     UTILITY                                          0.00    0.00 │
│     EXPENSES 32.00    0.00    0.00    0.00   0.00   32.00  -32.00 │
│     REVENUE                                          0.00    0.00 │
│     NET     -32.00    0.00    0.00    0.00   0.00  -32.00   32.00 │
│                                                                   │
│                                                                   │
│                                                                   │
│                                                                   │
│                                                                   │
└───────────────────────────────────────────────────────────────────┘
```

After you enter the values for the columns QTR1, QTR2, QTR3, QTR4, and BUDGET and the rows SALARY, BENEFITS, SUPPLIES, COMPUTER, RENT, UTILITY, and REVENUE, as shown in Display 5.13, you can execute the formulas.

Note: Do not enter values in the columns ACTUAL and VARIANCE or the rows EXPENSES and NET.

Display 5.13
Entered Values

```
┌CALC: SERVICE EASTERN.CALC (E)─────────────────────────────RECALC┐
│ File Edit View Execute Charts Locals Globals Help               │
│                                                                 │
│              QTR1    QTR2    QTR3    QTR4   BUDGET  ACTUAL  VARIANCE │
│                                                                 │
│   SALARY    32.00   34.00   34.00   34.50   130.00   32.00   -32.00 │
│   BENEFITS   6.40    6.40    6.60    6.70    25.50    0.00     0.00 │
│   SUPPLIES   3.00    3.00    3.50    3.70    11.00    0.00     0.00 │
│   COMPUTER  20.00   20.00   20.20   20.20    86.00    0.00     0.00 │
│   RENT       4.00    4.00    4.00    4.80    16.80    0.00     0.00 │
│   UTILITY    1.00    1.50    1.50    2.00     6.00    0.00     0.00 │
│   EXPENSES  32.00    0.00    0.00    0.00     0.00   32.00   -32.00 │
│   REVENUE   70.00   72.00   69.00   70.00   310.00    0.00     0.00 │
│   NET      -32.00    0.00    0.00    0.00     0.00  -32.00    32.00 │
│                                                                 │
└─────────────────────────────────────────────────────────────────┘
```

You can turn the AUTOCALC option on by following the same procedure you used to turn it off, except select **Autocalc on** from the Autocalc pull-down menu. However, even with the AUTOCALC option turned off, it is possible to execute formulas.

To execute formulas with the AUTOCALC option turned off:

1. Select **Execute** from the action bar.
2. Select **Recalc all** from the Execute pull-down menu, as shown in Display 5.14.

Display 5.14
Selecting Recalc All

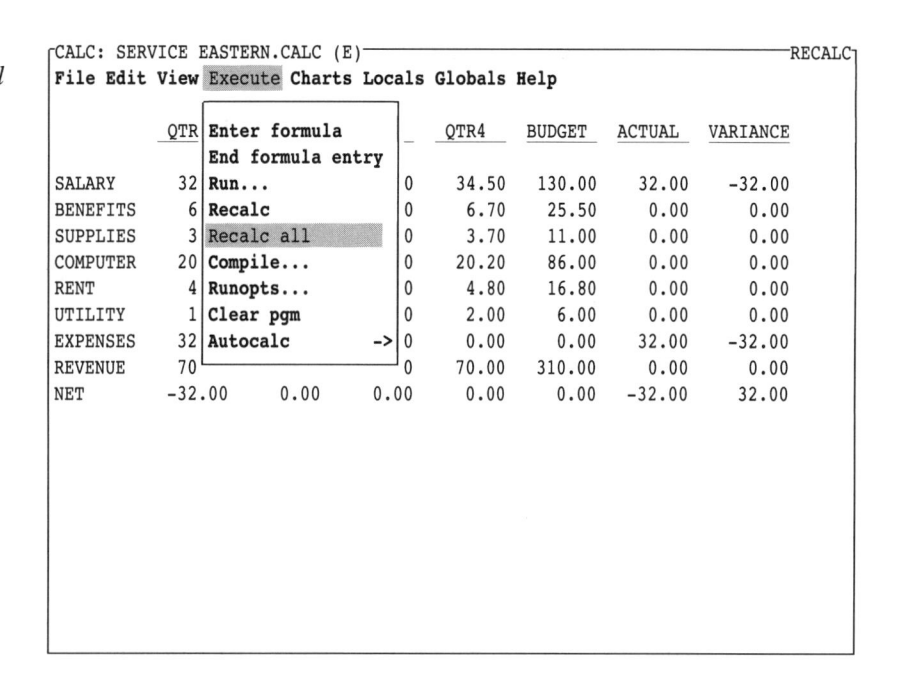

```
┌CALC: SERVICE EASTERN.CALC (E)──────────────────────────────RECALC┐
│File Edit View Execute Charts Locals Globals Help                 │
│                 ┌─────────────────┐                              │
│            QTR  │Enter formula    │    QTR4   BUDGET  ACTUAL  VARIANCE
│                 │End formula entry│
│SALARY       32  │Run...           │ 0  34.50  130.00   32.00   -32.00
│BENEFITS      6  │Recalc           │ 0   6.70   25.50    0.00     0.00
│SUPPLIES      3  │Recalc all       │ 0   3.70   11.00    0.00     0.00
│COMPUTER     20  │Compile...       │ 0  20.20   86.00    0.00     0.00
│RENT          4  │Runopts...       │ 0   4.80   16.80    0.00     0.00
│UTILITY       1  │Clear pgm        │ 0   2.00    6.00    0.00     0.00
│EXPENSES     32  │Autocalc      -> │ 0   0.00    0.00   32.00   -32.00
│REVENUE      70  └─────────────────┘ 0  70.00  310.00    0.00     0.00
│NET         -32.00      0.00     0.00    0.00    0.00  -32.00    32.00
│
│
│
│
│
└──────────────────────────────────────────────────────────────────┘
```

The formulas execute, the new values are displayed in the cells, and the word RECALC no longer appears in the upper-right corner of the window, indicating the spreadsheet is up-to-date and all formulas have executed. Be aware that using this technique leaves the AUTOCALC option turned off, so new modifications you make to the cell values do not cause the formulas to execute automatically again. Additionally, if you alter any cell values, RECALC is redisplayed in the upper-right corner of the window indicating the spreadsheet is not up-to-date.

The values for the SERVICE page of your spreadsheet should correspond to the values shown in Display 5.15. The SERVICE page is complete.

Display 5.15
The SERVICE Page

```
┌CALC: SERVICE EASTERN.CALC (E)─────────────────────────────────┐
│ File Edit View Execute Charts Locals Globals Help             │
│                                                                │
│            QTR1    QTR2    QTR3    QTR4   BUDGET  ACTUAL VARIANCE │
│                                                                │
│ SALARY    32.00   34.00   34.00   34.50  130.00  134.50  -4.50 │
│ BENEFITS   6.40    6.40    6.60    6.70   25.50   26.10  -0.60 │
│ SUPPLIES   3.00    3.00    3.50    3.70   11.00   13.20  -2.20 │
│ COMPUTER  20.00   20.00   20.20   20.20   86.00   80.40   5.60 │
│ RENT       4.00    4.00    4.00    4.80   16.80   16.80   0.00 │
│ UTILITY    1.00    1.50    1.50    2.00    6.00    6.00   0.00 │
│ EXPENSES  66.40   68.90   69.80   71.90  275.30  277.00  -1.70 │
│ REVENUE   70.00   72.00   69.00   70.00  310.00  281.00  29.00 │
│ NET        3.60    3.10   -0.80   -1.90   34.70    4.00  30.70 │
│                                                                │
│                                                                │
│                                                                │
└────────────────────────────────────────────────────────────────┘
```

Before you create PAGE3 for the summary data, turn on the AUTOCALC option.

Lesson 5.8: Turning On the AUTOCALC Option

To turn on the AUTOCALC option:

1. Select **Execute** from the action bar and **Autocalc** from the Execute pull-down menu.

2. Select **Autocalc on** from the Autocalc pull-down menu.

   A note is displayed indicating that the AUTOCALC option has been turned on.
   You are ready to create PAGE3, the summary page.

Lesson 5.9: Inserting a Page

To insert a page containing totals from both divisions:

1. Select **Edit** from the action bar and **Insert...** from the Edit pull-down menu to display the Insert... dialog box shown in Display 5.16.

Display 5.16
Inserting a Summary Page

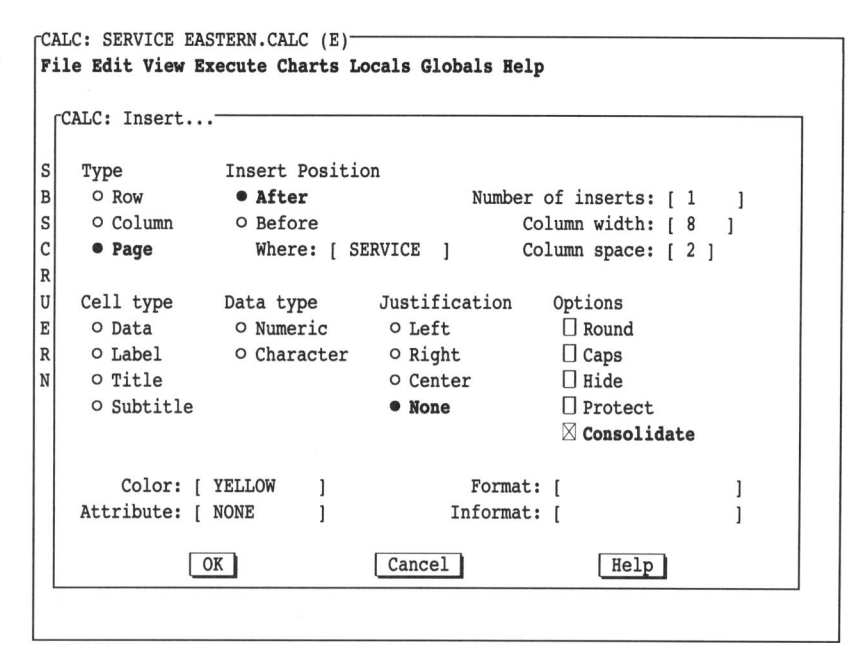

```
┌CALC: SERVICE EASTERN.CALC (E)─────────────────────────────
│File Edit View Execute Charts Locals Globals Help
│  ┌CALC: Insert...─────────────────────────────────────┐
│S │                                                     │
│B │  Type              Insert Position                  │
│S │  ○ Row             ● After         Number of inserts: [ 1  ]
│C │  ○ Column          ○ Before        Column width:     [ 8  ]
│R │  ● Page            Where: [ SERVICE ]  Column space: [ 2  ]
│U │                                                     │
│E │  Cell type         Data type       Justification   Options
│R │  ○ Data            ○ Numeric       ○ Left         ☐ Round
│N │  ○ Label           ○ Character     ○ Right        ☐ Caps
│  │  ○ Title                           ○ Center       ☐ Hide
│  │  ○ Subtitle                        ● None         ☐ Protect
│  │                                                   ☒ Consolidate
│  │
│  │      Color: [ YELLOW   ]         Format: [          ]
│  │  Attribute: [ NONE     ]       Informat: [          ]
│  │
│  │          [ OK ]       [ Cancel ]        [ Help ]
│  └─────────────────────────────────────────────────────┘
│
└────────────────────────────────────────────────────────────
```

2. Select **Page** in the **Type** field of the Insert... dialog box.

3. Specify that the desired location of the new page is after the SERVICE page by accepting the default **After** in the **Insert Position** field.

4. Specify the number of pages you want to insert. In this case, the default value of **1** in the **Number of inserts** field is correct, indicating that you want to insert one page after SERVICE.

5. Now, type SERVICE in the brackets following the **Where** field. You can type SERVICE in uppercase or lowercase.

    As you can see, there are numerous other fields in the dialog box, which you can use to supply additional information about the inserted row. In this example, you can accept the defaults. Consult *SAS/CALC Software: Usage and Reference* for more information about the Insert... dialog box.

6. After supplying the appropriate information, select **OK** to close the Insert... dialog box and redisplay the EASTERN spreadsheet with the new page, PAGE3, as shown in Display 5.17.

Display 5.17
PAGE3

```
┌CALC: PAGE3 EASTERN.CALC (E)─────────────────────────────────┐
│ File Edit View Execute Charts Locals Globals Help           │
│                                                             │
│              QTR1    QTR2    QTR3    QTR4   BUDGET  ACTUAL  VARIANCE │
│    SALARY                                                   │
│    BENEFITS                                                 │
│    SUPPLIES                                                 │
│    COMPUTER                                                 │
│    RENT                                                     │
│    UTILITY                                                  │
│    EXPENSES                                                 │
│    REVENUE                                                  │
│    NET                                                      │
│                                                             │
│                                                             │
│                                                             │
│                                                             │
│                                                             │
│                                                             │
└─────────────────────────────────────────────────────────────┘
```

You now have a 3D spreadsheet that contains one page for each division within the eastern region, and an additional page that summarizes the data from the two divisions. The new page, PAGE3, contains the same column and row names as PAGE1 and PAGE2, but it does not contain any cell values. All the values in this page are computed with formulas that sum corresponding cells from PAGE1 and PAGE2.

Lesson 5.10: Summarizing Data

To compute values for PAGE3, you first need to define a formula to compute the total salaries for the Sales and Service Divisions.

To define the formula:

1. Select **Execute** from the action bar.

2. Select **Enter formula** from the Execute pull-down menu.

3. Move the cursor to the formula entry area and type the following formula, as shown in Display 5.18. You can type the formula in uppercase or lowercase. When you press ENTER, the formula is translated to uppercase.

    =sum(sales.salary.qtr1,service.salary.qtr1)

Display 5.18
Computing Total Salaries

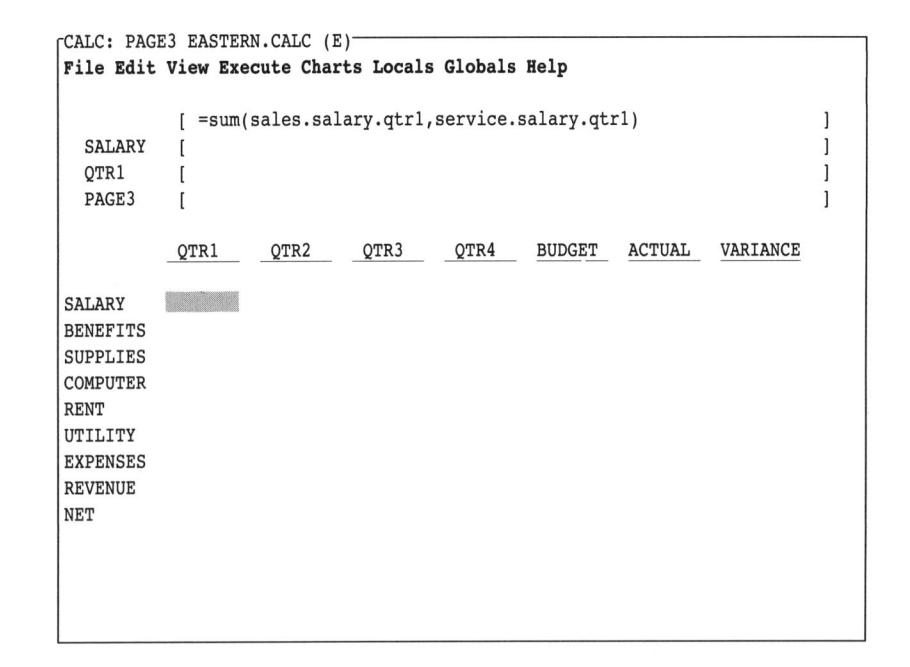

```
┌CALC: PAGE3 EASTERN.CALC (E)─────────────────────────────────────┐
│File Edit View Execute Charts Locals Globals Help                │
│                                                                 │
│              [ =sum(sales.salary.qtr1,service.salary.qtr1)    ] │
│    SALARY    [                                                ] │
│    QTR1      [                                                ] │
│    PAGE3     [                                                ] │
│                                                                 │
│              QTR1    QTR2    QTR3    QTR4    BUDGET  ACTUAL  VARIANCE │
│                                                                 │
│   SALARY     ▓▓▓▓                                               │
│   BENEFITS                                                      │
│   SUPPLIES                                                      │
│   COMPUTER                                                      │
│   RENT                                                          │
│   UTILITY                                                       │
│   EXPENSES                                                      │
│   REVENUE                                                       │
│   NET                                                           │
│                                                                 │
└─────────────────────────────────────────────────────────────────┘
```

Notice that in this formula, a three-level name is used to identify the appropriate cells to process. The three names specify the page, row, and column in the spreadsheet. Specifically, the value in the SALARY.QTR1 cell for SALES is added to the value in the SALARY.QTR1 cell for SERVICE and stored in the SALARY.QTR1 cell in PAGE3.

4. Press ENTER to execute the formula and display the computed value in the highlighted cell, as shown in Display 5.19.

Display 5.19
Result of the Formula

```
┌CALC: PAGE3 EASTERN.CALC (E)─────────────────────────────────────┐
│File Edit View Execute Charts Locals Globals Help                │
│                                                                  │
│               [ =SUM(SALES.SALARY.QTR1,SERVICE.SALARY.QTR1)    ] │
│     SALARY   [                                                 ] │
│     QTR1     [                                                 ] │
│     PAGE3    [                                                 ] │
│                                                                  │
│               QTR1    QTR2    QTR3    QTR4   BUDGET  ACTUAL  VARIANCE │
│                                                                  │
│     SALARY      62                                               │
│     BENEFITS                                                     │
│     SUPPLIES                                                     │
│     COMPUTER                                                     │
│     RENT                                                         │
│     UTILITY                                                      │
│     EXPENSES                                                     │
│     REVENUE                                                      │
│     NET                                                          │
│                                                                  │
└──────────────────────────────────────────────────────────────────┘
```

5. Select **Execute** from the action bar and **End formula entry** from the Execute pull-down menu to close the formula entry area.

You need to continue computing the total benefits, supplies, computer, rent, utility, expenses, revenue, and net values for the two divisions. Because all the cells in PAGE3 use the same basic formula (the sum of the corresponding cells in PAGE1 and PAGE2), you can copy the formula in PAGE3.SALARY.QTR1 to all the remaining cells in the page.

To copy the cell including the formula:

1. Mark the SALARY.QTR1 cell as the source cell by pressing the MARK BLOCK function key two times.

2. Mark the cells NET.VARIANCE through SALARY.QTR1 as the target cells.
   Be sure to mark NET.VARIANCE first and then mark SALARY.QTR1. Notice you have marked the SALARY.QTR1 cell as both a source cell and a target cell. Marking SALARY.QTR1 as part of the target range of cells enables you to copy the formula in SALARY.QTR1 to all cells in the spreadsheet at one time.

3. Select **Edit** from the action bar and **Copy marked areas** from the Edit pull-down menu to copy the formula.

The summary page (PAGE3) is shown in Display 5.20.

Display 5.20
PAGE3 with Computed Values

```
┌CALC: PAGE3 EASTERN.CALC (E)─────────────────────────────────────┐
│ File Edit View Execute Charts Locals Globals Help              │
│                                                                 │
│              QTR1    QTR2    QTR3    QTR4   BUDGET  ACTUAL  VARIANCE │
│                                                                 │
│  SALARY       62      67    69.5    71.5     265     270      -5    │
│  BENEFITS   12.4    13.4    14.3    14.7      53    54.8    -1.8    │
│  SUPPLIES    3.5     3.5     4.5     4.7      14    16.2    -2.2    │
│  COMPUTER     40    41.5    42.2    42.7     171   166.4     4.6    │
│  RENT          8       8       8     9.6    32.8    33.6    -0.8    │
│  UTILITY       2     2.5     2.5     3.5      10    10.5    -0.5    │
│  EXPENSES  127.9   135.9     141   146.7   545.8   551.5    -5.7    │
│  REVENUE     145   145.5     147     145     605   582.5    22.5    │
│  NET        17.1     9.6       6    -1.7    59.2      31    28.2    │
│                                                                 │
│                                                                 │
│                                                                 │
│                                                                 │
│                                                                 │
│                                                                 │
│                                                                 │
└─────────────────────────────────────────────────────────────────┘
```

PAGE3 is almost complete except that the cell values in the page are not formatted with two decimal places as they are in SALES and SERVICE. Remember, in Chapter 3 you learned how to select a specific format for your cells.

To define a format for PAGE3:

1. Move the cursor to the SALARY.QTR1 cell and press the MARK BLOCK function key.

2. Move the cursor to the NET.VARIANCE cell and press the MARK BLOCK function key.

3. Select **Edit** from the action bar and **Change...** from the Edit pull-down menu to display the Change dialog box.

4. Move the cursor to the **Format** field and type 7.2 over the current format, `BEST.`
    Make sure there is a mark in the selection field for **Format**. Remember to delete the default format name, BEST., completely. A format of 7.2T. is invalid.

5. Select **OK** to display the spreadsheet shown in Display 5.21. A message is displayed indicating that 63 cells have been changed.

Display 5.21
Formatted Values

```
┌CALC: PAGE3 EASTERN.CALC (E)─────────────────────────────────────┐
│ File Edit View Execute Charts Locals Globals Help               │
│                                                                 │
│              QTR1    QTR2    QTR3    QTR4   BUDGET  ACTUAL  VARIANCE │
│                                                                 │
│   SALARY    62.00   67.00   69.50   71.50   265.00  270.00   -5.00  │
│   BENEFITS  12.40   13.40   14.30   14.70    53.00   54.80   -1.80  │
│   SUPPLIES   3.50    3.50    4.50    4.70    14.00   16.20   -2.20  │
│   COMPUTER  40.00   41.50   42.20   42.70   171.00  166.40    4.60  │
│   RENT       8.00    8.00    8.00    9.60    32.80   33.60   -0.80  │
│   UTILITY    2.00    2.50    2.50    3.50    10.00   10.50   -0.50  │
│   EXPENSES 127.90  135.90  141.00  146.70   545.80  551.50   -5.70  │
│   REVENUE  145.00  145.50  147.00  145.00   605.00  582.50   22.50  │
│   NET       17.10    9.60    6.00   -1.70    59.20   31.00   28.20  │
│                                                                 │
└─────────────────────────────────────────────────────────────────┘
```

You now have a summary page of the Sales and Service Divisions within the eastern region.

You are almost finished with your 3D spreadsheet; however, currently, the page names are SALES, SERVICE, and PAGE3. The spreadsheet is easier to use if the last page name is SUMMARY. As you saw earlier in Lesson 5.3, you can rename pages in a spreadsheet. However, before you can rename PAGE3, you need to change your view of the spreadsheet.

To change the pespective:

1. Select **View** from the action bar.
2. Select **Change perspective** from the View pull-down menu.
3. Select **View pages and columns** from the Change perspective pull-down menu to display the pages and columns in the EASTERN spreadsheet.

Lesson 5.11: Renaming a Page

Notice the only page name displayed is **PAGE3**. You can display all three page names by pressing the BACKWARD function key or by using pull-down menus to go to the SALES page.

To use pull-down menus to go to the SALES page:

1. Select **View** from the action bar.

2. Select **Go to...** from the View pull-down menu.

3. In the Go to... dialog box, type `SALES` in the **Go to** field.

4. Select **OK** to display the pages and columns for all three pages.

To change the page name, type `SUMMARY` over `PAGE3`, and press ENTER. You can type `SUMMARY` in uppercase or lowercase. Pressing ENTER translates the name to uppercase, as shown in Display 5.22.

Display 5.22
Renamed Page

```
┌CALC: SALARY EASTERN.CALC (E)─────────────────────────────────┐
│ File Edit View Execute Charts Locals Globals Help            │
│                                                              │
│           QTR1     QTR2     QTR3     QTR4   BUDGET  ACTUAL  VARIANCE │
│                                                              │
│  SALES    30.00    33.00    35.50    37.00  135.00  135.50   -0.50  │
│  SERVICE  32.00    34.00    34.00    34.50  130.00  134.50   -4.50  │
│  SUMMARY  62.00    67.00    69.50    71.50  265.00  270.00   -5.00  │
│                                                              │
│                                                              │
└──────────────────────────────────────────────────────────────┘
```

After renaming the page, select **View** from the action bar and **Change perspective** from the View pull-down menu to change the perspective back to rows and columns. Notice the page name, **SALES**, in the upper-left corner of the spreadsheet, as shown in Display 5.23. You are currently viewing data for the Sales Division.

Display 5.23
The SALES Page

```
┌CALC: SALES EASTERN.CALC (E)─────────────────────────────────────┐
│ File Edit View Execute Charts Locals Globals Help               │
│                                                                 │
│               QTR1    QTR2    QTR3    QTR4   BUDGET  ACTUAL  VARIANCE │
│                                                                 │
│    SALARY    30.00   33.00   35.50   37.00   135.00  135.50   -0.50 │
│    BENEFITS   6.00    7.00    7.70    8.00    27.50   28.70   -1.20 │
│    SUPPLIES   0.50    0.50    1.00    1.00     3.00    3.00    0.00 │
│    COMPUTER  20.00   21.50   22.00   22.50    85.00   86.00   -1.00 │
│    RENT       4.00    4.00    4.00    4.80    16.00   16.80   -0.80 │
│    UTILITY    1.00    1.00    1.00    1.50     4.00    4.50   -0.50 │
│    EXPENSES  61.50   67.00   71.20   74.80   270.50  274.50   -4.00 │
│    REVENUE   75.00   73.50   78.00   75.00   295.00  301.50   -6.50 │
│    NET       13.50    6.50    6.80    0.20    24.50   27.00   -2.50 │
│                                                                 │
└─────────────────────────────────────────────────────────────────┘
```

To verify that the formulas have been automatically updated to reflect the new names, go to the SUMMARY page, open the formula entry area, and place the cursor on a cell.

You now have a completed 3D spreadsheet with a summary page for the Sales and Service Divisions within the eastern region, and you have completed Chapter 5.

You can end your spreadsheet and the SAS/CALC software session or continue with Chapter 6, ''Linking Spreadsheets.''

Note: Refer to Lessons 2.11 and 2.12 in Chapter 2 for information on closing your spreadsheet, ending the SAS/CALC software session, and ending the SAS System session.

Chapter Summary

This chapter teaches you how to change the two-dimensional EASTERN spreadsheet into a three-dimensional spreadsheet. A 2D spreadsheet consists of rows and columns. A 3D spreadsheet consists of rows, columns, and pages.

The EASTERN spreadsheet currently contains quarterly data for the Sales Division of the eastern region. As a result, EASTERN contains one page of data. In this chapter, you add a second page to the EASTERN spreadsheet. This second page, Service, contains the quarterly data for the Service Division of the eastern region. You create the SERVICE page by copying the existing SALES page. Copying is the appropriate choice because the new page, SERVICE, contains the same rows, columns, and formulas as the SALES page.

When you finish creating the SERVICE page, you add a third page to the EASTERN spreadsheet. This third page, SUMMARY, summarizes the data within the Sales and Service Divisions of the eastern region. You create the SUMMARY page by inserting a page after SERVICE. Inserting is the appropriate choice because the new page, SUMMARY, contains the same rows and columns as SALES and SERVICE, but different formulas.

Once the SUMMARY page is inserted, you define a formula that totals the data from both divisions to give you overall region totals.

In this chapter, you also learn the importance of turning the AUTOCALC option on and off. When AUTOCALC is turned on, all formulas automatically execute when you modify a cell value. By turning AUTOCALC off, the formulas execute when you turn AUTOCALC on again, or when you select RECALC ALL from the pull-down menu. Controlling when calculations occur can save you time and resources.

After completing this chapter, you are ready to learn how to link spreadsheets, one of the most powerful features of SAS/CALC software.

Chapter 6 Linking Spreadsheets

Linking Spreadsheets   131
　　Lesson 6.1: Copying a Spreadsheet   133
　　Lesson 6.2: Creating a New Spreadsheet   139
　　Lesson 6.3: Changing Column Widths   140
　　Lesson 6.4: Changing the Default Row and Column Names   141
　　Lesson 6.5: Linking Spreadsheets   142
　　Lesson 6.5: Defining a Formula   147
　　Lesson 6.6: Copying Formulas   149
　　Lesson 6.7: Using the Drilldown Facility   151
　　Lesson 6.8: Deactivating a Link   153
　　Lesson 6.9: Reactivating a Link   155
Chapter Summary   156

Linking Spreadsheets

In Chapter 5, "Creating a Three-Dimensional Spreadsheet," you inserted two pages into the EASTERN spreadsheet to create a three-dimensional spreadsheet containing separate pages for the Sales and Service Divisions and a SUMMARY page to summarize the Sales and Service data for the eastern region.

The western region of the company also has a 3D spreadsheet. The WESTERN spreadsheet contains a page for the Sales and Service Divisions and a summary page to summarize the Sales and Service data for the western region. The WESTERN spreadsheet already exists in the CALC catalog in the SASHELP library. Lesson 6.1 teaches you to how to copy the WESTERN spreadsheet from SASHELP.CALC to SASUSER.CALC.

In this chapter, you create a two-dimensional spreadsheet named COMPANY that summarizes the EASTERN and WESTERN spreadsheets and computes overall company totals. To compute these totals you create links from the COMPANY spreadsheet to the EASTERN and WESTERN spreadsheets.

Linking enables a current spreadsheet (COMPANY) to reference the rows, columns, pages, and cells within linked spreadsheets (EASTERN and WESTERN).

Before you create links to the COMPANY spreadsheet from the EASTERN and WESTERN spreadsheets, you copy the WESTERN spreadsheet from SASHELP.CALC and create the COMPANY spreadsheet.

Display 6.1
Enhanced COMPANY Spreadsheet

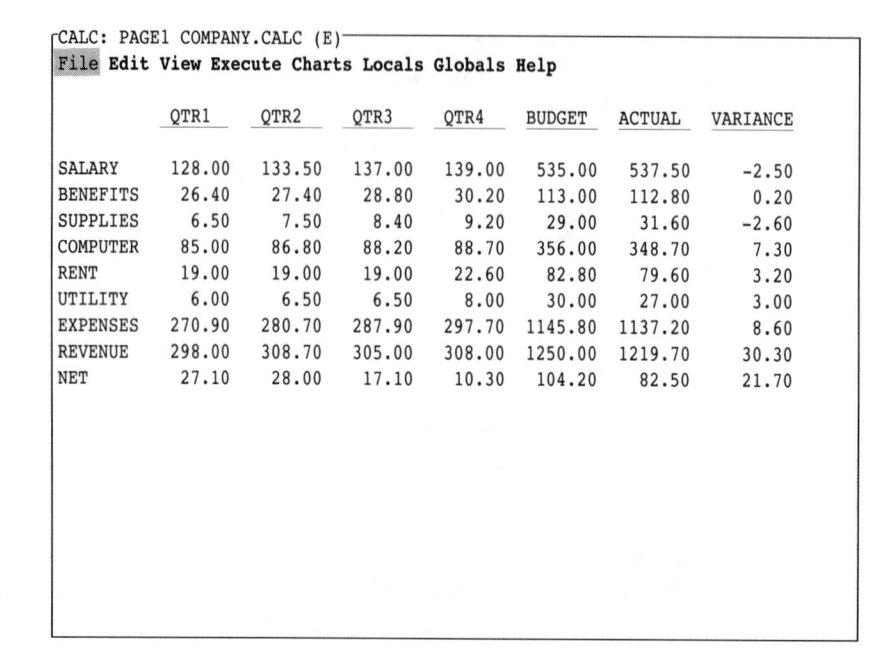

```
┌CALC: PAGE1 COMPANY.CALC (E)─────────────────────────────────────┐
│ File Edit View Execute Charts Locals Globals Help               │
│                                                                 │
│                QTR1    QTR2    QTR3    QTR4   BUDGET  ACTUAL  VARIANCE │
│                                                                 │
│   SALARY     128.00  133.50  137.00  139.00   535.00  537.50   -2.50  │
│   BENEFITS    26.40   27.40   28.80   30.20   113.00  112.80    0.20  │
│   SUPPLIES     6.50    7.50    8.40    9.20    29.00   31.60   -2.60  │
│   COMPUTER    85.00   86.80   88.20   88.70   356.00  348.70    7.30  │
│   RENT        19.00   19.00   19.00   22.60    82.80   79.60    3.20  │
│   UTILITY      6.00    6.50    6.50    8.00    30.00   27.00    3.00  │
│   EXPENSES   270.90  280.70  287.90  297.70  1145.80 1137.20    8.60  │
│   REVENUE    298.00  308.70  305.00  308.00  1250.00 1219.70   30.30  │
│   NET         27.10   28.00   17.10   10.30   104.20   82.50   21.70  │
│                                                                 │
│                                                                 │
│                                                                 │
│                                                                 │
└─────────────────────────────────────────────────────────────────┘
```

The COMPANY spreadsheet contains the following columns:

QTR1-QTR4	are the actual total expenditures for the quarters of the year for both divisions.
ACTUAL	represents actual year-to-date total expenses and revenues for both divisions.
BUDGET	is the total amount of money budgeted for the year for both divisions.
VARIANCE	represents the total difference between the columns ACTUAL and BUDGET for both divisions.

The spreadsheet contains the following rows:

SALARY	represents total salary values.
BENEFITS	represents total costs for employee benefits.
SUPPLIES	represents total costs for supplies.
COMPUTER	represents total costs for computer equipment.
RENT	represents total rental costs.
UTILITY	represents total costs for utilities.
EXPENSES	contains total costs for each quarter and the total budget.
REVENUE	represents total revenue amounts for each quarter and the projected yearly revenue for each division.
NET	represents the total difference between the rows REVENUE and EXPENSES.

Linking Spreadsheets □ *Linking Spreadsheets* **133**

If you ended the SAS/CALC software session after Chapter 5, refer to Lesson 3.1 in Chapter 3, "Modifying Your Spreadsheet," for information on invoking SAS/CALC software. If you did not close your spreadsheet and end the SAS/CALC software session after Chapter 5, continue with this chapter.

Lesson 6.1: Copying a Spreadsheet

To copy the WESTERN spreadsheet from SASHELP.CALC to SASUSER.CALC:

1. From the DIRECTORY window, select **File** from the action bar and **Open** from the File pull-down menu.

2. Select **Copy an entry** from the Open pull-down menu, as shown in Display 6.2.

Display 6.2
Selecting Copy an Entry

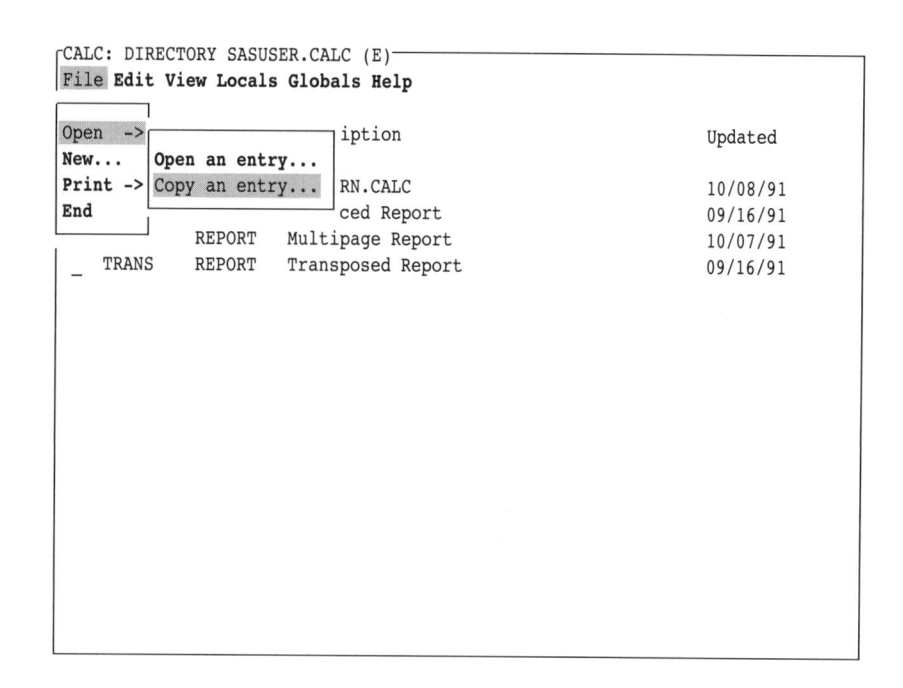

```
┌CALC: DIRECTORY SASUSER.CALC (E)─────────────────────────────────┐
│ File Edit View Locals Globals Help                              │
│                                                                 │
│┌─────────┐                                                      │
││Open  ->│─────────────────┐iption                    Updated    │
││New...  ││Open an entry...│                                     │
││Print ->││Copy an entry...│RN.CALC                   10/08/91   │
││End     │─────────────────┘ced Report                09/16/91   │
│└─────────┘       REPORT    Multipage Report          10/07/91   │
│  _    TRANS      REPORT    Transposed Report         09/16/91   │
│                                                                 │
│                                                                 │
│                                                                 │
│                                                                 │
│                                                                 │
│                                                                 │
│                                                                 │
│                                                                 │
└─────────────────────────────────────────────────────────────────┘
```

134 *Linking Spreadsheets* □ *Chapter 6*

3. Selecting **Copy an entry** displays the Copy An Entry... dialog box shown in Display 6.3.

Display 6.3
Copy An Entry...
Dialog Box

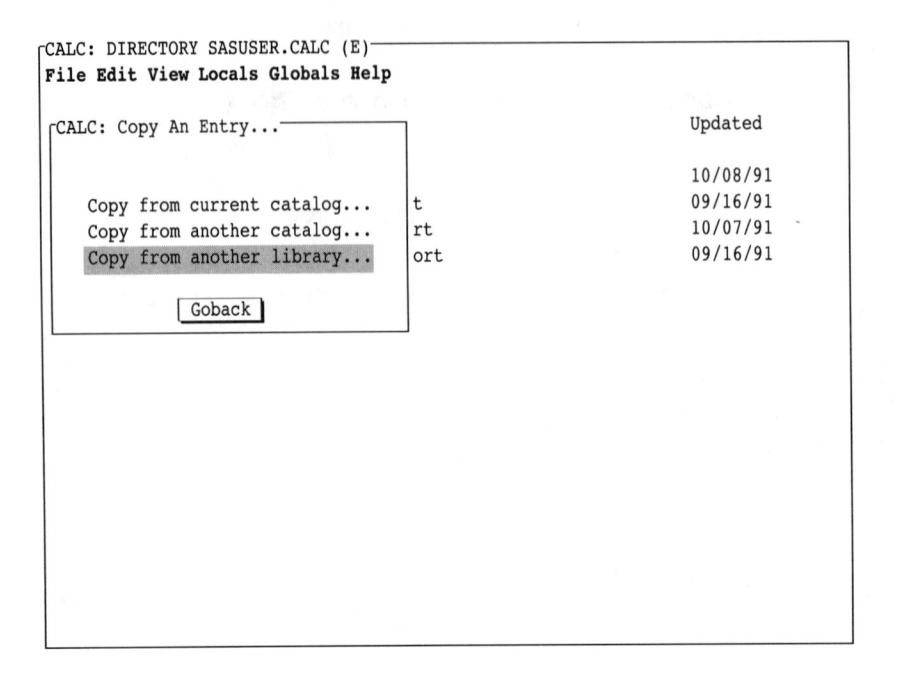

```
┌CALC: DIRECTORY SASUSER.CALC (E)─────────────────────────────┐
│File Edit View Locals Globals Help                           │
│                                                             │
│ ┌CALC: Copy An Entry...──────┐              Updated         │
│ │                            │                              │
│ │                            │              10/08/91        │
│ │   Copy from current catalog...│ t           09/16/91        │
│ │   Copy from another catalog...│ rt          10/07/91        │
│ │   Copy from another library...│ ort         09/16/91        │
│ │                            │                              │
│ │        [Goback]            │                              │
│ └────────────────────────────┘                              │
│                                                             │
│                                                             │
│                                                             │
└─────────────────────────────────────────────────────────────┘
```

4. Select **Copy from another library** to display the Libnames window shown in Display 6.4.

Display 6.4
Libnames Window

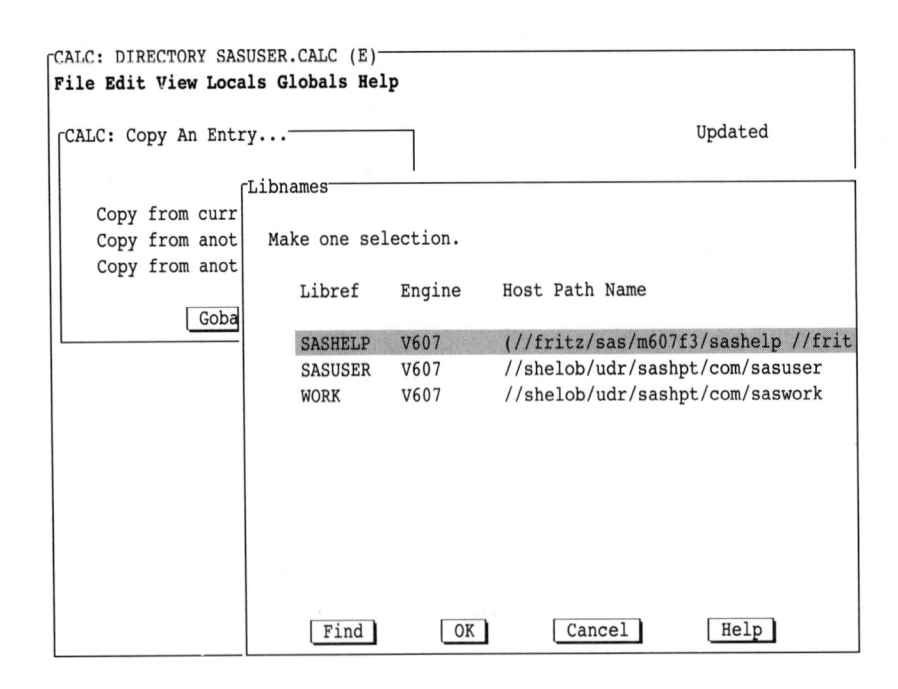

```
┌CALC: DIRECTORY SASUSER.CALC (E)─────────────────────────────┐
│File Edit View Locals Globals Help                           │
│                                                             │
│ ┌CALC: Copy An Entry...──────┐              Updated         │
│ │                 ┌Libnames──────────────────────────────┐  │
│ │  Copy from curr │                                      │  │
│ │  Copy from anot │  Make one selection.                 │  │
│ │  Copy from anot │                                      │  │
│ │                 │   Libref    Engine   Host Path Name  │  │
│ │       [Goba     │                                      │  │
│ └─────────────────│   SASHELP   V607     (//fritz/sas/m607f3/sashelp //frit│
│                   │   SASUSER   V607     //shelob/udr/sashpt/com/sasuser   │
│                   │   WORK      V607     //shelob/udr/sashpt/com/saswork   │
│                   │                                      │  │
│                   │                                      │  │
│                   │                                      │  │
│                   │      [Find]   [OK]   [Cancel]  [Help]│  │
│                   └──────────────────────────────────────┘  │
└─────────────────────────────────────────────────────────────┘
```

5. Select **SASHELP** from the list of librefs to display the Directory window for the SASHELP library, as shown in Display 6.5.

Display 6.5
SASHELP Directory Window

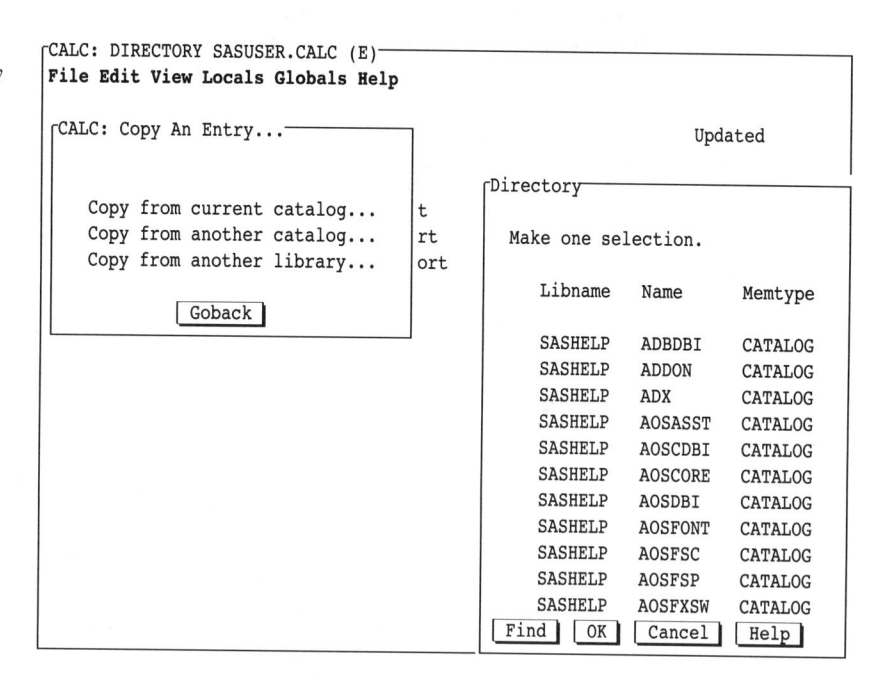

```
┌CALC: DIRECTORY SASUSER.CALC (E)─────────────────────────────┐
│ File Edit View Locals Globals Help                          │
│ ┌CALC: Copy An Entry...──────────┐         Updated          │
│ │                                │ ┌Directory─────────────┐ │
│ │ Copy from current catalog... t │ │ Make one selection.  │ │
│ │ Copy from another catalog... rt│ │                      │ │
│ │ Copy from another library... ort│ │ Libname  Name  Memtype│
│ │        [Goback]                │ │                      │ │
│ └────────────────────────────────┘ │ SASHELP  ADBDBI CATALOG│
│                                    │ SASHELP  ADDON  CATALOG│
│                                    │ SASHELP  ADX    CATALOG│
│                                    │ SASHELP  AOSASST CATALOG│
│                                    │ SASHELP  AOSCDBI CATALOG│
│                                    │ SASHELP  AOSCORE CATALOG│
│                                    │ SASHELP  AOSDBI CATALOG│
│                                    │ SASHELP  AOSFONT CATALOG│
│                                    │ SASHELP  AOSFSC CATALOG│
│                                    │ SASHELP  AOSFSP CATALOG│
│                                    │ SASHELP  AOSFXSW CATALOG│
│                                    │ [Find] [OK] [Cancel] [Help]│
└─────────────────────────────────────────────────────────────┘
```

6. Because the SASHELP catalog contains so many entries, press the function key assigned to the FORWARD command to scroll forward in the Directory window.

7. Select **SASHELP CALC CATALOG** as shown in Display 6.6.

Display 6.6
Selecting SASHELP CALC CATALOG

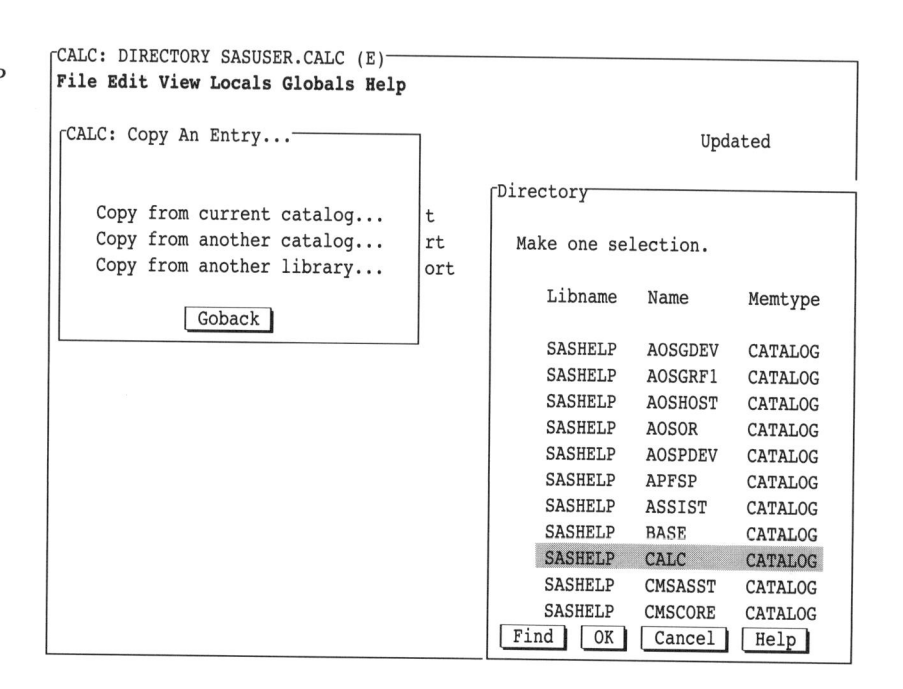

```
┌CALC: DIRECTORY SASUSER.CALC (E)─────────────────────────────┐
│ File Edit View Locals Globals Help                          │
│ ┌CALC: Copy An Entry...──────────┐         Updated          │
│ │                                │ ┌Directory─────────────┐ │
│ │ Copy from current catalog... t │ │ Make one selection.  │ │
│ │ Copy from another catalog... rt│ │                      │ │
│ │ Copy from another library... ort│ │ Libname  Name  Memtype│
│ │        [Goback]                │ │                      │ │
│ └────────────────────────────────┘ │ SASHELP  AOSGDEV CATALOG│
│                                    │ SASHELP  AOSGRF1 CATALOG│
│                                    │ SASHELP  AOSHOST CATALOG│
│                                    │ SASHELP  AOSOR  CATALOG│
│                                    │ SASHELP  AOSPDEV CATALOG│
│                                    │ SASHELP  APFSP  CATALOG│
│                                    │ SASHELP  ASSIST CATALOG│
│                                    │ SASHELP  BASE   CATALOG│
│                                    │ SASHELP  CALC   CATALOG│
│                                    │ SASHELP  CMSASST CATALOG│
│                                    │ SASHELP  CMSCORE CATALOG│
│                                    │ [Find] [OK] [Cancel] [Help]│
└─────────────────────────────────────────────────────────────┘
```

136 *Linking Spreadsheets* □ *Chapter 6*

Selecting **SASHELP CALC CATALOG** displays the Catalog Directory window for SASHELP.CALC, as shown in Display 6.7.

8. Select **WESTERN CALC** from the Catalog Directory window, as shown in Display 6.7, and select **OK** to close the Catalog Directory window.

Display 6.7
Selecting WESTERN CALC from the Catalog Directory Window

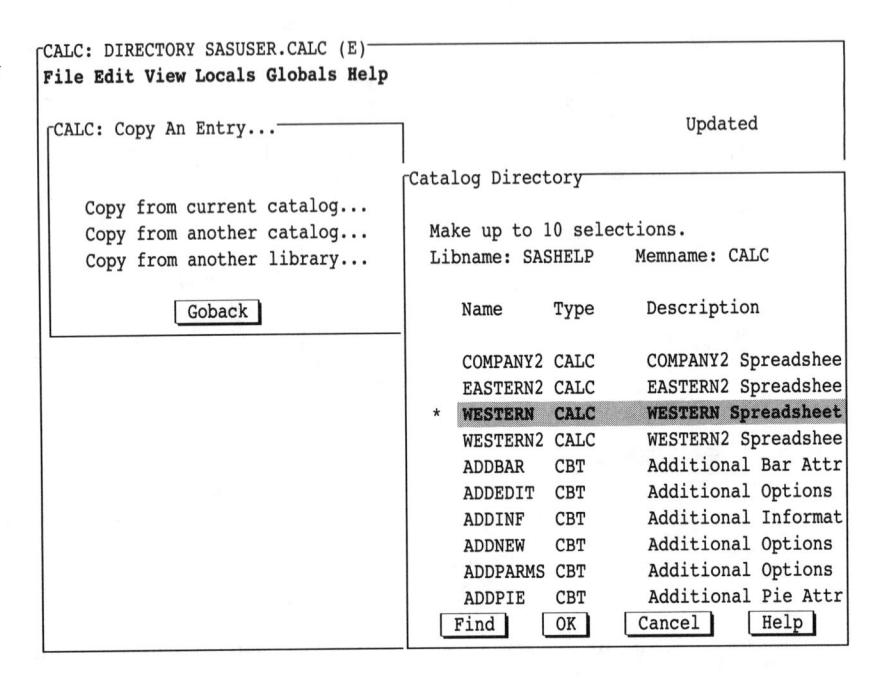

```
┌CALC: DIRECTORY SASUSER.CALC (E)─────────────────────────────────────┐
│ File Edit View Locals Globals Help                                  │
│                                                                     │
│┌CALC: Copy An Entry...──────────┐                    Updated        │
││                                │                                   │
││                                │ ┌Catalog Directory──────────────┐ │
││ Copy from current catalog...   │ │                               │ │
││ Copy from another catalog...   │ │ Make up to 10 selections.     │ │
││ Copy from another library...   │ │ Libname: SASHELP   Memname: CALC│
││                                │ │                               │ │
││         ┌──────┐               │ │   Name      Type   Description│ │
││         │Goback│               │ │                               │ │
││         └──────┘               │ │   COMPANY2  CALC   COMPANY2 Spreadshee│
│└────────────────────────────────┘ │   EASTERN2  CALC   EASTERN2 Spreadshee│
│                                   │ * WESTERN   CALC   WESTERN Spreadsheet│
│                                   │   WESTERN2  CALC   WESTERN2 Spreadshee│
│                                   │   ADDBAR    CBT    Additional Bar Attr│
│                                   │   ADDEDIT   CBT    Additional Options│
│                                   │   ADDINF    CBT    Additional Informat│
│                                   │   ADDNEW    CBT    Additional Options│
│                                   │   ADDPARMS  CBT    Additional Options│
│                                   │   ADDPIE    CBT    Additional Pie Attr│
│                                   │  ┌────┐ ┌──┐ ┌──────┐ ┌────┐   │ │
│                                   │  │Find│ │OK│ │Cancel│ │Help│   │ │
│                                   │  └────┘ └──┘ └──────┘ └────┘   │ │
│                                   └───────────────────────────────┘ │
└─────────────────────────────────────────────────────────────────────┘
```

9. Selecting **OK** displays the Assign New Names dialog box, as shown in Display 6.8, which enables you to change the name of the WESTERN spreadsheet.

10. Accept the spreadsheet name WESTERN by selecting **OK** to confirm the copy of the WESTERN spreadsheet.

Display 6.8
Assign New Names Dialog Box

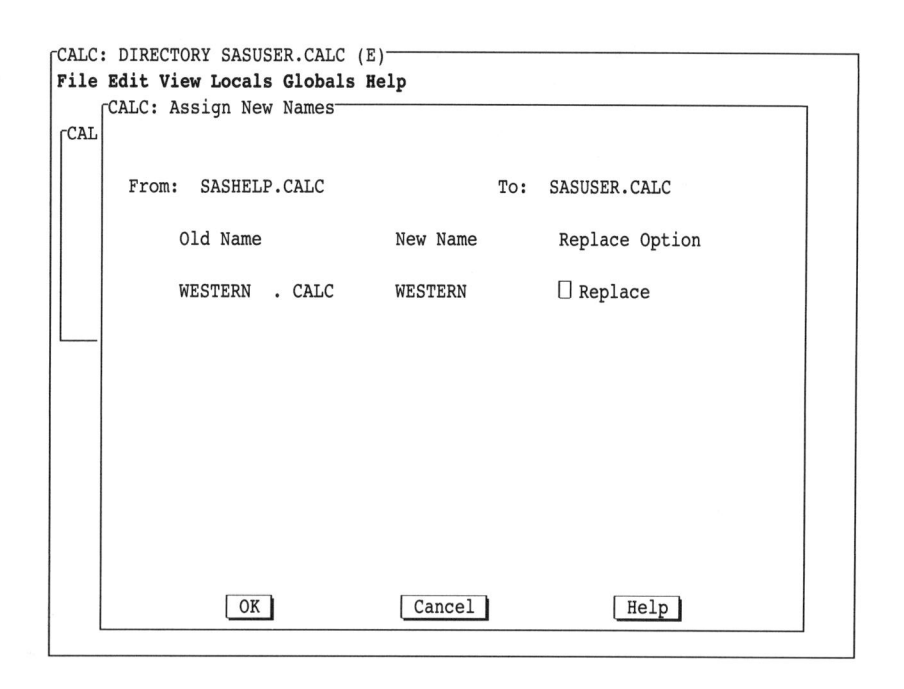

```
┌CALC: DIRECTORY SASUSER.CALC (E)─────────────────────────┐
│File Edit View Locals Globals Help                       │
│  ┌CALC: Assign New Names──────────────────────────────┐ │
│ ┌CAL                                                    │
│ │                                                       │
│ │   From:  SASHELP.CALC          To:  SASUSER.CALC     │
│ │                                                       │
│ │      Old Name          New Name      Replace Option  │
│ │                                                       │
│ │      WESTERN  . CALC   WESTERN       ☐ Replace       │
│ │                                                       │
│ │                                                       │
│ │                                                       │
│ │                                                       │
│ │                                                       │
│ │       [ OK ]         [ Cancel ]       [ Help ]       │
│ └───────────────────────────────────────────────────────┘
└─────────────────────────────────────────────────────────┘
```

138 *Linking Spreadsheets* □ *Chapter 6*

Selecting **OK** redisplays the Copy An Entry... dialog box.

11. Select **Goback** to close the Copy An Entry... dialog box and redisplay the DIRECTORY window shown in Display 6.9.

    Notice the WESTERN CALC entry.

Display 6.9
DIRECTORY Window with WESTERN Entry

```
┌CALC: DIRECTORY SASUSER.CALC (E)─────────────────────────────────┐
│File Edit View Locals Globals Help                               │
│                                                                 │
│    Name     Type     Description                      Updated   │
│                                                                 │
│ _  EASTERN  CALC     EASTERN.CALC                     10/08/91  │
│ _  WESTERN  CALC     WESTERN Spreadsheet for Chapter 5 10/08/91 │
│ _  ENHANCED REPORT   Enhanced Report                  09/16/91  │
│ _  MULTI    REPORT   Multipage Report                 10/07/91  │
│ _  TRANS    REPORT   Transposed Report                09/16/91  │
│                                                                 │
│                                                                 │
│                                                                 │
└─────────────────────────────────────────────────────────────────┘
```

After copying the WESTERN spreadsheet, you can open it and browse the cell values on each page of the spreadsheet.

To open the WESTERN spreadsheet, type the letter O in the selection field beside **WESTERN** and press ENTER to display the SALES page of the spreadsheet shown in Display 6.10.

Display 6.10
The WESTERN Spreadsheet

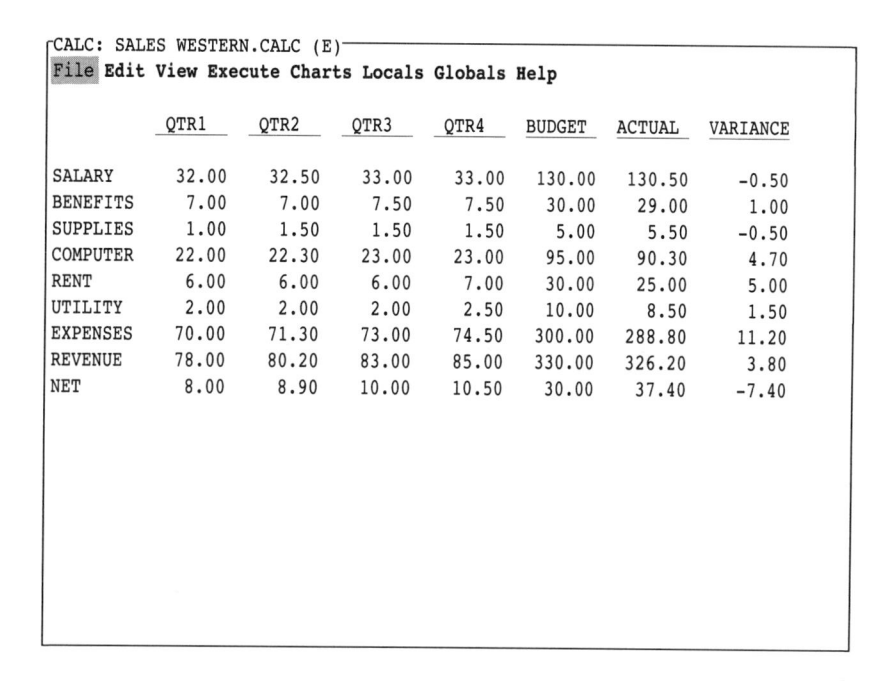

```
┌CALC: SALES WESTERN.CALC (E)─────────────────────────────────┐
│ File Edit View Execute Charts Locals Globals Help           │
│                                                             │
│          QTR1    QTR2    QTR3    QTR4   BUDGET  ACTUAL  VARIANCE │
│                                                             │
│ SALARY   32.00   32.50   33.00   33.00  130.00  130.50   -0.50 │
│ BENEFITS  7.00    7.00    7.50    7.50   30.00   29.00    1.00 │
│ SUPPLIES  1.00    1.50    1.50    1.50    5.00    5.50   -0.50 │
│ COMPUTER 22.00   22.30   23.00   23.00   95.00   90.30    4.70 │
│ RENT      6.00    6.00    6.00    7.00   30.00   25.00    5.00 │
│ UTILITY   2.00    2.00    2.00    2.50   10.00    8.50    1.50 │
│ EXPENSES 70.00   71.30   73.00   74.50  300.00  288.80   11.20 │
│ REVENUE  78.00   80.20   83.00   85.00  330.00  326.20    3.80 │
│ NET       8.00    8.90   10.00   10.50   30.00   37.40   -7.40 │
│                                                             │
│                                                             │
│                                                             │
└─────────────────────────────────────────────────────────────┘
```

If you want to view the SERVICE and SUMMARY pages:

1. Select **View** from the action bar and **Go to...** from the View pull-down menu.
2. Type the page name, SERVICE or SUMMARY, in the **Go to** field and select **OK**.

When you are finished viewing the WESTERN spreadsheet, select **File** from the action bar and **End** from the File pull-down menu to close and save the WESTERN spreadsheet.

You are now ready to create the COMPANY spreadsheet.

Lesson 6.2: Creating a New Spreadsheet

To create a new spreadsheet:

1. Select **File** from the action bar at the top of the DIRECTORY window and **New...** from the File pull-down menu.
2. In the New... dialog box, type the name of the spreadsheet, COMPANY, in the **Entry name** field.
3. Accept the default type of **CALC** in the **Type** field.

4. Select **Additional options** to define initial parameters for your spreadsheet.

5. Set the initial number of rows to 9.

6. Set the initial number of columns to 7.

7. Select **OK** to redisplay the New... dialog box.

8. Select **OK** to display the COMPANY spreadsheet with default row and column names.

Note: If your display is not wide enough to display all the columns, you can scroll to the right to see all the columns by pressing the function key assigned to the RIGHT command.

The first thing you need to do to the COMPANY spreadsheet is change the column widths.

Lesson 6.3: Changing Column Widths

To change the column widths:

1. Mark the column name **QTR1** by pressing the MARK BLOCK function key.

2. Mark the column name **ACTUAL** by pressing the MARK BLOCK function key.

3. Select **Edit** from the action bar and **Change...** from the Edit pull-down menu. Notice the **Target** field contains the range **QTR1:ACTUAL**.

4. Notice that no other fields contain values. Make sure the **Width** field is selected, and change the width to 7.

5. Select **OK** to redisplay the spreadsheet shown in Display 6.11. Notice the note indicating that six columns have been changed.

Display 6.11
New Column Width

```
┌CALC: PAGE1 COMPANY.CALC (E)─────────────────────────────────┐
│File Edit View Execute Charts Locals Globals Help            │
│NOTE: 6 column(s) have been changed.                         │
│          QTR1    QTR2    QTR3    QTR4   BUDGET  ACTUAL  VARIANCE │
│                                                             │
│SALARY                                                       │
│BENEFITS                                                     │
│SUPPLIES                                                     │
│COMPUTER                                                     │
│RENT                                                         │
│UTILITY                                                      │
│EXPENSES                                                     │
│REVENUE                                                      │
│NET                                                          │
│                                                             │
│                                                             │
│                                                             │
│                                                             │
│                                                             │
└─────────────────────────────────────────────────────────────┘
```

Now you need to define the row and column names for the COMPANY spreadsheet.

Lesson 6.4: Changing the Default Row and Column Names

Change the column names COL1 through COL7 to QTR1, QTR2, QTR3, QTR4, BUDGET, ACTUAL, and VARIANCE, respectively.

To define the column names:

1. Move the cursor to each column name.

2. Type the new name over the existing name. Be sure to delete the default column name completely.

3. Press ENTER.

Note: The column names are centered and translated to uppercase.

Change the row names ROW1 through ROW9 to SALARY, BENEFITS, SUPPLIES, COMPUTER, RENT, UTILITY, EXPENSES, REVENUE, and NET, respectively.

To define the row names:

1. Move the cursor to each row name.

2. Type the new name over the existing name. Be sure to delete the default row name completely.

3. Press ENTER.

Note: The row names are left aligned and translated to uppercase.

Now that you have a COMPANY spreadsheet, you are ready to link the EASTERN and WESTERN spreadsheets to the COMPANY spreadsheet.

Your COMPANY spreadsheet currently contains no data values. You obtain the data values by summing values from the EASTERN and WESTERN spreadsheets through linking. By linking to the EASTERN and WESTERN spreadsheets, you can write formulas that reference values in those spreadsheets.

Lesson 6.5: Linking Spreadsheets

To add a link from the COMPANY spreadsheet to the EASTERN spreadsheet:

1. Select **Locals** from the action bar.

2. Select **Set link...** from the Locals pull-down menu, as shown in Display 6.12.

Display 6.12
Selecting Set Link...

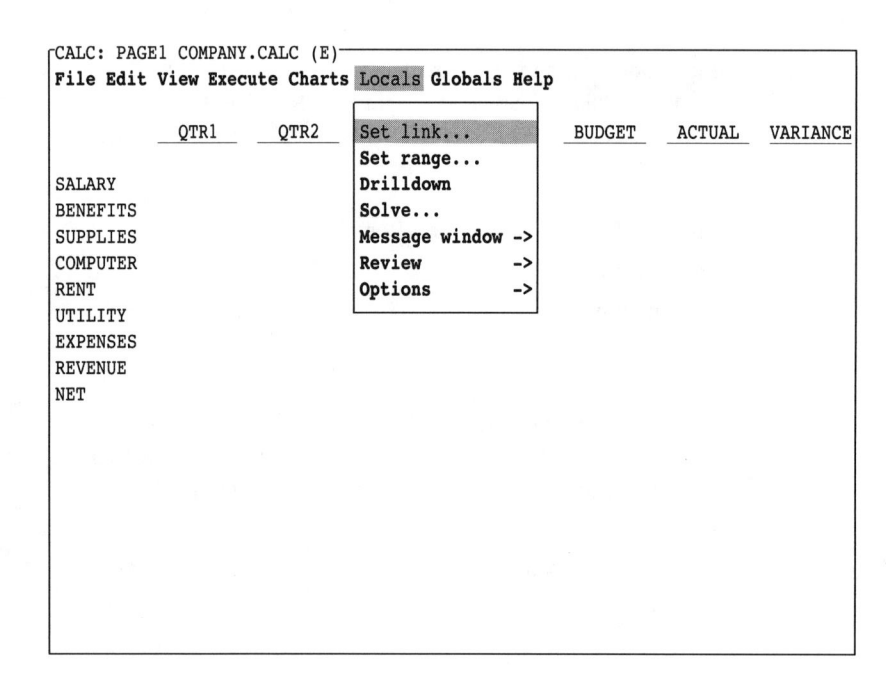

```
┌CALC: PAGE1 COMPANY.CALC (E)─────────────────────────────────────┐
│File Edit View Execute Charts Locals Globals Help                │
│                                                                 │
│              QTR1      QTR2    ┌─Set link...──┐ BUDGET  ACTUAL  VARIANCE
│                                │ Set range... │
│  SALARY                        │ Drilldown    │
│  BENEFITS                      │ Solve...     │
│  SUPPLIES                      │ Message window -> │
│  COMPUTER                      │ Review       -> │
│  RENT                          │ Options      -> │
│  UTILITY                       └──────────────┘
│  EXPENSES
│  REVENUE
│  NET
│
│
│
│
│
│
└─────────────────────────────────────────────────────────────────┘
```

After selecting **Set link...** the Define a New Link dialog box opens, as shown in Display 6.13, enabling you to name your link.

Display 6.13
Define a New Link Dialog Box with ELINK

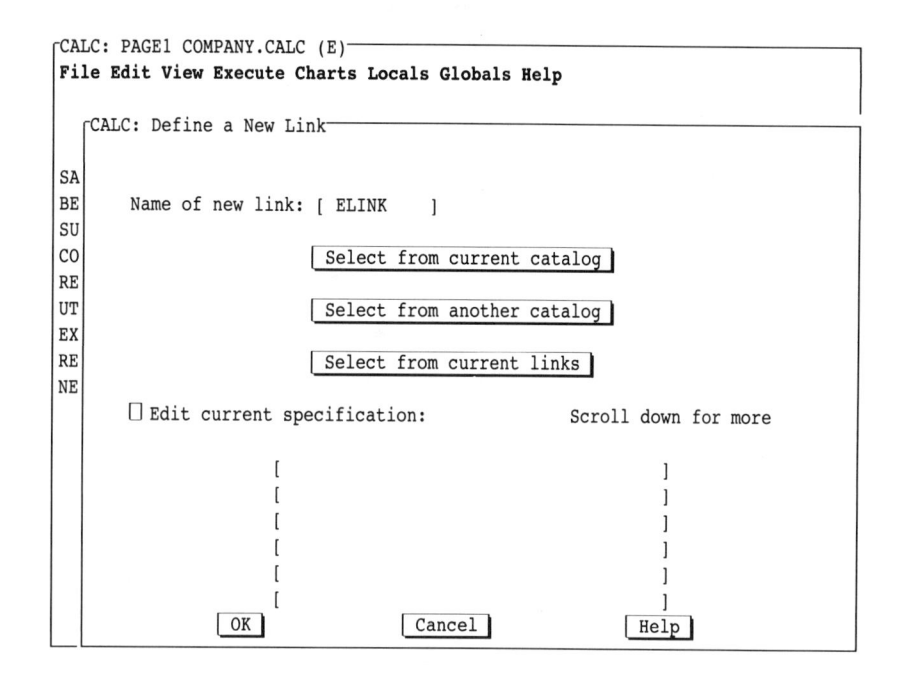

```
┌CALC: PAGE1 COMPANY.CALC (E)─────────────────────────────┐
│File Edit View Execute Charts Locals Globals Help        │
│  ┌CALC: Define a New Link──────────────────────────────┐ │
│SA│                                                     │ │
│BE│    Name of new link: [ ELINK    ]                   │ │
│SU│                                                     │ │
│CO│              ┌Select from current catalog┐          │ │
│RE│              └───────────────────────────┘          │ │
│UT│              ┌Select from another catalog┐          │ │
│EX│              └───────────────────────────┘          │ │
│RE│              ┌ Select from current links ┐          │ │
│NE│              └───────────────────────────┘          │ │
│  │  □ Edit current specification:    Scroll down for more│ │
│  │                  [              ]      [          ]  │ │
│  │                  [              ]      [          ]  │ │
│  │                  [              ]      [          ]  │ │
│  │                  [              ]      [          ]  │ │
│  │                  [              ]      [          ]  │ │
│  │         ┌──┐           ┌──────┐         ┌────┐       │ │
│  │         │OK│           │Cancel│         │Help│       │ │
│  │         └──┘           └──────┘         └────┘       │ │
│  └─────────────────────────────────────────────────────┘ │
└─────────────────────────────────────────────────────────┘
```

3. Move the cursor to the **Name of new link** field and type the name of your link. A link name must be a valid SAS name and acts as a reference for the linked spreadsheet. In this case, you might select a name that starts with the letter E, such as ELINK, to remind you that the name references the EASTERN spreadsheet.

4. Type `ELINK` and press ENTER. After pressing ENTER, you need to define which spreadsheet ELINK references.

144 *Linking Spreadsheets* □ *Chapter 6*

5. Because the EASTERN spreadsheet is in the current catalog, select the **Select from current catalog** button to display the Catalog Directory window.

6. Select **EASTERN** as shown in Display 6.14.

Display 6.14
Selecting EASTERN from the Catalog Directory Window

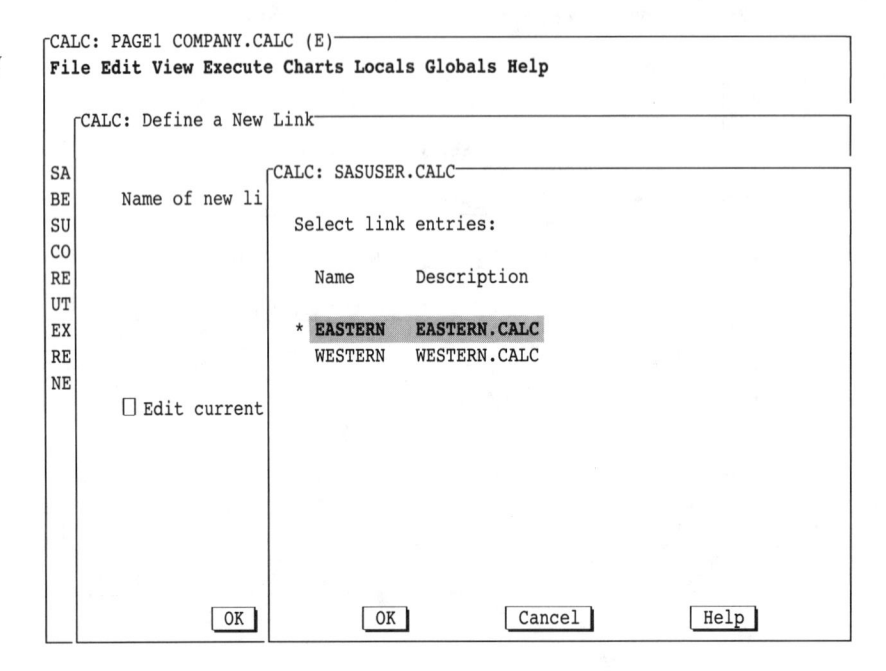

```
┌CALC: PAGE1 COMPANY.CALC (E)─────────────────────────────────────┐
│File Edit View Execute Charts Locals Globals Help                │
│  ┌CALC: Define a New Link──────────────────────────────────────┐│
│SA│                                                             ││
│BE│                    ┌CALC: SASUSER.CALC──────────────────┐   ││
│SU│  Name of new li    │                                    │   ││
│CO│                    │  Select link entries:              │   ││
│RE│                    │                                    │   ││
│UT│                    │     Name       Description         │   ││
│EX│                    │                                    │   ││
│RE│                    │  *  EASTERN    EASTERN.CALC        │   ││
│NE│                    │     WESTERN    WESTERN.CALC        │   ││
│  │                    │                                    │   ││
│  │  ☐ Edit current    │                                    │   ││
│  │                    │                                    │   ││
│  │                    │                                    │   ││
│  │                    │                                    │   ││
│  │                                                             ││
│  │             [ OK ]   [ OK ]   [ Cancel ]   [ Help ]         ││
│  └─────────────────────────────────────────────────────────────┘│
└─────────────────────────────────────────────────────────────────┘
```

7. Select **OK** to redisplay the Define a New Link dialog box shown in Display 6.15.

Display 6.15
Define a New Link Dialog Box

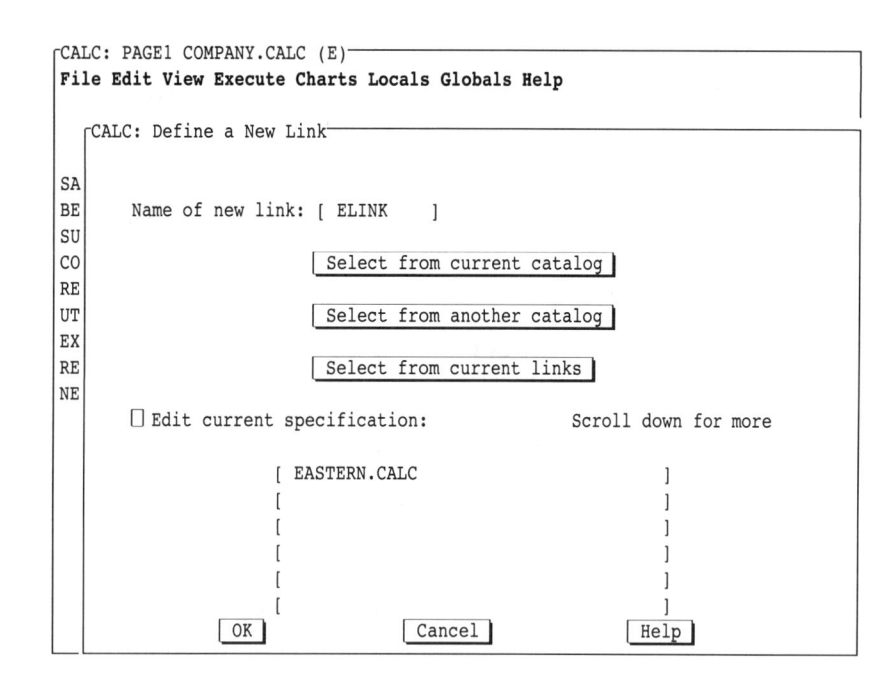

```
┌CALC: PAGE1 COMPANY.CALC (E)──────────────────────────────┐
│File Edit View Execute Charts Locals Globals Help         │
│  ┌CALC: Define a New Link─────────────────────────────┐  │
│SA│                                                    │  │
│BE│   Name of new link: [ ELINK    ]                   │  │
│SU│                                                    │  │
│CO│              [ Select from current catalog ]       │  │
│RE│                                                    │  │
│UT│              [ Select from another catalog ]       │  │
│EX│                                                    │  │
│RE│              [ Select from current links ]         │  │
│NE│                                                    │  │
│  │  □ Edit current specification:   Scroll down for more│  │
│  │                                                    │  │
│  │              [ EASTERN.CALC              ]         │  │
│  │              [                           ]         │  │
│  │              [                           ]         │  │
│  │              [                           ]         │  │
│  │              [                           ]         │  │
│  │        [ OK ]        [ Cancel ]      [ Help ]      │  │
│  └────────────────────────────────────────────────────┘  │
└──────────────────────────────────────────────────────────┘
```

8. Select **OK** to redisplay the COMPANY spreadsheet shown in Display 6.16. A note is displayed confirming the link ELINK has been assigned.

Display 6.16
ELINK Has Been Assigned

```
┌CALC: PAGE1 COMPANY.CALC (E)──────────────────────────────┐
│File Edit View Execute Charts Locals Globals Help         │
│NOTE: Link ELINK has been assigned.                       │
│         QTR1      QTR2      QTR3      QTR4    BUDGET   ACTUAL   VARIANCE
│
│SALARY
│BENEFITS
│SUPPLIES
│COMPUTER
│RENT
│UTILITY
│EXPENSES
│REVENUE
│NET
│
│
│
└──────────────────────────────────────────────────────────┘
```

Now that you have defined a link for the EASTERN and COMPANY spreadsheets, you can define a link for the WESTERN and COMPANY spreadsheets by following the same steps:

1. Select **Locals** from the action bar and **Set link...** from the Locals pull-down menu. Selecting **Set link...** displays the Define a New Link dialog box.

2. Type the name of your link, `WLINK`, in the **Name of new link** field and press ENTER.

3. Since the WESTERN spreadsheet is in the current catalog, select the **Select from current catalog** button to display the Catalog Directory window.

4. Select **WESTERN** and then select **OK** to redisplay the Define a New Link dialog box.

5. Select **OK** to redisplay the COMPANY spreadsheet. A note is displayed confirming the link WLINK has been assigned.

Note: Because SAS/CALC software saves the link information with the COMPANY spreadsheet, the links are available across sessions.

Consult *SAS/CALC Software: Usage and Reference, Version 6, First Edition* for more information on defining links.

Now that you have linked the COMPANY, EASTERN, and WESTERN spreadsheets, formulas in the COMPANY spreadsheet can access values in the EASTERN and WESTERN spreadsheets.

Lesson 6.5: Defining a Formula

Remember that you want to determine the total amount of money that was spent for salaries in the first quarter. To obtain the total, you add the cell value in SUMMARY.SALARY.QTR1 from the EASTERN spreadsheet to the cell value in SUMMARY.SALARY.QTR1 from the WESTERN spreadsheet.

To create a formula to compute the total salaries for the eastern and western regions:

1. Select **Execute** from the action bar and **Enter formula** from the Execute pull-down menu.

2. Select the SALARY.QTR1 cell in the COMPANY spreadsheet.

3. Type the formula, as shown in Display 6.17, in the formula entry area.

Display 6.17
Formula for SALARY.QTR1

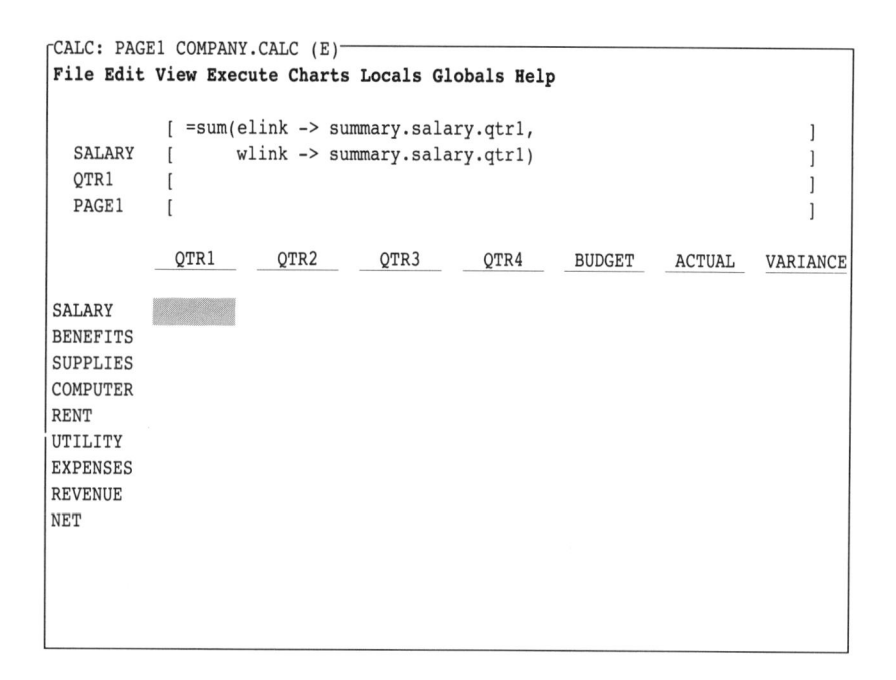

```
┌CALC: PAGE1 COMPANY.CALC (E)─────────────────────────────┐
│File Edit View Execute Charts Locals Globals Help        │
│                                                         │
│          [ =sum(elink -> summary.salary.qtr1,        ]  │
│  SALARY  [      wlink -> summary.salary.qtr1)        ]  │
│  QTR1    [                                           ]  │
│  PAGE1   [                                           ]  │
│                                                         │
│          QTR1    QTR2    QTR3    QTR4   BUDGET  ACTUAL  VARIANCE │
│                                                         │
│  SALARY  ▓▓▓▓▓                                          │
│  BENEFITS                                               │
│  SUPPLIES                                               │
│  COMPUTER                                               │
│  RENT                                                   │
│  UTILITY                                                │
│  EXPENSES                                               │
│  REVENUE                                                │
│  NET                                                    │
│                                                         │
└─────────────────────────────────────────────────────────┘
```

▶ *Caution* .... *Pressing ENTER in the Formula Entry Area*
Pressing ENTER while the formula entry area is open automatically executes the formula. If you press ENTER before you have finished typing the formula, you are executing an incomplete formula. ▲

Remember to type an equals sign (=) in front of the expression. The syntax for the formula is the link name followed by -> followed by the item from the linked spreadsheet. In this case, you want to add the value of the SUMMARY.SALARY.QTR1 cell of the EASTERN spreadsheet to the value of the SUMMARY.SALARY.QTR1 cell of the WESTERN spreadsheet. Thus, the cell names in the formula are preceded by the appropriate link name (ELINK for EASTERN and WLINK for WESTERN) and the special character ->.

This expression has a specific purpose, as Figure 6.1 illustrates.

Figure 6.1 *Purpose of the Expression*

Expression:	Instructs SAS/CALC Software to:
=sum(elink -> summary.salary.qtr1, wlink -> summary.salary.qtr1)	1. resolve the link names ELINK and WLINK to the actual spreadsheet names EASTERN and WESTERN, respectively. 2. locate each of the spreadsheets 3. locate the summary page of the two spreadsheets and return the values to the current spreadsheet 4. sum the values and store the results in the corresponding cells in the COMPANY spreadsheet.

Once you press ENTER, the computed value is displayed in the highlighted cell as shown in Display 6.18.

Display 6.18
Result of the Formula

```
┌CALC: PAGE1 COMPANY.CALC (E)─────────────────────────────────────┐
│File Edit View Execute Charts Locals Globals Help                │
│                                                                 │
│            [ =SUM(ELINK -> SUMMARY.SALARY.QTR1,              ]  │
│   SALARY   [     WLINK -> SUMMARY.SALARY.QTR1)               ]  │
│   QTR1     [                                                 ]  │
│   PAGE1    [                                                 ]  │
│                                                                 │
│             QTR1    QTR2    QTR3    QTR4   BUDGET  ACTUAL  VARIANCE │
│                                                                 │
│   SALARY     128                                                │
│   BENEFITS                                                      │
│   SUPPLIES                                                      │
│   COMPUTER                                                      │
│   RENT                                                          │
│   UTILITY                                                       │
│   EXPENSES                                                      │
│   REVENUE                                                       │
│   NET                                                           │
│                                                                 │
└─────────────────────────────────────────────────────────────────┘
```

4. Select **Execute** from the action bar and **End formula entry** from the Execute pull-down menu to close the formula entry area.

Now that you have computed the value for SALARY.QTR1, you need to compute the total values for all other cells in the COMPANY spreadsheet. Because you are totaling cell values across the EASTERN and WESTERN spreadsheets by adding the information in cells in the EASTERN spreadsheet to information in the corresponding cells in the WESTERN spreadsheet, the same basic formula is used for all cells. Therefore, you can copy the formula in SALARY.QTR1 to all other cells in the COMPANY spreadsheet.

Lesson 6.6: Copying Formulas

To copy the cells including the formula:

1. Mark the SALARY.QTR1 cell as the source cell.

2. Select **Edit** from the action bar and **Copy marked areas** from the Edit pull-down menu.

3. Mark the cells SALARY.QTR1 through NET.VARIANCE as the target cells.

4. Select **Edit** from the action bar and **Paste** from the Edit pull-down menu.

You now have a COMPANY spreadsheet, shown in Display 6.19, containing yearly totals for the eastern and western regions of a company.

Note: Consult Chapter 7, ''Using Programs with SAS/CALC Software,'' in this book for information on defining and using programs in SAS/CALC spreadsheets.

Display 6.19
The COMPANY Spreadsheet with Computed Values

```
CALC: PAGE1 COMPANY.CALC (E)
File Edit View Execute Charts Locals Globals Help

             QTR1     QTR2     QTR3     QTR4    BUDGET   ACTUAL   VARIANCE

SALARY        128    133.5      137      139      535    537.5      -2.5
BENEFITS     26.4     27.4     28.8     30.2      113    112.8       0.2
SUPPLIES      6.5      7.5      8.4      9.2       29     31.6      -2.6
COMPUTER       85     86.8     88.2     88.7      356    348.7       7.3
RENT           19       19       19     22.6     82.8     79.6       3.2
UTILITY         6      6.5      6.5        8       30       27         3
EXPENSES    270.9    280.7    287.9    297.7   1145.8   1137.2       8.6
REVENUE       298    308.7      305      308     1250   1219.7      30.3
NET          27.1       28     17.1     10.3    104.2     82.5      21.7
```

The COMPANY spreadsheet is almost complete except that the cell values are not formatted with two decimal places as they are in the EASTERN and WESTERN spreadsheets.

Remember, to define a format for the COMPANY spreadsheet cells:

1. Mark the cells SALARY.QTR1 through NET.VARIANCE indicating that all cells in the spreadsheet will be affected by the format change.

2. Select **Edit** from the action bar and **Change...** from the **Edit** pull-down menu.

3. In the Change dialog box, type 7.2 in the **Format** field. Remember to delete the default format, `BEST.`, completely.

4. Select **OK** to display the spreadsheet shown in Display 6.20.

Display 6.20
Enhanced COMPANY Spreadsheet

```
┌CALC: PAGE1 COMPANY.CALC (E)─────────────────────────────────────┐
│ File Edit View Execute Charts Locals Globals Help               │
│ NOTE: 63 cell(s) have been changed.                             │
│            QTR1     QTR2     QTR3     QTR4    BUDGET   ACTUAL   VARIANCE
│
│ SALARY    128.00   133.50   137.00   139.00   535.00   537.50    -2.50
│ BENEFITS   26.40    27.40    28.80    30.20   113.00   112.80     0.20
│ SUPPLIES    6.50     7.50     8.40     9.20    29.00    31.60    -2.60
│ COMPUTER   85.00    86.80    88.20    88.70   356.00   348.70     7.30
│ RENT       19.00    19.00    19.00    22.60    82.80    79.60     3.20
│ UTILITY     6.00     6.50     6.50     8.00    30.00    27.00     3.00
│ EXPENSES  270.90   280.70   287.90   297.70  1145.80  1137.20     8.60
│ REVENUE   298.00   308.70   305.00   308.00  1250.00  1219.70    30.30
│ NET        27.10    28.00    17.10    10.30   104.20    82.50    21.70
│
│
│
│
│
│
└─────────────────────────────────────────────────────────────────┘
```

You are finished defining the links from the COMPANY spreadsheet to the eastern and western spreadsheets. Linking is an efficient way of managing multiple spreadsheets. Users at the eastern and western regions have access to their respective spreadsheets while users at the headquarters have access to all three spreadsheets. As a matter of fact, whenever a cell is changed in the EASTERN or WESTERN spreadsheets that change is automatically reflected in the COMPANY spreadsheet.

To monitor and manipulate the links to your spreadsheets, you use the drilldown facility in SAS/CALC software.

The drilldown facility enables you to verify the links to the COMPANY spreadsheet and the data contributing to the COMPANY spreadsheet.

▶ *Caution* .... ***Graphics Device***

If you do not have a graphics device, your drilldown displays may look different from the ones in this chapter. Although your displays appear different, you use the drilldown facility as described below. Before using the drilldown facility you may want to contact the SAS Software Consultant at your site to verify your graphics device. ▲

Lesson 6.7: Using the Drilldown Facility

To use the drilldown facility:

1. Select **Locals** from the action bar.

2. Select **Drilldown** from the Locals pull-down menu, as shown in Display 6.21.

Display 6.21
Selecting Drilldown

```
┌CALC: PAGE1 COMPANY.CALC (E)─────────────────────────────────┐
│File Edit View Execute Charts Locals Globals Help            │
│                                                             │
│              QTR1    QTR2   ┌─Set link...─┐ DGET   ACTUAL   VARIANCE
│                             │ Set range...│
│   SALARY   128.00  133.50   │ Drilldown   │  35.00  537.50   -2.50
│   BENEFITS  26.40   27.40   │ Solve...    │  13.00  112.80    0.20
│   SUPPLIES   6.50    7.50   │ Message window ->│ 29.00  31.60  -2.60
│   COMPUTER  85.00   86.80   │ Review         ->│ 56.00 348.70   7.30
│   RENT      19.00   19.00   │ Options        ->│ 82.80  79.60   3.20
│   UTILITY    6.00    6.50   └─────────────┘  30.00   27.00    3.00
│   EXPENSES 270.90  280.70   287.90  297.70  1145.80 1137.20   8.60
│   REVENUE  298.00  308.70   305.00  308.00  1250.00 1219.70  30.30
│   NET       27.10   28.00    17.10   10.30   104.20   82.50  21.70
│                                                             │
└─────────────────────────────────────────────────────────────┘
```

Selecting **Drilldown** displays the Drilldown window shown in Display 6.22. This graphic representation illustrates the links defined in the COMPANY spreadsheet.

Display 6.22
Drilldown Window

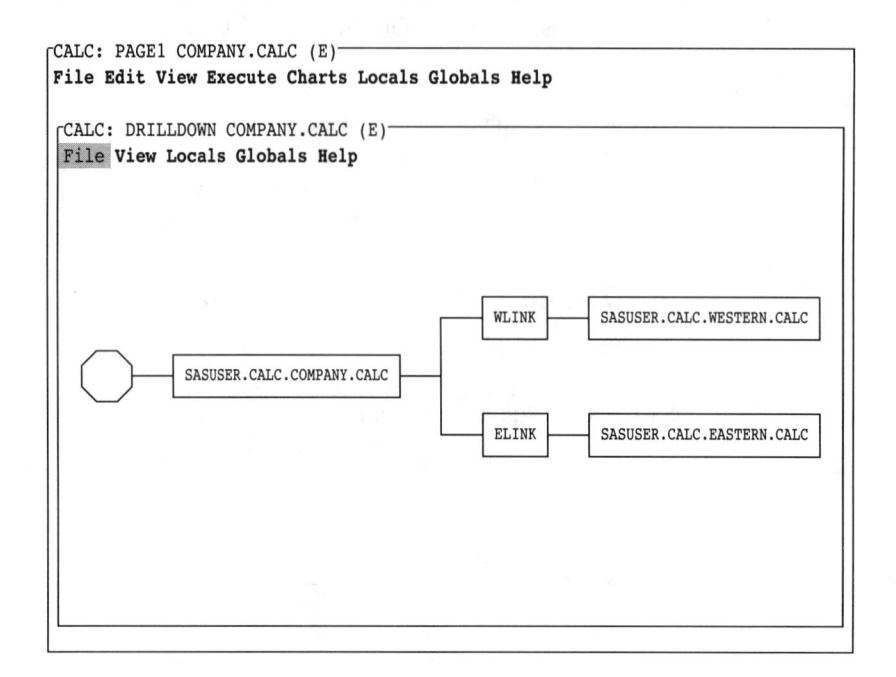

```
┌CALC: PAGE1 COMPANY.CALC (E)─────────────────────────────────────┐
│ File Edit View Execute Charts Locals Globals Help               │
│ ┌CALC: DRILLDOWN COMPANY.CALC (E)──────────────────────────────┐│
│ │ File View Locals Globals Help                                ││
│ │                                                              ││
│ │                                                              ││
│ │                                       ┌───────┐  ┌─────────────────────────┐
│ │                                       │ WLINK ├──┤ SASUSER.CALC.WESTERN.CALC │
│ │                                       └───────┘  └─────────────────────────┘
│ │            ╱╲      ┌──────────────────────────┐  │
│ │           ╱  ╲─────┤ SASUSER.CALC.COMPANY.CALC├──┤
│ │           ╲  ╱     └──────────────────────────┘  │
│ │            ╲╱                                    │
│ │                                       ┌───────┐  ┌─────────────────────────┐
│ │                                       │ ELINK ├──┤ SASUSER.CALC.EASTERN.CALC │
│ │                                       └───────┘  └─────────────────────────┘
│ │                                                              ││
│ └──────────────────────────────────────────────────────────────┘│
└─────────────────────────────────────────────────────────────────┘
```

Verifying that links do exist is an important aspect of the drilldown facility. Another important feature is the ability to activate and deactivate links. For example, suppose you want to see what effect eliminating the EASTERN spreadsheet has on the COMPANY spreadsheet.

Lesson 6.8: Deactivating a Link

1. Select **ELINK**, as shown in Display 6.23, to display the Drilldown Actions dialog box.

Display 6.23
Selecting ELINK

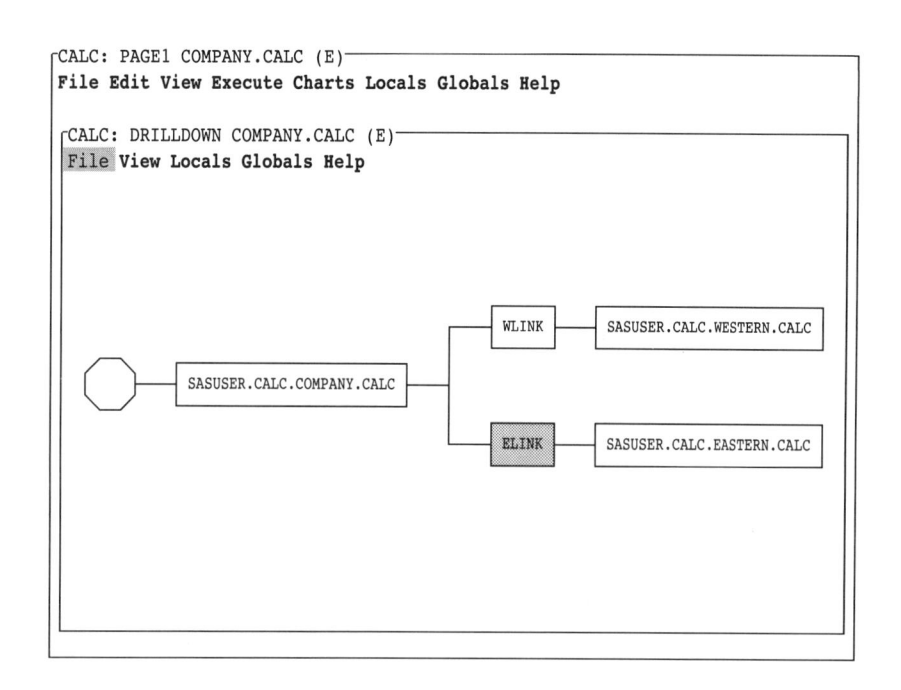

```
┌CALC: PAGE1 COMPANY.CALC (E)─────────────────────────────────┐
│File Edit View Execute Charts Locals Globals Help            │
│                                                             │
│┌CALC: DRILLDOWN COMPANY.CALC (E)────────────────────────────┐│
││File View Locals Globals Help                               ││
││                                                            ││
││                                      ┌─WLINK─┐  ┌─SASUSER.CALC.WESTERN.CALC─┐
││                                      └───────┘  └───────────────────────────┘
││       ┌─SASUSER.CALC.COMPANY.CALC─┐                        ││
││       └───────────────────────────┘                        ││
││                                      ┌─ELINK─┐  ┌─SASUSER.CALC.EASTERN.CALC─┐
││                                      └───────┘  └───────────────────────────┘
│└────────────────────────────────────────────────────────────┘│
└─────────────────────────────────────────────────────────────┘
```

2. Select **Deactivate**, as shown in Display 6.24 to display the Select Data dialog box.

Display 6.24
Selecting Deactivate

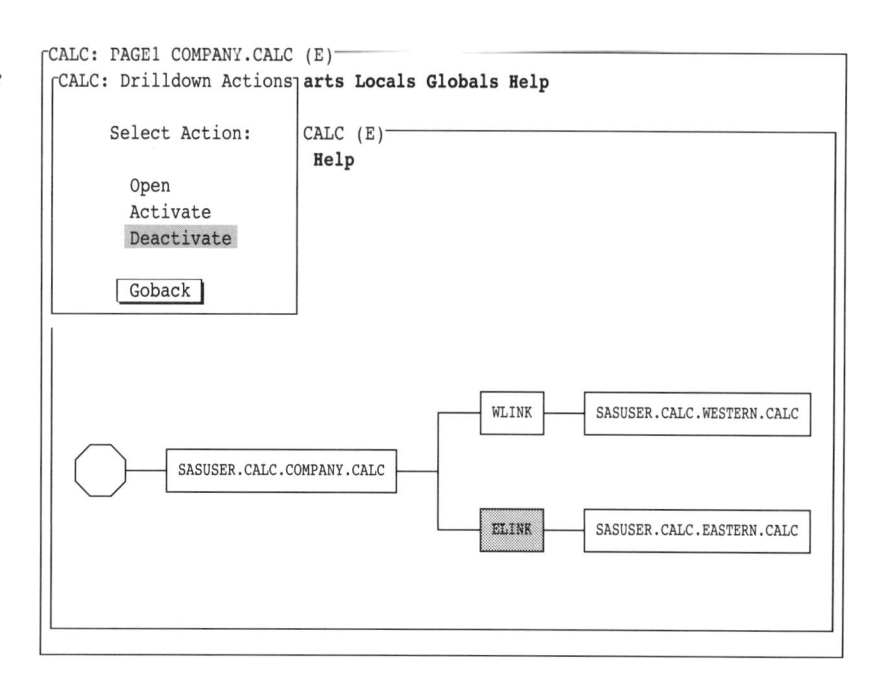

```
┌CALC: PAGE1 COMPANY.CALC (E)─────────────────────────────────┐
│┌CALC: Drilldown Actions─┐arts Locals Globals Help           │
││                        │                                   │
││  Select Action:        │ CALC (E)────────────────────────┐ │
││                        │ Help                            │ │
││    Open                │                                 │ │
││    Activate            │                                 │ │
││    Deactivate          │                                 │ │
││                        │                                 │ │
││   ┌Goback┐             │                                 │ │
│└────────────────────────┘                                 │ │
│                                                           │ │
│                                      ┌─WLINK─┐  ┌─SASUSER.CALC.WESTERN.CALC─┐
│       ┌─SASUSER.CALC.COMPANY.CALC─┐                         │
│                                      ┌─ELINK─┐  ┌─SASUSER.CALC.EASTERN.CALC─┐
└─────────────────────────────────────────────────────────────┘
```

3. Select **SASUSER.CALC.EASTERN.CALC** in the Select Data dialog box to deactivate the EASTERN spreadsheet.

154 *Linking Spreadsheets* □ *Chapter 6*

    4. Select **OK** to close the Select Data dialog box and redisplay the drilldown graphic.

    5. Select the spreadsheet name, **SASUSER.CALC.COMPANY.CALC**, to display the Drilldown Actions dialog box.

    6. Select **Open**, as shown in Display 6.26, to display the COMPANY spreadsheet, shown in Display 6.27.

Display 6.25
Selecting Open

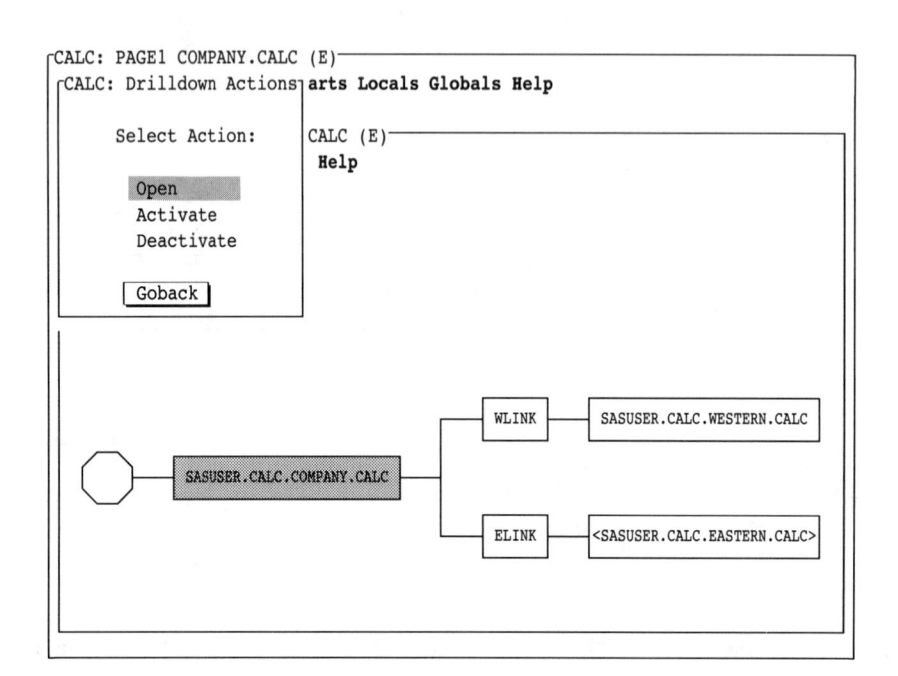

```
┌CALC: PAGE1 COMPANY.CALC (E)─────────────────────────────────┐
│ ┌CALC: Drilldown Actions┐arts Locals Globals Help          │
│ │                       │ ┌CALC (E)────────────────────┐   │
│ │   Select Action:      │ │  Help                      │   │
│ │                       │ │                            │   │
│ │   ▓Open▓              │ │                            │   │
│ │    Activate           │ │                            │   │
│ │    Deactivate         │ │                            │   │
│ │                       │ │                            │   │
│ │   [Goback]            │ │                            │   │
│ └───────────────────────┘ │                            │   │
│                                                            │
│                                        ┌──────┐  ┌────────────────────────┐
│                                        │WLINK │──│SASUSER.CALC.WESTERN.CALC│
│                                        └──────┘  └────────────────────────┘
│     ○──────▓SASUSER.CALC.COMPANY.CALC▓                      │
│                                        ┌──────┐  ┌────────────────────────┐
│                                        │ELINK │──│<SASUSER.CALC.EASTERN.CALC>│
│                                        └──────┘  └────────────────────────┘
└────────────────────────────────────────────────────────────┘
```

Display 6.26
The COMPANY Spreadsheet without EASTERN Cell Values

```
┌CALC: PAGE1 COMPANY.CALC (E)─────────────────────────────────────────────┐
│ File Edit View Execute Charts Locals Globals Help                      │
│                                                                         │
│              QTR1      QTR2      QTR3      QTR4    BUDGET   ACTUAL   VARIANCE │
│ SALARY      66.00     66.50     67.50     67.50    270.00   267.50     2.50 │
│ BENEFITS    14.00     14.00     14.50     15.50     60.00    58.00     2.00 │
│ SUPPLIES     3.00      4.00      3.90      4.50     15.00    15.40    -0.40 │
│ COMPUTER    45.00     45.30     46.00     46.00    185.00   182.30     2.70 │
│ RENT        11.00     11.00     11.00     13.00     50.00    46.00     4.00 │
│ UTILITY      4.00      4.00      4.00      4.50     20.00    16.50     3.50 │
│ EXPENSES   143.00    144.80    146.90    151.00    600.00   585.70    14.30 │
│ REVENUE    153.00    163.20    158.00    163.00    645.00   637.20     7.80 │
│ NET         10.00     18.40     11.10     12.00     45.00    51.50    -6.50 │
│                                                                         │
└─────────────────────────────────────────────────────────────────────────┘
```

The COMPANY spreadsheet no longer includes data from the EASTERN spreadsheet. The displayed values are identical to the SUMMARY page in the WESTERN spreadsheet.

Lesson 6.9: Reactivating a Link

1. Once you are finished viewing the COMPANY spreadsheet, select **Locals** from the action bar and **Drilldown** from the Locals pull-down menu to redisplay the drilldown graphic.

2. Select **ELINK**.

3. Select **Activate** in the Drilldown Actions dialog box.

4. Select **SASUSER.CALC.EASTERN.CALC** in the Select Data dialog box.
   The EASTERN spreadsheet has been reactivated.

5. Select **File** from the action bar and **End** from the File pull-down menu to close the drilldown facility and redisplay the COMPANY spreadsheet.

You have now completed Chapter 6. You can end your SAS/CALC software session, or you can continue with Chapter 7.

If you want to end your spreadsheet and end the SAS/CALC software session, refer to Lessons 2.11 and 2.12 in Chapter 2, "Creating Your First Spreadsheet," for assistance.

Chapter Summary

This chapter introduces the concept of spreadsheet linking. Linking enables a current spreadsheet to reference the rows, columns, pages, and cells within other linked spreadsheets.

This chapter uses three spreadsheets: EASTERN, which contains data for the eastern region; WESTERN, which contains data for the western region; and COMPANY, which summarizes the EASTERN and WESTERN spreadsheets and computes overall company totals. To compute these company totals you create links from the COMPANY spreadsheet to the EASTERN and WESTERN spreadsheets.

To begin the chapter, you learn how to copy the three-dimensional WESTERN spreadsheet from an existing SAS System catalog, SASHELP.CALC. The WESTERN spreadsheet is identical to the EASTERN spreadsheet except it contains the sales, service, and summary data for the western region of the company.

After viewing the WESTERN spreadsheet, you create a new two-dimensional spreadsheet named COMPANY, which contains the same rows and columns as EASTERN and WESTERN. After defining the rows and columns for COMPANY, you learn how to define links to the EASTERN and WESTERN spreadsheets using the action bar and pull-down menus. You assign the link names ELINK and WLINK to the EASTERN and WESTERN spreadsheets, respectively.

These links enable you to compute totals across both the EASTERN and WESTERN spreadsheets and to assign the totals to corresponding cells in the COMPANY spreadsheet. To compute the totals, you define a formula that resolves your link names, locates the SUMMARY page within the EASTERN and WESTERN spreadsheets, returns the values to the COMPANY spreadsheet, sums the values and stores the results in the corresponding cells in the COMPANY spreadsheet.

When you finish defining the formula for COMPANY, you copy the formula to all cells in the COMPANY spreadsheet. As a result, you end this chapter with a COMPANY spreadsheet summarizing the eastern and western regions.

Before ending this chapter, you learn to use the drilldown facility to monitor and manipulate the links to your spreadsheet. The drilldown facility provides an interactive facility enabling you to verify the links and activate and deactivate the links.

After completing this chapter, you are ready to learn how to use programs with SAS/CALC software.

Chapter 7 Using Programs with SAS/CALC™ Software

Using Programs with SAS/CALC Software   157
   Lesson 7.1: Copying Spreadsheets   158
   Lesson 7.2: Opening and Viewing the EASTERN2 Spreadsheet   160
   Lesson 7.3: Defining a SAS/CALC Program for EASTERN2   163
   Lesson 7.4: Running a SAS/CALC Program   169
   Lesson 7.5: Running REGION.PGM for WESTERN2   175
   Lesson 7.6: Defining a SAS/CALC Program for COMPANY2   178
   Lesson 7.7: Running SUMMARY.PGM for COMPANY2   182
Chapter Summary   186
Conclusion   187

Using Programs with SAS/CALC Software

So far, you have learned to compute cell values by defining a formula for a specific cell and then copying the formula to other cells within a spreadsheet. An alternative to computing cell values with formulas is to use SAS/CALC programs.

A SAS/CALC program consists of one or more SAS/CALC language statements that are stored in a PGM entry in a SAS catalog such as SASUSER.CALC.REGION.CALC. These language statements can affect single spreadsheet cells or multiple cells across multiple pages. They also enable you not only to compute cell values, but also to validate, modify, and assign cell values.

In the previous tutorial chapters, you created the EASTERN spreadsheet using formulas, worked with the WESTERN spreadsheet containing formulas, and created the COMPANY spreadsheet using a formula. Each time you defined or copied a formula in those spreadsheets, the formula was stored in the corresponding cell. For example, the EASTERN spreadsheet alone has 115 cells containing formulas. Needless to say, these cell formulas can require a lot of storage space. Also, if you ever need to change the way a cell is computed in the EASTERN spreadsheet, you need to redefine the formula in, or copy the formula to, all corresponding cells. This redefining and recopying can be very time consuming.

In this chapter, you create and work with those same spreadsheets, but you use SAS/CALC programs rather than formulas for computing cell values. With programs, you define the programming statements one time. The statements are saved with the spreadsheet rather than each individual cell, and they execute everytime you modify a cell value. Also, if you need to change the way a cell value is computed, you alter and re-execute the program. There is no need to redefine or recopy individual formulas.

In Chapter 6, "Linking Spreadsheets," you copied the WESTERN spreadsheet from the SASHELP.CALC catalog to the SASUSER.CALC catalog. You probably noticed other spreadsheets, EASTERN2, WESTERN2, and COMPANY2, in the DIRECTORY window. Those spreadsheets are used in this chapter to illustrate SAS/CALC programs.

EASTERN2 and WESTERN2 are identical to the EASTERN and WESTERN spreadsheets except they do not contain values or formulas for the EXPENSES and NET rows, the ACTUAL and VARIANCE columns, and the SUMMARY page. COMPANY2 is identical to the COMPANY spreadsheet except it contains no cell values or formulas. To give COMPANY2 its values, you compute the totals across EASTERN2 and WESTERN2 using a SAS/CALC program.

158 *Using Programs with SAS/CALC Software □ Chapter 7*

Before you begin working with SAS/CALC programs, you need to copy EASTERN2, WESTERN2, and COMPANY2 from SASHELP.CALC to SASUSER.CALC.

Lesson 7.1: Copying Spreadsheets

To copy the EASTERN2, WESTERN2, and COMPANY2 spreadsheets:

1. From the DIRECTORY window, select **File** from the action bar and **Open** from the File pull-down menu.

2. Select **Copy an entry...** from the Open pull-down menu to display the Copy An Entry... dialog box.

3. Select **Copy from another library...** to display the Libnames window.

4. Select **SASHELP** from the list of librefs in the Libnames window.
   Selecting **SASHELP** closes the Libnames window and displays the Directory window for the SASHELP library.

5. Because the SASHELP catalog contains so many entries, press the function key assigned to the FORWARD command to scroll forward in the Directory window.

6. Select **SASHELP CALC CATALOG** to display the Catalog Directory window for SASHELP.CALC.

7. Select **COMPANY2 CALC**, **EASTERN2 CALC**, and **WESTERN2 CALC** from the Catalog Directory window, as shown in Display 7.1.

Display 7.1
Selecting the Spreadsheets

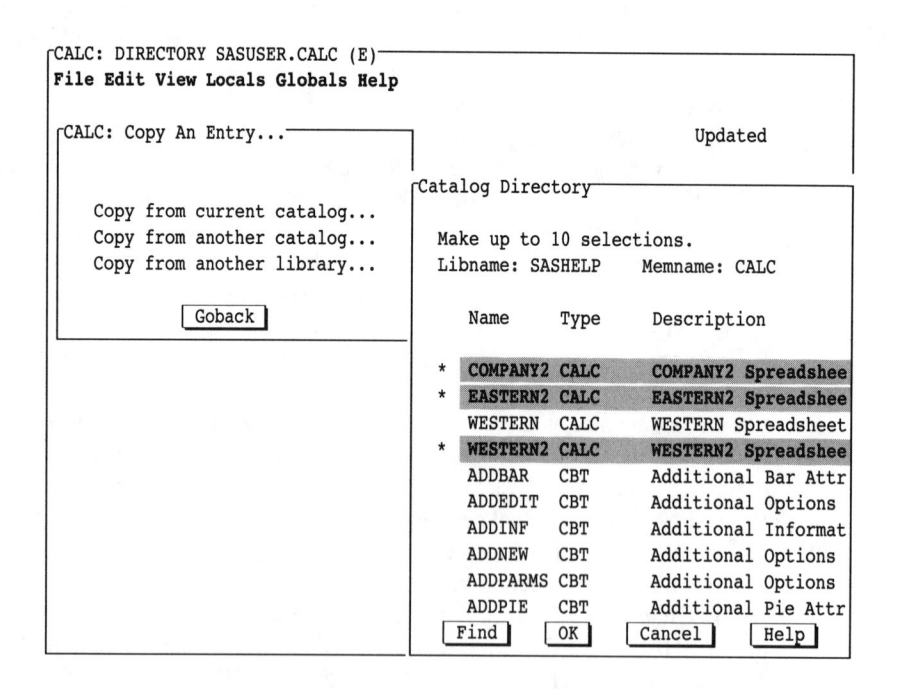

```
┌CALC: DIRECTORY SASUSER.CALC (E)─────────────────────────────────────┐
│ File Edit View Locals Globals Help                                  │
│┌CALC: Copy An Entry...─────┐                            Updated     │
││                           │                                        │
││                           │┌Catalog Directory─────────────────────┐│
││ Copy from current catalog.││                                      ││
││ Copy from another catalog.││ Make up to 10 selections.            ││
││ Copy from another library.││ Libname: SASHELP    Memname: CALC    ││
││                           ││                                      ││
││        [Goback]           ││   Name      Type    Description      ││
││                           ││                                      ││
││                           ││ * COMPANY2  CALC    COMPANY2 Spreadshee
││                           ││ * EASTERN2  CALC    EASTERN2 Spreadshee
││                           ││   WESTERN   CALC    WESTERN Spreadsheet
││                           ││ * WESTERN2  CALC    WESTERN2 Spreadshee
││                           ││   ADDBAR    CBT     Additional Bar Attr
││                           ││   ADDEDIT   CBT     Additional Options
││                           ││   ADDINF    CBT     Additional Informat
││                           ││   ADDNEW    CBT     Additional Options
││                           ││   ADDPARMS  CBT     Additional Options
││                           ││   ADDPIE    CBT     Additional Pie Attr
│└───────────────────────────┘│ [Find]  [OK]  [Cancel]  [Help]       ││
│                             └──────────────────────────────────────┘│
└─────────────────────────────────────────────────────────────────────┘
```

8. Select **OK** to close the Catalog Directory window and display the the Assign New Names dialog box, as shown in Display 7.2, which enables you to change the names of the three spreadsheets.

Display 7.2
Assign New Names Dialog Box

```
┌CALC: DIRECTORY SASUSER.CALC (E)─────────────────────────┐
│File Edit View Locals Globals Help                        │
│  ┌CALC: Assign New Names──────────────────────────────┐  │
│┌CAL                                                    │ │
│                                                        │ │
│   From:  SASHELP.CALC           To:   SASUSER.CALC     │ │
│                                                        │ │
│          Old Name              New Name     Replace Option │
│                                                        │ │
│          COMPANY2 . CALC       COMPANY2     ☐ Replace  │ │
│          EASTERN2 . CALC       EASTERN2     ☐ Replace  │ │
│          WESTERN2 . CALC       WESTERN2     ☐ Replace  │ │
│                                                        │ │
│                                                        │ │
│                                                        │ │
│                                                        │ │
│             ┌────┐         ┌──────┐        ┌────┐     │ │
│             │ OK │         │Cancel│        │Help│     │ │
│             └────┘         └──────┘        └────┘     │ │
│  └────────────────────────────────────────────────────┘  │
└──────────────────────────────────────────────────────────┘
```

9. Accept the spreadsheet names by selecting **OK** to confirm the spreadsheet names, copy the three spreadsheets, and return to the Copy An Entry... dialog box.

10. Select **Goback** to close the Copy An Entry... dialog box and redisplay the DIRECTORY window shown in Display 7.3.
    Notice the COMPANY2, EASTERN2, and WESTERN2 entries.

Display 7.3
DIRECTORY Window

```
┌CALC: DIRECTORY SASUSER.CALC (E)──────────────────────────┐
│File Edit View Locals Globals Help                         │
│                                                           │
│   Name      Type     Description                Updated   │
│                                                           │
│ _ COMPANY   CALC     COMPANY.CALC               10/08/91  │
│ _ COMPANY2  CALC     COMPANY2 Spreadsheet for Chapter 6  10/08/91  │
│ _ EASTERN   CALC     EASTERN.CALC               10/08/91  │
│ _ EASTERN2  CALC     EASTERN2 Spreadsheet for Chapter 6  10/08/91  │
│ _ WESTERN   CALC     WESTERN Spreadsheet for Chapter 5   10/08/91  │
│ _ WESTERN2  CALC     WESTERN2 Spreadsheet for Chapter 6  10/08/91  │
│ _ ENHANCED  REPORT   Enhanced Report            09/16/91  │
│ _ MULTI     REPORT   Multipage Report           10/07/91  │
│ _ TRANS     REPORT   Transposed Report          09/16/91  │
│                                                           │
└───────────────────────────────────────────────────────────┘
```

160 *Using Programs with SAS/CALC Software* □ *Chapter 7*

After copying the three spreadsheets, you are ready to define the SAS/CALC programs.

Lesson 7.2: Opening and Viewing the EASTERN2 Spreadsheet

Before you define a program for the EASTERN2 spreadsheet, you open the the spreadsheet.

To open the EASTERN2 spreadsheet, type the letter O beside EASTERN2 and press ENTER to display the SALES page of the EASTERN2 spreadsheet, as shown in Display 7.4.

Display 7.4
SALES Page of EASTERN2

```
┌CALC: SALES EASTERN2.CALC (E)────────────────────────────────┐
│ File Edit View Execute Charts Locals Globals Help           │
│                                                             │
│               QTR1    QTR2    QTR3    QTR4   BUDGET  ACTUAL   VARIANCE │
│                                                             │
│   SALARY     30.00   33.00   35.50   37.00   135.00         │
│   BENEFITS    6.00    7.00    7.70    8.00    27.50         │
│   SUPPLIES    0.50    0.50    1.00    1.00     3.00         │
│   COMPUTER   20.00   21.50   22.00   22.50    85.00         │
│   RENT        4.00    4.00    4.00    4.80    16.00         │
│   UTILITY     1.00    1.00    1.00    1.50     4.00         │
│   EXPENSES                                                  │
│   REVENUE    75.00   73.50   78.00   75.00   295.00         │
│   NET                                                       │
│                                                             │
│                                                             │
│                                                             │
└─────────────────────────────────────────────────────────────┘
```

The EASTERN2 spreadsheet contains three pages, SALES, SERVICE, and SUMMARY. However, SALES and SERVICE do not contain values for the EXPENSES and NET rows, and the ACTUAL and VARIANCE columns. The SUMMARY page contains no cell values.

To verify the missing cell values, go to the SERVICE and SUMMARY pages using the pull-down menus.

To go to each page:

1. Select **View** from the action bar and **Go to...** from the View pull-down menu.

2. Type the page name, SERVICE or SUMMARY, in the **Go to** field and select **OK**.

Display 7.5 shows the SERVICE page.

Display 7.5
SERVICE Page of EASTERN2

```
┌CALC: SERVICE EASTERN2.CALC (E)────────────────────────────────┐
│ File Edit View Execute Charts Locals Globals Help             │
│                                                                │
│              QTR1     QTR2     QTR3     QTR4    BUDGET   ACTUAL   VARIANCE │
│                                                                │
│   SALARY    32.00    34.00    34.00    34.50    130.00         │
│   BENEFITS   6.40     6.40     6.60     6.70     25.50         │
│   SUPPLIES   3.00     3.00     3.50     3.70     11.00         │
│   COMPUTER  20.00    20.00    20.20    20.20     86.00         │
│   RENT       4.00     4.00     4.00     4.80     16.80         │
│   UTILITY    1.00     1.50     1.50     2.00      6.00         │
│   EXPENSES                                                     │
│   REVENUE   70.00    72.00    69.00    70.00    310.00         │
│   NET                                                          │
│                                                                │
│                                                                │
│                                                                │
│                                                                │
└────────────────────────────────────────────────────────────────┘
```

Display 7.6 shows the SUMMARY page.

Display 7.6
SUMMARY Page of EASTERN2

```
┌CALC: SUMMARY EASTERN2.CALC (E)─────────────────────────────────┐
│ File Edit View Execute Charts Locals Globals Help              │
│                                                                │
│              QTR1    QTR2    QTR3    QTR4   BUDGET  ACTUAL  VARIANCE │
│     SALARY                                                     │
│     BENEFITS                                                   │
│     SUPPLIES                                                   │
│     COMPUTER                                                   │
│     RENT                                                       │
│     UTILITY                                                    │
│     EXPENSES                                                   │
│     REVENUE                                                    │
│     NET                                                        │
│                                                                │
│                                                                │
│                                                                │
│                                                                │
└────────────────────────────────────────────────────────────────┘
```

When you finish viewing the SERVICE and SUMMARY pages, go to the SALES page. You are ready to define a SAS/CALC program to compute the values of EXPENSES, NET, ACTUAL, VARIANCE, and the SUMMARY page.

Lesson 7.3: Defining a SAS/CALC Program for EASTERN2

To define a SAS/CALC program:

1. Select **File** from the action bar and **New...** from the File pull-down menu to display the New... dialog box shown in Display 7.7.

Display 7.7
Default New...
Dialog Box

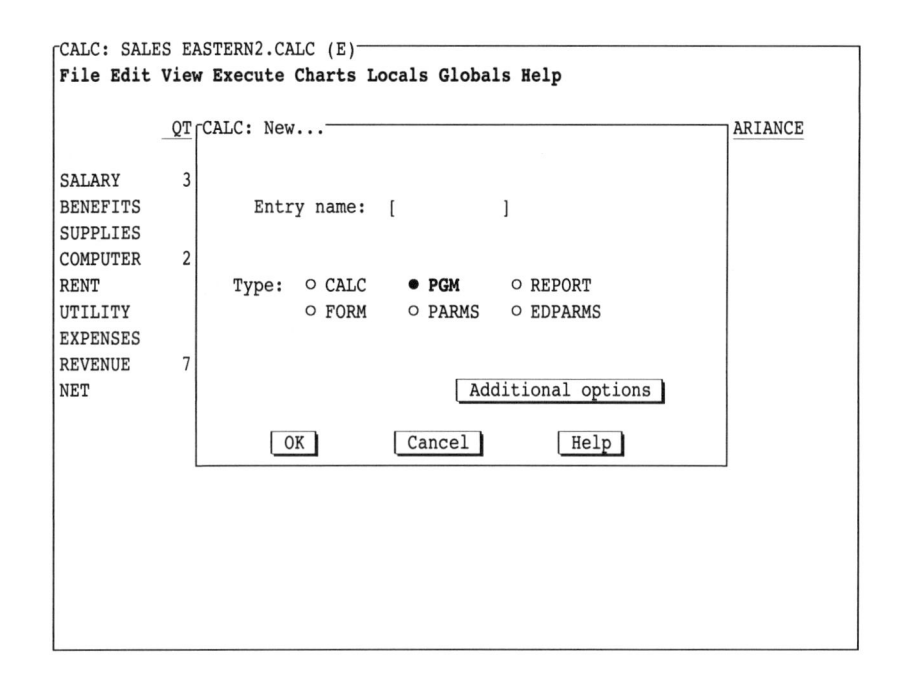

```
┌CALC: SALES EASTERN2.CALC (E)─────────────────────────────┐
│File Edit View Execute Charts Locals Globals Help         │
│                                                          │
│          QT ┌CALC: New...──────────────────────┐ ARIANCE │
│             │                                  │         │
│ SALARY    3 │                                  │         │
│ BENEFITS    │    Entry name:  [          ]     │         │
│ SUPPLIES    │                                  │         │
│ COMPUTER  2 │                                  │         │
│ RENT        │    Type:  ○ CALC   ● PGM   ○ REPORT │      │
│ UTILITY     │           ○ FORM   ○ PARMS  ○ EDPARMS │    │
│ EXPENSES    │                                  │         │
│ REVENUE   7 │                                  │         │
│ NET         │                  [Additional options]   │  │
│             │                                  │         │
│             │   [ OK ]   [Cancel]      [Help]  │         │
│             └──────────────────────────────────┘         │
│                                                          │
│                                                          │
└──────────────────────────────────────────────────────────┘
```

164 *Using Programs with SAS/CALC Software* □ *Chapter 7*

2. Type the name of the program, `REGION`, in the **Entry name** field, as shown in Display 7.8. You can type `REGION` in uppercase or lowercase.

3. Select **PGM** in the **Type** field.

Display 7.8
New... Dialog Box with REGION

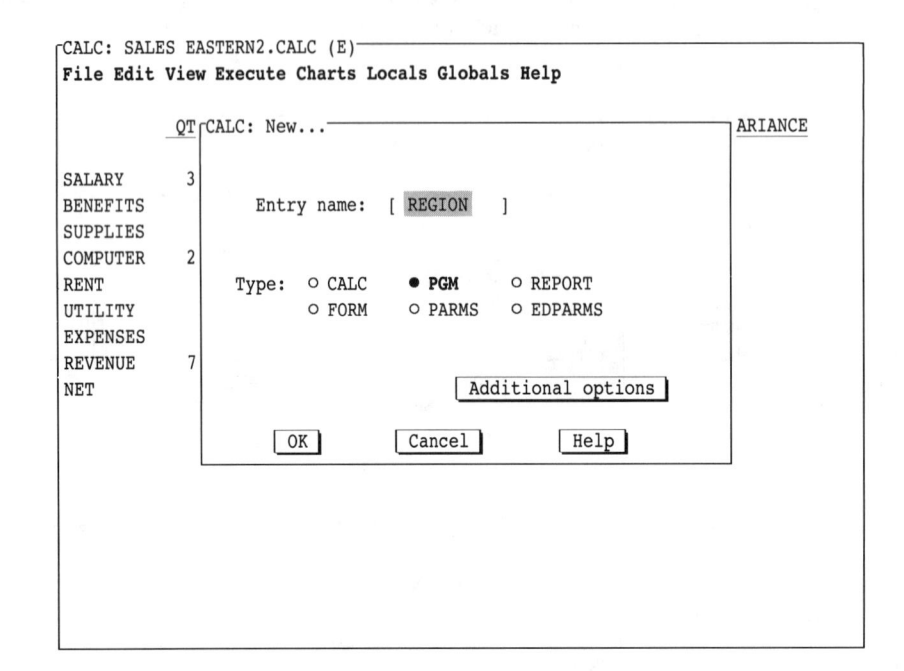

```
┌CALC: SALES EASTERN2.CALC (E)─────────────────────────────────┐
│File Edit View Execute Charts Locals Globals Help             │
│            QT ┌CALC: New...──────────────────────┐  ARIANCE  │
│               │                                  │           │
│ SALARY     3  │                                  │           │
│ BENEFITS      │   Entry name:  [ REGION     ]    │           │
│ SUPPLIES      │                                  │           │
│ COMPUTER   2  │                                  │           │
│ RENT          │   Type:  ○ CALC    ● PGM   ○ REPORT │         │
│ UTILITY       │          ○ FORM    ○ PARMS ○ EDPARMS │        │
│ EXPENSES      │                                  │           │
│ REVENUE    7  │              ┌─Additional options─┐│         │
│ NET           │                                  │           │
│               │   ┌ OK ┐   ┌ Cancel ┐   ┌ Help ┐ │           │
│               │                                  │           │
│               └──────────────────────────────────┘           │
│                                                              │
└──────────────────────────────────────────────────────────────┘
```

4. Select **OK** to display the PGM window shown in Display 7.9. This window enables you to type the SAS/CALC language statements for your program.

   You can issue line commands for deleting, copying, and moving lines by typing the commands on the line numbers in the display and pressing ENTER.

   Note: Consult *SAS Language: Reference, Version 6, First Edition,* Chapter 19, "SAS Text Editor Commands," for information regarding these line commands.

Display 7.9
PGM Window

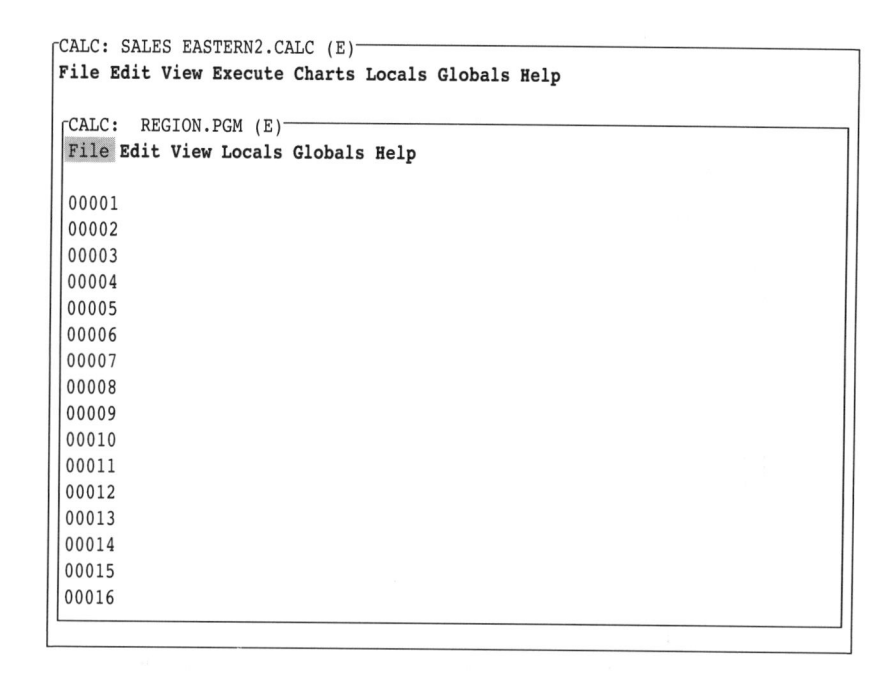

```
┌CALC: SALES EASTERN2.CALC (E)─────────────────────────────
│File Edit View Execute Charts Locals Globals Help
│
│┌CALC:  REGION.PGM (E)────────────────────────────────────┐
││File Edit View Locals Globals Help                       │
││                                                          │
││00001                                                     │
││00002                                                     │
││00003                                                     │
││00004                                                     │
││00005                                                     │
││00006                                                     │
││00007                                                     │
││00008                                                     │
││00009                                                     │
││00010                                                     │
││00011                                                     │
││00012                                                     │
││00013                                                     │
││00014                                                     │
││00015                                                     │
││00016                                                     │
│└──────────────────────────────────────────────────────────┘
```

166 *Using Programs with SAS/CALC Software* □ *Chapter 7*

5. Type the assignment statements, as shown in Display 7.10, on the first five lines of the PGM window. You can type these statements in uppercase or lowercase. Press the RETURN, ENTER, or TAB key at the end of each line to advance to the next line.

Display 7.10
Assignment Statements for the REGION.PGM Entry

```
┌CALC: SALES EASTERN2.CALC (E)─────────────────────────────────┐
│File Edit View Execute Charts Locals Globals Help             │
│┌CALC:  REGION.PGM (E)────────────────────────────────────────┤
││File Edit View Locals Globals Help                           │
││                                                             │
││00001 expenses=sum(salary,benefits,supplies,computer,rent,utility);
││00002 net=revenue-expenses;                                  │
││00003 actual=sum(qtr1,qtr2,qtr3,qtr4);                       │
││00004 variance=budget-actual;                                │
││00005 summary=sum(sales,service);                            │
││00006                                                        │
││00007                                                        │
││00008                                                        │
││00009                                                        │
││00010                                                        │
││00011                                                        │
││00012                                                        │
││00013                                                        │
││00014                                                        │
││00015                                                        │
││00016                                                        │
└──────────────────────────────────────────────────────────────┘
```

These assignment statements begin with a column, row, or page name, followed by an equal sign (=), followed by an expression, followed by a semicolon. As with formulas, the expression can be arithmetic or logical and can contain comparison operators, such as less than, greater than, or equal to; and logical operators, such as OR, AND, and NOT.

▶ *Caution* . . . . **Ending Semicolon**
All SAS/CALC software statements end with a semicolon. Omitting the semicolon results in programming errors. Consult Appendix 2, ''Troubleshooting Information,'' in this book for more information on programming errors. ▲

Each assignment statement has a distinct purpose, as illustrated in Figure 7.1.

Figure 7.1 *Purpose of Assignment Statements in REGION.PGM*

Assignment statement for:	Instructs SAS/CALC software to:
EXPENSES	sum the values for the expense items and assign the sum to the appropriate cells in the EXPENSES row across all pages.
NET	calculate the difference between REVENUE and EXPENSES and assign the difference to the appropriate cells in the NET row across all pages.
ACTUAL	sum the values of the four quarters and assign the sum to the appropriate cells in the ACTUAL column across all pages.
VARIANCE	calculate the difference between ACTUAL and BUDGET and assign the difference to the appropriate cells in the VARIANCE column across all pages.
SUMMARY	sum the cell values in the SALES page with the cell values in the SERVICE page and assign the sum to the corresponding cells in the SUMMARY page. You are actually defining an entire page of the EASTERN spreadsheet.

6. When you finish entering the statements, select **File** from the action bar and **End** from the File pull-down menu to close the PGM window and redisplay the EASTERN2 spreadsheet shown in Display 7.11.

168 *Using Programs with SAS/CALC Software* □ *Chapter 7*

Display 7.11
EASTERN2 without Computed Cell Values

```
┌CALC: SALES EASTERN2.CALC (E)─────────────────────────────────┐
│ File Edit View Execute Charts Locals Globals Help            │
│ NOTE: Member REGION.PGM has been saved.                      │
│            QTR1    QTR2    QTR3    QTR4   BUDGET   ACTUAL   VARIANCE │
│                                                              │
│ SALARY     30.00   33.00   35.50   37.00   135.00            │
│ BENEFITS    6.00    7.00    7.70    8.00    27.50            │
│ SUPPLIES    0.50    0.50    1.00    1.00     3.00            │
│ COMPUTER   20.00   21.50   22.00   22.50    85.00            │
│ RENT        4.00    4.00    4.00    4.80    16.00            │
│ UTILITY     1.00    1.00    1.00    1.50     4.00            │
│ EXPENSES                                                     │
│ REVENUE    75.00   73.50   78.00   75.00   295.00            │
│ NET                                                          │
│                                                              │
└──────────────────────────────────────────────────────────────┘
```

A note is displayed indicating that REGION.PGM has been saved. Also, notice the values for EXPENSES, NET, ACTUAL, and VARIANCE have not been calculated. Unlike formulas, which automatically execute when you press the ENTER key, you must run a new program, such as REGION.PGM, to execute the SAS/CALC language statements.

Lesson 7.4: Running a SAS/CALC Program

To run the program:

1. Select **Execute** from the action bar and **Run...** from the Execute pull-down menu, as shown in Display 7.12.

Display 7.12
Selecting Run

```
┌CALC: SALES EASTERN2.CALC (E)─────────────────────────────────────┐
│ File Edit View Execute Charts Locals Globals Help                │
│                                                                  │
│              QTR  Enter formula          QTR4   BUDGET  ACTUAL   VARIANCE
│                   End formula entry                              │
│   SALARY      30  Run...                 0     37.00   135.00    │
│   BENEFITS     6  Recalc                 0      8.00    27.50    │
│   SUPPLIES     0  Recalc all             0      1.00     3.00    │
│   COMPUTER    20  Compile...             0     22.50    85.00    │
│   RENT         4  Runopts...             0      4.80    16.00    │
│   UTILITY      1  Clear pgm              0      1.50     4.00    │
│   EXPENSES        Autocalc      ->                               │
│   REVENUE     75                         0     75.00   295.00    │
│   NET                                                            │
│                                                                  │
└──────────────────────────────────────────────────────────────────┘
```

170 *Using Programs with SAS/CALC Software* □ *Chapter 7*

2. Selecting **Run...** displays the Run dialog box, shown in Display 7.13, enabling you to name the SAS/CALC program you want to run.

Display 7.13
Default Run Dialog Box

```
┌CALC: SALES EASTERN2.CALC (E)─────────────────────────────┐
│ File Edit View Execute Charts Locals Globals Help        │
│                                                          │
│           QTR1    QTR2    QTR3    QTR4   BUDGET  ACTUAL  VARIANCE │
│                                                          │
│ SALARY   ┌Calc: Run──────────────────────┐ 00            │
│ BENEFITS │                               │ 50            │
│ SUPPLIES │   Run:                        │ 00            │
│ COMPUTER │                               │ 00            │
│ RENT     │      Program:  [           ]  │ 00            │
│ UTILITY  │                               │ 00            │
│ EXPENSES │      □ All formulas           │               │
│ REVENUE  │                               │ 00            │
│ NET      │     OK     Cancel    Help     │               │
│          └───────────────────────────────┘               │
└──────────────────────────────────────────────────────────┘
```

3. Type REGION in the **Program** field, as shown in Display 7.14, indicating you want to run REGION.PGM. You can type the program name in uppercase or lowercase.

Display 7.14
Specifying REGION in the Run Dialog Box

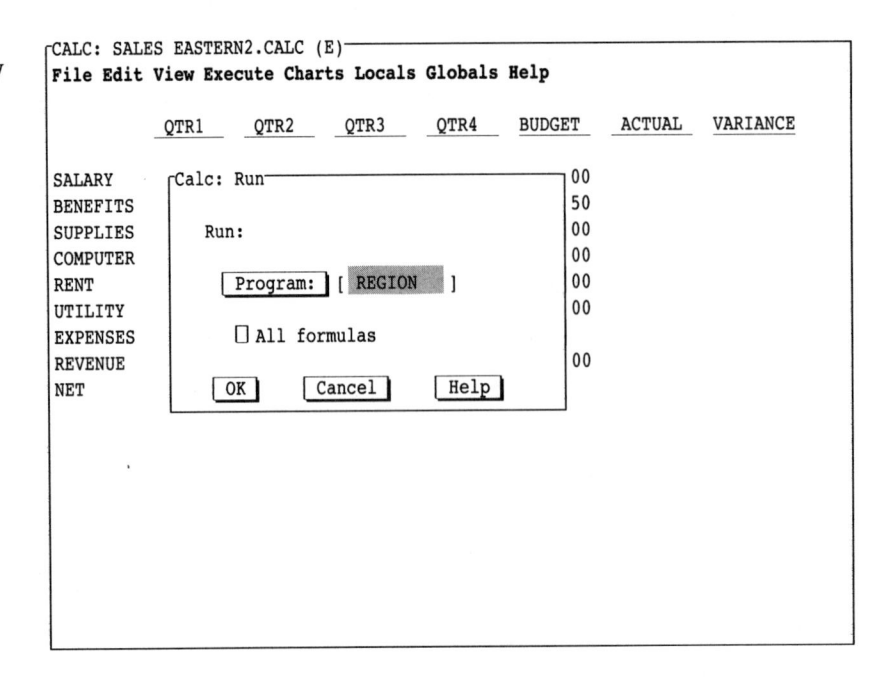

```
┌CALC: SALES EASTERN2.CALC (E)─────────────────────────────┐
│ File Edit View Execute Charts Locals Globals Help        │
│                                                          │
│           QTR1    QTR2    QTR3    QTR4   BUDGET  ACTUAL  VARIANCE │
│                                                          │
│ SALARY   ┌Calc: Run──────────────────────┐ 00            │
│ BENEFITS │                               │ 50            │
│ SUPPLIES │   Run:                        │ 00            │
│ COMPUTER │                               │ 00            │
│ RENT     │      Program:  [ REGION    ]  │ 00            │
│ UTILITY  │                               │ 00            │
│ EXPENSES │      □ All formulas           │               │
│ REVENUE  │                               │ 00            │
│ NET      │     OK     Cancel    Help     │               │
│          └───────────────────────────────┘               │
└──────────────────────────────────────────────────────────┘
```

4. Select **OK** to close the Run dialog box, execute the program, and redisplay the EASTERN2 spreadsheet, as shown in Display 7.15.

Selecting **OK** enables SAS/CALC software to check the syntax of the assignment statements, including correct spelling of the row, column, and page names, proper placement of the equal signs (=) and the semicolons. Once SAS/CALC software verifies the syntax, the program executes, and values are displayed in the appropriate cells in the EASTERN2 spreadsheet. Copying computed cell values from cell to cell is not necessary.

▶ *Caution* .... *Execution Errors*
If you receive an execution error message, consult Appendix 2 in this book for information on reading error messages and correcting programming errors. ▲

You are currently viewing the SALES page of the EASTERN2 spreadsheet. Notice the computed cell values for EXPENSES, NET, ACTUAL, and VARIANCE.

Display 7.15
SALES Page of EASTERN2 with Computed Cell Values

```
┌CALC: SALES EASTERN2.CALC (E)──────────────────────────────────┐
│ File Edit View Execute Charts Locals Globals Help             │
│                                                                │
│            QTR1    QTR2    QTR3    QTR4   BUDGET  ACTUAL  VARIANCE │
│                                                                │
│ SALARY     30.00   33.00   35.50   37.00  135.00  135.50   -0.50 │
│ BENEFITS    6.00    7.00    7.70    8.00   27.50   28.70   -1.20 │
│ SUPPLIES    0.50    0.50    1.00    1.00    3.00    3.00    0.00 │
│ COMPUTER   20.00   21.50   22.00   22.50   85.00   86.00   -1.00 │
│ RENT        4.00    4.00    4.00    4.80   16.00   16.80   -0.80 │
│ UTILITY     1.00    1.00    1.00    1.50    4.00    4.50   -0.50 │
│ EXPENSES   61.50   67.00   71.20   74.80  270.50  274.50   -4.00 │
│ REVENUE    75.00   73.50   78.00   75.00  295.00  301.50   -6.50 │
│ NET        13.50    6.50    6.80    0.20   24.50   27.00   -2.50 │
│                                                                │
│                                                                │
│                                                                │
└────────────────────────────────────────────────────────────────┘
```

Note: SAS/CALC software runs the program every time you modify a cell value.
Note: SAS/CALC software automatically saves the compiled REGION program with the EASTERN2 spreadsheet.
Note: Using programs for computing cell values is more efficient than using formulas because all calculations are performed as a set. You do not have to copy the computed cell values from cell to cell in the spreadsheet.

172 *Using Programs with SAS/CALC Software* □ *Chapter 7*

To verify that values have been calculated for the entire spreadsheet:

1. Select **View** from the action bar and **Go to...** from the View pull-down menu.

2. Type the page name, `SERVICE` or `SUMMARY`, in the **Go to** field and select **OK**. Display 7.16 shows the SERVICE page.

Display 7.16
SERVICE Page with Computed Cell Values

```
┌CALC: SERVICE EASTERN2.CALC (E)────────────────────────────────────┐
│ File Edit View Execute Charts Locals Globals Help                 │
│                                                                   │
│              QTR1    QTR2    QTR3    QTR4   BUDGET  ACTUAL VARIANCE│
│                                                                   │
│   SALARY    32.00   34.00   34.00   34.50  130.00  134.50   -4.50 │
│   BENEFITS   6.40    6.40    6.60    6.70   25.50   26.10   -0.60 │
│   SUPPLIES   3.00    3.00    3.50    3.70   11.00   13.20   -2.20 │
│   COMPUTER  20.00   20.00   20.20   20.20   86.00   80.40    5.60 │
│   RENT       4.00    4.00    4.00    4.80   16.80   16.80    0.00 │
│   UTILITY    1.00    1.50    1.50    2.00    6.00    6.00    0.00 │
│   EXPENSES  66.40   68.90   69.80   71.90  275.30  277.00   -1.70 │
│   REVENUE   70.00   72.00   69.00   70.00  310.00  281.00   29.00 │
│   NET        3.60    3.10   -0.80   -1.90   34.70    4.00   30.70 │
│                                                                   │
│                                                                   │
│                                                                   │
│                                                                   │
│                                                                   │
└───────────────────────────────────────────────────────────────────┘
```

Display 7.17 shows the SUMMARY page.

Display 7.17
SUMMARY Page with Computed Cell Values

```
┌CALC: SUMMARY EASTERN2.CALC (E)─────────────────────────────────┐
│ File Edit View Execute Charts Locals Globals Help              │
│                                                                │
│             QTR1    QTR2    QTR3    QTR4   BUDGET  ACTUAL  VARIANCE │
│                                                                │
│ SALARY     62.00   67.00   69.50   71.50   265.00  270.00   -5.00 │
│ BENEFITS   12.40   13.40   14.30   14.70    53.00   54.80   -1.80 │
│ SUPPLIES    3.50    3.50    4.50    4.70    14.00   16.20   -2.20 │
│ COMPUTER   40.00   41.50   42.20   42.70   171.00  166.40    4.60 │
│ RENT        8.00    8.00    8.00    9.60    32.80   33.60   -0.80 │
│ UTILITY     2.00    2.50    2.50    3.50    10.00   10.50   -0.50 │
│ EXPENSES  127.90  135.90  141.00  146.70   545.80  551.50   -5.70 │
│ REVENUE   145.00  145.50  147.00  145.00   605.00  582.50   22.50 │
│ NET        17.10    9.60    6.00   -1.70    59.20   31.00   28.20 │
│                                                                │
│                                                                │
│                                                                │
│                                                                │
└────────────────────────────────────────────────────────────────┘
```

Note: The format 7.2 was previously assigned to the EASTERN2 spreadsheet. As a result, you do not need to define a format.

174 *Using Programs with SAS/CALC Software ◻ Chapter 7*

3. When you finish viewing the EASTERN2 spreadsheet, select **File** from the action bar and **End** from the File pull-down menu to redisplay the DIRECTORY window, as shown in Display 7.18.

   Notice the REGION.PGM entry.

Display 7.18
DIRECTORY Window with REGION.PGM Entry

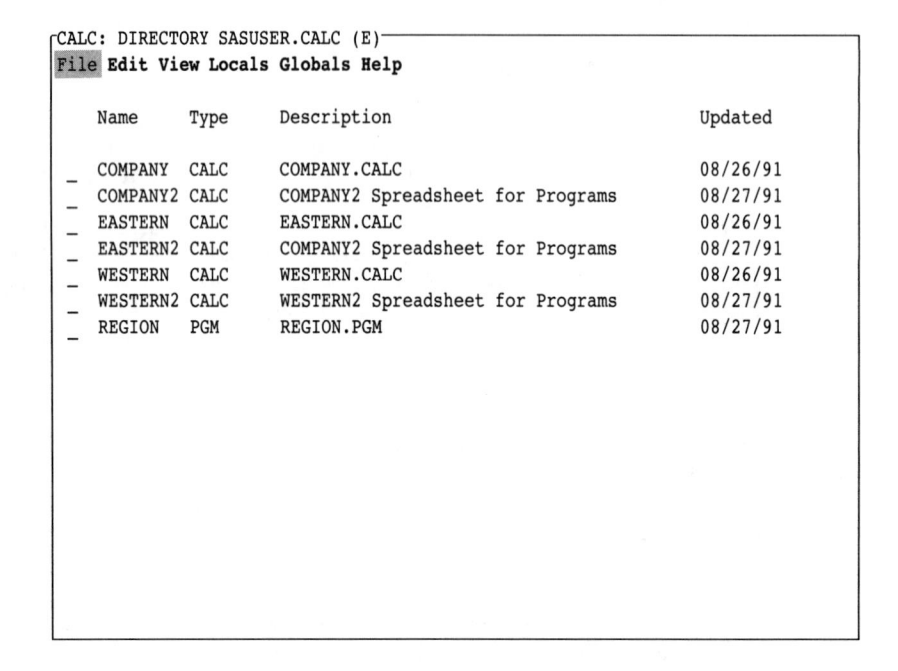

```
┌CALC: DIRECTORY SASUSER.CALC (E)─────────────────────────────────┐
│ File Edit View Locals Globals Help                              │
│                                                                 │
│    Name      Type   Description                    Updated      │
│                                                                 │
│  _ COMPANY   CALC   COMPANY.CALC                    08/26/91    │
│  _ COMPANY2  CALC   COMPANY2 Spreadsheet for Programs 08/27/91  │
│  _ EASTERN   CALC   EASTERN.CALC                    08/26/91    │
│  _ EASTERN2  CALC   COMPANY2 Spreadsheet for Programs 08/27/91  │
│  _ WESTERN   CALC   WESTERN.CALC                    08/26/91    │
│  _ WESTERN2  CALC   WESTERN2 Spreadsheet for Programs 08/27/91  │
│  _ REGION    PGM    REGION.PGM                      08/27/91    │
│                                                                 │
│                                                                 │
│                                                                 │
│                                                                 │
│                                                                 │
└─────────────────────────────────────────────────────────────────┘
```

You are ready to work with the WESTERN2 and COMPANY2 spreadsheets.

Lesson 7.5: Running REGION.PGM for WESTERN2

Type the letter O beside WESTERN2 and press ENTER to display the SALES page of the WESTERN2 spreadsheet, as shown in Display 7.19. Notice there are no values for EXPENSES, NET, ACTUAL, and VARIANCE. The SUMMARY page also contains no values.

Display 7.19
SALES Page of WESTERN2

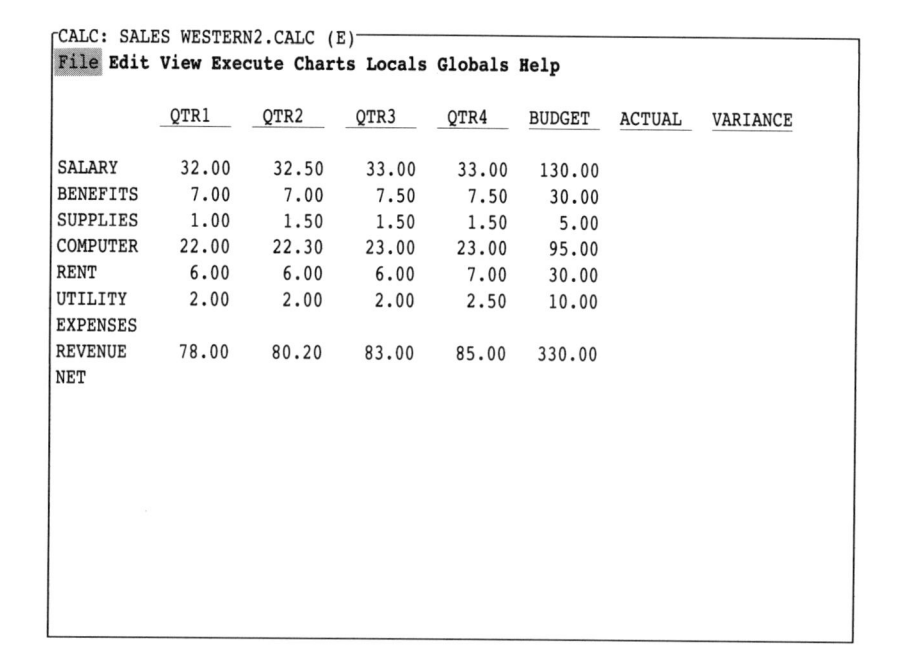

```
┌CALC: SALES WESTERN2.CALC (E)─────────────────────────────────┐
│ File Edit View Execute Charts Locals Globals Help            │
│                                                              │
│              QTR1    QTR2    QTR3    QTR4   BUDGET  ACTUAL  VARIANCE │
│                                                              │
│  SALARY     32.00   32.50   33.00   33.00   130.00           │
│  BENEFITS    7.00    7.00    7.50    7.50    30.00           │
│  SUPPLIES    1.00    1.50    1.50    1.50     5.00           │
│  COMPUTER   22.00   22.30   23.00   23.00    95.00           │
│  RENT        6.00    6.00    6.00    7.00    30.00           │
│  UTILITY     2.00    2.00    2.00    2.50    10.00           │
│  EXPENSES                                                    │
│  REVENUE    78.00   80.20   83.00   85.00   330.00           │
│  NET                                                         │
│                                                              │
└──────────────────────────────────────────────────────────────┘
```

The EASTERN2 and WESTERN2 spreadsheets are identical. They

- contain the same number of pages, rows, and columns
- have the same names defined for the pages, rows, and columns
- perform the same computations.

176 *Using Programs with SAS/CALC Software* □ *Chapter 7*

As a result, you can execute REGION.PGM to calculate values for WESTERN2. To run the program:

1. Select **Execute** from the action bar and **Run...** from the Execute pull-down menu.

2. Type REGION in the **Program** field, as shown in Display 7.20, indicating you want to run REGION.PGM.

Display 7.20
Specifying REGION in the Run Dialog Box

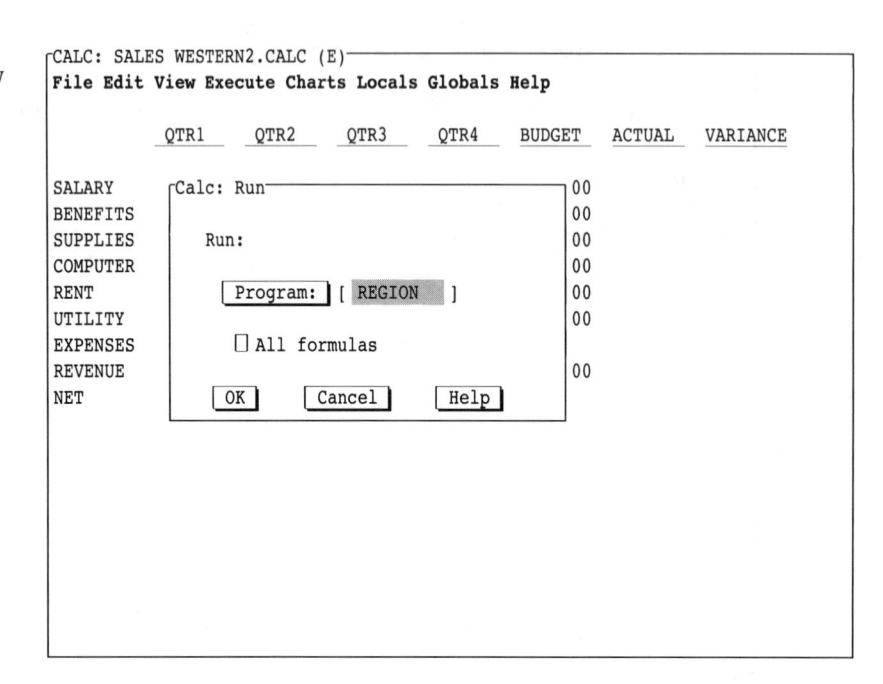

```
┌CALC: SALES WESTERN2.CALC (E)─────────────────────────────────────┐
│File Edit View Execute Charts Locals Globals Help                 │
│                                                                  │
│            QTR1     QTR2     QTR3     QTR4    BUDGET  ACTUAL  VARIANCE│
│                                                                  │
│SALARY     ┌Calc: Run──────────────────────────────┐ 00           │
│BENEFITS   │                                       │ 00           │
│SUPPLIES   │   Run:                                │ 00           │
│COMPUTER   │                                       │ 00           │
│RENT       │      [ Program: ] [ REGION    ]       │ 00           │
│UTILITY    │                                       │ 00           │
│EXPENSES   │           □ All formulas              │              │
│REVENUE    │                                       │ 00           │
│NET        │      [ OK ]   [ Cancel ]   [ Help ]   │              │
│           └───────────────────────────────────────┘              │
│                                                                  │
│                                                                  │
│                                                                  │
└──────────────────────────────────────────────────────────────────┘
```

3. Select **OK** to close the Run dialog box, execute the program, and redisplay the WESTERN2 spreadsheet, as shown in Display 7.21.

Display 7.21
SALES Page of WESTERN2 with Computed Cell Values

```
┌CALC: SALES WESTERN2.CALC (E)─────────────────────────────────┐
│ File Edit View Execute Charts Locals Globals Help            │
│ NOTE: Member WESTERN2.CALC has been saved.                   │
│            QTR1    QTR2    QTR3    QTR4   BUDGET  ACTUAL  VARIANCE │
│                                                              │
│ SALARY    32.00   32.50   33.00   33.00   130.00  130.50   -0.50 │
│ BENEFITS   7.00    7.00    7.50    7.50    30.00   29.00    1.00 │
│ SUPPLIES   1.00    1.50    1.50    1.50     5.00    5.50   -0.50 │
│ COMPUTER  22.00   22.30   23.00   23.00    95.00   90.30    4.70 │
│ RENT       6.00    6.00    6.00    7.00    30.00   25.00    5.00 │
│ UTILITY    2.00    2.00    2.00    2.50    10.00    8.50    1.50 │
│ EXPENSES  70.00   71.30   73.00   74.50   300.00  288.80   11.20 │
│ REVENUE   78.00   80.20   83.00   85.00   330.00  326.20    3.80 │
│ NET        8.00    8.90   10.00   10.50    30.00   37.40   -7.40 │
│                                                              │
│                                                              │
│                                                              │
└──────────────────────────────────────────────────────────────┘
```

▶ *Caution* .... *Execution Errors*

If you receive an execution error message, consult Appendix 2 in this book for information on reading error messages and correcting programming errors. ▲

SAS/CALC software automatically saves the REGION program with the WESTERN2 spreadsheet.

178 *Using Programs with SAS/CALC Software* □ *Chapter 7*

To verify that values have been calculated for the entire spreadsheet:

1. Select **View** from the action bar and **Go to...** from the View pull-down menu.
2. Type the page name, `SERVICE` or `SUMMARY`, in the **Go to** field and select **OK**.

When you finish viewing the WESTERN2 spreadsheet, select **File** from the action bar and **End** from the File pull-down menu to redisplay the DIRECTORY window.

Lesson 7.6: Defining a SAS/CALC Program for COMPANY2

You are ready to define a SAS/CALC program for the COMPANY2 spreadsheet.

The SAS/CALC program for COMPANY2 summarizes the EASTERN2 and WESTERN2 spreadsheets and computes overall COMPANY2 totals. Remember, to compute these totals, links must be defined between COMPANY2 and EASTERN2 and between COMPANY2 and WESTERN2. For your convenience, these links have already been defined.

To open the COMPANY2 spreadsheet, type the letter O beside COMPANY2 and press ENTER to display PAGE1 of the COMPANY2 spreadsheet, as shown in Display 7.22.

Display 7.22
COMPANY2 with No Cell Values

```
┌CALC: PAGE1 COMPANY2.CALC (E)──────────────────────────────────┐
│ File Edit View Execute Charts Locals Globals Help             │
│                                                               │
│            QTR1    QTR2    QTR3    QTR4   BUDGET  ACTUAL  VARIANCE │
│                                                               │
│ SALARY                                                        │
│ BENEFITS                                                      │
│ SUPPLIES                                                      │
│ COMPUTER                                                      │
│ RENT                                                          │
│ UTILITY                                                       │
│ EXPENSES                                                      │
│ REVENUE                                                       │
│ NET                                                           │
│                                                               │
│                                                               │
│                                                               │
│                                                               │
│                                                               │
└───────────────────────────────────────────────────────────────┘
```

Notice COMPANY2 contains no cell values. You calculate the cell values using a SAS/CALC program.

First, you should verify the links between COMPANY2 and EASTERN2, and COMPANY2 and WESTERN2.
To verify the links:

1. Select **Locals** from the action bar and **Drilldown** from the Locals pull-down menu to display the drilldown graphic.
   Verify the link names ELINK2 and WLINK2.

2. When you finish viewing the drilldown graphic or display, select **File** from the action bar and **End** from the File pull-down menu to close the drilldown facility.

You are ready to define the program for COMPANY2.

1. Select **File** from the action bar and **New...** from the File pull-down menu to display the New... dialog box.

2. Type the name of the program, SUMMARY, in the **Entry name** field.

3. Select **PGM** in the **Type** field, as shown in Display 7.23.

Display 7.23
Naming the SUMMARY PGM Entry

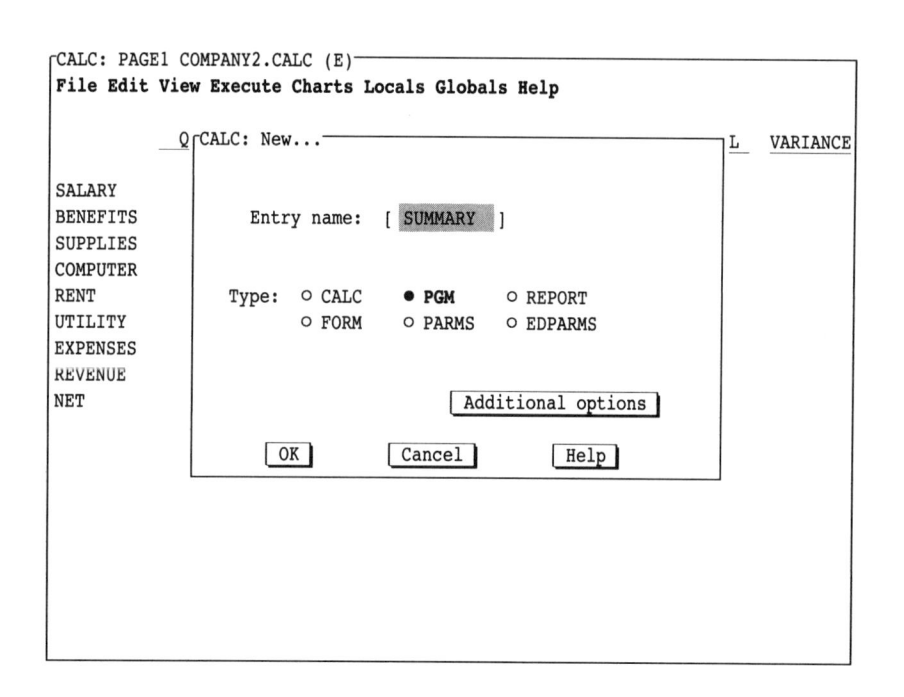

```
┌CALC: PAGE1 COMPANY2.CALC (E)─────────────────────────────┐
│File Edit View Execute Charts Locals Globals Help         │
│        Q┌CALC: New...──────────────────────────┐  L  VARIANCE
│         │                                      │
│ SALARY  │                                      │
│ BENEFITS│   Entry name:  [ SUMMARY  ]          │
│ SUPPLIES│                                      │
│ COMPUTER│                                      │
│ RENT    │   Type:  o CALC    • PGM    o REPORT │
│ UTILITY │          o FORM    o PARMS  o EDPARMS│
│ EXPENSES│                                      │
│ REVENUE │                                      │
│ NET     │                    [Additional options]│
│         │   [ OK ]   [Cancel]      [Help]      │
│         └──────────────────────────────────────┘
│                                                          │
└──────────────────────────────────────────────────────────┘
```

4. Select **OK** to display the PGM window.

180 *Using Programs with SAS/CALC Software* □ *Chapter 7*

5. Type the assignment statement, shown in Display 7.24, on the first line of the PGM window.

Display 7.24
Assignment Statement for PAGE1 of COMPANY2

```
┌CALC: PAGE1 COMPANY2.CALC (E)─────────────────────────┐
│File Edit View Execute Charts Locals Globals Help     │
│                                                      │
│┌CALC:  SUMMARY.PGM (E)──────────────────────────────┐│
││File Edit View Locals Globals Help                  ││
││                                                    ││
││00001 page1=sum(elink2 -> summary, wlink2 -> summary);│
││00002                                               ││
││00003                                               ││
││00004                                               ││
││00005                                               ││
││00006                                               ││
││00007                                               ││
││00008                                               ││
││00009                                               ││
││00010                                               ││
││00011                                               ││
││00012                                               ││
││00013                                               ││
││00014                                               ││
││00015                                               ││
││00016                                               ││
└──────────────────────────────────────────────────────┘
```

▶ *Caution* .... **Ending Semicolon**

All SAS/CALC software statements end with a semicolon. Omitting the semicolon results in programming errors. Consult Appendix 2 in this book for more information on programming errors. ▲

Remember to type the page name, PAGE1, followed by an equal sign (=) in front of the expression. The syntax for the expression is the SUM function with the link names followed by ->, followed by the item from the linked spreadsheet. Notice the arguments for the SUM function are separated by commas. In this case, you want to add the values of the SUMMARY page of the EASTERN2 spreadsheet to the values of the SUMMARY page of the WESTERN2 spreadsheet. Thus, the page names in the formula are preceded by the appropriate link name (ELINK2 for EASTERN2 and WLINK2 for WESTERN2) and the special character ->.

The assignment statement for PAGE1 has a specific purpose, as Figure 7.2 illustrates.

Figure 7.2 *Purpose of Assignment Statement in SUMMARY.PGM*

Assignment statement for:	Instructs SAS/CALC software to:
PAGE1	1. resolve the link names ELINK2 and WLINK2 to the actual spreadsheet names EASTERN2 and WESTERN, respectively 2. locate each of the spreadsheets 3. locate the summary page of the two spreadsheets and return the values to the current spreadsheet 4. sum the values and store the results in the corresponding cells in the COMPANY2 spreadsheet.

6. When you finish entering the assignment statement, select **File** from the action bar and **End** from the File pull-down menu to close the PGM window and redisplay the COMPANY2 spreadsheet shown in Display 7.25. A note is displayed indicating SUMMARY.PGM has been saved.

Display 7.25
COMPANY2 without Computed Cell Values

```
┌CALC: PAGE1 COMPANY2.CALC (E)─────────────────────────────────────────┐
│ File Edit View Execute Charts Locals Globals Help                    │
│ NOTE: Member SUMMARY.PGM has been saved.                             │
│         QTR1     QTR2     QTR3     QTR4    BUDGET   ACTUAL  VARIANCE │
│                                                                      │
│ SALARY                                                               │
│ BENEFITS                                                             │
│ SUPPLIES                                                             │
│ COMPUTER                                                             │
│ RENT                                                                 │
│ UTILITY                                                              │
│ EXPENSES                                                             │
│ REVENUE                                                              │
│ NET                                                                  │
│                                                                      │
│                                                                      │
│                                                                      │
│                                                                      │
│                                                                      │
└──────────────────────────────────────────────────────────────────────┘
```

Notice the values for COMPANY2 are not automatically calculated.

182 *Using Programs with SAS/CALC Software* □ *Chapter 7*

Lesson 7.7: Running SUMMARY.PGM for COMPANY2

To run the program:

1. Select **Execute** from the action bar and **Run...** from the Execute pull-down menu to display the Run dialog box. The Run dialog box enables you to name the SAS/CALC program you want to run.

2. Type SUMMARY in the **Program** field, as shown in Display 7.26, indicating you want to run SUMMARY.PGM.

Display 7.26
Running the SUMMARY.PGM Entry

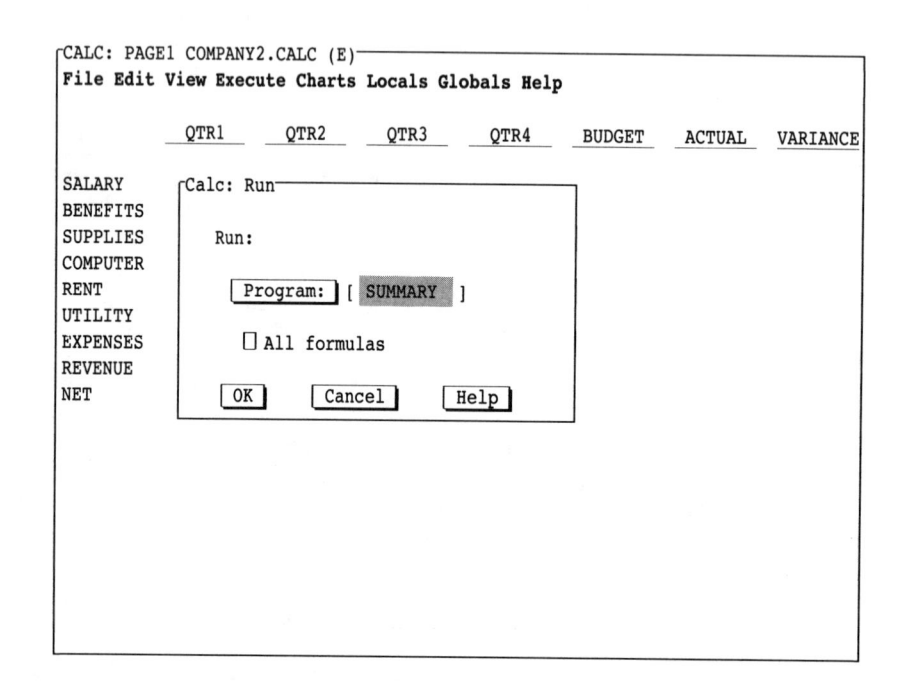

```
┌CALC: PAGE1 COMPANY2.CALC (E)─────────────────────────────────────┐
│ File Edit View Execute Charts Locals Globals Help                │
│                                                                  │
│            QTR1      QTR2      QTR3      QTR4    BUDGET  ACTUAL  VARIANCE
│  SALARY  ┌Calc: Run─────────────────────────────────┐
│  BENEFITS│                                          │
│  SUPPLIES│   Run:                                   │
│  COMPUTER│                                          │
│  RENT    │     Program:  [ SUMMARY       ]          │
│  UTILITY │                                          │
│  EXPENSES│         □ All formulas                   │
│  REVENUE │                                          │
│  NET     │     [ OK ]    [ Cancel ]   [ Help ]      │
│          └──────────────────────────────────────────┘
│                                                                  │
└──────────────────────────────────────────────────────────────────┘
```

3. Select **OK** to close the Run dialog box, execute the program, and redisplay the COMPANY2 spreadsheet, as shown in Display 7.27.

   Selecting **OK** enables SAS/CALC software to check the syntax of the assignment statements, including correct spelling of the link and page names, and proper placement of the ->, equal sign, and the semicolon. Once SAS/CALC software verifies the syntax, the program executes, and values are displayed in the corresponding cells in the COMPANY2 spreadsheet.

Display 7.27
COMPANY2 with Computed Cell Values

```
┌CALC: PAGE1 COMPANY2.CALC (E)─────────────────────────────────────────┐
│ File Edit View Execute Charts Locals Globals Help                    │
│                                                                      │
│              QTR1    QTR2    QTR3    QTR4   BUDGET  ACTUAL  VARIANCE │
│                                                                      │
│   SALARY    128.00  133.50  137.00  139.00  535.00  537.50    -2.50  │
│   BENEFITS   26.40   27.40   28.80   30.20  113.00  112.80     0.20  │
│   SUPPLIES    6.50    7.50    8.40    9.20   29.00   31.60    -2.60  │
│   COMPUTER   85.00   86.80   88.20   88.70  356.00  348.70     7.30  │
│   RENT       19.00   19.00   19.00   22.60   82.80   79.60     3.20  │
│   UTILITY     6.00    6.50    6.50    8.00   30.00   27.00     3.00  │
│   EXPENSES  270.90  280.70  287.90  297.70 1145.80 1137.20     8.60  │
│   REVENUE   298.00  308.70  305.00  308.00 1250.00 1219.70    30.30  │
│   NET        27.10   28.00   17.10   10.30  104.20   82.50    21.70  │
│                                                                      │
│                                                                      │
│                                                                      │
│                                                                      │
│                                                                      │
└──────────────────────────────────────────────────────────────────────┘
```

184 *Using Programs with SAS/CALC Software* □ *Chapter 7*

4. When you finish viewing the COMPANY2 spreadsheet, select **File** from the action bar and **End** from the File pull-down menu to close the spreadsheet and redisplay the DIRECTORY window shown in Display 7.28.

    Notice the SUMMARY.PGM entry.

Display 7.28
DIRECTORY Window with SUMMARY.PGM Entry

```
CALC: DIRECTORY SASUSER.CALC (E)
File Edit View Locals Globals Help

    Name      Type    Description                         Updated

_   COMPANY   CALC    COMPANY.CALC                        09/04/91
_   COMPANY2  CALC    COMPANY2 Spreadsheet for Programs   09/04/91
_   EASTERN   CALC    EASTERN.CALC                        09/04/91
_   EASTERN2  CALC    EASTERN2 Spreadsheet for Programs   09/04/91
_   WESTERN   CALC    WESTERN.CALC                        09/04/91
_   WESTERN2  CALC    WESTERN2 Spreadsheet for Programs   09/04/91
_   REGION    PGM     REGION.PGM                          09/04/91
_   SUMMARY   PGM     SUMMARY.PGM                         09/04/91
```

Figure 7.3 provides some guidelines for deciding whether to use formulas or programs. You should choose the method that best benefits your spreadsheet application.

Figure 7.3 *Formulas versus Programs*

You should you use formulas when:	You should use programs when:
1. There are only a few calculations per spreadsheet.	1. There are multiple calculations per spreadsheet.
2. Calculations are unique to one spreadsheet.	2. Calculations are common to more than one spreadsheet.
3. You have simple expressions.	3. You have complex programs that perform data validation and modification and decision-making processes.
4. You want to store the formulas with each individual cell.	4. You want to store the SAS/CALC language statements with the spreadsheet.
	5. You want to be able to view, analyze, and modify all spreadsheet calculations location. (Spreadsheet formulas are spread across pages, rows, and columns.)

Chapter Summary

This chapter introduces SAS/CALC programs and teaches you how to use them to compute cell values.

This chapter uses three new spreadsheets: EASTERN2, WESTERN2, and COMPANY2.

To begin the chapter, you copy EASTERN2, WESTERN2, and COMPANY2 from the SASHELP.CALC data library.

To generate a program for the EASTERN2 spreadsheet, you learn how to create a PGM entry. A *PGM entry* contains SAS/CALC language statements that compute, validate, modify, and assign cell values. You create a PGM entry named REGION that computes values for the EXPENSES and NET rows, the ACTUAL and VARIANCE columns, and the SUMMARY page.

Unlike formulas, which immediately execute when a cell value is modified, a new program does not automatically execute when it is first created. Executing SAS/CALC programs is different from executing formulas. So, after defining REGION.PGM, you learn how to execute the program statements using the action bar and pull-down menus.

Once the EASTERN2 spreadsheet contains the appropriate values, you open WESTERN2. Because EASTERN2 and WESTERN2 contain the same number of pages, rows, and columns with the same names, and because both spreadsheets perform the same computations, you can execute REGION.PGM for WESTERN2.

Once the WESTERN2 spreadsheet contains all of its values, you open COMPANY2. As with the formula for COMPANY, the program you create, SUMMARY, summarizes the EASTERN2 and WESTERN2 spreadsheets to compute overall company totals. Again, you execute the new program SUMMARY.PGM for COMPANY2.

This chapter also provides guidelines for when to use formulas and when to use programs.

Conclusion

You have finished the SAS/CALC software tutorial. During this tutorial you have learned many of the features and options for creating spreadsheets. These spreadsheets can be as simple as a single page of rows and columns, or they can be three-dimensional spreadsheets linking vast amounts of data to a single spreadsheet.

SAS/CALC software provides more power than discussed in these tutorial chapters. Consult *SAS/CALC Software: Usage and Reference, Version 6, First Edition* for more information on basic and advanced features of SAS/CALC software, including

- creating a SAS data set from a SAS/CALC software spreadsheet
- creating a SAS/CALC software spreadsheet from a SAS data set
- splitting a display so you can view multiple spreadsheets and graphics at once
- creating more advanced spreadsheet display features, such as titles, subtitles, and cell labels
- using advan ed programming features such as interfacing to SAS/AF software, using Screen Cont. ıl Language, and accessing SAS data sets, catalogs, and external files.

Part 3
Appendices

Appendix 1	Accessing and Using the Online Help Facility and COPY Command
Appendix 2	Troubleshooting Information
Appendix 3	Video References

Appendix 1 Accessing and Using the Online Help Facility and COPY Command

Accessing the Online Help Facility 191

Using the COPY Command 197

Accessing the Online Help Facility

To assist you in using SAS/CALC software, an online help facility accompanies the software. To access the online facility:

1. From the DIRECTORY window, select **Help** from the action bar and **CALC Index** from the Help pull-down menu, as shown in Display A1.1.

Display A1.1
Selecting Help and CALC Index

```
┌CALC: DIRECTORY SASUSER.CALC (E)─────────────────────────────────────┐
│File Edit View Locals Globals Help                                    │
│                                                                      │
│      Name      Type     Descrip┌Extended help┐           Updated     │
│                                │Keys         │                       │
│      COMPANY   CALC     COMPANY│SAS System   │           09/16/91    │
│   _  COMPANY2  CALC     COMPANY│CALC Index   │ r Chapter 6  09/16/91 │
│   _  EASTERN   CALC     EASTERN└─────────────┘           09/16/91    │
│   _  EASTERN2  CALC     EASTERN2 Spreadsheet for Chapter6  09/16/91  │
│   _  WESTERN   CALC     WESTERN.CALC                     09/16/91    │
│   _  WESTERN2  CALC     WESTERN2 Spreadsheet for Chapter 6 09/16/91  │
│   _  REGION    PGM      REGION.PGM                       09/16/91    │
│   _  SUMMARY   PGM      SUMMARY.PGM                      09/16/91    │
│   _  ENHANCED  REPORT   Enhanced Report                  09/16/91    │
│   _  MULTI     REPORT   Multipage Report                 09/16/91    │
│   _  TRANS     REPORT   Transposed Report                09/16/91    │
│                                                                      │
│                                                                      │
│                                                                      │
│                                                                      │
└──────────────────────────────────────────────────────────────────────┘
```

192 Accessing the Online Help Facility □ Appendix 1

Selecting **CALC Index** displays the help index shown in Display A1.2. Notice you get a brief description of SAS/CALC software with four specific topics. To obtain specific information, select one of the four topics.

Display A1.2
CALC: Index Window

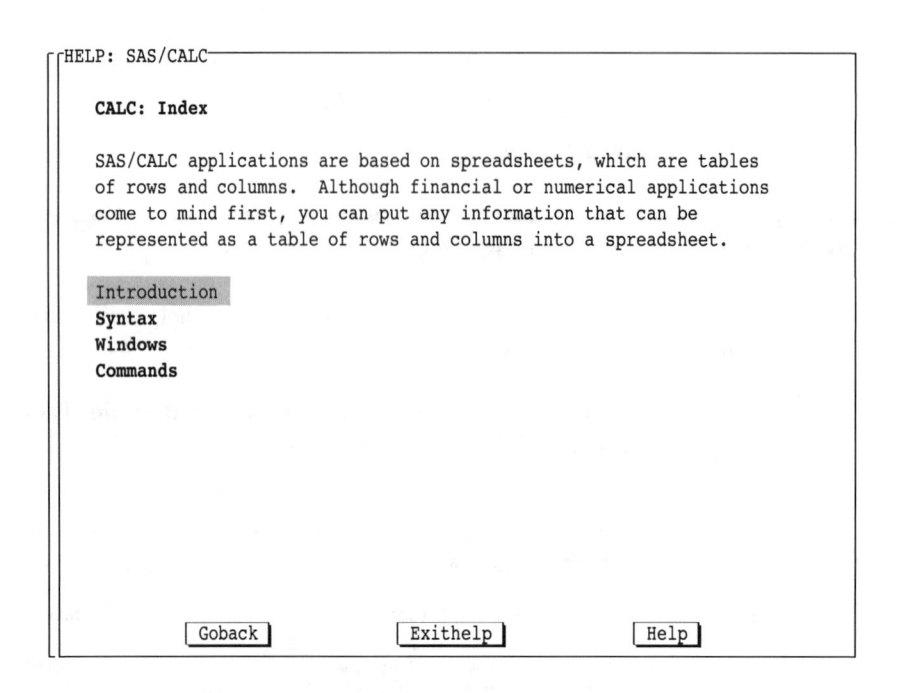

```
┌─HELP: SAS/CALC─────────────────────────────────────────────┐
│                                                            │
│   CALC: Index                                              │
│                                                            │
│   SAS/CALC applications are based on spreadsheets, which are tables
│   of rows and columns.  Although financial or numerical applications
│   come to mind first, you can put any information that can be
│   represented as a table of rows and columns into a spreadsheet.
│                                                            │
│   Introduction                                             │
│   Syntax                                                   │
│   Windows                                                  │
│   Commands                                                 │
│                                                            │
│                                                            │
│                                                            │
│                                                            │
│                                                            │
│                                                            │
│                                                            │
│                                                            │
│       [Goback]          [Exithelp]         [Help]          │
└────────────────────────────────────────────────────────────┘
```

2. Select **Introduction** to display a brief explanation of SAS/CALC software, as shown in Display A1.3.

Display A1.3
SAS/CALC Software Introduction

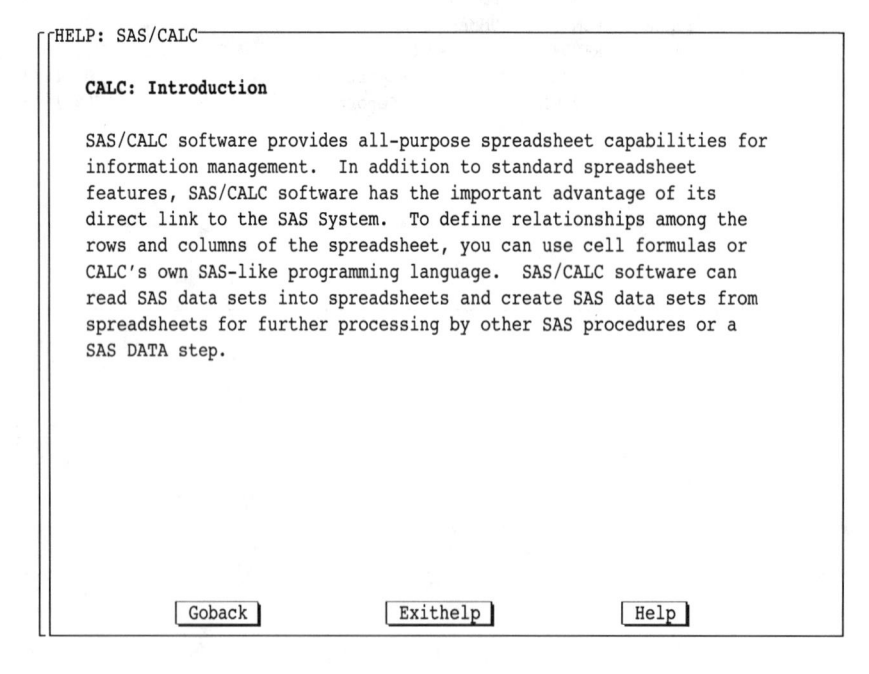

```
┌─HELP: SAS/CALC─────────────────────────────────────────────┐
│                                                            │
│   CALC: Introduction                                       │
│                                                            │
│   SAS/CALC software provides all-purpose spreadsheet capabilities for
│   information management.  In addition to standard spreadsheet
│   features, SAS/CALC software has the important advantage of its
│   direct link to the SAS System.  To define relationships among the
│   rows and columns of the spreadsheet, you can use cell formulas or
│   CALC's own SAS-like programming language.  SAS/CALC software can
│   read SAS data sets into spreadsheets and create SAS data sets from
│   spreadsheets for further processing by other SAS procedures or a
│   SAS DATA step.                                           │
│                                                            │
│                                                            │
│                                                            │
│                                                            │
│       [Goback]          [Exithelp]         [Help]          │
└────────────────────────────────────────────────────────────┘
```

3. Select **Goback** to redisplay the help index.
4. Select **Syntax** to display an overview of the programming syntax for the PROC CALC step, as shown in Display A1.4.

Display A1.4
PROC CALC Syntax

```
┌─HELP: SAS/CALC────────────────────────────────────────┐
│                                                        │
│  CALC: Syntax                                          │
│                                                        │
│  PROC CALC CATALOG|CAT|C= <libref>.catalog<.entry.type>│
│            CTYPE= ADD|DIFFERENCE|REPLACE               │
│            DATA= SAS-data-set<( data-set options )>    │
│            EDIT | OPEN                                 │
│            FIRSTOBS= obsnumber                         │
│            LASTOBS= obsnumber                          │
│            NODIR                                       │
│            NOMSG                                       │
│            TRANSPOSE;                                  │
│     COMPILE options;                                   │
│     FETCH options;                                     │
│     ID id_variable;                                    │
│     MERGE CATALOG=libref.catalog options;              │
│     VAR variable-list;                                 │
│                                                        │
│                                                        │
│                                                        │
│       [ Goback ]      [ Exithelp ]      [ Help ]       │
│                                                        │
└────────────────────────────────────────────────────────┘
```

5. Select a highlighted option, such as **CATALOG|CAT|C=**, to display specific information for that option, as shown in Display A1.5.

Display A1.5
CATALOG Option Information

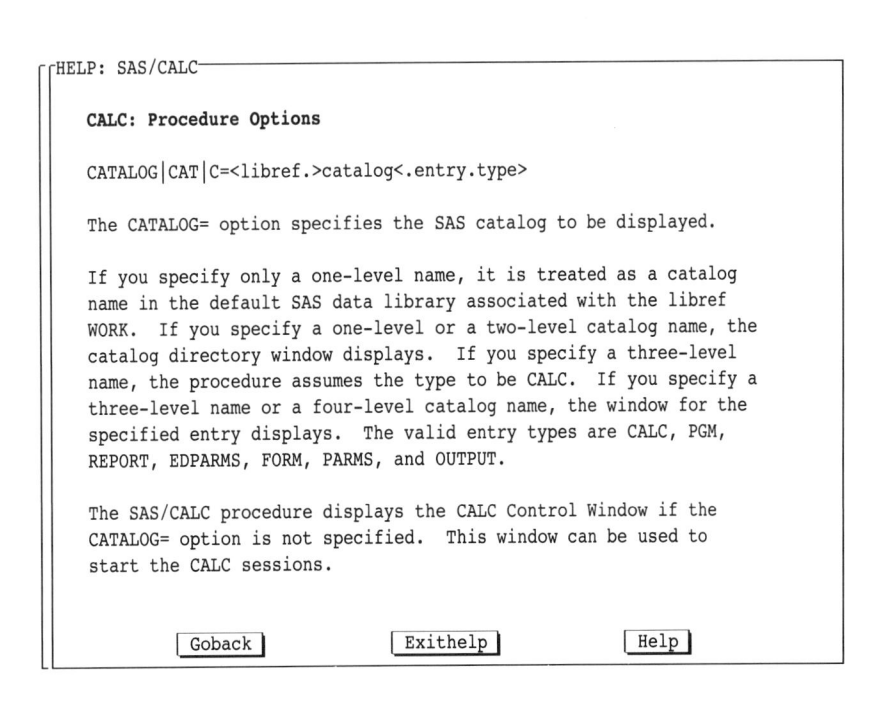

```
┌─HELP: SAS/CALC────────────────────────────────────────┐
│                                                        │
│  CALC: Procedure Options                               │
│                                                        │
│  CATALOG|CAT|C=<libref.>catalog<.entry.type>           │
│                                                        │
│  The CATALOG= option specifies the SAS catalog to be displayed. │
│                                                        │
│  If you specify only a one-level name, it is treated as a catalog │
│  name in the default SAS data library associated with the libref │
│  WORK.  If you specify a one-level or a two-level catalog name, the │
│  catalog directory window displays.  If you specify a three-level │
│  name, the procedure assumes the type to be CALC.  If you specify a │
│  three-level name or a four-level catalog name, the window for the │
│  specified entry displays.  The valid entry types are CALC, PGM, │
│  REPORT, EDPARMS, FORM, PARMS, and OUTPUT.             │
│                                                        │
│  The SAS/CALC procedure displays the CALC Control Window if the │
│  CATALOG= option is not specified.  This window can be used to │
│  start the CALC sessions.                              │
│                                                        │
│       [ Goback ]      [ Exithelp ]      [ Help ]       │
│                                                        │
└────────────────────────────────────────────────────────┘
```

6. Select **Goback** to redisplay the syntax help.

7. Select **Goback** again to redisplay the help index.

8. Select **Windows** to display a list of the windows available in SAS/CALC software, as shown in Display A1.6. Selecting a highlighted window name provides additional information for that window.

Display A1.6
Windows Information

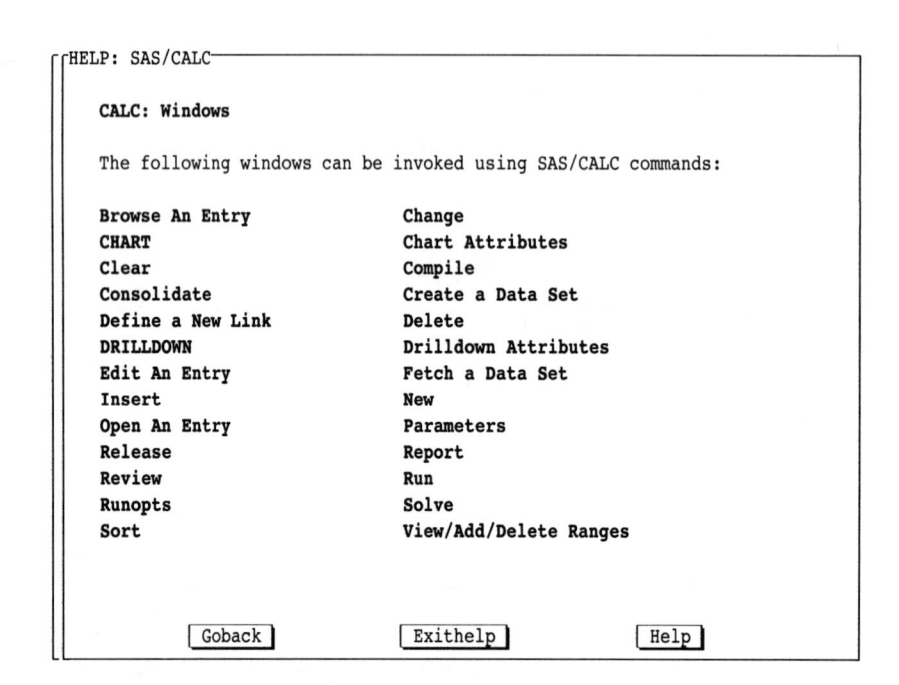

```
┌─HELP: SAS/CALC────────────────────────────────────────────┐
│                                                            │
│   CALC: Windows                                            │
│                                                            │
│   The following windows can be invoked using SAS/CALC commands: │
│                                                            │
│   Browse An Entry         Change                           │
│   CHART                   Chart Attributes                 │
│   Clear                   Compile                          │
│   Consolidate             Create a Data Set                │
│   Define a New Link       Delete                           │
│   DRILLDOWN               Drilldown Attributes             │
│   Edit An Entry           Fetch a Data Set                 │
│   Insert                  New                              │
│   Open An Entry           Parameters                       │
│   Release                 Report                           │
│   Review                  Run                              │
│   Runopts                 Solve                            │
│   Sort                    View/Add/Delete Ranges           │
│                                                            │
│         [Goback]        [Exithelp]         [Help]          │
└────────────────────────────────────────────────────────────┘
```

9. Select **Goback** to redisplay the help index.

10. Select **Commands** to display an overview of the commands available in SAS/CALC software. Display A1.7 shows the first list of commands.

Display A1.7
First Display of Available SAS/CALC Software Commands

```
┌─HELP: SAS/CALC Commands──────────────────────────────────────────┐
│                                                                   │
│  CALC: Commands                                                   │
│                                                      Viewing      │
│  Spreadsheet Editing     Formulas         Scrolling  Entries      │
│  AUTOSAVE    MOVE        EXEC     REVIEW  BACKWARD   BROWSE       │
│  CHANGE      NAMES       FORMULA  VALUE   BOTTOM     EDIT         │
│  CLEAR       PARMS       RECALC   VERIFY  DOWN       NEW          │
│  COPY        PASTE       RESET            EQUAL      OPEN         │
│  DELETE      RELEASE                      FORWARD                 │
│  HOLD        UNDO        Catalog          HSCROLL    Charting     │
│  INSERT                  Maintenance      LEFT       ATTR         │
│  Window Management       COPY             RIGHT      BAR          │
│  ARRANGE     SETWSZ      DELETE           SETCR      CHART        │
│  CANCEL      SHOWTYPE                     TOP        HOTLINK      │
│  END         SPLIT       Calculation      UP         PIE          │
│  SAVE        SWAP        Control          VSCROLL    PLOT         │
│  SETCR       VIEW        AUTOCALC  RUN               SEQUENCE     │
│  SETHELP     WREGION     COMPILE   RUNOPTS Security               │
│  SETPMENU    WSIZE       RECALC            PASSWORD               │
│                                                                   │
│  MORE                                                             │
│         ┌Goback┐          ┌Exithelp┐          ┌Help┐             │
└───────────────────────────────────────────────────────────────────┘
```

11. Select **MORE** at the bottom of the display to see the second list of available commands, as shown in Display A1.8.

Display A1.8
Second Display of Available SAS/CALC Software Commands

```
┌─HELP: SAS/CALC Commands──────────────────────────────────────────┐
│                                                                   │
│  CALC: Commands (cont'd)                                          │
│                                                                   │
│  Accessing        Accessing                                       │
│  Spreadsheets     SAS Data Sets   Printing      Miscellaneous     │
│  ACTIVATE         CREATE          FONT          EDPARMS           │
│  CONSOLIDATE      FETCH           FORMNAME      HELP              │
│  DEACTIVATE                       PRINT         MSG               │
│  DRILLDOWN                        PRTFILE       REVIEW            │
│  LINK                             REPORT        SOLVE             │
│  RANGE                            SEND          SORT              │
│                                   SPRINT        TYPE              │
│                                                                   │
│         ┌Goback┐          ┌Exithelp┐          ┌Help┐             │
└───────────────────────────────────────────────────────────────────┘
```

196 *Accessing the Online Help Facility* □ *Appendix 1*

12. Select **Goback** to redisplay the first list of available commands.

    You can obtain additional information for a specific command by moving the cursor to the command name and pressing ENTER, or pointing and clicking with a mouse. For example, select **COPY** to display additional information for the COPY command, as shown in Display A1.9.

Display A1.9
COPY Command Help

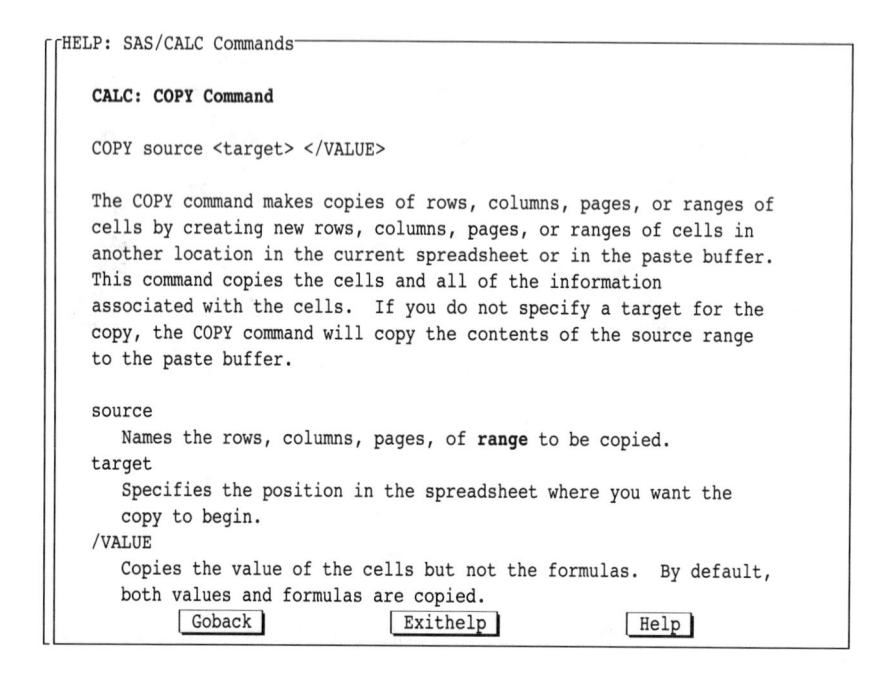

```
┌─HELP: SAS/CALC Commands─────────────────────────────────────┐
│                                                             │
│  CALC: COPY Command                                         │
│                                                             │
│  COPY source <target> </VALUE>                              │
│                                                             │
│  The COPY command makes copies of rows, columns, pages, or  │
│  ranges of cells by creating new rows, columns, pages, or   │
│  ranges of cells in another location in the current         │
│  spreadsheet or in the paste buffer. This command copies    │
│  the cells and all of the information associated with the   │
│  cells.  If you do not specify a target for the copy, the   │
│  COPY command will copy the contents of the source range    │
│  to the paste buffer.                                       │
│                                                             │
│  source                                                     │
│     Names the rows, columns, pages, of range to be copied.  │
│  target                                                     │
│     Specifies the position in the spreadsheet where you     │
│     want the copy to begin.                                 │
│  /VALUE                                                     │
│     Copies the value of the cells but not the formulas.     │
│     By default, both values and formulas are copied.        │
│      ┌────────┐           ┌─────────┐         ┌──────┐      │
│      │ Goback │           │ Exithelp│         │ Help │      │
│      └────────┘           └─────────┘         └──────┘      │
└─────────────────────────────────────────────────────────────┘
```

13. Select **Goback** to redisplay the help index.

14. Select **Goback** or **Exithelp** to close the help index and redisplay the DIRECTORY window.

   Note: Consult *SAS/CALC Software: Usage and Reference, Version 6, First Edition* for more information regarding the online help facility for SAS/CALC software.

Using the COPY Command

Now that you have seen the commands available with SAS/CALC software, look at an example using the COPY command.

Before you can use the COPY command, you must display a command line. One way to display a command line is to:

1. Select **Globals** from the action bar and **Global options** from the Globals pull-down menu, as shown in Display A1.10.

Display A1.10
Selecting Global Options

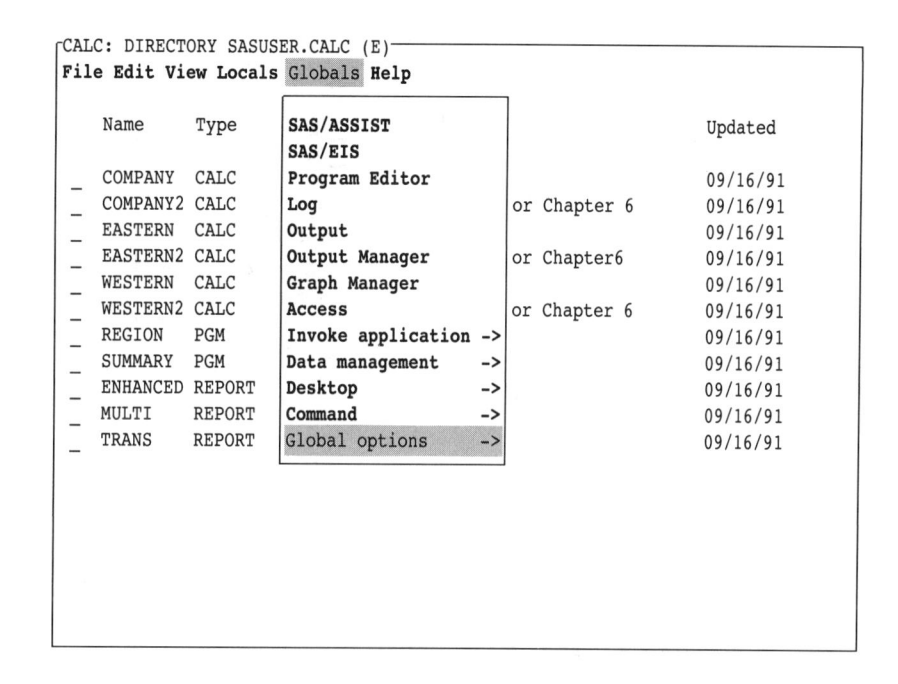

```
┌CALC: DIRECTORY SASUSER.CALC (E)─────────────────────────────────────┐
│File Edit View Locals Globals Help                                   │
│                                                                     │
│      Name      Type    ┌SAS/ASSIST─────────────┐         Updated    │
│                        │SAS/EIS                │                    │
│   _  COMPANY   CALC    │Program Editor         │         09/16/91   │
│   _  COMPANY2  CALC    │Log             │ or Chapter 6   09/16/91   │
│   _  EASTERN   CALC    │Output          │                09/16/91   │
│   _  EASTERN2  CALC    │Output Manager  │ or Chapter6    09/16/91   │
│   _  WESTERN   CALC    │Graph Manager   │                09/16/91   │
│   _  WESTERN2  CALC    │Access          │ or Chapter 6   09/16/91   │
│   _  REGION    PGM     │Invoke application ->│             09/16/91 │
│   _  SUMMARY   PGM     │Data management    ->│             09/16/91 │
│   _  ENHANCED  REPORT  │Desktop            ->│             09/16/91 │
│   _  MULTI     REPORT  │Command            ->│             09/16/91 │
│   _  TRANS     REPORT  │Global options     ->│             09/16/91 │
│                        └─────────────────────┘                      │
│                                                                     │
└─────────────────────────────────────────────────────────────────────┘
```

198 *Using the COPY Command □ Appendix 1*

2. Select **Action bar off** from the Global options pull-down menu, as shown in Display A1.11, to turn the action bar off and display a command line.

Display A1.11
Selecting Action Bar Off

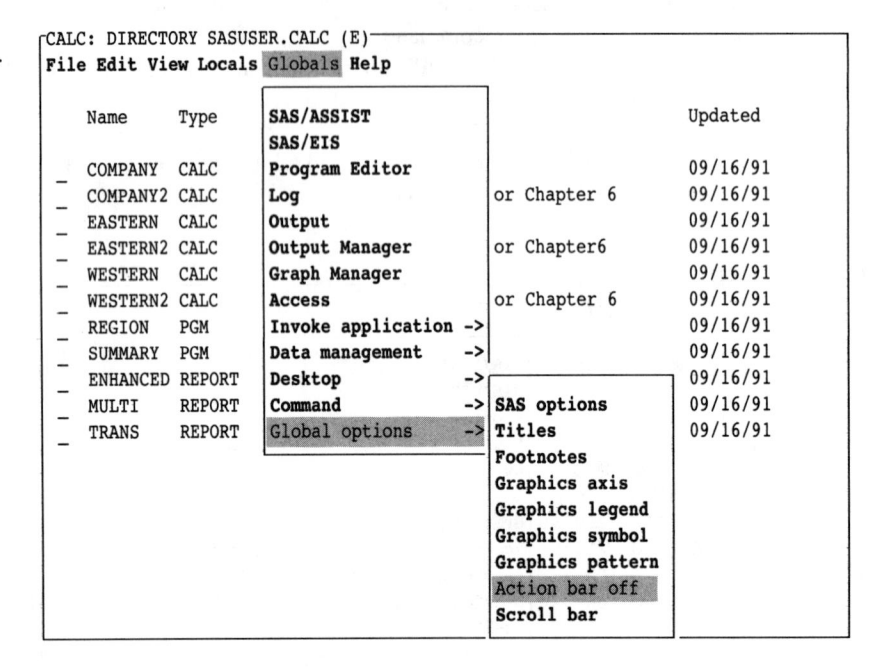

```
┌CALC: DIRECTORY SASUSER.CALC (E)─────────────────────────────────────┐
│File Edit View Locals Globals Help                                   │
│                                                                      │
│      Name      Type    SAS/ASSIST                      Updated       │
│                        SAS/EIS                                       │
│    _ COMPANY   CALC    Program Editor                  09/16/91      │
│    _ COMPANY2  CALC    Log              or Chapter 6   09/16/91      │
│    _ EASTERN   CALC    Output                          09/16/91      │
│    _ EASTERN2  CALC    Output Manager   or Chapter6    09/16/91      │
│    _ WESTERN   CALC    Graph Manager                   09/16/91      │
│    _ WESTERN2  CALC    Access           or Chapter 6   09/16/91      │
│    _ REGION    PGM     Invoke application ->           09/16/91      │
│    _ SUMMARY   PGM     Data management  ->             09/16/91      │
│    _ ENHANCED  REPORT  Desktop          ->             09/16/91      │
│    _ MULTI     REPORT  Command          -> SAS options 09/16/91      │
│    _ TRANS     REPORT  Global options   -> Titles      09/16/91      │
│                                            Footnotes                 │
│                                            Graphics axis             │
│                                            Graphics legend           │
│                                            Graphics symbol           │
│                                            Graphics pattern          │
│                                            Action bar off            │
│                                            Scroll bar                │
│                                                                      │
└──────────────────────────────────────────────────────────────────────┘
```

Display A1.12 shows the command line and a note indicating that pull-down menus are turned off for all windows.

Display A1.12
A Command Line

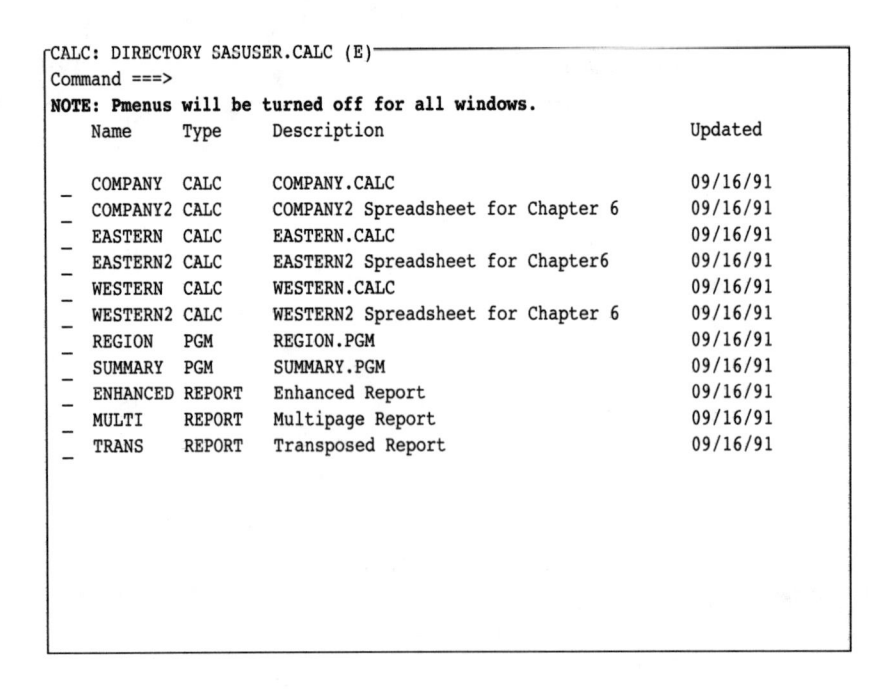

```
┌CALC: DIRECTORY SASUSER.CALC (E)─────────────────────────────────────┐
│Command ===>                                                          │
│NOTE: Pmenus will be turned off for all windows.                      │
│      Name      Type    Description                     Updated       │
│                                                                      │
│    _ COMPANY   CALC    COMPANY.CALC                    09/16/91      │
│    _ COMPANY2  CALC    COMPANY2 Spreadsheet for Chapter 6  09/16/91  │
│    _ EASTERN   CALC    EASTERN.CALC                    09/16/91      │
│    _ EASTERN2  CALC    EASTERN2 Spreadsheet for Chapter6   09/16/91  │
│    _ WESTERN   CALC    WESTERN.CALC                    09/16/91      │
│    _ WESTERN2  CALC    WESTERN2 Spreadsheet for Chapter 6  09/16/91  │
│    _ REGION    PGM     REGION.PGM                      09/16/91      │
│    _ SUMMARY   PGM     SUMMARY.PGM                     09/16/91      │
│    _ ENHANCED  REPORT  Enhanced Report                 09/16/91      │
│    _ MULTI     REPORT  Multipage Report                09/16/91      │
│    _ TRANS     REPORT  Transposed Report               09/16/91      │
│                                                                      │
│                                                                      │
│                                                                      │
│                                                                      │
└──────────────────────────────────────────────────────────────────────┘
```

Once you have a command line, you are ready to issue commands.

In Lesson 1.8, you learned how to copy a formula from the EXPENSES.QTR1 cell to the EXPENSES.QTR2 cell through EXPENSES.BUDGET. You used the MARK BLOCK function key, action bar, and pull-down selections to perform the copy.

To use the COPY command:

1. Type the command on the command line, as shown in Display A1.13.

Display A1.13
Copying a Formula with the COPY Command

```
┌CALC: PAGE1 EASTERN.CALC (E)─────────────────────────────────────┐
│Command ===> copy expenses.qtr1 expenses.qtr2:expenses.budget    │
│                                                                  │
│               QTR1      QTR2      QTR3      QTR4     BUDGET     │
│                                                                  │
│   SALARY       30        33       35.5       37       135       │
│   BENEFITS      6         7        7.7        8       27.5      │
│   SUPPLIES    0.5       0.5        1          1         3       │
│   COMPUTER     20       21.5      22        22.5       85       │
│   RENT          4         4        4         4.8       16       │
│   UTILITY       1         1        1         1.5        4       │
│   EXPENSES   61.5                                                │
│   REVENUE      75       73.5      78         75       295       │
│                                                                  │
│                                                                  │
│                                                                  │
│                                                                  │
└──────────────────────────────────────────────────────────────────┘
```

2. Press ENTER to execute the COPY command and copy the formula to the designated cells, as shown in Display A1.14.

Display A1.14
Result of the COPY Command

```
┌CALC: PAGE1 EASTERN.CALC (E)─────────────────────────────────┐
│Command ===>                                                 │
│                                                             │
│                QTR1      QTR2      QTR3      QTR4    BUDGET │
│                                                             │
│   SALARY         30        33      35.5        37       135 │
│   BENEFITS        6         7       7.7         8      27.5 │
│   SUPPLIES      0.5       0.5         1         1         3 │
│   COMPUTER       20      21.5        22      22.5        85 │
│   RENT            4         4         4       4.8        16 │
│   UTILITY         1         1         1       1.5         4 │
│   EXPENSES     61.5        67      71.2      74.8     270.5 │
│   REVENUE        75      73.5        78        75       295 │
│                                                             │
│                                                             │
│                                                             │
│                                                             │
└─────────────────────────────────────────────────────────────┘
```

In Lesson 4.2, you learned how to copy PAGE1 of the EASTERN spreadsheet to create PAGE2. Again, you changed the spreadsheet perspective to pages and columns, and used the MARK BLOCK function key, action bar, and pull-down menu selections to perform the copy.

To use the COPY command, you do not need to change the spreadsheet perspective, you type the command on the command line, as shown in Display A1.15, and press ENTER.

Display A1.15
Copying a Formula with the COPY Command

```
┌CALC: PAGE1 EASTERN.CALC (E)──────────────────────────────────────┐
│Command ===> copy page1 page1                                     │
│                                                                  │
│            QTR1    QTR2    QTR3    QTR4   BUDGET   ACTUAL  VARIANCE│
│                                                                  │
│ SALARY    30.00   33.00   35.50   37.00   135.00   135.50   -0.50│
│ BENEFITS   6.00    7.00    7.70    8.00    27.50    28.70   -1.20│
│ SUPPLIES   0.50    0.50    1.00    1.00     3.00     3.00    0.00│
│ COMPUTER  20.00   21.50   22.00   22.50    85.00    86.00   -1.00│
│ RENT       4.00    4.00    4.00    4.80    16.00    16.80   -0.80│
│ UTILITY    1.00    1.00    1.00    1.50     4.00     4.50   -0.50│
│ EXPENSES  61.50   67.00   71.20   74.80   270.50   274.50   -4.00│
│ REVENUE   75.00   73.50   78.00   75.00   295.00   301.50   -6.50│
│ NET       13.50    6.50    6.80    0.20    24.50    27.00   -2.50│
│                                                                  │
│                                                                  │
│                                                                  │
│                                                                  │
└──────────────────────────────────────────────────────────────────┘
```

202 *Using the COPY Command* □ *Appendix 1*

Pressing ENTER executes the COPY command and displays PAGE2, as shown in Display A1.16.

Display A1.16
Result of the COPY Command

```
┌CALC: PAGE2 EASTERN.CALC (E)─────────────────────────────┐
│Command ===>                                              │
│                                                          │
│             QTR1    QTR2    QTR3    QTR4   BUDGET  ACTUAL  VARIANCE │
│                                                          │
│   SALARY    30.00   33.00   35.50   37.00  135.00  135.50   -0.50  │
│   BENEFITS   6.00    7.00    7.70    8.00   27.50   28.70   -1.20  │
│   SUPPLIES   0.50    0.50    1.00    1.00    3.00    3.00    0.00  │
│   COMPUTER  20.00   21.50   22.00   22.50   85.00   86.00   -1.00  │
│   RENT       4.00    4.00    4.00    4.80   16.00   16.80   -0.80  │
│   UTILITY    1.00    1.00    1.00    1.50    4.00    4.50   -0.50  │
│   EXPENSES  61.50   67.00   71.20   74.80  270.50  274.50   -4.00  │
│   REVENUE   75.00   73.50   78.00   75.00  295.00  301.50   -6.50  │
│   NET       13.50    6.50    6.80    0.20   24.50   27.00   -2.50  │
│                                                          │
│                                                          │
│                                                          │
│                                                          │
│                                                          │
└──────────────────────────────────────────────────────────┘
```

These are just two examples of using the COPY command. Many of the tasks performed with the action bar and pull-down menus can be performed using commands. Consult *SAS/CALC Software: Usage and Reference* for a full description including proper syntax of all available commands.

Appendix 2 Troubleshooting Information

Common User Errors 203

Common Programming Errors 205

Common User Errors

Tables A2.1 and A2.2 describe common user problems and errors.

Table A2.1
Common User Problems

Problem	Result	Often caused by	Solution
A command line appears in the windows instead of an action bar.	You cannot use the action bars and pull-down menus as instructed.	By default, SAS software displays a command line.	Type the PMENU command on the command line and press ENTER.
After Chapter 2, you open SASUSER.CALC and no entries are listed.	SAS/CALC software is invoked but you are not in SASUSER.CALC. As a result, no entries are listed.	Misspelling CALC in the **CATALOG** field in the Spreadsheet... dialog box or in the *CATALOG=* option in the PROC CALC statement.	Reopen the Spreadsheet... dialog box or recall the PROC CALC statement and type CALC correctly.

Table A2.2
Common User Errors

Error	Result	Often caused by	Solution
Libname SASUSER is not assigned.	SAS/CALC software is not invoked.	Misspelling SASUSER in the **LIBNAME** field in the Spreadsheet... dialog box or in the *CATALOG=* option in the PROC CALC statement	Reopen the Spreadsheet... dialog box or recall the PROC CALC statement and type CALC correctly. To recall the PROC CALC statement, select **Locals** from the action bar and **Recall text**.
Invalid SAS name.	The new spreadsheet is not created.	Typing a name that violates spreadsheet naming conventions in the **Entry name** field of the New... dialog box.	Type a valid SAS name in the **Entry name** field.

204 *Common User Errors* □ *Appendix 2*

Error	Result	Often caused by	Solution
QTR1 1 is not a valid SAS name.	The column name is reset to the default.	Typing a valid column but not deleting the default name completely	Type a valid column name and delete the default column name completely.
Errors encountered in the formula. See LOG or MSG window.	The formula does not execute.	Pressing ENTER before you complete the formula. Misspelling a page, row, or column name. Omitting a comma between arguments in a function. Omitting a parenthesis or the equal sign. Splitting a row or column name across lines.	Select **Locals** from the action bar, then **Go to message window** to view the error messages. Select **File** and **End** to close the message window. Fix the formula.
You must mark in a scrollable area.	The mark cannot be issued.	Pressing the MARK BLOCK function in an invalid location	Move the cursor to the correct row, column, or page name and press the MARK BLOCK function key.
The specified format is invalid.	Requested action cannot be performed.	Specifying an invalid format in the **Format** field of the Change dialog box. The default format, BEST., was not deleted completely when specifying the 7.2 format.	Specify a valid format. Delete the default format completely.

Common Programming Errors

When working with formulas and programs, you may encounter problems or error messages. This section describes error messages you may receive.

If you receive compile or execution error messages when defining formulas or programs:

1. Select **Locals** from the action bar and **Message window** from the Locals pull-down menu.

2. Select **Go to message window** to open the MESSAGE window and read the error messages.

3. Once you determine the cause of the error, select **View** from the action bar and **Clear** from the View pull-down menu to clear the contents of the Message window.

4. Select **File** from the action bar and **End** from the File pull-down menu to close the Message window and redisplay the appropriate spreadsheet.

To correct an error in a formula, move the cursor to the formula entry area, correct the error, and press ENTER.

To correct an error in a program:

1. Select **File** from the action bar and **Open...** from the File pull-down menu to display the Edit An Entry dialog box.

2. Select **PGM** in the **Type** field.

3. Select the **Select entry** button to display the Catalog Directory window for the SASUSER.CALC catalog.

4. Select the appropriate PGM entry name, such as REGION PGM, to redisplay the Edit An Entry dialog box.

5. Select **OK** to open the PGM window for the PGM entry you selected.

6. Correct the error or errors.

7. Select **Execute** from the action bar and **Run** from the Execute pull-down menu to rerun the program.

8. Select **File** from the action bar and **End** from the File pull-down menu to close the PGM window.

Table A2.3 lists some error messages you may receive when executing formulas and programs:

Table A2.3
Error Messages

Error	Result	Often caused by	Solution
Compile errors. Please see the Message window.	The program does not execute.	Omitting a semicolon, comma, parenthesis, operator, or misspelling a keyword	Check the Message window, open the PGM window, correct the program, re-execute the program.
Expecting a semicolon.	The program does not execute.	Omitting a semicolon	Edit the program and re-execute the program.
Expecting one of the following: Operator, Delimiter.	The program does not execute.	Omitting a semicolon	Edit the program and re-execute the program.
Attempt to reference the uninitialized variable 'SLARY'.	The program does not execute.	Misspelling a row, column, page, or link name in an expression	Edit the program and re-execute the program.

Appendix 3 Video References

The video titled *Getting Started with SAS/CALC Spreadsheet Applications* covers most of the information provided in this book. Table A3.1 is a list of the video segments and their corresponding chapters in this book.

Table A3.1
Video References

Video Segment	Book Chapter
Segment 1: Introduction to SAS/CALC Software	Chapter 1: "Introducing SAS/CALC Software"
Segment 2: Creating Your First Spreadsheet	Chapter 2: "Creating Your First Spreadsheet"
Segment 3: Modifying Your Spreadsheet	Chapter 3: "Modifying a Spreadsheet"
Segment 4: Producing Spreadsheet Reports	Chapter 4: "Producing Spreadsheet Reports and Generating Graphics"
Segment 5: Creating a 3D Spreadsheet	Chapter 5: "Creating a Three-Dimensional Spreadsheet"
Segment 6: Linking Spreadsheets	Chapter 6: "Linking Spreadsheets"

Glossary

action bar
a list of selections that appears when the PMENU command is executed. The action bar is used by placing your cursor on the item that you want and pressing the ENTER key or, if you are using a mouse, by pointing and clicking on the item you want. This either executes a command or displays a pull-down menu or dialog box.

argument
(1) the data values within parentheses on which a SAS function or CALL routine performs the indicated operation. (2) in syntax descriptions, any keyword in a SAS statement other than the statement name.

arithmetic operator
(1) a built-in operator that performs a numeric computation. (2) an infix operator used to perform arithmetic calculations, such as addition, subtraction, multiplication, division, and exponentiation.

assignment statement
in SAS/CALC software, a statement that assigns data values to spreadsheet cells.

base SAS software
software that includes a programming language that manages your data, procedures that are software tools for data analysis and reporting, a macro facility, help menus, and a windowing environment for text editing and file management.

carriage-control character
a specific symbol that tells the printer how many lines to advance the paper, when to begin a new page, when to skip a line, and when to hold the current line for overprint.

catalog
See SAS catalog.

catalog entry
See entry type.

cell
See spreadsheet cell.

command
a request you issue to SAS/CALC software, often from the command line. For example, COPY is a command.

comparison operator
an infix operator that tests a relationship between two values. If the comparison (or relationship) is true, the result of carrying out the operation is the value 1; if the comparison is false, the result is the value 0.

constant
a literal value in a program or formula.

current spreadsheet
the spreadsheet that you are editing.

data value
(1) a unit of information. (2) the intersection of a row (observation) and a column (variable) in the rectangular form of a SAS data set or SAS/CALC spreadsheet.

default spreadsheet
See current spreadsheet.

dialog box
a feature of the PMENU facility that appears in response to an action, usually selecting a menu item. The purpose of dialog boxes is to obtain information, which you supply by filling in a field or choosing a selection from a group of fields. You can execute the CANCEL command to exit the dialog box.

dimension
in SAS/CALC software, the row, column, or page of a spreadsheet.

directory
(1) a list of the members and associated information in a SAS data library. (2) a list of entries and associated information in a SAS catalog.
    Note: Directory has a different meaning outside of the SAS System under some operating systems.

display manager
See SAS Display Manager System.

entry
a unit of information stored in a SAS catalog.

entry type
a part of the name for an entry in a SAS catalog that is assigned by the SAS System to identify what type of information is stored in the entry. For example, CALC is the entry type for an entry containing a spreadsheet created with SAS/CALC software.

expression
a sequence of operators and operands that form a set of instructions used to produce a value.

first-level name
See libref (first-level name).

FORM entry
a catalog entry that contains specifications for formatting and printing full-screen output.

format
the instructions the SAS System uses to write each value of a variable. There are two types of formats: formats supplied by SAS software and user-written formats created using the FORMAT procedure.

formula
an expression assigned to a cell in a spreadsheet.

function
(1) a built-in expression that returns a value resulting from zero or more arguments.
(2) a computation invoked by its name.

function key
a keyboard key that can be assigned commands to perform specific tasks.

graphics device
See graphics output device.

graphics output device
any terminal, printer, or other output device capable of displaying or producing graphics output.

infix operator
an operator that appears between two operands (for example, the greater-than symbol in 8>6). There are four general kinds of infix operators: arithmetic, comparison, logical or Boolean, and others (minimum, maximum, and concatenation).

item
one of the choices displayed in a pull-down menu or an action bar of the PMENU facility. Selecting an item either executes a command, displays a pull-down menu, or displays a dialog box.

library reference
another name for libref.

libref (first-level name)
the name temporarily associated with a SAS data library. The libref is the first-level name of a two-level name. For example, A is the libref in the two-level name A.B. The default libref is WORK unless the USER libref is defined.

linked spreadsheet
a spreadsheet that has been linked so that data may be read from it and operated upon.

linking
in SAS/CALC software, the process of defining links between spreadsheets that enables a current spreadsheet to reference the rows, columns, pages, and cells within linked spreadsheets.

literal
(1) a SAS constant. There are numeric, character string, and missing literals.

logical operator (Boolean operator)
an operator used in expressions to link sequences of comparisons. The logical operators are AND, OR, and NOT.

member
(1) a file in a SAS data library. (2) a single element of a partitioned data set under the MVS operating system.

member name
(1) the name of a file in a SAS data library. When you reference a file with a two-level name, such as A.B, the member name is the second part of the name (the libref is the first part). (2) the name of a single element of a partitioned data set under the MVS operating system.

member type
the classification of a file in a SAS data library that is assigned by the SAS System to identify what type of information is stored in the file. For example, CATALOG is the member type for catalogs.

message window
in SAS/CALC software, a window where programming errors, warning messages, and notes are written.

operands
the variables and constants in a comparison operation or calculation.

operator
a symbol that requests a comparison, logical operation, or arithmetic calculation. The SAS System uses two major kinds of operators: prefix operators and infix operators.

paste buffer
a temporary storage location that holds the contents of text stored with the STORE or CUT commands. The contents of the paste buffer remain in effect only for the current SAS session.

permanent SAS data library
a library that is not deleted when the SAS session terminates; it is available for subsequent SAS sessions. Unless the USER libref is defined, you use a two-level name to access a file in a permanent library. The first-level name is the libref, and the second-level name is the member name.

permanent SAS file
a SAS file in a library that is not deleted when the SAS session or job terminates.

perspective
in SAS/CALC software, one of three views of a spreadsheet; rows and columns, pages and rows, and pages and columns.

PGM entry
a catalog entry that contains one or more SAS/CALC software language statements.

PMENU facility
a menuing system that is used instead of the command line as a way to execute commands.

prefix operator
an operator that is applied to the variable, constant, function, or parenthetical expression immediately following it (for example, the minus sign in -A).

print file
an external file containing carriage-control (printer-control) information.

PROC step
a group of SAS statements that calls and executes a procedure, usually with a SAS data set as input.

procedures
(1) often called SAS procedures, a collection of built-in SAS programs that are used to produce reports, manage files, and analyze data. They enable you to accept default output or

to tailor your output by overriding defaults. (2) usually called user-written procedures, a self-contained user-written program, written in a language other than the SAS language, that interfaces with the SAS System and is accessed with a PROC statement.

program
a collection of statements that are executed to transform input data into output data. In SAS/CALC software, the input and output data are typically spreadsheets, although they can be SAS data sets, external data files, full-screen data, graphics, reports, and so on.

programming error
an execution-time logic error that causes a SAS program to fail or to produce incorrect results.

pull-down menu
the list of choices that appears when you choose an item from an action bar or from another pull-down menu in the PMENU facility. The choices in the list are called items.

range
a fixed subset of spreadsheet cells delimited by an anchor cell and a free cell.

REPORT entry
a catalog entry that contains specifications such as titles, headings, formats, and additional options for specific reports.

SAS catalog
a SAS file that stores many different kinds of information in smaller units called entries. Some catalog entries contain system information such as key definitions. Other catalog entries contain application information such as window definitions, help windows, formats, informats, macros, or graphics output.

SAS command
a command that invokes the SAS System. This command may vary depending on operating system and site.

SAS data library
a collection of one or more SAS files that are recognized by the SAS System. Each file is a member of the library.

SAS Display Manager System
an interactive windowing environment in which actions are performed with a series of commands or function keys. Within one session, multiple tasks can be accomplished. It can be used to prepare and submit programs, view and print the results, and debug and resubmit the programs.

SAS file
a specially structured file that is created, organized, and, optionally, maintained by the SAS System. A SAS file can be a SAS data set, a catalog, a stored program, or an access descriptor.

SAS language
(1) the statements that direct the execution of the SAS System. (2) as a grouping in SAS documentation, all parts of base SAS software except procedures.

SAS log
a window that can contain the SAS statements you enter and messages about the execution of your program.

SAS name
a name that can appear in a SAS statement, including items such as names of variables and SAS data sets. SAS names can be up to eight characters long. The first character must be a letter or an underscore. Subsequent characters can be letters, numbers, or underscores. Blanks and special characters (except the underscore) are not allowed.

SAS operator
See operator.

SAS procedures
See procedures.

SAS program
a sequence of related SAS statements.

SAS statement
a string of SAS keywords, SAS names, and special characters and operators ending in a semicolon that instructs the SAS System to perform an operation or gives information to the SAS System.

SAS Text Editor
a full-screen editing facility available in some windows of the SAS Display Manager System, as well as in windows of SAS/CALC, SAS/AF, SAS/FSP, and SAS/GRAPH software.

SAS windowing environment
See SAS Display Manager System.

SASHELP library
a SAS data library supplied by SAS software that stores the text for HELP windows, default function key and window definitions, and menus.

SASUSER library
the library that contains a profile catalog that stores the tailoring features you specify for the SAS System.

second-level name
See member name.

selection field
the portion of a display manager window (shown on the display as an underscore) where you can enter a short command to perform an action, such as O for Open.

selection-field command
a command that enables you to perform actions from a display manager window. For example, entering the letter O in the DIRECTORY window's selection field beside the name of a SAS/CALC software spreadsheet enables you to open the spreadsheet for editing.

simple expression
an expression that uses only one operator.

spreadsheet
a collection of data organized into rows, columns, and pages. SAS/CALC programs operate on spreadsheets.

spreadsheet cell
one data cell in a spreadsheet, found at the intersection of a row, column, and page.

syntax
the rules specifying how to assemble literals, keywords, and other text to form valid expressions and statements.

syntax checking
a process in which the SAS System checks each statement to be sure it is used properly, that all keywords are spelled correctly, that all names meet the requirements for SAS names, and so on.

syntax error
an error in the spelling or grammar of SAS/CALC statements. The SAS System finds syntax errors as it compiles each SAS/CALC program before execution.

temporary file
a SAS file in a SAS data library (usually the WORK library) that is deleted at the end of the SAS session or job.

text editing command
a command specific to the text editor.

three-dimensional spreadsheet
a SAS/CALC software spreadsheet containing rows and columns arranged in several pages.

two-dimensional spreadsheet
a SAS/CALC software spreadsheet containing rows and columns.

title
a heading printed at the top of each page of SAS output or the log.

window
a resizable, movable object on the display.

windowing environment
See SAS Display Manager System.

Index

A

action bar
    activating with PMENU command 20
    available selections 9
    turning off 198
activating links using drilldown facility 155
Additional options dialog box
    defining initial parameters 29-30, 140
    modified, illustration 31
Additional Pie Attributes dialog box
    default selections, illustration 98
    exploding pie slices 99-101
    selecting 97
Assign New Names dialog box 137, 158-159
assignment statements
    ending with semicolon (;) 166, 180
    entering for SAS/CALC programs 166
    equal sign (=) 166, 171, 180, 183
    purpose of statements in SAS/CALC programs 167, 181
    syntax 166
    verified by SAS/CALC software before running 171, 183
asterisk (*)
    indicating deleted rows 36
AUTOCALC option
    controlling execution of formulas 115
    executing formulas when turned off 119
    turning off 116-120
    turning on 120
Autocalc pull-down menu
    Autocalc off 116
    Autocalc on 118, 120

B

BACKWARD command 11, 127
bar charts 102-104
    creating 102-104
    default bar chart 103
    default bar chart, illustration 78, 103
    legends 103
BEST. format 69

C

CALC entry type as default 29
CALC Index 191-196
CALC procedure 25-27
    CATALOG= option 25
    invoking SAS/CALC software 25-27
    online help for options 193
    submitting from Locals pull-down menu 26-27
Cancel button 8
carriage-control information 81
Catalog Directory window
    copying spreadsheets 158
    selecting spreadsheet for linking 136, 144, 146
CATALOG= option, CALC procedure 25
catalogs
    SASHELP catalog 135-136
    specifying in Spreadsheet... dialog box 22, 24, 56
cells
    See also formulas
    assigning cell formats 70-71, 125-126
    BEST. format 69
    clearing cell values 113-114
    copying formulas 44-49
    copying formulas to range of cells 47
    copying formulas with COPY command 199-200
    copying values from source ranges 47
    correcting incorrectly marked cells 46, 62, 67
    default number of cells 30
    definition 5
    entering cell values 115
    entering values 38
    identifying 5
    methods for assigning values 5
    verifying attributes 72
    verifying formats with HELP command 71
Change perspective pull-down menu
    View pages and columns 108, 126
    View rows and columns 111, 128
Change... dialog box
    assigning cell formats 70, 125
    changing cell attributes 63
CHART window
    Additional Pie Attributes dialog box 97-99
    closing 102, 103
    displaying 96, 103
    Label Attributes dialog box 101
    Select Data dialog box 100
charts
    See bar charts
    See pie charts
Charts pull-down menu
    Bar chart... 103
    definition 9
    displaying CHART window 103
    Pie chart... 96
CHECK command 85
Clear marked areas... pull-down menu 113-114
closing spreadsheets 50, 94, 139, 184
colon (:)
    specifying ranges of cells in formulas 65

columns
   changing default column names 32–33,
      141–142
   changing widths 61–64, 140
   default names 4
   default number of columns 30
   defining initial parameters 30–31
   deleting 37
   inserting 57, 60–61
   sample COMPANY spreadsheet 132
   sample EASTERN spreadsheet 20
   scrolling to right and left 61
   transposing rows and columns for reports
      87–88
   truncated column names 62
comma (,)
   separating elements of formulas 42
command line, displaying 197–198
Command pull-down menu 11
Command... dialog box 11
commands
   BACKWARD 11, 127
   CHECK 85
   COPY 196–202
   displaying command line 197–198
   END 11, 91
   FORWARD 11, 135
   HELP 71, 72
   LEFT 11, 61
   MARK BLOCK 11, 44–47, 61–63, 67–69,
      95, 102, 109, 113, 124–125, 140
   methods for issuing 7
   NUMS 89–90
   O (Open) selection field command 56, 73,
      139, 160
   online help 195–196
   PMENU 20
   RIGHT 11, 61, 140
Copy An Entry... dialog box
   closing 138, 159
   Copy from another library 134
   copying spreadsheets 134, 158–159
COPY command
   copying formulas from one cell to another
      199–200
   copying formulas from one page to another
      201–202
   online help 196
Copy marked areas(values only), Edit pull-down
   menu 47
Copy marked areas, Edit pull-down menu 47,
   69, 109, 125, 149
copying formulas
   See formulas
copying spreadsheets
   See spreadsheets
Customize pull-down menu
   Set labels... 101
   Set specific attributes 97

D

deactivating links using drilldown facility
   153–155

defaults
   altering default features of reports 83
   bar chart defaults 103
   bar chart, illustration 78, 103
   CALC entry type 29
   changing default row and column names
      32–33, 141–142
   number of columns, rows, and cells 30
   numeric values right-justified by default 38
   pie chart defaults 96–97
   pie chart, illustration 14, 77, 96
   row and column names 4
   sending default report 80–81
   spreadsheet defaults 5
   spreadsheet report, illustration 75, 83
   spreadsheet, illustration 5
   suppressing default report formatting
      options 86
Define a New Link dialog box
   naming links 143, 146
   redisplaying 145
   Select from current catalog button 144, 146
defining formulas
   See formulas
defining initial parameters 29–32, 140
Delete dialog box 35–37
Delete pull-down menu 34
deleting rows and columns 34–37
Desktop pull-down menu 22, 56
dialog boxes
   definition 8
   exiting 8
   illustration 8
DIRECTORY window
   displaying 24–25, 27, 56
   displaying REPORT entries 94
   displaying spreadsheet entries 138
   selecting spreadsheet for copying 133
Drilldown Actions dialog box 153–154
drilldown facility 151–152
   deactivating links 153–155
   graphic display 151
   purpose 151
   verifying links between spreadsheets
      151–152, 179

E

Edit pull-down menu
   assigning cell formats 70, 150
   changing cell attributes 63
   changing column widths 140
   clearing cell values 113
   copying cell values only 47
   copying formulas 47, 69, 125, 149
   copying pages 109–110
   correcting incorrectly marked cells 46, 62,
      67
   definition 9
   deleting rows and columns 34
   illustration 7
   inserting columns 60–61

inserting pages 121
inserting rows 58–59
END command
   closing Free Style Specification window 91
   definition 11
End, File pull-down menu
   closing CHART window 102, 103
   closing drilldown facility 155
   closing ENHANCED.REPORT dialog box 87
   closing Keys window 12
   closing MULTI.REPORT dialog box 91
   closing PGM window 167, 181
   closing spreadsheets 50, 94, 139, 184
   closing TRANS.REPORT dialog box 88
   ending SAS/CALC software sessions 51
   ending SAS System session 52
   not used for closing formula entry area 43
ENHANCED REPORT entry 83–87
   See also ENHANCED.REPORT dialog box
   altering default features 83
   creating 83–87
   enhanced spreadsheet report, illustration 76, 93
   saving 87
   sending to print file 91–92
ENHANCED.REPORT dialog box 84–86
   CHECK command 85
   Form field 85
   Page Format dialog box 85–87
   Report description field 85
   Report title field 85
   suppressing options in Page Format dialog box 86
ENTER key for executing formulas 41, 65, 147
entering cell values 38
Entry Definition dialog box 92
equal sign (=)
   required to begin formulas 42, 147
   using in assignment statements 166, 180
   verification of placement by SAS/CALC software 171, 183
errors
   See troubleshooting
Execute pull-down menu
   closing formula entry area 43, 49, 66, 124, 148
   definition 9
   displaying formula entry area 64, 122, 147
   running programs 169, 182
   turning off Autocalc 116
   turning on Autocalc 120
   verifying copied formulas 49
exploding pie slices 99–101

F

File pull-down menu
   closing CHART window 102, 103
   closing drilldown facility 155
   closing ENHANCED.REPORT dialog box 87
   closing Keys window 12

closing PGM window 167, 181
closing spreadsheets 50, 94, 139, 184
closing TRANS.REPORT dialog box 88
copying spreadsheets 133, 158
creating enhanced REPORT entry 84
creating multipage REPORT entry 89
creating new spreadsheets 27–28, 139
creating transposed report 87
defining SAS/CALC programs 163, 179
definition 9
ending SAS/CALC software sessions 51
ending SAS System session 52
freeing print files 82, 93–94
not used for closing formula entry area 43
saving spreadsheets 49
sending default reports 80
sending reports 91
transposing rows and columns for reports 87
FORM entries 84
formats
   assigning cell formats 70–71, 125–126
   BEST. format 69
   defining in linked spreadsheets 150
formulas 39–44
   See also SAS/CALC programs
   automatic protection 44
   closing formula entry area 43–44, 49, 66, 124, 148
   compared with SAS/CALC programs 157, 171
   controlling execution with AUTOCALC option 115–120
   copying 44–49, 67–69, 124–125, 149–151
   copying with COPY command 199–202
   defining 39–44, 64–67
   defining for linked spreadsheets 147–149
   definition 39
   entering long formulas 41
   equal sign (=) required to begin 42, 147
   errors during entry 43
   executing by pressing ENTER 41, 65, 147
   executing prematurely 41, 147
   executing when AUTOCALC is turned off 119
   formula entry area 40–41
   guidelines for using formulas or programs 185
   reexecuting 115
   results, illustration 43, 66, 124, 148
   specifying cell ranges with colon (:) 65
   SUM function 42
   summarizing data in three-dimensional spreadsheets 122–126
   syntax 39
   syntax in linked spreadsheets 147
   TAB key not used for moving into cells containing formulas 45, 64, 67
   three-level names used in three-dimensional spreadsheets 123
   turning off AUTOCALC option 116–120
   turning on AUTOCALC option 120
   verifying accuracy of copied formulas 49

220 *Index*

FORWARD command 135
   assigning to function key 11
   definition 11
Free Style Specification window 89–91
freeing print files 82–83, 93–94
function keys 9–12
   commands frequently assigned 11
   definition 9
   Keys window 10
   viewing or changing definitions 10–11, 44

G

generating graphics
   See graphics, generating
generating reports
   See reports, generating
Global options pull-down menu 198
Globals pull-down menu
   creating new spreadsheet 21
   defining function keys 11
   definition 9
   displaying command line 197
   opening existing spreadsheet 56
Go to... dialog box 112, 127, 139, 161, 172, 178
Goback button
   closing Copy an Entry... dialog box 138, 159
   closing Help window 72
   moving between online help windows 193–194, 196
graphics device
   required for generating graphics 95
   using with drilldown facility 151
graphics, generating 95–103
   See also reports, generating
   chapter summary 104
   creating bar charts 102–104
   creating pie charts 95–97
   default bar chart 103
   default bar chart, illustration 78
   default pie chart 96–97
   default pie chart, illustration 77
   enhancing pie charts 97–102

H

HELP command
   displaying Help window 72
   verifying cell formats 71
help facility, online
   See online help facility
Help pull-down menu
   definition 9
   viewing or changing function key definitions 10, 44, 71
Help window
   Goback button 72
   verifying cell attributes 72

I

initial parameters 30–32
   Additional Options dialog box 29–30, 140
   defining 30–32
Insert... dialog box
   inserting columns 60–61
   inserting pages 121
   inserting rows 59
invoking SAS/CALC software 20–27, 56–57

K

Keys window
   assigning function keys 10
   closing 11
   illustration 10

L

Label Attributes dialog box 101
LEFT command
   definition 11
   scrolling columns 61
Libnames window 134–135, 158
libnames, assigning to spreadsheets 23, 56
link names 143
link symbol (->) 147–148, 180, 183
linked spreadsheets 131–156
   availability of links across sessions 146
   changing column widths 140
   changing default row and column names 141–142
   COMPANY spreadsheet, illustration 132
   copying formulas 149–151
   copying spreadsheets 133–139
   creating links 142–146
   creating new spreadsheets 139–140
   deactivating links 153–155
   defining formats 150
   defining formulas 147–149
   defining SAS/CALC programs 178–181
   definition of linking 131
   link names 143
   reactivating links 155
   summary 156
   using drilldown facility 151–152
Locals pull-down menu
   definition 9
   displaying Drilldown window 151, 155, 179
   linking spreadsheets 142
   opening Message window 43
   submitting CALC procedure 26–27

M

MARK BLOCK command
   assigning cell formats 70, 125
   changing column widths 61–63, 140
   clearing cell values 113

Index 221

copying formulas 44-47, 67-69, 124-125
copying pages 109
correcting incorrectly marked cells 46, 62, 67
creating bar charts 102
creating pie charts 95
definition 11
Message window
    checking errors in formulas 43
    viewing error messages 204
    viewing programming errors 206
modifying spreadsheets
    See spreadsheets, modifying
MULTI.REPORT dialog box
    Form field 89
    Report description field 89
    Report title field 89
multipage reports
    creating 89-91
    Free Style Specification window 89-91
    illustration 77, 94
    sending to print file 91-92
    slashes (/) indicating page breaks 90

N

naming spreadsheets 29
New... dialog box
    Additional options button 29
    creating enhanced REPORT entry 84
    defining SAS/CALC programs 179
    naming spreadsheets 28-29, 139, 163-164
numeric values, default justification 38
NUMS command 89-90

O

O (Open) selection field command 56, 73, 139, 160
online help facility 191-196
    accessing 191
    CALC: Index window 192
    command information 195-196
    procedure option information 193
    SAS/CALC software introduction 192
    syntax information 193
    window information 194
Open pull-down menu 133, 158
Outside label selection group 98-99

P

Page Format dialog box
    enhanced reports 85-87
    multipage reports 91
    Print date 86
    Print global title 86
    Print page number 86
    Print report title 86, 88, 91
    Print time 86
    transposed reports 87-88

pages of three-dimensional spreadsheets
    copying 109-110
    copying formulas with COPY command 201-202
    going to specific page 112
    inserting pages .-109
    renaming 111, 127-128
paste buffer 109
Paste, Edit pull-down menu 110, 149
percentage amounts for pie slices, selecting 97-99
perspective, changing 108-109, 111, 126, 128
PGM entries
    See SAS/CALC programs
PGM window 165, 180
pie charts 95-102
    adding titles 101-102
    Additional Pie Attributes dialog box 97-100
    creating 95-97
    default pie chart 96-97
    default pie chart, illustration 14, 77, 96
    enhanced pie chart, illustration 101
    enhancing 97-102
    exploding pie slices 99-101
    Label Attributes dialog box 101
    numbers outside pie slices 97
    Select Data dialog box 100
    selecting percentage amounts for slices 97-99
PMENU command 20
PMENU facility 7-9
    action bar and pull-down menu selections 9
    dialog boxes 8
    moving the cursor 7
    pull-down menus 7-8
print files
    definition 81
    freeing print files 82-83, 93-94
Print pull-down menu
    freeing print files 82, 93
    sending alternate reports 91-92
    sending default report 81
PROGRAM EDITOR window
    invoking SAS/CALC software 21
    running CALC procedure 25-26
protection of cells containing formulas 44
pull-down menus
    See also specific menus
    activating with PMENU command 20
    available selections 9
    dialog boxes 8
    exiting 8
    illustration 7

R

reactivating links using drilldown facility 155
renaming pages of three-dimensional spreadsheets 111, 127-128
reports, generating 75-95
    See also ENHANCED.REPORT dialog box
    See also graphics, generating

reports, generating *(continued)*
    See also MULTI.REPORT dialog box
    See also TRANS.REPORT dialog box
    altering default features 83
    CHECK command 85
    creating enhanced REPORT entry 84–87
    creating multipage REPORT entry 89–91
    default features 83
    default spreadsheet report, illustration 75, 83
    displaying REPORT entries in DIRECTORY window 94
    enhanced spreadsheet report, illustration 76, 93
    Entry Definition dialog box 92
    Free Style Specification window 89–91
    freeing print files 82–83, 93–94
    multipage report, illustration 77, 94
    Page Format dialog box 85–87, 88, 91
    saving reports 87, 88, 91
    sending default report 80–81
    sending reports to print file 91–92
    steps for generating printed reports, chart 79
    summary
    suppressing default formatting options 86, 91
    transposed spreadsheet report, illustration 76, 93
    transposing rows and columns 87–88
    verifying printers available at your site 78
RIGHT command
    definition 11
    scrolling columns 61, 140
rows
    changing default row names 32–33, 141–142
    default names 4
    default number of rows 30
    defining initial parameters 30–31
    deleting 34–36
    inserting 57–60
    transposing rows and columns for reports 87–88
Run dialog box 170–171, 176–178, 182–184

S

sample spreadsheets
    See also defaults
    columns in COMPANY spreadsheet 132
    columns in EASTERN spreadsheet 20
    COMPANY spreadsheet 132
    default spreadsheet report, illustration 75
    default spreadsheet, illustration 5
    EASTERN spreadsheet 12–13, 19
    EASTERN spreadsheet, illustration 107
    enhanced COMPANY spreadsheet, illustration 150
    enhanced EASTERN spreadsheet 13, 55
    enhanced spreadsheet report, illustration 76
    multipage report, illustration 77
    saved spreadsheet 49
    spreadsheet with entered values, illustration 6
    three-dimensional spreadsheet, illustration 6, 106
    transposed spreadsheet report, illustration 76
    WESTERN spreadsheet, illustration 139
SAS/CALC programs 157–186
    assignment statements 166, 180
    automatic execution after modification of cell values 171
    common programming errors 205–206
    compared with formulas 157, 171
    copying spreadsheets 158–159
    defining programs 163–168
    defining programs for linked spreadsheets 173–181
    ending statements with semicolon (;) 166, 180
    equal sign (=) in assignment statements 166, 180
    guidelines for using formulas or programs 185
    link symbol (->) in assignment statements 180
    online help with syntax 193
    opening existing spreadsheets 160
    PGM window 165
    purpose of assignment statements 167, 181
    running programs 169–174, 182–184
    running programs for identical spreadsheets 175–178
    saving 167, 181
    saving with specific spreadsheets 171, 177
    summary 186
    syntax verification by SAS/CALC software 171, 183
    verifying calculation of values 172–174, 178
    verifying links with drilldown facility 179
    viewing existing spreadsheets 160–162
SAS/CALC software 3–16
    action bar 4, 9
    default spreadsheet 5
    ending a session 51–52
    fundamental spreadsheet concepts 3–7
    introduction 3–12
    invoking 20–27, 56–57
    issuing commands 7
    PMENU facility 7–9
    pull-down menu selections 9
    Spreadsheet window, illustration 4
    three-dimensional spreadsheet, illustration 6
    tutorial topics 12–16
    two-dimensional spreadsheet, illustration 6
    using function keys 9–12
SAS catalogs
    See catalogs
SAS System session, ending 52
SAS Text Editor 89–90
SASHELP catalog 135, 158
SASHELP Directory window 135, 158
SASUSER libname 23, 56

Select Data dialog box 100
semicolon (;)
   ending assignment statements 166, 180
   verification of placement by SAS/CALC software 171, 183
Set specific attributes pull-down menu 97
slashes (/)
   indicating page breaks in multipage reports 90
spreadsheet
   See also three-dimensional spreadsheets
spreadsheet examples
   See sample spreadsheets
Spreadsheet window 4
Spreadsheet... dialog box 22–24
spreadsheets
   See also cells
   See also columns
   See also linked spreadsheets
   See also rows
   See also spreadsheets, creating
   See also spreadsheets, modifying
   See also three-dimensional spreadsheets
   closing 50, 94, 139, 184
   copying 133–139, 158–159
   default spreadsheet, illustration 5
   definition 3
   fundamental concepts 3–7
   opening existing spreadsheets 56–57, 139, 160
   saving 49
   Spreadsheet window 4
   storing 21
   viewing 160–162, 172–174
spreadsheets, creating 19–53, 139–140
   CALC entry type 29
   changing default row and column names 32–33
   closing spreadsheets 50–51
   copying formulas 44–49
   default number of columns and rows 30
   defining formulas 39–44
   defining initial parameters 29–32
   deleting rows and columns 34–37
   ending SAS/CALC software sessions 51–52
   entering cell values 38
   invoking SAS/CALC software using CALC procedure 25–27
   invoking SAS/CALC software using pull-down menus 20–21
   linked spreadsheets 139–140
   naming spreadsheets 28–29
   saving spreadsheets 49
   storing spreadsheets 21
   summary 53
   using pull-down menus 21
   using pull-down menus 27–30
spreadsheets, linked
   See linked spreadsheets
spreadsheets, modifying 55–73
   assigning cell formats 70–71
   changing column widths 61–64

copying formulas 67–69
defining formulas 64–67
inserting new columns 57, 60–61
inserting new rows 57–60
invoking SAS/CALC software 56–57
opening existing spreadsheet 56–57
summary 73
verifying cell attributes 72
spreadsheets, three-dimensional
   See three-dimensional spreadsheets
Submit, Locals pull-down menu 26–27
SUM function
   defining range of cells 65
   summarizing data in three-dimensional spreadsheets 122–126
   using in formulas 42
   using in SAS/CALC programs 180

T

TAB key
   moving the cursor in PMENU facility 7
   not used for moving into cells containing formulas 45, 64, 67
three-dimensional spreadsheets 105–129
   changing perspective 108–109, 111, 126
   clearing cell values 113–114
   copying formulas 124–125
   copying pages 109–110
   creating 105–129
   defining formats for cell values 125–126
   definition 105
   entering cell values 115
   going to a page 112
   illustration 6, 106
   inserting a page 121–122
   reexecuting formulas 115
   renaming pages 111, 127–128
   summarizing data 122–126
   summary 129
   turning off AUTOCALC option 116–120
   turning on AUTOCALC option 120
titles, adding to pie charts 101–102
TRANS.REPORT dialog box 88
   Form field 88
   Page Format dialog box 88
   Report columns field 88
   Report description field 88
   Report rows field 88
   Report title field 88
transposed reports
   See also TRANS.REPORT dialog box
   creating 87–88
   illustration 76, 93
   saving 88
   sending to print file 91–92
   TRANS entry 87
troubleshooting 203–206
   common programming errors 205–206

troubleshooting (*continued*)
  common user errors 203–204
  common user problems 203

V

video references 207
View pull-down menu
  changing perspective 108, 111, 126, 128
  definition 9
  going to specific pages 112, 127, 139, 161, 172, 178

7

7.2 format 70, 125, 150

Special Characters

/ (slashes)
  See slashes (/)
= (equal sign)
  See equal sign (=)
* (asterisk)
  See asterisk (*)
; (semicolon)
  See semicolon (;)
-> (link symbol)
  See link symbol (->)
, (comma)
  See comma (,)
: (colon)
  See colon (:)

Your Turn

If you have comments or suggestions about SAS/CALC software or *Getting Started with SAS/CALC Spreadsheet Applications, Version 6, First Edition*, please send them to us on a photocopy of this page.

    Please return the photocopy to the Publications Division (for comments about this book) or the Technical Support Division (for suggestions about the software) at SAS Institute Inc., SAS Campus Drive, Cary, NC 27513.